Bomber Command

Max Hastings has been studying warfare in libraries and on the battlefield since he left school. A scholar at Charterhouse and University College, Oxford, he has reported from more than fifty countries for the London *Evening Standard* and BBC TV's *24 Hours* and *Panorama*. He has seen action in the Middle East, India, southern Africa and Vietnam, where he flew on several air force ground attack sorties. *Bomber Command* is his fifth book. Most recently he has published a biography of Montrose, Charles I's brilliant commander in Scotland during the Civil War, and made a special study of the Israeli Army for a biography of one of their most distinguished commando officers who was killed at Entebbe. Now thirty-five, he is married with two children. *Bomber Command* was awarded the W. Somerset Maugham Award for Non-Fiction in 1980. His new book on D-Day and the French Resistance in June 1944 will be published in 1981.

Max Hastings

Bomber Command

Pan Books London and Sydney

for Charles,
who will one day be as moved by
their courage as I have been

How can I live among this gentle
Obsolescent breed of heroes, and not weep?
Unicorns, almost,
For they are fading into two legends
In which their stupidity and chivalry
Are celebrated. Each, fool and hero, will be an immortal.
Keith Douglas, 1943

First published 1979 by Michael Joseph Ltd
This edition published 1981 by Pan Books Ltd,
Cavaye Place, London SW10 9PG
© Max Hastings 1979
ISBN 0 330 26236 X
Made and printed in Great Britain by
Hazell Watson & Viney Ltd, Aylesbury Bucks

Contents

Illustrations

Plates

F/Sgt Herbert Ruse being briefed
Harry Jones of 37 Squadron
Marshal of the RAF Lord Trenchard*
Sir Edgar Ludlow-Hewitt*
Sir Richard Peirse*
Sir Archibald Sinclair*
A Halifax of Bomber Command*

Albert Speer addresses German armament workers†
Night images of Germany, as seen by the crews of
Bomber Command*
Speer with Field-Marshal Erhard Milch†
The Prime Minister with Lord Cherwell, Sir Charles
Portal and Sir Dudley Pound*
Some aircrew of Bomber Command
Sir Arthur Harris, his wife and daughter*

*Imperial War Museum
†Speer Archives

Foreword

Bomber Command's offensive against Germany in the Second World War was one of the most remarkable passages of arms in history. It began when Winston Churchill could see no other road to victory, as England stood alone in 1940. It was undertaken with almost messianic fervour by a generation of senior airmen determined to prove that strategic air power could make a unique and decisive contribution to war. It ended in a controversy, moral and strategic, which has been unresolved ever since.

The cost was very high. 55,573 aircrew,* almost all officers and NCOs, among the finest and most highly trained material in the British Empire, were killed. A further 9,784 were shot down and taken prisoner. The sacrifice was greater than the British Army's total loss of officers in the First World War. Bomber Command's casualties amounted to almost one-seventh of all British deaths in action by land, sea and air from 1939 to 1945. The pitiful prospects of surviving a tour of bomber operations were only matched in hazard on either side by the German U-boat crews. Germany's losses in the bomber offensive were also awe-inspiring. All statistical estimates are unreliable, but somewhere between 300,000 and 600,000 people, most of them civilians, were killed by the bombs of the RAF and the USAAF. A further five million were 'de-housed'. By 1945 the major city centres of the Third Reich had been razed to rubble.

But was this *decisive* in making Allied victory possible, as leading airmen have claimed ever since, or merely *catastrophic*, as that very perceptive scientific civil servant Sir Henry Tizard feared would prove to be the case, as far back as 1942?

*Royal Air Force: 38,462 (69.2 per cent); Royal Canadian Air Force: 9,919 (17.8 per cent); Royal Australian Air Force: 4,050 (7.3 per cent); Royal New Zealand Air Force: 1,679 (3.0 per cent); other Allied air forces: 1,463 (2.7 per cent).

In his post-war memoirs, Bomber Command's C-in-C Sir Arthur Harris argued that 'in spite of all that happened at Hamburg, bombing proved a comparatively humane method. For one thing, it saved the flower of the youth of this country and of our Allies from being mown down by the military in the field, as it was in Flanders in the war of 1914–18.'[1]

Harris's claim deserves the most careful consideration from a Western Allied point of view, if not for the reasons that he himself would advance. The Second World War cost Britain 400,000 dead, America 300,000. It cost Germany at least 5,000,000, Russia at least 20,000,000. If there had been no bomber offensive from 1941 to 1944, while Germany was being reduced in the terrible war of attrition in the east, would it have been possible for the Allies to justify the interminable delay before opening the Second Front in Europe? Would it also have been possible to avoid the enormous casualties that would have followed a D-Day in 1943?

It is unlikely that important new evidence will be found about the nature of what was done to Germany by the bomber offensive. Each generation of historians can only seek to reinterpret the post-war reports of the American and British bombing survey units, and the testimony of vital witnesses such as Albert Speer. But a succession of fascinating, interwoven questions still surround Bomber Command: beyond what was done, why was it done? How was it done? What was it like to do it? What was it like to be a victim of it? I have tried to examine all these aspects, chiefly with the help of first-hand accounts from those who took part. It is a decade since the last significant book on the bomber offensive appeared, and in the interval all the relevant official files have at last been released for public scrutiny; and the Speer memoirs and other important studies have been published.

This is not the comprehensive story of the offensive, for it deals only incidentally with the American contribution. Nor is it an exhaustive account of everything that was done by Bomber Command, for which it is necessary to turn to the four volumes of the Official History, published in 1961. I have omitted or dealt very briefly with legendary episodes, such as the Dambusters' Raid, which have been fully described in the past. Instead, I have pieced together some less widely known epics of courage and endurance. I have tried to look at the key issues of the offensive as they appeared at the time, with generous use of contemporary material, much of it hitherto unpublished. Thirty-five years after the event, I think that most men's memories have gained in frankness what they have lost in precision. The mood of almost childlike bravado in some of the war stories published in the 1950s has faded.

Because Bomber Command's losses were so terrible, those who survived have always been specially sensitive to criticism of the campaign. Yet only a charlatan would seek to entangle the men who flew the aircraft in the strategic controversy. Even one of the most cynical critics of the air force, Professor D. C. Watt, has written in his essay 'The RAF View of History':[2] 'We do not think less of Leonidas's three hundred Spartans at Thermopylae because, reviewed objectively, their deaths had little effect one way or another on the Persian invasion of Greece.'

As far as possible in this book, I have separated the story of the aircrew from that of the struggle in Whitehall, Washington and High Wycombe. It is impossible to describe everything that every unit did, because Bomber Command was an enormous organization, so I have chosen six more or less typical line squadrons, whose experience illustrates the nature of the bomber offensive at various stages, and examined their men and their operations in some detail. Through their stories, it may become possible to understand something of what it was like to fly in the darkness over Germany.

The third section of Chapter 8, headed 'Courage', has been extensively rewritten for this the second edition of the book, after it had been suggested to me that I had dealt unjustly and incorrectly with some aspects of the story and personalities of 76 Squadron in 1943. I have been able to consider material which was not available to me in writing the first edition and which has caused me to revise my view of the squadron's story. I am pleased to have been able to correct the fine record of 76 Squadron in this period and to acknowledge the role played by its Commanding Officer.

I have quoted extensively from unpublished letters, diaries and manuscripts, and interviewed almost a hundred former aircrew, together with many former senior officers and civil servants. Each section of my draft manuscript was read by a former officer who took part in the events described. This is no protection against error, and indeed some senior officers concerned took the strongest exception to my judgements and comments. But it was intended at least to ensure that I clearly understood the Service view of what took place.

At the strategic level, I must express my deep gratitude to the former Commander-in-Chief of Bomber Command, Sir Arthur Harris; to his former Group commanders, Air Vice-Marshal Donald Bennett, the late Air Chief Marshal Sir Ralph Cochrane, and Air Vice-Marshal E. B. Addison; and to the former Director of Bomber Operations at the Air Ministry, Air Vice-Marshal S. O. Bufton. These are only the most prominent of the distinguished airmen who have given me time and help. They will find much to disagree with in what I have written, but I hope that they will accept that I have tried honestly to review their achievements, recognizing the extraordinary conditions and difficulties amidst which they fought.

As for those who flew, it was deeply moving to sit through long evenings in suburban bungalows, listening to very ordinary middle-aged men describing the quite extraordinary things that they did as young aircrew over Germany. I am grateful that my generation has been spared the need to discover whether we could match the impossible sacrifices that they made.

Max Hastings
Jerpoint House
Co. Kilkenny
January 1979

Prologue: Norfolk and Heligoland Bight, 18 December 1939

On Monday, 18 December 1939, Leading Aircraftsman Harry Jones of 37 Squadron, Bomber Command, ate his last breakfast in England for five and a half years at home in Feltwell with his wife Mary. The war was already more than three months old, yet the Joneses' lives still had the tidy discipline of suburban commuters. Feltwell was a tiny Norfolk village on the edge of the empty horizons of the Fens, where they had a small flat. Every morning, LAC Jones kissed Mary, boarded his squadron bicycle, and pedalled for ten minutes down the road to the airfield where 37 Squadron was based. A rigger by trade, he spent his working days tending the airframes of the twin-engined Vickers Wellington I bombers with which Feltwell was equipped. The previous day, Sunday, he had been in the hangars until lunchtime carrying out a routine sixty-hour check on his aircraft, and sorting out some trouble with an oleo leg. Today he would go home again at lunchtime for steak and chips with a poached egg on top. Mary, a pretty, jolly bespectacled farmer's daughter who had defied her family's direst warnings about servicemen by marrying Harry fourteen months before, was spending the morning putting the finishing touches to her Christmas pudding.

Harry Jones loved the Royal Air Force. The son of a Birmingham brewery worker, like so many other boys of his generation he had yearned to be a pilot. The day in 1935 that he reported to the recruiting office just short of eighteen years old, this first ambition was brought back to earth with a bump: 'You've got to be a gentleman to fly, my lad!' So Harry Jones did the next best thing and became a rigger. In 1938 he was posted to Feltwell.

For sixpence a day extra pay, however, ground crew could volunteer for occasional flying duties. After five weeks training on drum-fed Lewis guns at North Coates, LAC Jones qualified to wear the brass winged bullet of an air gunner on his arm and to fly when required as a rear gunner in one of the squadron's Wellingtons. The privilege of flying had to be fitted in with routine ground duties, of course. Non-commissioned aircrew volunteers were invariable targets for persecution by a station's senior NCOs, who regarded them as 'spoilt brats' trying to escape fire drill, guard details and other real airman's business. It was not unusual for Harry Jones and his kind to return from a six-hour exercise and find themselves rostered for a 24-hour picket while their pilots adjourned to bed or the mess. The Other Ranks' cookhouse closed according to ground duties schedules, and remained impervious to special pleading from aircrew late for breakfast after a night flight. The Royal Air Force was a young service, demanding technical flair, imagination, initiative. Yet its hierarchy and routines were still those devised for the armies, and the baser human material, of an earlier age. It was a frustrating paradox, but one which didn't trouble Harry Jones. He loved to fly, he loved 37 Squadron and the Wellingtons and the smell of high-octane fuel and, yes, perhaps even the bull and brass-polishing and cracking discipline of a pre-war RAF station.

37 was one of 3 Group's six operational squadrons at the outbreak of war. Like the rest of Bomber Command, none of them had so far been permitted to attack any land target on enemy territory, while the British Government cautiously debated the future of aerial bombardment. When it was suggested that the RAF might bomb the Ruhr, the Air Minister, Sir Kingsley Wood, declared with affronted decency that factories were private property. Even after the German *blitzkrieg* on Warsaw, Allied politicians still fervently hoped to avoid provoking such an assault on their own civilians. Since 3 September, 3 Group had staged three ineffectual attacks on naval targets off the German coast and a number of other minor sorties. But 37 Squadron had yet to engage the enemy for the first time. The squadron's only casualties since the outbreak of war had been the crew of an old Harrow, which crashed while lost on an exercise. After the first fortnight, when the squadron was shuttled round England in a fever of panicky diversions to avoid an expected German attack, they came home to Feltwell and stayed there.

The war, and even training for it, returned to its usual gentlemanly pace. Once or twice the squadron took part in desultory affiliation exercises with Fighter Command's Spitfires. After the most recent, in November with a flight from Tangmere, the fighter pilots reported that they could have wiped out 37 Squadron in ten minutes, but nobody believed them. Rivalry with Fighter Command and ill-concealed disdain for its flamboyant habits precluded close cooperation in training. Bomber Command was full of pride in itself, one mess of the most delightful flying club in the world. Tangmere could save their line-shoots for the Luftwaffe. A Wellington could take care of itself. 37 Squadron settled back into Norfolk village life, marching on Sundays to church for the sermons of the local vicar, 'Jubilate Joe'. An official request was sent to the station to make less noise on take-off, because an aged local resident was dying in a cottage close to the flight path.

But at 8.15 a.m. on 18 December, as Harry Jones cycled up to 'A' Flight hangar, Feltwell's usual disciplined Monday morning calm was already shattered. Six aircraft had been taxied in from their dispersals and were being warmed up on the stands by the ground crews. Armourers were traversing turrets and checking bomb loads. 'Come on, Jonah, you're flying!' somebody shouted. Harry hurried into the hangar and checked the roster in the Flight Book on the table. He was down for duty as rear gunner with Sergeant Ruse.

Amidst the hustle of aircrew pulling on flying clothes and seizing maps and equipment, they drew flying rations of sandwiches and chocolate, to be returned intact if the exercise was for any reason uncompleted. Harry had no time to talk to the other four members of the crew before he swung himself into the turret of Ruse's aircraft behind his twin Browning .303s. The Wellington began to move forward across the grass, past the squadron commander Joe Fogarty, standing beside the runway, saluting as 'A' Flight rolled past one by one. They bumped towards take-off. At last Harry called to Ruse on the intercom: 'What's going on, skipper?'

'They've found the German navy, and we're going to Wilhelmshaven to attack them . . .'

The operation on which 37 Squadron was now embarked had been conceived months before the war, by the Air Ministry's Directorate of Plans. Among the thick file of alternative attacks to be carried out by Bomber Command, Western Air Plan 7B called for the bombing of the German fleet in or around its base at Wilhelmshaven. In the immediate aftermath of the outbreak of war, while the Government shrank from authorizing an assault on German industry, they seized enthusiastically upon WAP 7B. The German navy was obviously a legitimate target, surrounded by water and therefore safe from the risk that ill-aimed bombs might fall on civilians. Bomber Command was impatient to flex its muscles. On 4 September, fourteen Wellingtons of 3 Group and fifteen Blenheims of 2 Group carried out the first of a series of attacks on the German navy in its bases. The Blenheims attacked the pocket-battleship *Admiral Scheer* in the Schillig Roads with great gallantry at low level, hitting the ship four times. None of the bombs exploded. Five Blenheims were lost. The Wellingtons, bombing the *Scharnhorst* and the *Gneisenau* in the Elbe at higher level, scored no hits on their targets, but lost only two of their own number.

The concept of the self-defending bomber formation, fighting its way over enemy lines to attack vital targets miles behind any battlefield, was at the core of the theory of strategic air power. The power-operated gun turrets fitted to the Wellingtons and Whitleys of Bomber Command represented one of the major British breakthroughs in armament technology, and it was believed that they gave the RAF's bombers a decisive margin of defence against an attacking fighter. Group and Bomber Command headquarters studied closely the reports on the events of 4 September, and professed themselves very encouraged by the failure of German Me109 fighters to close with the Wellingtons. Although in reality one Wellington and one Blenheim had been destroyed by fighters, it was believed at Bomber Command that enemy anti-aircraft fire – 'flak' – had accounted for all the RAF losses. Tactics were adjusted accordingly. Henceforth attacks would be carried out at higher levels.

On 3 December, after a prolonged lull provoked by digestion of the lessons of September, by lack of suitable targets and weather, and by the general lack of urgency about prosecuting the war that characterized all British activities at this period, a formation of twenty-four Wellingtons from 3 Group carried out a second abortive operation against German cruisers off Heligoland and returned without loss, despite a series of German fighter attacks. These relatively large British forces had failed to damage the enemy, but Bomber Command was encouraged by their very survival. Even when a third 'armed patrol of the Schillig Roads' by twelve Wellingtons on 12 December ended in tragedy, with the loss of half the force, there was no weakening of confidence at the top. It was believed that most if not all the losses had been inflicted by flak and not fighters, despite repeated attacks by Me109s.

'The failure of the enemy,' noted Air Commodore Norman Bottomley, Bomber Command's Senior Air Staff Officer and the future Deputy Chief of Air Staff from 1941, 'must be ascribed to good formation flying. The maintenance of tight, unshaken formations in the face of the most powerful enemy action, is the test of bomber force fighting efficiency and morale. In our service, it is the equivalent of the old "Thin Red Line", or the "Shoulder to Shoulder" of Cromwell's Ironsides . . .'

There can be no doubt that these raids were deliberately conceived as a means of testing Germany's defences and Bomber Command's tactics, rather than a serious assault on German sea power. There is no other way to explain the Command's lack of concern about the failure of their aircraft to sink or damage a single enemy ship. Even after the experience of 12 December – which he himself had compared to the Charge of the Light Brigade – 3 Group's AOC, the cheerfully energetic and popular Air Vice-Marshal John 'Jackie' Baldwin, was impatient to get his squadrons once again to grips with the enemy.

At 3 p.m. on the afternoon of 17 December, Baldwin telephoned on the scrambler to Air Commodore Bottomley at Bomber Command HQ at High Wycombe, to urge a further operation against the German fleet:

The Group commander pointed out the importance of seizing the very first suitable day in view of the few such occasions which were likely to present themselves under winter conditions. He stated that from the point of view of preparation, the details of the plan had been thoroughly considered by all concerned, and he was satisfied that if Monday the

18th of December were given as zero day, there would be no undue haste in planning and preparation right down to the crews engaged.[1]

Air Chief Marshal Sir Edgar Ludlow-Hewitt, C-in-C Bomber Command, concurred. He approved Baldwin's proposal to mount a new attack on the German fleet at Wilhelmshaven on the 18th, subject only to a proviso that the Wellingtons bomb from at least 10,000 feet, which should take them above effective flak. Group-Captain Goodwin, SASO at 3 Group HQ, drafted orders for the operation to be carried out by twenty-four Wellingtons. Nine aircraft would come from 149 Squadron at Mildenhall, including that of the formation leader, Wing-Commander Richard Kellett, who had also led the 3 December sweep; nine would come from 9 Squadron at Honington; the remaining six from 37 Squadron at Feltwell. 'Task: to attack enemy warships in the Schillig Roads or Wilhelmshaven,' began the Operation Order. 'Great care is to be taken that no bombs fall on shore, and no merchant ships are to be attacked. Formations shall not loiter in the target area, and all aircraft are to complete bombing as soon as possible after the sighting signal has been made.'

'Not only did I have all the leaders into the Operations Room the night before the mission went out,' wrote Baldwin to Ludlow-Hewitt a few days later, 'but I personally explained to each of them my ideas on formation flying and what I meant by mutual assistance, and they all professed that they agreed and understood.'

Late in the afternoon of Sunday the 17th, the order went out to the squadrons taking part in the operation to stand-by at two hours' notice for take-off from 0730 hrs on the morning of the 18th. Pilots and observers were briefed by squadron and station commanders. Part-time crew members such as Harry Jones were thought to need no enlightenment beyond their time of take-off, and many of them learnt this only the next morning.

Before dawn on the 18th, a Whitley of 4 Group, from 78 Squadron at Dishforth in Yorkshire, flew out across the North Sea, approaching the island of Heligoland at 0800 in patchy cloud, ideal cover for a daylight bomber operation. The crew signalled their weather report, and turned homewards towards England. 3 Group HQ passed the final readiness order to the

Wellington squadrons: take-off would be at 0930; squadrons would take up formation over King's Lynn before crossing the North Sea. The attack on Wilhelmshaven was on.

Most of 9 Squadron's officers had been out playing rugger on their home pitch at Honington the previous afternoon, when word reached 'Donkeydrop' Horsefall, the adjutant, that nine crews would be required for operations the next day. 3 Group's young pilots probably had fewer illusions about the likelihood of their own survival than their senior officers. It had been an affectionate cliché of Bomber Command since long before the war that they were a club of which a member landing at any airfield in England would meet someone he knew. 9 Squadron had heard about the losses of 12 December. They vaguely perceived that this would be a hard war, in which it was unlikely that those who were in at the beginning would remain to see the end, and of course they were perfectly correct. Perhaps the very uncertainty about the nature of the battle that they would be called upon to fight made it worse for these young men of December 1939 than for those who came after them, to whom at least the reality was brutally apparent.

Within the year, attrition would destroy the continuity and character of 9 Squadron's officers' mess as inexorably as it attacked that of every other unit in the RAF. But in these days before the slaughter began in earnest, Honington's welcoming leather armchairs and white-jacketed mess servants knew their thirty-odd brash young men as intimately as any public school prefects' club or university junior common room: James Smalley, big and untidy, bringing showgirls down from London to their parties and bewildering colleagues on idle evenings by sitting quietly knitting on a sofa: Parrot, who had been a ladies' hairdresser; Bill Macrae, a wild, brave, passionately alcoholic Canadian short-service officer who delighted in stunting his lumbering Wellington over the churches of Norfolk, lifting his wingtip at the last second before crashing into the spires; Peter Grant, fairhaired and elegant, almost a Hollywood caricature of the sporting young English public school boy, a general's son who had joined the RAF after failing to get into Cambridge. Half the mess secretly envied his stylish approach to life on the ground and in the air. The previous winter he had driven in the Monte Carlo Rally in his own Talbot 10 with Appleby, a fellow-pilot chum from 37 Squadron. Everybody remembered the squadron CO standing roaring with laughter outside the mess as Peter's Wellington came in at nought feet over the rugger pitch, scattering players to all points of the compass. Spirited flying, the CO believed, bred spirited fighters.

There was less interest in education for war. Charlie Vann, another squadron pilot, had taken his leave in Spain in the midst of her civil war, to see what real fighting looked like. He ended up in front of the Group AOC for going abroad without permission. He was an exception. Most officers were happy to let Command dictate the leisurely pace and nature of their training.

They were, on average, three or four years older than the twenty and twenty-one year olds who would be the mainstay of Bomber Command at the height of its offensive five years later, but then that later generation was older by so many seasons' experience of war. These young men of 9 Squadron and their kin were the innocents. Even their faces in the inevitable squadron photographs look somehow different from those who followed in 1943, 1944 and 1945: Challes, Fordham, Lines, Allison, Bailey – these were young men who cut their hair and cultivated rakish little moustaches, precursors of the later handlebars. They drank at The Angel in Bury St Edmunds and The Bell at Thetford – always beer. Once a month they climbed into formal messkit for Dining-In nights, and when they were paid they cashed a cheque for five pounds and sped off to London crammed into somebody's car for a night of noisy, gauche wickedness that usually ended unconscious on a bed at the Regent Palace Hotel.

In the early summer of 1939, 9 Squadron had represented the RAF at the Brussels International Air Exhibition, where they had exchanged warily chivalrous compliments with their Luftwaffe counterparts, and then been sent to stage a 'Show The Flag' flight the length of France and back. Even since the outbreak of war there had been plenty of social diversions. The Duke of Grafton did his bit for the war effort by inviting the whole of Honington officers' mess to Euston, his stately home near Thetford. Then, one winter morning, the first contingent of Women's Auxiliary Air Force girls, the WAAFs, arrived at the airfield, creating unprecedented excitement and causing the Station Commander to make one of his rare public appearances to supervise the rigging of barbed-wire entanglements round their quarters. The only discordant note, forerunner of many more social upheavals to come, was struck when the most glamorous and sought-after of the girls ended up, of all places, in the arms of a non-commissioned sergeant pilot.

Even by the standards of the other two services, the young pre-war RAF pilot was the least long-sighted of warriors. At least a few of the young men who joined the British army and the Royal Navy did so because they aspired to end up as generals or admirals. Those who came to the RAF did so because they passionately, single-mindedly, unashamedly wanted to fly. The Hendon Air Displays, the barnstormers of the 1920s and 1930s, the hugely publicized exploits of Lindberg, Hinckler, Amy Johnson, all these had seized the imagination of their generation. Above all, perhaps, it had captured that of the young grammar school boys of modest, conventional lower middle-class backgrounds from which they yearned to escape. Some day there is an intriguing essay to be written on the social origins of senior British airmen of this period, and the effects of these on their attitudes to the other two services. It is enough to say that pre-war RAF officers' messes offered young men a unique opportunity to be paid for living the life of gentlemen fliers, and yet public school boys were slower to take it up than Lord Trenchard and his colleagues had hoped. There was a rueful pre-war air force chestnut about the young man who told his mother he had become a pianist in a brothel rather than reveal that he had joined the RAF.

But they behaved as English public school boys of the period were expected to behave. One messnight, they locked a racehorse in James Smalley's bedroom, and bravely faced the difficulties next morning when it was found impossible to get it out again. They were woken in the morning by civilian batmen who had already run their baths, and who uncomplainingly collected the debris of the previous night's clothes and ironed them while their owners soaked, then made the beds while their charges strolled to the mess for ham and eggs. There was usually some flying in the morning, then after lunch squash and tennis and time to clean up before tea. They spurned the vulgarity of a bar – drinks were brought to the ante-room by a waiter summoned by the bell, and signed for by chit (only in the sergeants' mess was it necessary to pay cash). The pre-war stations had been built to standards of spacious, solid comfort that ate deep into the RAF Estimates even when aircraft design and production were being cut to the bone.

That December of 1939 the war had still made little impact on Honington. Three armoured cars arrived to take over the station's defence against invasion, and slit trenches were dug everywhere. The hangars had been draped in huge camouflage nets. Dining-In nights in full messkit had been abandoned. Blue bulbs were substituted for the white ones in every socket, a lurid contribution to the blackout. Every morning aircrew spent an inordinate amount of time hanging around the hangars waiting for orders that never came. Peter Grant and a handful of others had been sent on one abortive operation against the Kiel Canal at the very outbreak of war, from which they returned almost drained of petrol and utterly exhausted, with a bleak inkling that operational flying would be at best very dreary and at worst terrifyingly dangerous. They had been ordered to bomb at extreme low level to avoid risking hitting the neighbouring land, and lost two aircraft. Since September, however, operations had been ordered again and again, only to be cancelled before take-off.

At the evening briefing of 17 December nine captains were detailed. Guthrie, Petts and Macrae, and Allison, Challes and Lines, would fly in two vics – V formations – of three, on the left of the big diamond formation led by six aircraft of 149 Squadron. Peter Grant, with sergeants Ramshaw and Purdy, would fly on the right of the diamond with three aircraft from 149. 37 Squadron would bring up the rear. Wireless silence would be observed, although leaders would maintain a listening watch on 3190 Kilocycles. The only communication within the formation would be by Aldis signal lamp. Each aircraft would carry three 500-pound Semi Armour-Piercing bombs.

At 0930 on the morning of 18 December they took off on schedule from Honington at two-minute intervals. They rendezvoused according to plan with 149's aircraft led by Kellett, and

22

took up formation over the coastal town of King's Lynn. Then, mostly in silent apprehension, they settled to keep station on the long haul across the North Sea.

Feltwell's six aircraft were late taking off, and caught up the formation over the sea. Some of 37 Squadron had been lucky. An observer, Sergeant Butcher, had been found the previous day to be suffering from mumps. His crew was withdrawn from the operation. Others were less fortunate. LAC Jack Greaves was in bed in his barrack room when an NCO put his head in to call: 'Come on, you lucky lads, you're "On" this morning!' As the sleepy gunners roused themselves and dressed, Greaves, a wireless operator/gunner who had been posted to Feltwell only a few days before and had not yet been attached to a crew, made himself busy in the accumulator charging room. He had heard enough about daylight sweeps to know that this was not a good morning on which to make his operational début. Then he heard the Tannoy calling 'LAC Greaves to "A" Flight Office'. A stocky, sharp little flight-lieutenant, 'Cheese' Lemon, had a sick wireless-operator. Greaves was to replace him.

Sergeant Herbert Ruse, the pilot of Harry Jones's aircraft, had joined the RAF as a technical apprentice at Trenchard's famous Halton school at the age of sixteen, in 1930. A Suffolk butcher's son, he had decided that the air force could not be worse than sweating for school certificate at Sudbury grammar school, and discovered too late that the discipline at Halton exceeded that of the most remorseless teacher. In 1936 he was a metal rigger when he was offered the chance to train as an NCO pilot under the ungenerous scheme of the period which allowed selected ground crew to fly for five years before returning to ground duties in their original rank. But Herbie Ruse thought that if he became an experienced bomber pilot, there might be a career for him in civil aviation. He qualified and was posted to Feltwell in September 1937. That December Sunday of 1939 he was at home in Long Melford when he was telephoned to return at once to the station: 'Some practice do,' they said. At briefing he was surprised to learn that they were to bomb above ten thousand feet, for he could never remember any crew scoring hits in bombing practice on a target as small as a ship from that height. Enemy fighters were an unknown quantity. In fighter affiliation exercises, the gunners would call exultantly: 'Got him, skip!' But neither he nor they had any scientific means of judging whether they were right. They had seldom fired live ammunition in the air, and on exercises they had trained to attack in succession in pairs, making a series of runs over the target to judge their own errors. On this occasion, there would clearly be no opportunity for these refinements.

As Ruse's Wellington climbed slowly over Norfolk, Harry Jones in the rear turret tested his twin guns, while Corporal Fred Taylor the wireless operator/gunner fired a few rounds from the front turret. 37 Squadron had been practising a new formation, flying 'stepped-down' in pairs above each other, rather than in the vics customary in other squadrons. Herbie Ruse's only concern was to keep station with Flying Officer Thompson in the Wellington beside him, to bomb when he did, to change course as he did. Sergeant Tom May, in the second-pilot's seat beside Ruse, had no need to concern himself with dead-reckoning navigation on this trip. It was simply a case of follow-my leader. 37's section were over the North Sea before they took up station at the rear of Kellett's formation, and throughout the flight they lagged some way behind. As the day grew around them, they noted with concern that the broken cloud over England had cleared completely. It was now a bright, crystal-clear morning with visibility approaching fifty miles, ideal conditions for an enemy interception.

They had climbed to 15,000 feet, and were becoming acutely conscious of the numbing December cold that was spilling through the draughty turrets, blowing relentlessly down the un-heated fuselage, seeping into their hands and feet, closing its grip on their tautening limbs as the hours went on. They could now see the island of Heligoland before them. They were approaching German waters, the familiar naval battle grounds of the First World War, where Beatty's battlecruisers and the Royal Navy's dashing submarine captains had played tip-and-run with the German High Seas Fleet for so long. They would be making a landfall close to the Danish–German frontier, then turning on a long leg southwards, down the German coast, searching for enemy naval units. In the leading aircraft perhaps two miles in front of them, Wing-Commander Kellett, who had made his name before the war chasing long-distance flying records, was for the first time carrying as a member of his crew a naval officer, Lieutenant-Commander Rotherham, to identify suitable targets.

In his lonely turret in the tail of Ruse's Wellington, Harry Jones tightened the twenty-foot scarf Mary had knitted for him as close as he could around his throat, to fight the dreadful cold. The turret was even more cramped than was usual in Wellingtons, for after acute difficulty with the ammunition feeds, 37 Squadron had improvised a system of canvas trays to hold the folded belts beneath the guns, and in consequence the gunners were hemmed in by .303 rounds up to their knees. Herbie Ruse was not one of those captains who tried to enforce silence on the intercom on long flights. Harry chatted for a few minutes to Fred Taylor, at the front guns, gazing down at the dirty grey sea below them, occasionally traversing his turret. It was moving sluggishly, the hydraulic oil already thickening at the unaccustomed height and temperature. Harry stamped his feet on the ammunition below him to keep circulation moving.

Two hours out from Mildenhall, in the midst of the North Sea Flight-Lieutenant Duguid of 149 Squadron, leading the second vic of the forward section, began to have trouble maintaining the revolutions of his starboard engine. Accurate formation flying was no longer possible as his speed dropped. His observer signalled his two wingmen by Aldis lamp to close up on Kellett's vic just ahead, when he himself dropped back. His no. 2, Riddlesworth, obediently closed up on Kellett. His no. 3 apparently failed to see Duguid's signal, and with what seemed remarkable lack of imagination, followed the ailing Wellington down and on to the homeward track. The two bombers landed at Mildenhall at 1.25 p.m. that afternoon. There were now twenty-two aircraft remaining in the formation.

At 12.30 p.m., three hours out from Norfolk, Kellett sighted the north German coast, a smudge fifty miles ahead across the gin-clear sky. For the next one-and-a-half hours, his force would be within range of German fighter aircraft. The long run southwards had brought them over Wilhelmshaven as far as possible from the concentration of flak ships among the Friesian Islands. But the price of the dog's leg was that the German defences had maximum warning of their coming.

Yet, in the event, it was the German flak which saved the formation from the first fighters into the air. Six Messerschmitt Bf109 single-engined night-fighters scrambled to approach the Wellingtons as they closed the Jade Roads. But as the fighters made their first attack, the German anti-aircraft batteries on shore opened a furious bombardment on the Wellingtons. The Bf109s* broke away, and hung off the flanks of the formation, expecting the barrage to stop. In fact, however, as the Wellingtons approached Wilhelmshaven, the ground fire intensified. The fighters waited for their turn.

To Harry Jones in his turret, the black puffs hanging in the air around them looked like buckets of coal that some madman was hurling into the sky. Ruse's aircraft bucked in the concussions, but the formation was too high for effective flak, just as Ludlow-Hewitt had hoped. Jack Greaves, in the front turret of 'Cheese' Lemon's aircraft, thought that if this was German flak, there was nothing to it. He was relieved, for there was no room in the turret for his parachute, and he felt acutely vulnerable to any sudden disaster to the aircraft.

The most serious consequence of the flak was that it caused the formation, and especially 9 Squadron, its port section, and 37 in the rear, to open ranks and lose their delicate cohesion. Both Squadron-Leader Guthrie of 9 and Squadron-Leader Hue-Williams of 37 were some distance ahead of their sections, and those at the rear were straggling. As Kellett in the leading aircraft opened his bomb doors on the approach to Wilhelmshaven, many of his crews were already dangerously scattered across the sky.

The fact that the Wellingtons had now survived an hour inside German fighter range without loss was the result of an extra-

---

*As an abbreviation readily understood by a lay audience, henceforth I shall refer to Messerschmitt fighters as Me109s and 110s, although their correct designation was Bf109 and Bf110. I trust that aviation specialists will not carp.

ordinary series of lapses by the Luftwaffe. The British pilots were only sketchily aware that their own country possessed the capability to detect the approach of enemy aircraft by radar, and certainly had no notion that the Germans did also. In the upper reaches of Bomber Command, it was known that the Germans had been carrying out radar experiments parallel with those of the RAF, but there was a tacit reluctance to believe that Hun technology could already have matched the British achievement. In reality, on this 18 December, at about the same time that Kellett sighted the north German coast fifty miles ahead, the Wellingtons were picked up by the Luftwaffe's *Freya* radar station among the sand dunes of the offshore island of Wangerooge, and by the naval radar station on Heligoland. Yet it would be an hour before the fighters made their first effective attack. Fifty-three doomed men among the 114 in the British formation were granted that much extra life because of simple disbelief on the part of the Germans that the Royal Air Force could flaunt itself in the face of the Luftwaffe on a brilliant day that promised only a massacre.

Despite the adequacy of their technology, the Germans had failed to match the British in marrying radar to an effective fighter direction system. The naval radar report was only hesitantly passed through their own HQ exchange to the Luftwaffe at Jever. When the young lieutenant commanding the air-force's own radar station telephoned Jever direct, he was caustically dismissed: 'Tommies approaching in weather like this? You're plotting seagulls or there's interference on your set!'[2] The Luftwaffe officer then tried to telephone the CO of the neighbouring Me110 squadron direct, only to learn that he was absent at headquarters. Kellett's men, now cruising majestically down the coast of Schleswig-Holstein, had gained a few more minutes. Only after a visual sighting report by German naval observers, whose message was duplicated in transmission and reached HQ as a warning of forty-four approaching enemy aircraft, did the Luftwaffe at last grasp the reality of attack. Belatedly the fighters began to scramble.

Even as the Messerschmitts were climbing to engage the Wellingtons, the Germans suffered another moment of bewildered astonishment. The bombers came high over Wilhelmshaven, over a battleship and cruiser lying in Bau Haven, with bomb doors open. Yet not a bomb fell. With the flak still splashing and blackening the sky around them, the British aircraft turned slowly westwards towards the North Sea and home. The formation's orders not to bomb if there was any danger of hitting the shore gave Kellett no discretion. He had concluded that the warships were too close to land to risk attack. As an operation of war against the German navy, the Wellington's mission had thus been a total, indeed a grotesque, failure. Yet as the bombers cruised away from Wilhelmshaven and emerged from the flak barrage, a few minutes before 1.30 p.m., their own destruction began.

In the Luftwaffe's previous encounters with Wellington formations, they had probed the bombers' weaknesses with some circumspection. Two important conclusions had emerged from the fighter pilots' reports. First, although the Wellington's rear turret could be very effective against attacks from astern, the guns were incapable of traversing to a full right-angle with the aircraft, and Wellingtons were thus unable to make any reply to an attack from the beam. Second, through a criminal omission on the part of the Air Ministry, the aircraft lacked self-sealing tanks. If hit in a fuel tank, especially that in the port wing, a Wellington could be transformed within seconds into a flying bonfire. Even if the tanks did not ignite, rapid loss of fuel would almost certainly bring down a crippled aircraft on a long run home. The Luftwaffe fighter squadron commanders urged their pilots to knock out the British rear turrets at long range, where the Wellington's .303s were useless, then close in for the kill.

Many of the men flying the bombers had joined the RAF in the early and mid-1930s, before the era of the 350-mph cannon fighter. As they lumbered westwards at less than 200 mph over the north German island towards the open sea, a succession of stabbing, slashing assaults by the Me109s and 110s began. P/O Speirs of 149 Squadron was flying no. 3 in the leading section behind Kellett, when a twin-engined Me110 dived across the formation hosing fire that suddenly lanced into the fuselage of Speirs' aircraft. There was an explosion to the rear of the cockpit close to the wing root, almost certainly in a fuel tank. The

Wellington fell away from the formation, flames pouring from the fuselage, to plunge headlong into the sea 10,000 feet below. There were no parachutes. Riddlesworth, the only survivor of Duguid's vic, since the other two had turned back, now closed up to take Speirs' place behind Kellett. The three Wellingtons began twenty minutes of desperate fighting against a procession of Messerschmitts. The 109s seemed to follow the 110s into attack. As they flew over Schillig Point, to their dismay the British could see a further squadron of fighters taking off to join the battle.

'The enemy pressed home their attacks in a splendid manner,' wrote Kellett in his report, striking a curiously gallant note in describing an ill-matched slaughter. But at last an Me109 gave the British their chance. Tiring of beam attacks and difficult deflection shots, the German swung in to attack Riddlesworth from dead astern. This was the situation for which the RAF had developed 'mutual supporting fire'. All three Wellington rear gunners in the lead vic ripped into him. Spuming smoke, the fighter curled away to the sea. The pilot escaped from his sinking cockpit only to drown under the weight of his flying gear. Kellett's three aircraft, with the advantage of being in the van of the formation and aided by some disciplined and determined flying, pressed on towards England.

But behind them, the bomber force was crumbling. In 9 Squadron's section on the port side of the formation, the fierce little Canadian Bill Macrae cursed his gunner as he kicked and banked the Wellington under attack and heard no sound of answering fire from his own rear turret: 'I'm trying, skip, but my fingers are too stiff to get the guns to bear!' shouted the frozen, desperate gunner, who was wounded moments later. Fabric was flapping from the great gashes torn in the wings and fuselage, and fuel leaking from the tanks. In Petts' aircraft nearby, the first burst from an Me109 wounded the rear gunner. Heathcote, the second pilot, scrambled down the fuselage and dragged the gunner out. He emptied burst after burst into the attacking fighters until at last the guns clicked dead. The ammunition trays were empty. Heathcote crawled forward to the front gunner, wounded in the thigh, and took over his turret instead. Sergeant Petts threw the aircraft into a tortured dive to sea level to shake off the Messerschmitts.

Miraculously he succeeded. With his bleeding gunners and his rudder controls partly jammed, he nursed the Wellington home to a forced landing at Sutton Bridge in Lincolnshire. Macrae made an emergency landing at the coastal airfield of North Coates.

These were the only two aircraft from the port section to reach home. S/Ldr Guthrie, whom Baldwin was to charge with 'lack of interest' in his report, flew his blazing aircraft headlong into the North Sea. Douglas Allison, a quiet, serious Londoner, dropped away with his port engine on fire, and no trace of himself or his crew was ever found. The Wellington of Challes, beside him, broke up in mid-air after being hit amidships by fire from an Me110. Lines, the last of the section, vanished shortly afterwards, probably at the hands of an Me110 of the Luftwaffe's 2 Squadron ZG 76.

The starboard section of the big diamond – two vics of three, led respectively by S/Ldr Harris of 149 and F/Lt Grant of 9 Squadron – held formation under attack better than their counterparts on the port side. Grant had just given the order to close bomb doors after passing Wilhelmshaven when the fighters fell on them. It was the first time that they had seen Me110s and as they droned steadily west they were shocked by the ruthless ease with which the Germans took station abreast of them, and hammered fire into the bombers with impunity, the Wellingtons' turrets traversed to their impotent maximum of 80 degrees. Glancing out of the cockpit, Grant was dismayed to see fuel spuming out of his holed tanks. He began urgently pumping what remained into those that seemed unhit: 'There was absolutely nothing that we could do except sit there being picked off one by one . . .'[3] On Grant's port side Sergeant Ramshaw, his aircraft hit repeatedly by attacks which came almost certainly from the Messerschmitt of Gordon Gollob – later to become a famous ace with 150 alleged victories – was appalled to find all his turrets jammed and his rear gunner mortally wounded. Defenceless, he dropped his Wellington under the rest of the section and flew on homewards, clinging beneath the shelter of their guns, fuel pouring from his tanks. In Harris's aircraft in front of them, fire cut into the front turret, one round smashing through the sole of

30

the gunner's boot, another burst damaging sections of the geodetic frame and an elevator. Behind Harris, Briden was staggering onwards in an aircraft heavily damaged and losing fuel fast.

It was the performance of this starboard section and that of Kellett in the lead which later caused one of the German fighter squadron commanders to note in his report the 'tight formation and excellent rear gunners of the Wellington bombers'. One Me110 had already been compelled to pull out of action and make an emergency landing with its crew wounded by turret fire from a Wellington. The German squadron CO himself forced-landed with a badly damaged aircraft, and most of his fighters had been hit by the British guns. But the fact remained that none of the 110s had been totally destroyed, and as the German also stated in his report: 'The Wellingtons' maintenance of formation and rigid adherence to course made them easy targets to find.'

While the leading sections of the British force fought a savage battle for survival, it was at the rear, among the aircraft of 37 Squadron, that disaster became almost absolute. Even before Kellett's formation closed Wilhelmshaven, the second pilot of 'Cheese' Lemon's aircraft reached down to open the bomb doors. On a Wellington, the control was set beside the flap lever. He accidentally put on full flap. The results were dramatic. The Wellington soared abruptly upwards, causing chaos among the crew and uproar on the intercom. The aircraft then stalled and began to dive steeply towards the earth, as Lemon and his second pilot struggled to regain control.

By the time they had done so, they were alone, very low, over the sea. 'Christ, we've lost everything now. We're on our own,' thought Greaves. It was at this moment that the rear gunner, Kidd, shouted: '109s!' Lemon clung desperately to the waves as the gunner called out the attacks: 'They're coming in . . . now . . . left! Now, right, right! He's overshooting!' They were hit repeatedly in the fuselage, the aircraft still streaking along with spray breaking on the perspex of the front turret, where Greaves tried in vain to bring his guns to bear. 'If we go down now, we've had it,' he thought, struck by the ghastly vision of the aircraft plunging unhesitating to the sea bottom if Lemon lost control for a moment. The observer at the mid-upper hatch was commentating on the German attacks. Suddenly, as one of the fighters closed again, there was a cry of choked astonishment from the rear turret: 'Christ! He's gone straight in!' The German's wingtip seemed to have touched the water, and in an instant had vanished. The other fighter broke away. They were alone. There was an outburst of nervous hilarity on the intercom about the German's collision with the North Sea. Then Lemon cut in: 'Come on, cut the chatter, we've got to get home.' Silent, exhausted by fear, they settled for the long run back to Feltwell, flying all the way almost at sea level. Greaves swore that he could taste the salt. After their half-hearted debriefing on landing at 3.30 p.m., they waited for the next Feltwell aircraft to return. Yet by evening, none had come.

As the rear section of the Wellington force, 37 Squadron were the first and easiest targets for the German fighters. The experiment with the 'stepped down' formation in pairs must be considered a failure, by results. Lemon had been flying as wingman to S/Ldr Hue-Williams. In the chaotic nightmare of the battle, as each bomber struggled for its own survival, men caught only momentary glances at the plight of others. Peter Grant glimpsed Hue-Williams' aircraft diving for the sea, starboard wing on fire. Hue-Williams' second pilot was that same Appleby who had driven so gaily to Monte Carlo with Grant that spring. There were no survivors.

Just north of Wangerooge a second pair – Wimberley and Lewis – broke away westwards in an attempt to make a low-level escape for home over the sandbanks. They were at once spotted by Lieutenant Helmut Lent in his Me110. Lent had scrambled from Jever with his armourer still lying on the wing loading cannon shells into the magazines – the man was scarcely able to roll to the ground before Lent accelerated to take off. After one abortive beam attack on the blindspot of Wimberley's Wellington, the impatient Lent closed astern and abruptly silenced the rear gunner. His second burst set fire to the aircraft, which dived and crashed in the sea close to Borkum Island. 'Pete' Wimberley, the only survivor, was picked up by a German patrol boat. Lent turned in pursuit of Lewis, now struggling ten feet above the sea to escape in the same style as Lemon. Lent, unlike his colleague in the Me109 which had attacked Lemon, made no mistake. After a single burst, the Wellington caught fire and broke up as it hit the water. There were no survivors. Lent was later to become one of the most celebrated German fighter aces of the war.

Herbie Ruse, concentrating on keeping formation with F/O Thompson in the middle pair of the 37 Squadron section, was one of the few British pilots to drop aimed bombs that day. Thompson opened his bomb doors, apparently on his own initiative, as they approached a German vessel a few miles west of Schillig Point. Ruse followed suit, and Tom May, himself a former seaman who had joined up during the Slump, took position forward by the bomb release. 'He's going for that ship!' called May, 'He's going to overshoot!' 'Are you sure it's naval?' asked Ruse, as he struggled to hold the aircraft steady amidst a new surge of flak. Then as Thompson's bombs fell away, May released their own. The aircraft lifted as the weight vanished. They saw the sticks splash harmlessly into the sea at the same moment that Herbie Ruse spotted a German fighter underneath them 'climbing like a lift'. Thompson put his nose down and dived steeply northwestwards, Ruse close behind him. The leading Wellington had obviously decided that they must try to make a break for it on their own. Although Ruse instinctively regretted breaking away from the formation, 37 Squadron's section had become a straggling litter of aircraft. This might be their only hope.

The Wellington was racing downwards at an incredible 300 mph, shaking in every rivet. Harry Jones was irrelevantly startled to see red roofs on the coast to port of them: 'The roofs can't be red!' he muttered. 'Those are German houses. We have red roofs in England.' Then he saw a German fighter streaking towards them at a closing speed of more than 100 mph. 'My God, isn't it small!' he thought, as so many thousands of air gunners would think in their turn in the next five years as the slim silhouette of the fighter swung in, guns winking, to attack. At 600 yards Harry touched his triggers. The guns fired a single round and stopped. They were frozen. He tried to traverse the turret. It was jammed by the cold. Fighting with the cocking handles, he glimpsed Thompson's Wellington sliding by beneath them, its tail shot to pieces. Its rear turret had simply disappeared, and with it Harry's friend Len Stock, a little instrument-repairer from North London. There would be no survivors from Thompson's aircraft.

Harry was still wrestling with his guns when the fighter came in again. There was a violent explosion in the turret and a savage pain in his ankle and back. 'Skip, I've been hit!' he called down the intercom. 'Can you do anything back there? No? Then for God's sake get out of the turret,' answered Ruse. Harry dragged himself up the fuselage towards the rest bed, half-conscious, with his back scored by one bullet, his ankle shattered by a second. The Wellington I was equipped with a bizarre mid-under turret known to the crews as 'the dustbin'. Because of its fierce drag on the aircraft's speed in the firing position, it was lowered only in action. Now Tom Holly, the wireless operator, was struggling to bring it to bear as the Messerschmitts raked the Wellington yet again. Fred Taylor bent over Harry Jones, morphia in hand, trying to lift his leg on to the rest bed. A burst smashed through the port side of the fuselage, shattering Taylor's head and back. Harry had persuaded the quiet northern boy to put aside his wartime scruples and get married only a few weeks before. Now Taylor collapsed on him, dying. The next burst caught Tom Holly as he struggled to pull himself out of the dustbin turret, jammed and useless. Hit in the face and side, Holly fell dead, draped half in, half out of the gun position.

Herbie Ruse could smell the cordite from the explosions in the fuselage, and feel the Wellington being cut to pieces as he laboured to keep it in the air, still diving towards the sea with the revolutions counter gone mad and the engines in coarse pitch. Calmly he wound back the actuating wheel controlling the aircraft's trim, so that if he himself was hit and fell from the controls, the Wellington should automatically seek to recover from the dive. Then the elevator controls collapsed, and he knew that the aircraft was doomed. Beside him Tom May fought to help pull back the control column. Jones, lying behind them, was astounded to see a burst of fire tear up the floor between May's legs as he stood straddled in the cockpit. May was hit only once, slightly wounded in the buttock. They saw the sand dunes of an island rushing up to meet them. It was Borkum, just a few miles east of neutral Dutch waters. With a grinding, wrenching, protracted shriek of metal and a whirlwind of sparks from the frozen ground beneath, Ruse brought the Wellington to rest. There were a few seconds of merciful silence. May jettisoned the canopy and jumped down. Ruse was about to follow when he heard Jones' painful cry: 'I'm trapped!' As flames began to seep up the fuselage, Ruse hoisted Jones off the floor. 'My God, you're heavy, Jonah,' he complained. Then he half-dragged, half-carried the gunner out of the wrecked aircraft. The three men lay silent, in pain and exhaustion behind a dune in the sandy, frozen waste as their aircraft burned. At last a German patrol arrived to greet them with the time-honoured cliché: 'For you the war is over!' The rear section of the Wellington formation had ceased to exist.

It is a measure of the fierceness of the struggle that continued for almost thirty minutes around Kellett's Wellingtons that of those aircraft which survived, 9 Squadron claimed six certain 'kills' and six 'probables' among the German fighters, 149 Squadron the same, and Lemon of 37 Squadron a single. Their turrets were strewn with cartridge cases, their wings, tanks and fuselages holed repeatedly. Almost all had jettisoned their bombs in the sea. Three aircraft remained of the leading section under Kellett. The port and rear sections had vanished entirely. On the starboard side, Sergeant Ramshaw's aircraft was still tucked in underneath, streaming fuel, while immediately ahead of Peter Grant, Briden of 149 Squadron was also heavily damaged and losing fuel fast.

Then, perhaps ninety miles west of Wilhelmshaven, Grant glanced up for a moment to find that 'quite suddenly, there were just a few Wellingtons flying alone in the clear sky'.[4] The German fighters had reached the limit of their endurance. They had retired, to claim thirty-four victories, twenty-six of which were confirmed by the Reich Air Ministry. They had lost two Me109s, a further one which was written off after crashlanding, and almost all the Me110s which took part in the action had been more or less damaged. In reality, ten British aircraft had already been totally destroyed out of the original twenty-four. It had not been an impressive performance by the Germans. Even after their belated interception, they had made repeated ineffectual long-range attacks. If their tactics had been better, it would have been remarkable if any British aircraft had survived at all. But for the British, by any objective assessment, it had been a disastrous day.

As the remnants of the formation lumbered home, the Wellingtons of Briden and Ramshaw were dropping back. Briden signalled Harris, his section leader: could they take the shortest possible route home, because he was losing petrol very fast? Forty miles out from the English coast, a few minutes after 3 p.m., Briden's engines spluttered and died. The Wellington glided smoothly down towards the icy sea below, cartwheeled to starboard as it touched, then settled. Harris circled above them, watching the crew struggling around their dinghy. He ordered his own crew to throw out their dinghy to assist. After a struggle, they set it free. But it inflated as it fell away from the aircraft, struck the tail and jammed there. With his rudder controls crippled, Harris with difficulty flew on to forced land at Coltishall. Lifeboats put out from Cromer and Sheringham to Briden's last reported position, but the North Sea in December is not a welcoming refuge. Like so many men who ditched in its waters in the next five years, neither Briden nor his crew were ever seen again. They had been warned in training that they might expect to survive for fifteen minutes under such conditions.

Sergeant Ramshaw of 9 Squadron was more fortunate. His engines died at last just short of Grimsby. Lilley, his rear gunner, was already critically wounded when they ditched and was lost with the aircraft. Ramshaw and the remainder of his crew were picked up by a trawler and by nightfall lay in Grimsby hospital.

Thus twelve surviving aircraft – ten, discounting the two which had not attacked – came home. Soon after 4 p.m., after almost seven hours in the air, the eight remaining in the formation touched down. At Honington, only Peter Grant and Sergeant Purdy landed. Grant told his tale to the CO and the Adjutant in the officers' mess, then went exhausted to bed. An officer who put his head into the mess a little later found it deserted but for the CO, who sat bowed and old, alone by the fireplace.

*

Slaughter of these proportions at this, still squeamish, moment of the war provoked an unprecedented upheaval and post-mortem both at 3 Group and at Bomber Command. Ludlow-Hewitt, a C-in-C already well known for his sensitivity to casualties, flew in person to Norfolk to hear first-hand accounts of the operation. Group-Captain Hugh Pughe-Lloyd, a 3 Group staff officer who had commanded 9 Squadron until a few weeks before, said in one of a mass of reports inspired by the disaster: 'I dislike the course taken to the target. On this occasion we make a land-fall near the German–Danish frontier and run the whole way down it, giving the enemy all the warning he can get.' This was almost the only instance of open criticism of the planning of the operation.

Most senior officers studied the events of 18 December and drew much more hopeful and face-saving conclusions. They readily accepted that the Wellingtons had to be provided with beam guns and self-sealing tanks. But granted these measures, it seemed to them that the elements of Kellett's formation which had stuck rigidly together as ordered had fared astonishingly well. Only one of Kellett's own section of four aircraft had been lost, an impressive list of enemy fighters destroyed had been accepted. Of the six aircraft on the starboard side, all would have survived the battle had they been fitted with self-sealing tanks.

Why therefore had the port and rear sections of the formation fared so badly? Air Vice-Marshal Baldwin's report to Ludlow-Hewitt contained no breath of criticism of the strategic and tactical concepts underlying the operation:

I am afraid [he wrote firmly on 23 December] there is no doubt that the heavy casualties experienced by 9 and 37 Squadrons were due to poor leadership and consequent poor formation flying. Squadron-Leader Guthrie is reported as being almost a mile ahead of his formation. For some unknown reason Hue-Williams, who, I thought, was a very sound leader, appears to have done the same thing . . .

I have not by any means given up hope of being able to drive home the lessons learnt . . . I have already taken steps to prevent a repetition, but I was allowing a certain period to elapse before pinning results on to individual actions, although instances of bad leadership have already been pointed out to all units.

3 Group's summary of the lessons to be derived from the events of 18 December concluded: 'There is every reason to believe that a very close formation of six Wellington aircraft will emerge from a long and heavy attack by enemy fighters with very few, if any, casualties to its own aircraft.' 3 Group's operational instruction No. 21 of 23 December 1939 stated: 'With the intention of combining useful training and operations, sweeps will continue to be carried out . . . If enemy aircraft are encountered, gunners will be able to practise shooting at real targets instead of drogues . . .'

On 2 January 1940, Air Vice-Marshal A. T. Harris, the future C-in-C of Bomber Command, then serving as AOC of 5 Group, told HQ at High Wycombe that so long as three bombers were in company in daylight, the pilots 'considered themselves capable of taking on anything'.

Peter Grant was sent to lecture to a Bomber Command gunnery school on the realities of facing attack in daylight. On his return, he was reprimanded for having given 'an unpatriotic talk likely to cause dismay and demoralization'.

The Germans at Wilhelmshaven were unaware that Ruse had dropped his bombs in the sea before crashing, and were therefore bewildered to find that his Wellington had apparently flown the operation unloaded. The only logical conclusion that they could reach about the behaviour of Kellett's formation was that the British had been carrying out some suicidal form of exercise, which was indeed not far from the truth.

On the night of 18 December, there was a knock on the door of Mary Jones' little flat in Feltwell. It was 37 Squadron's adjutant, struggling to mask his embarrassment in harshness: 'You know your husband's not coming back, don't you?' That night, Mary dreamt of Harry's golden hair floating on the sea. She was quickly gone from Feltwell. The station made it apparent that they were anxious to rid themselves of their dreadful crop of widows as hastily as possible. It was weeks before she heard confirmation of German radio claims that Harry, with May and Ruse, was a prisoner. It was Christmas 1945 before the Joneses sat down together to eat the pudding that she had made that winter of 1939, and which she stored so hopefully through the six Christmases of war that followed.

Most of the other men who survived 18 December were killed on operations in the years that followed. Many of the German aircrew who triumphed that day were killed eight months later in the Battle of Britain. Among the Wellington crews, Bill Macrae, 9 Squadron's tough little Canadian, died perhaps most pathetically of all, on collecting a Distinguished Flying Cross from Buckingham Palace a few weeks following the Wilhelmshaven raid. After a celebration with his crew, he took off from Weybridge to fly home to Norfolk, and crashed.

But if it had not been Weybridge, the odds were overwhelming that it would have been Cologne, Hanover, Berlin, or Frankfurt, some night in the five years that were to come. The Wilhelmshaven raid had been merely a blooding, one episode in the first weeks of a long war. Its importance was that it struck a major blow at the strategic and tactical concepts on which the Royal Air Force had based itself for twenty years – although its leaders declined to see the battle in these terms. The Wilhelmshaven raid was the beginning of the confrontation between the theory and practice of warfare that would dominate the long campaign of Bomber Command.

1 In the beginning, Trenchard: British bomber policy, 1917-40

'From the time when the first experiments were made in air power during the First World War until the great Bomber Command attack on Dresden and the discharge of the first atomic bombs by the USAAF thirty years later, the whole development and direction of strategic bombing was a highly and continuously controversial matter . . . The controversy raged over the whole field of the offensive which embraced questions of strategic desirability, operational possibility, economic, industrial and moral vulnerability, and legal and moral responsibility . . . '
The Strategic Air Offensive against Germany 1939–45[1]

One clear May morning in 1917, a formation of German Gotha bombers droned high over the Kent coastal town of Folkestone and the neighbouring army camp of Shorncliffe. In the few minutes that followed, their bombs killed 95 people and injured 175. The seventy-four British aircraft which took off to intercept them were able to shoot down only one Gotha. Three weeks later, on 17 June, twenty-one Gothas mounted a second daylight attack. Seven bombers attacked small towns in Kent and Essex, while the remaining fourteen flew on in diamond formation to attack London itself. 162 people were killed and 432 injured. A third attack on 7 July killed 65 people and injured 245. It was the inauguration of strategic air bombardment, the first significant attempt by an air force to take advantage of this third dimension of warfare to pass above protecting armies and navies and strike direct at the nation of the enemy.

The consternation, indeed panic, provoked by the German attack was considerably greater among British politicians and in the Press than among Britons at large. All governments in wartime are nervous about the effects of unexpected shocks on national morale, and the Gothas came at a moment when mounting war-weariness was apparent in Britain. The bombings seemed to signal the inception of a new, ghastly age, vividly foretold as far back as 1908 by England's most celebrated contemporary prophet, H. G. Wells, in his book *The War in the Air*. Extraordinary efforts were made to strengthen the air defences, specially around London. Fighters were recalled from France. Guns and searchlights were deployed for the first time in depth. Lloyd George, the Prime Minister, appointed himself and one of the Empire's foremost heroes, the rehabilitated Boer General Smuts, as a committee of two, to study how best Britain's air forces could be reorganized to meet the German threat; above all, to consider whether the national interest was best served by maintaining the air forces as subordinate corps within the British Army and Royal Navy. In the event, Smuts conducted the inquiry single-handed, with the assistance of army and Royal Flying Corps officers. The Smuts Report, as it became known, inspired the creation of the Royal Air Force as an independent service alongside the army and navy. More than this, Smuts sowed the seed of the vast British strategic air offensive in the Second World War.

Somewhere in the midst of his rather cursory investigation, Smuts became captivated by the vision of air power. He was fascinated by the concept of a New Force in warfare – this, at a moment when in France the Old Forces were achieving the most spectacular and ghastly débâcle in their history. His report, completed on 17 August 1917, would form the foundation on which British airmen would build a complete theory of warfare in the next twenty years:

An air service [Smuts wrote to the War Cabinet] can be used as an independent means of war operations. Nobody that witnessed the attack on London on 11 July could have any doubt on that point . . . As far as can at present be foreseen there is absolutely no limit to the scale of its future independent war use. And the day may not be far off when aerial operations with their devastation of enemy lands and destruction of industrial and populous centres on a vast scale may become the principal operations of war, to which the older forms of military and naval operations may become secondary and subordinate.

The magnitude and significance of the transformation now in progress are not easily recognized. It requires some imagination to realize that next summer, while our Western Front may still be moving forward at a snail's pace in Belgium and France, the air battle front will be far behind on the Rhine, and that its continuous and intense pressure against the chief industrial centres of the enemy as well as on his lines of communication may form an important factor in bringing about peace.

Here indeed was a vision, and one which sent as great a shock of anger and scorn through the ranks of the generals and admirals as of excitement and enthusiasm through those of the airmen. At another time, the combined hostility of the War Office and the Admiralty would have been enough to kill the Smuts Report without notice. But in the autumn of 1917 the political stock of the leaders of the two established services had sunk to a very low ebb indeed in the eyes of the British Government. Service objections to Smuts's recommendations were interpreted as rearguard actions to prevent any transfer of forces from their own commands. Lloyd George overruled them. He approved the creation of an 'Independent Air Force' to begin bombing operations against Germany. He authorized the build-up of a powerful fighter force in England to meet the German bomber threat. He decreed the union of the Royal Flying Corps and the Royal Naval Air Service to form the new Royal Air Force from 1 April 1918. The RFC's commander, Sir Hugh Trenchard, was brought back from France to become the first Chief of Air Staff.

To the Government's satisfaction, this extraordinary wave of activity produced results. The Germans abandoned daylight bombing in the face of stiffening opposition and, for the rest of the war, troubled England with only desultory night attacks by Gothas and Zeppelins. Although the merger of the RFC and the RNAS had provoked such heat at high level, on the squadrons themselves it was accomplished without excessive ill will. Trenchard, who had earlier opposed the creation of a Royal Air Force as an independent service, now surprised and confused everybody by the fierce single-mindedness with which he adopted the care of his fledgling against the army and navy's rapacious designs. His initial tenure as Chief of Air Staff was short-lived, for he quarrelled with the Air Minister and returned to France to command the Independent Air Force – the Allies' embryo strategic bombing force – for the remaining months of the war. The 543 tons of explosives his aircraft dropped on Germany before the armistice made only a pinprick impact on the enemy, but enormously enlarged Trenchard's vision of the potential of air power. At the end of the war, after a change of Air Minister, Trenchard returned to England not only as Chief of Air Staff, but as the messiah of the new form of warfare. Trenchard's passionate commitment to the concept of a bomber offensive against an enemy nation was to dominate the Royal Air Force for more than twenty years.

At the armistice, the RAF was larger than the British Army had been in 1914. But in the first months of peace, this vast organization was almost totally dismantled. Like the other two services, the air force found its annual financial estimates cut to the bone. Indeed, throughout the 1920s it would have been difficult for the RAF to resist total dismemberment but for Trenchard's invention of the new scheme of 'Air Control' for some of the wilder frontiers of the Empire, notably Iraq. Trenchard persuaded the Government that rather than maintain expensive standing garrisons of troops and dispatch punitive expeditions against recalcitrant tribesmen, the RAF could keep them at bay with occasional prescriptions of air attack. In the next twenty years, the RAF's only operational experience was gained dropping bombs, usually without opposition, on the hillside villages of rebellious peasants. Local Political Officers remained sceptical of Air Control and its achievements, but Trenchard and his followers were convinced that, in the years between the two world wars, it was only their well-publicized activities abroad which saved the RAF from extinction at home.

Between 1920 and 1938 the air force commanded only an average 17 per cent of Britain's paltry defence budget. The RAF share fell to a low of less than £11 million in 1922, and never passed £20 million a year until the great drive for rearmament had begun, in 1935. There was no question in Trenchard's mind of trying to do everything, of seeking a balanced force. With such tiny resources, he concentrated them where he believed that they mattered – on his bomber squadrons. He was convinced that fighters had no chance of effectively countering a bomber attack, and he grudged every fighter unit that he was compelled to keep in being as a sop to public and political opinion. Trenchard's air force was to be devoted decisively to strategic rather than tactical ends.

In my view [he wrote, in an important and controversial memorandum to his fellow Chiefs of Staff in May 1928] the object of all three services is the same, to defeat the enemy nation, not merely its army, navy or air force.

For an army to do this, it is almost always necessary as a preliminary step to defeat the enemy's army, which imposes itself as a barrier that must first be broken down.

It is not, however, necessary for an air force, in order to defeat the enemy nation, to defeat its armed forces first. Air power can dispense with that intermediate step, can pass over the enemy navies and armies, and penetrate the air defences and attack direct the centres of production, transportation and communication from which the enemy war effort is maintained . . . The stronger side, by developing the more powerful offensive, will provoke in his weaker enemy increasingly insistent calls for the protective employment of aircraft. In this way he will throw the enemy on to the defensive and it will be in this manner that air superiority will be obtained, and not by direct destruction of air forces.

In the struggle to retain a *raison d'être* for the RAF as an independent service, Trenchard argued that aircraft provided an opportunity to wage an entirely new kind of war. The army and the Royal Navy greeted his prophecies with memoranda in which conventional courtesies did little to mask withering scorn. But Trenchard was uncrushable. Although often completely inarticulate at a conference table, 'Boom' (a nickname his remarkable voice had earned for him) possessed much personal presence and the power of inspiring great affection. Through the 1920s he gathered around himself in the middle ranks of the air force a body of passionate young disciples, not only captured by his vision of air power, but devoted to the old man himself.

Portal, Harris, Cochrane and Slessor were among the most prominent. The Hon. Ralph Cochrane, for example, who would be Harris's outstanding wartime group commander, met Trenchard in Egypt one day in 1921. He had joined the Royal Navy in 1908 and flown airships on convoy escort during the First World War. He had once tried to hit a German submarine with four 8-lb bombs without successfully convincing either himself or the enemy of the efficacy of air power. He was still an airship man when 'Boom' entered his life. 'Young man,' said the fatherly Trenchard, 'you're wasting your time. Go and learn to fly an aeroplane.' Within a few years of this Damascene conversion Cochrane was a flight commander in Iraq, where Harris was converting his Vernon troop carriers into bombers on his own initiative, and experimenting with the prone position for bomb-aiming.

In the years between the wars, air power and the threat of bombing offensives against great cities became a matter of growing public debate and concern. It provoked an enormous literature, much of it fanciful, on bombers and air defence, on air-raid precautions and the morality of bombing. It is generally accepted that the godfather of air power was the Italian General Guilo Douhet, whose book *The Command of the Air* was published in 1921. Douhet ranks alongside Trenchard and Billy Mitchell in America, the most important advocates of assault on the heart of a nation by self-contained, self-defending bomber formations. Captain Basil Liddell Hart and Colonel J. F. C. Fuller would later come to be regarded as the foremost British military thinkers of the twentieth century, and in later life became formidable opponents of Bomber Command's strategic air offensive. But in 1920 Fuller foresaw that in the next war 'Fleets of aeroplanes will attack the enemy's great industrial and governing centres. All these attacks will be made against the civil population in order to compel it to accept the will of the attacker . . .'[2] Liddell Hart wrote in 1925, in his book *Paris, or the Future of War:*

A modern state is such a complex and interdependent fabric that it offers a target highly sensitive to a sudden and overwhelming blow from the air . . . Imagine for a moment London, Manchester, Birmingham and half a dozen other great centres simultaneously attacked, the business localities and Fleet Street wrecked, Whitehall a heap of ruins, the slum districts maddened into the impulse to break loose and maraud, the railways cut, factories destroyed. Would not the general will to resist vanish, and what use would be the still determined fractions of the nation, without organization and central direction?[3]

Here, from a soldier, was a prophecy that Trenchard himself might have hesitated to match. The concept of limitless terror from the air grew throughout the 1920s. In 1925 the Air Staff were asked by the Government to project the casualties in the event of an attack on Britain by the air force of France, with whom British relations were then strained almost to breaking point. They answered: 1,700 killed and 3,300 wounded in the first twenty-four hours; 1,275 killed and 2,475 wounded in the second twenty-four hours; 850 killed and 1,650 wounded in every twenty-four hours thereafter. This was merely a crude projection of the casualties suffered during the German surprise attack of 1917. The War Office was highly critical of the figures, but the public – to whom such forecasts eventually filtered through as rumour – was appalled. There were further anxious questions from politicians. Trenchard and his colleagues declared insistently that the only effective precaution against an enemy bomber attack was the possession of a British bomber force capable of inflicting comparable damage on an enemy. Fighter defence was useless. As late as 1934 the RAF's fighter squadrons were still outnumbered two to one by the bomber units, and depended heavily on reservists and auxiliaries to provide pilots on mobilization. The Battle of Britain would make the fighter pilot the most glamorous figure in the RAF, but in the years between the wars the bomber pilots considered themselves the élite of the service.

The most celebrated writers of the day launched forth upon the horrors of air attack with a passion a later generation would bring to those of the atomic bomb. Beverley Nichols and A. A. Milne denounced the barbarity. *The Times* declared in 1933 that 'it would be the bankruptcy of statesmanship to admit that it is a legitimate form of warfare for a nation to destroy its rival capital from the air'. Bernard Shaw reflected gloomily on 'cities where millions of inhabitants are dependent for light and heat, water and food, on centralized mechanical organs like great steel hearts and arteries that can be smashed in half an hour by a boy in a bomber'.[4] The Royal Navy, which still clung to the conviction that war could be waged with chivalry, was foremost in the assault on the RAF and its weapons. Admiral of the Fleet Lord Beatty wrote a letter to *The Times*, Admiral Sir Herbert Richmond delivered a lecture to the Royal United Services Institution in which he declared gloomily that 'frightfulness, expressly repudiated in the case of sea warfare, appears to be a fundamental principle in the air'.

There was also, however, a highly articulate air lobby, championing the cause of the new force. The airmen themselves argued – as they would reiterate repeatedly for the next half century – that in the age of industrialized mass slaughter it was ridiculous to draw an artificial line at some point between a tank factory and the front line, at which the tank and those responsible for it became morally acceptable targets. A body called 'The Hands Off Britain Air Defence League' was distributing pamphlets in 1933: 'Why wait for a bomber to leave Berlin at four o'clock and wipe out London at eight? Create a new winged army of long range British bombers to smash the foreign hornets in their nests!'

Air Power has its dreams [wrote one of the RAF's foremost public advocates, a civil servant at the Air Ministry, Mr J. M. Spaight]. It knows that its qualities are unique. The armoury of the invincible knight of old held no such weapon as that which it wields. It dreams of using its powers to the full. It dreams of victory achieved perhaps by a swift, sudden, overwhelming stroke at the heart and nerve centre of a foe, perhaps by a gathering wave of assaults that will submerge the morale and the will to war of the enemy people, perhaps by ventures as yet but dimly apprehended. Its mystery is half its power . . .[5]

In a remarkable passage of his book *Air Power and Cities*, the lyrical Mr Spaight recommended an interesting moral compromise to validate air bombardment of cities: 'The destruction of property not strictly classifiable as military should be legitimized under strict conditions designed to prevent loss of life, e.g. by confining bombardments of establishments tenanted only by day (as many large factories are) to the hours of darkness. . .'

In the last decade before the Second World War, it is no exaggeration to say that the threat of aerial bombardment and the possibilities of defence against it became a public obsession in Britain and France – in Germany, propaganda had already too far eclipsed free debate to allow any similar national neurosis to develop. Americans alone could view aerial bombardment with detachment, conscious that no likely enemy bomber force possessed the range to reach their shores. For the rest of the civilized world, it was a horrifying vision that the apostles of air power laid before them. Baldwin, Britain's former Prime Minister and a prominent member of the Coalition Cabinet, confirmed the worst fears of the world when he addressed the House of Commons on 10 November 1932, winding up a debate on international affairs:

I think it is well for the man in the street to realize that there is no power on earth that can protect him from being bombed. Whatever people may tell him, the bomber will always get through. The only defence is in offence, which means that you have to kill more women and children more quickly than the enemy if you want to save yourselves. I just mention that ... so that people may realize what is waiting for them when the next war comes.

One cannot help reflecting that, after the hundreds of millions of years during which the human race has been on this earth, it is only within our generation that we have secured the mastery of the air. I certainly do not know how the youth of the world may feel, but it is not a cheerful thought to the older men that, having got that mastery of the air, we are going to defile the earth from the air as we have defiled the soil during all the years that mankind has been on it. This is a question for the younger men far more than for us. They are the men who fly in the air.

'By 1933, and even more by 1934, Baldwin had developed what can best be described as the "Armada Complex",' in the words of a political historian of these years.[6] 'The Defence of the Realm – particularly from the air – was his personal and almost total obsession.'

Thus the Royal Air Force and its bombers stood at the very heart of the political and public debate between the wars. Yet in 1941, after two years in action, it was to come as a paralysing shock to Britain's leaders to discover that Bomber Command was not only incapable of hitting a precise objective, but even of locating a given enemy city by night. The theory of the self-defending daylight bomber formation would be tested and found wanting over the Heligoland Bight and finally exploded by the American 8th Air Force. Seldom in the history of warfare has a force been so sure of the end it sought – fulfilment of the Trenchard doctrine – and yet so ignorant of how this might be achieved, as the RAF between the wars.

As a bomber squadron commander, Arthur Harris explored such techniques as marking a target at night, but was compelled to abandon the experiment because the flares then available were quite inadequate for the task. Harris and his contemporary Charles Portal, who would be Chief of Air Staff for much of the war, competed fiercely year after year for squadron bombing trophies, but the exercises for which these were awarded bore as much relation to the reality of wartime bomber operations as a funfair rifle-range to the front line at Stalingrad. Although efforts were made to improve the quality of weather forecasting, there was no attempt to face the fact that wartime operations would take place in difficult conditions, that indeed the weather would dominate the conduct of bomber offensive. Before 1939 crews simply did not fly in bad weather. Cross-country exercises over England taught them nothing about the difficulties of navigating at night for long distances over blacked-out countries, for they grew accustomed to following railway lines and city lights. In the last two years before war, 478 Bomber Command crews forced landed on exercises in England, having lost their way. Realistic training might have been carried out over the Atlantic or the North Sea, but the loss of aircraft and crews that would undoubtedly have ensued seemed quite unacceptable in the climate of peace.

These were the years when if there was to be any hope of striking effectively when the war came, it was vital to build a comprehensive intelligence picture of the German economy. But as late as 1938, the British Secret Service budget was only equal to the annual cost of running one destroyer. Economics were scarcely comprehended outside the ranks of a few specialists. A very small branch of Air Intelligence was created to study targeting under a retired squadron leader. The Secret Service officer Major Desmond Morton controlled the Industrial Intelligence Centre, but devoted the weight of his limited resources to the study of arms-related industries rather than to assessing the broad industrial potential of the German economy.

Until the mid-1930s at least, the Air Staff showed no awareness of the speed with which aircraft technology was changing. Specifications were issued for biplanes a few miles an hour faster than those already in service, when designers were already feeling their way towards the 400 mph, retractable-undercarriage monoplanes that would dominate the war. Because there had been no scientific analysis of the problems of destroying a modern aircraft, there was no understanding of the need for heavy calibre automatic weapons on both fighters and bombers – the grossly inadequate .303 machine-gun was the basis of all RAF armament in 1939, and until the end of the war, in Bomber Command. Barnes Wallis, the Vickers designer who would later become famous as the creator of the dambusting bomb and other remarkable weapons, notes that it was not until after the outbreak of war that there was any understanding in the RAF of the need for big bombs because there had been no analysis of the problems of destroying large structures.[7] Most officers preferred a load of eight 250-lb bombs on an aircraft rather than one 2,000-lb bomb, according to Wallis, because they thus increased the chance of hitting a target at least with something. For the first three years of the war, the RAF used an explosive markedly inferior to that of the Luftwaffe, having failed to develop anything comparable for themselves in twenty years of peace. When Wallis first proposed the creation of really big bombs in the 1930s, Air Ministry 'experts' replied that they doubted whether it was possible to detonate large quantities of explosive in a bomb, and argued that it would probably go off with a mere damp-squib effect. Likewise, the development of bombsights was lamentably sluggish. The early Mark 7 automatic bombsight, with which the RAF went to war, lacked any facility for taking account of the aircraft's gyrations on the bombing run, and required a pilot to make an absolutely steady approach to the target – suicidal under operational conditions.

The RAF trained for more than two decades guided only by a Trenchardian faith that it would somehow be 'all right on the night'. The Air Staff stand condemned for failure to inspire advanced aircraft design – the Spitfire, the Hurricane and the Mosquito are the most famous examples of aircraft that reached production only thanks to independent initiatives by British manufacturers. In his anxiety to create a strong organizational base for the new RAF, Trenchard devoted a surprisingly generous proportion of his budget to the building of solid, elegant stations and the staffing of a grossly overweight Air Ministry, while almost totally neglecting research and development. There were three Air Ministry officials for every aircraft in squadron service, and in the 1920s one-fifth of the RAF's budget was spent on buildings. It is possible to blame the politicians for all the quantitative shortcomings of the RAF at the outbreak of war, but the airmen themselves must accept overwhelming responsibility for the qualitative failures.

Much of the above has been often remarked. Yet there has never been a satisfactory explanation of *why* these huge omissions were made. Many of them stemmed from a reluctance to discuss openly the real nature of a strategic bomber offensive. Both in those years and up to the present day, RAF officers have asserted that they were planning for an attack on the industrial infrastructure of the enemy, by destroying his factories and vital installations. Air Vice-Marshal Sir John Steel, later Bomber Command's first C-in-C, declared in 1928 that 'there has been a lot of nonsense talked about killing women and children. Every objective I have given my bombers is a point of military importance which the guns would shell if they could reach it. Otherwise the pilots, if captured, would be liable to be treated as war criminals.' Both the pre-war plans of Bomber Command and the early operations of war undertaken by its crews invariably specified strategic targets: factories, rail yards, power stations.

Yet it is impossible to accept the airmen's intentions at face value. Trenchard said in 1919 that 'at present, the moral effect of bombing stands undoubtedly to the material effect in a proportion of twenty to one', and ever since it had been the prospect of destroying the enemy's morale, bringing about the collapse of his will to produce or resist by bombing, that had been at the heart of the airmen's vision of a bomber offensive. They understood perfectly well that attack upon an enemy nation and its morale meant the killing of civilians, but they were reluctant to say so, and even at the height of their offensive in the Second World War, their political masters would be most circumspect about revealing the nature of what was being done to Germany. In 1927 and even 1937, it would have been unthinkable to make the kind of mathematical projection carried out as a routine daily exercise at Bomber Command headquarters in 1943, in which 'Effort' measured 'tons of bombs claimed dropped per built-up acre attacked', 'Efficiency' measured 'acres of devastation per ton of bombs claimed dropped', and 'Success' was calculated by 'acres of devastation per acre of built-up area attacked'.

No scientific study had been conducted in 1917 (of the sort that would be made so thoroughly and with such startling conclusions in the Second World War) of the effects on British morale and productivity of the German air attacks. Airmen merely remembered the shock and outcry among the civilian population, and the political panic which followed. The notion had bitten deep of a 'soft centre' at the heart of a nation behind its shield of armies and navies, that air forces might and must attack.

In air operations against production [wrote a future Chief of Air Staff, Group-Captain John Slessor, in 1936] the weight of attack will inevitably fall upon a vitally important, and not by nature very amenable, section of the community – the industrial workers, whose morale and sticking power cannot be expected to equal that of the disciplined soldier. And we should remember that if the moral effect of air bombardment was serious seventeen years ago, it will be immensely more so under modern conditions.[8]

Perhaps the central conscious or subconscious reason that the RAF devoted so little thought to the successful execution of a precision air attack between the wars was that, on the evidence of the 1917 experience, no very accurate aim seemed necessary to provoke the desired moral collapse. In a memorandum of 1938 the Air Staff distinguished two forms of bombing against: '(1) the "precise target", e.g. a power station . . . (2) the "target group", of considerable area in which are concentrated many targets of equal or nearly equal importance on which accurate bombing is not necessary to achieve valuable hits, e.g. parts of cities, industrial towns, distribution centres or storage areas'. If a few tons of German bombs had caused a major political crisis in London in 1917, it seemed reasonable to assume that many times more bombs on such a 'target group' as Berlin would provoke a veritable cataclysm. It is also worth remembering that when airmen conceived a future enemy moral collapse in which a crazed and deprived civilian population roamed the streets shooting and looting and demanding peace behind the back of their own armies, they were not weaving a fantasy but remembering the reality of Germany in 1918, albeit forgetting the military collapse that simultaneously took place.

Yet at a time when fierce public controversy raged around the legitimacy of air bombardment, when there were attempts to outlaw the very existence of the bomber at the international conference table, it was unthinkable publicly to debate a strategic air offensive in terms of terrorizing a nation into suing for peace. And this, for all the talk of 'centres of production and communication', was really the point at issue. The RAF's belief in attacking industrial areas stemmed not from realistic analysis of the prospects of smashing enough industrial plant to break the German economy (although lip-service was paid to that end), but from belief that the will of industrial workers would collapse when bombs rained around their factories and homes. The pre-war RAF was geared to the execution of a strategic terror bombing campaign and this was at the core of the Trenchard doctrine.

Perhaps the central flaw of this concept was that it was already obsolete. It rested on the old assumption of armies as professional bodies, behind which rested the unprotected and undisciplined civilian heart of the nation, divorced from the battle and thus totally unconditioned to take part in it. Yet the essence of warfare since the mid-nineteenth century was that the world had left behind the era of the *condottieri* and entered upon the new age of the nation in arms. The old gulf between fighting man and civilian had ceased to exist. The Japanese bomber operations in Manchuria and the Condor Legion's adventures over Guernica were throwbacks no more related to total war between modern industrial states than Air Control in Iraq. Among the great western powers, it had become impossible to conduct a major war without the support of an overwhelming consensus within the nation. In a fascinating paper which he wrote as Minister of Munitions as far back as 1917, Winston Churchill dismissed the arguments for morale bombing before Trenchard and the airmen had even developed them:

It is improbable that any terrorization of the civil population which could be achieved by air attack would compel the Government of a great nation to surrender. Familiarity with bombardment, a good system of dug-outs or shelters, a strong control by police and military authorities, should be sufficient to preserve the national fighting spirit unimpaired. In our own case, we have seen the combative spirit of the people roused, and not quelled, by the German air raids. Nothing that we have learned of the capacity of the German population to endure suffering justifies us in assuming that they could be cowed into submission by such methods, or indeed, that they would not be rendered more desperately resolved by them. Therefore our air offensive should consistently be directed at striking at the bases and communications upon whose structure the fighting power of his armies and his fleets of the sea and of the air depends. Any injury which comes to the civil population from this process of attack must be regarded as incidental and inevitable.

. . . But the indispensable preliminary to all results in the air, as in every other sphere of war, is to defeat the armed forces of the enemy.[9]

If Churchill's paper had been made a basic text at the RAF Staff College between the wars, much heartbreak in the first four years of the bomber offensive might have been avoided. The airmen might have addressed themselves intensively to the problems of ground and naval air support, instead of allowing their obsession with an independent role for the RAF to distort the thinking of a generation. They might have focused on the decisive problem of air warfare, the defeat of the enemy's air force, and thus conceived the need for a long-range fighter in 1933 rather than 1943. Instead, their thinking was directed towards means of bypassing the enemy's defences, either by the power of the bomber's guns in daylight, or by using the cover of darkness, in order to attack his allegedly vulnerable heart. The RAF might also have avoided the fatal disparity between its public commitment to precision bombing – which its line aircrew would offer so much devotion and sacrifice to fulfilling when war came – and a half-articulated faith in terror bombing in the higher ranks of the service. The gulf between the alleged function of Bomber Command as a precision-bombing force, and its real nature as an area-bombing one, would be revealed at the end of 1941. Harris, who then became C-in-C with a mandate to conduct a full-blooded area campaign, was far more truly Trenchard's disciple than those diligent staff officers at the Air Ministry who continued throughout the war to try to direct Bomber Command's efforts to the destruction of selected precision, industrial targets.

*

In the last five years, and most dramatically in the last two years before the outbreak of war, the face of the British and German air forces changed beyond recognition. As the political sky darkened, the Cabinet approved a succession of Royal Air Force rearmament programmes that tripped upon each other in the haste with which one was overtaken by the next. Air defence loomed larger and larger in Government priorities until by 1938 the RAF share of the combined services budget had risen to 40 per cent from its inter-war average of 17 per cent. Yet the bomber still seized the lion's share of the available cash: under Scheme A, approved in July 1934, RAF strength in Britain would expand by April 1939 from 316 to 476 bombers, from 156 to 336 fighters. Schemes C, F, H succeeded each other in May 1935, February 1936 and February 1937 respectively. Then in December 1937 there was a sudden check: Sir Thomas Inskip, Minister for the Co-Ordination of Defence, declined to accept Scheme J, by which the Air Staff proposed an increased strength of 1,442 bombers and 532 fighters by April 1941. Inskip argued that the total cost would be too great, and that the proportion of fighters was too low. After prolonged debate, in April 1938 the Cabinet finally adopted Scheme L, by which the RAF would reach a strength of 1,352 bombers and 608 first-line fighters by April 1940. Airmen argue that Inskip was an indifferent minister who forced these measures through – at the cost of severe delays in creating a four-engined bomber force – merely for financial and political reasons, because fighters are cheaper than bombers. But modern historians of the Battle of Britain are disposed to believe that it was Inskip's insistence on higher priority for fighter production that gave Fighter Command the tiny margin of strength by which it achieved victory against the Luftwaffe in 1940. In September 1939, Britain would enter the war with 608 first-line fighters against the 1,215 of the Luftwaffe, and with 536 bombers against 2,130.

But more important than mere numbers were the aircraft types in production and coming off the drawing board. It is impossible to overstate the significance of design decisions taken before the outbreak of war in both Britain and Germany, decisions that would have a critical effect on the struggle in the air right through to 1945. Although the Luftwaffe had achieved overwhelming superiority over the RAF in both quantity and quality in the mid-1930s, in the last two years before war, British designers were creating aircraft that Germany proved disastrously unable to match in 1942, 1943, even 1944. In 1936 the Air Staff had issued specifications P/13/36 and B/12/36 for four-engined heavy bombers and twin-engined 'heavy-medium' bombers that would create, in 1941, the Stirling, the Halifax, the Manchester and its ultimate modification, the Lancaster. Whatever debate is possible about the proportion of national resources ultimately devoted to heavy-bomber production, and about the manner in which the bomber force was employed, it is difficult to dispute the value to the British war effort of possessing heavy bombers with capabilities no other nation in the world could match, although the best brains in the German aircraft industry struggled to do so.

The heavy bomber was the visible expression of the RAF's determination to make a contribution to the war independent of the other two services, as was the weakness of its air-ground and air-sea coordination techniques. Germany and France, on the other hand, had throughout the 1930s devoted their resources to producing light and medium bombers primarily for army support, and both the German Army and the Luftwaffe were imbued with the doctrines of mobile warfare preached by De Gaulle, Guderian and Liddell Hart. From the Stuka in 1939 to Hitler's obsession with the jet Me262 as a fighter-bomber in 1944, Germany was preoccupied with tactical air power, and would desperately feel the lack of an adequate four-engined long-range bomber.

The American Flying Fortress, designed as a strategic bomber, achieved remarkable performance and packed powerful defensive armament only at the cost of carrying a severely limited bombload. The early Flying Fortresses also lacked the power-operated turrets which proved a vital advance in aircraft defence – albeit still insufficient to make the day bomber self-defending.

But in Britain, until the new generation of 'heavies' began to come off the production line – and with aircraft of such radical design there would be serious teething troubles – the RAF would go to war with stop-gap bombers of much less satisfactory pedigree – the twin-engined Hampden, Blenheim, Whitley and Wellington, and worst of all the single-engined Battle. The

Battle had been an unwanted aircraft in 1933, yet such was the pressure to increase the RAF's numbers in the last days of peace that production was even accelerated: 3,100 Battles would be produced before the end of 1940. As the pre-war expansion schemes reached their climax with Scheme M, approved in November 1938, there was no possibility of meeting requirements with new designs. Instead, bombers such as the Battle and the Blenheim, already known to be quite outclassed for modern warfare, continued to pour off the production lines. It seemed better to have something than to have nothing, at least in Whitehall. Those who would be flying the Battles and Blenheims in action were not consulted. One of the brutal lessons of the war would be that obsolete aircraft could contribute nothing whatever on the battlefield. They merely served as deathtraps for precious aircrew.

In 1936 the old area organization of the Air Defence Of Great Britain was abolished and replaced by functional commands: Bomber, Fighter, Training and Coastal. Bomber Command's squadrons were redeployed, moving from the stations in southern England that they had occupied throughout the 1920s when the Government was looking with such alarm towards France, taking up the eastern airfields closest to Germany, from which they would fight the Second World War, and ranging southwards from 4 Group in Yorkshire to 2 and 3 Groups* in Norfolk.

The very nature of air war changed so rapidly in the last years of peace that few airmen understood what had happened. In March 1939, chafing noisily from his retirement, Trenchard deplored 'the continuous clamouring for defence measures' from an ignorant and optimistic public. Yet the German Me109 and the British Spitfire could now intercept bombers at closing speeds of better than 150 mph. Most important of all, the birth of radar had transformed overnight the power of the defence to plot an attacking bomber and direct fighters to intercept. The total dominance that radar was to achieve over aerial warfare between 1939 and 1945 cannot be overemphasized, nor can the contribution of Watson-Watt, its inventor, and Sir Henry Tizard, the brilliant scientific civil servant whose Committee for the

*A Bomber Command Group comprised anything between six squadrons of sixteen aircraft in 1939 and eighteen squadrons of twenty aircraft in 1945.

Scientific Survey of Air Defence was largely responsible for bringing Britain's radar network into being. It was Tizard who personally presided over the critical 'Biggin Hill Experiment' in 1938, when the fighter station was used as a laboratory for creating the Fighter Direction organization, linking radar to the defending aircraft, which made victory possible in the Battle of Britain.

Yet it is important to notice that Fighter Command's brilliant achievement in 1940 only became possible in a situation in which disaster had befallen British strategy. While the Luftwaffe had trained and equipped for mobile operations from improvised airstrips, the RAF was wedded to the concept of controlled operations from secure bases. The performance of the 261 Hurricane fighters supporting the 160 Battles of the Advanced Air Striking Force in the Battle of France in 1940 was not impressive. Divorced from Fighter Command's sophisticated warning and direction system, which could only operate in defence of Britain itself, the British fighter squadrons were at a loss. Had the Battle of France continued for even a few more weeks instead of ending so abruptly in disaster, the RAF's inability to support the British Army effectively might have been even more embarrassingly exposed.

The composition of the Royal Air Force in 1939 reflected the twenty-year struggle about its purpose: there was a substantial bomber force to pursue the airmen's strategic offensive theories, and a fighter arm equipped with short-range, lightly built and armed aircraft called into being almost entirely by public and political pressure, organized solely for the defence of Britain. And whereas politicians, scientists and civil servants had taken the keenest interest in the development of Fighter Command, Bomber Command was the subject of much less public concern, and the airmen had been left to develop it as they saw fit. Professor R. V. Jones, the scientist who would play so prominent a part in the key radar Intelligence discoveries of the war, was one of those who noted its shortcomings in the last days of peace:

I was . . . astonished by the complacency that existed regarding our ability to navigate at long range at night. The whole of our bombing policy depended on this assumption, but I was assured that by general instrument flying, coupled with navigation by the stars, Bomber Command was confident that it could find pinpoint targets in Germany at night, and that there was therefore no need for any such radio aids as I had proposed . . .[10]

Yet the prospect of war concentrates minds wonderfully. In the last months of peace, as urgent inquiries began to flow to the airmen from Whitehall about their state of readiness, the first tremors of awareness of their desperate plight became apparent within Bomber Command. In the wake of Munich, the C-in-C and the Air Ministry advised the Government that it would be in Britain's interests to accept any restrictions on bombing that could be internationally agreed. The Joint Planners confirmed this advice on 24 October 1938. A scheme was devised for a raid on Munich by two stand-by squadrons of bombers if the crisis exploded without warning: the Staff predicted 100 per cent losses. In May 1939 the AOC of 3 Group reported to Bomber Command HQ that 'Dead Reckoning navigation by day above cloud can only be expected to get aircraft within fifty miles of the target.' In July, Bomber Command's C-in-C Sir Edgar Ludlow-Hewitt was writing: 'As things are at present, the gunners have no real confidence in their ability to use this equipment efficiently in war, and captains and crews have, I fear, little confidence in the ability of the gunners to defend them against destruction by enemy aircraft.' After a generation in which, at Trenchard's insistence, the RAF had dismissed the need to make provision for fighter escorts for bomber formations, only months before the outbreak of war Ludlow-Hewitt sprang a thunderbolt:

Experience in China and in Spain seems clearly to indicate that with the aircraft in use in these two theatres of war at present, Fighter Escorts are considered absolutely essential for the protection of Bomber aircraft. So far as I am aware this policy runs counter to the view long held by the Air Staff.

It did indeed. There had never been any Bomber Command counterpart of Fighter Command's Biggin Hill experiment, designed to test equipment under operation conditions. Ludlow-Hewitt had pressed in vain for the creation of a Bombing Development Unit. He met Sir Henry Tizard for the first time only on 4 July 1939. More and more airmen were becoming convinced that most, if not all, of Bomber Command's operations would have to be carried out at night, yet the art of night bombing in the RAF was no more technically advanced than blindfold practice at a coconut shy.

As his *coup de théâtre*, final judgement on the RAF's twenty-year commitment to a strategic bomber offensive, Ludlow-Hewitt informed the Air Ministry before the outbreak of war that if his Command was ordered to undertake an all-out offensive against Germany, he anticipated that his medium bombers – the Blenheims – would be destroyed in three and a half weeks. The heavy bombers – Hampdens, Whitleys and Wellingtons – would be totally destroyed in seven and a half weeks. The Chief of Air Staff, Sir Cyril Newall, reluctantly bowed to the inevitable. On 23 August 1939 he wrote to Ludlow-Hewitt that since it had already been agreed that the odium of inaugurating the air war should be left to the Germans,

Our plans must to some extent be dependent on the initial reaction of the enemy . . . it would be manifestly unwise to expend a high proportion of our best aircraft and crews at the beginning, when there are so many unknown factors in air warfare of which we have to gain experience. This would be all the more undesirable during a phase when for political reasons we are confined to a course of action which is neither economical nor fully effective . . .

This 'course of action' committed Bomber Command to attack only definable military targets where there was no reasonable risk of bombs falling on civilians. The British Government hoped fervently to avoid provoking a mass air assault upon their own people. Now, instead of seeking to convince the politicians that their scruples were misguided, the airmen gratefully assented to a policy that would avoid exposing the inadequacy of Bomber Command at the outbreak of war. The tasks of the bomber force, it now appeared, would be precisely those for which no effective preparation had been made at all: attack on the German navy at sea and close support of the British Army in France under Western Air Plan 4b.

Both among his contemporaries and among historians, Sir Edgar Ludlow-Hewitt has incurred hostility and even scorn for his outbreak of realism at one of the most critical, if inglorious, moments of the RAF's history. A teetotal Christian Scientist of acute humanitarian sensitivities, he insisted upon being informed personally when an aircraft under his command was lost, and he always spoke personally to the responsible Station Commander. As the RAF prepared to plunge into war, many of his young staff officers believed that the austere Ludlow lacked the steel in his soul to lead Bomber Command in battle, and indeed he was to be replaced on 4 April 1940, before the war began in earnest. But Ludlow-Hewitt was a highly intelligent man, who made a great contribution by speaking so frankly about the shortcomings of his command. In all forces at war, there is a fear that voicing unpleasant truths may be construed as defeatism. In Bomber Command in the next six years, there would be many occasions when men shrank from discussing the emperor's absence of clothes, of which they were silently aware. Most fighting men believe that it is preferable to do something, however undesirable, rather than merely to stand passive. Ludlow's reluctance to lead Bomber Command on the course which had been set since its birth seemed unmilitary, even old-womanish. His departure from Bomber Command in 1940 would be greeted with relief, a sense that at last the real business of fighting the war could begin.

Yet whose judgement was justified by events? It is worth comparing Ludlow-Hewitt's relentlessly pessimistic minutes with a memorandum drafted four days after the outbreak of war by one of the young turks, John Slessor, Director of Plans, who wrote:

Although our numerical inferiority in the air is a most important factor it should not be allowed to obscure other potent considérations. We are now at war with a nation which possesses an imposing façade of armed might, but which, behind that façade, is politically rotten, weak in financial and economic resources, and already heavily engaged on another front [Poland]. The lessons of history prove that victory does not always go to the big battalions. At present we have the initiative. If we seize it we may gain important results; if we lose it by waiting we shall probably lose more than we gain . . .

It was fortunate for the crews of the first generation of Bomber Command that Ludlow-Hewitt had his way and Slessor did not get his.*

*As Slessor himself conceded with disarming grace in his memoirs twenty years later.

It is one of the small ironies of history that the British, who had forged a strategic bomber force with the specific intention of striking at the cities of the enemy, should have left to the Germans, who had prepared their air force for an army support role, the dubious honour of laying waste the first city blocks. 'Some amazing stories of the opportunities forgone by Great Britain in observance of the law will be told some day,' declared an editorial in *The Aeroplane* of 29 March 1940. 'Pilots, confronted with perfect targets, have had to keep the law, grind their teeth in chagrin, and hope for a change in the temper of the war.' The writer may have been thinking of Wing-Commander Kellett and his Wellingtons cruising over the German warships in Bau Haven. But in this matter moral restraint and imperative operational expediency marched together.

At the outbreak of war, Britain hastened to accept President Roosevelt's appeal to the belligerents to renounce the bombing of civilian targets. Bomber Command launched its spasmodic attacks on the German fleet; flew scores of monotonous weather, maritime reconnaissance and mining sorties; and sent the Whitleys and Hampdens forth over Germany night after night, inundating the enemy with propaganda leaflets. The CO of 51 Squadron in desperation entered some of his crews for navigation courses at Southampton University. Slessor, the Director of Plans, pressed for more aggressive policies. Although he noted carefully in his memorandum to the Chief of Air Staff on 7 September 1939 that 'indiscriminate attacks on civilian populations as such will never form part of our policy', he urged that Bomber Command commence bombing oil plants and power stations in the Ruhr. In the spring of 1940 he put forward a proposal for adapting the RAF's old Iraqi Air Control techniques by 'proscribing' listed German industrial cities, leafleting the population in warning, and then commencing air bombardment.

But throughout the long months of the Phoney War that ended in May 1940, Government, public and senior airmen alike were very content to stand passive. 'We are fighting for a moral issue,' declared a *Daily Mail* editorial in January 1940, denouncing proposals for bombing Germany. 'We should do nothing unworthy of our cause.' At an Air Ministry conference as late as 28 April 1940, when the battle of Norway was already all but lost, the Vice-Chief of Air Staff, Air Marshal Peirse, said that since a German bomber effort against Britain would be four times as heavy as anything Bomber Command could mount, 'it would therefore be foolish to provoke such an attack needlessly unless Bomber Command could promise decisive results'.

In the first months of war the nature of the air force that Trenchard had created was clearly revealed by its deployments. The bulk of the British Army was in France, where it was expected that sooner or later, the great German blow would fall. But whatever their differences on other issues, the airmen were united in their determination that they would not spend the war acting as long-range artillery for the British Army, or for that matter for the Royal Navy. The 'Advanced Air Striking Force' that went to France under the command of Air Marshal Sir Arthur 'Ugly' Barratt comprised ten squadrons of Battles – 160 aircraft, well known to be the 'expendables' of Bomber Command. The overwhelming weight of the Command's striking power remained at the stations in England, poised for the strategic offensive against Germany. In September 1939 the average daily availability of aircraft stood at 280 out of a total strength of 349 – 77 Wellingtons, 61 Whitleys, 71 Hampdens, 140 Blenheims. The Blenheim 'medium' bombers were notionally available for operations as part of the Advanced Air Striking Force, and indeed during the spring of 1940 a number were moved to France. But when the German onslaught descended with the full weight of the Luftwaffe behind it, it was on the Battle and Hurricane squadrons of Barratt's force that responsibility fell for the direct support of the British army, and tragically inadequate they proved to be. Bomber Command, like Fighter Command, was indeed 'conserved' for the future rather than destroyed in the Battle of France, but as the British army waded into the Channel from the beaches of Dunkirk, the broken battalions which cursed the RAF for its absence could not be expected to understand the airmen's excellent and historically inevitable reasons why.

The RAF's misfortune was that it had believed its own public image. For twenty years it had luxuriated in the conviction 'We are, *ergo* we are capable of a strategic bombing offensive.' Now, in the first years of war, the RAF would become the victim of its own pre-war propaganda. The British army and the Royal Navy would vent their spleen upon the air marshals for their inability to fulfil the promises of peace. In reality, the RAF's strengths were considerable and its qualitative shortcomings were little worse than those of its enemies, far less grave than those of its allies. In September 1939 the Luftwaffe possessed no bomb larger than 1,100 lb, and was chronically short of hardware because Hitler had halted bomb production in expectation of a short war. Luftwaffe aircraft were experiencing acute technical problems with oxygen equipment and guns freezing at high altitude. The Germans possessed no power-operated turrets for their bombers, their fighter cannon were inadequate, and they lacked sufficient reserves of aircraft to back up the imposing strength of their first-line. Above all, the Luftwaffe's He111, Do17 and even Ju88 bombers were no more capable than Bomber Command's Hampdens, Whitleys and Wellingtons of attacking in daylight at acceptable cost *unless local air superiority had first been obtained* by the defeat of the defending fighter force. At night the Luftwaffe's capability to 'bomb on the beam' by radio navigation aids of the kind that Bomber Command so signally lacked would count for something, and Britain would be punished severely by the blitz. But the Luftwaffe was unable to achieve decisive results. Germany would win the first airbattles of the war, but would lose the Battle of Britain even while operating its bombers under massive fighter escort at short range from its bases.

Bomber Command and its leading airmen, however, would be judged not by comparison with the Luftwaffe but by the standard of their pre-war promises. It was the core of Trenchard's thesis that it was unnecessary first to defeat the enemy's air force in order to wage an effective bomber offensive, and – by implication revealed in the RAF's conduct of its own affairs between the wars – that it was not necessary to concentrate much attention where the bombs fell on enemy territory in order to achieve results. Now, the airmen perceived with bleak clarity that they had made no attempt to reconcile their ends with the means available to achieve them. Nothing would persuade them to renounce their purpose before the Government or the other two services. But by the spring of 1940, the Air Staff's confident strategy of twenty years' standing had been replaced by a courageous yet empty determination to make the best of a bad job, and pray for the time to build the means to pursue their great strategic ambitions.

Only Trenchard's faith flew on sublime. On 4 April 1940 one of his protégés, Sir Charles Portal, succeeded Ludlow-Hewitt as Commander-in-Chief of Bomber Command. Trenchard wrote to congratulate Portal on his first month in his post, and on the achievements of British air power ' . . . though I am sorry that you could not use it where I and others think it probably would have ended the war by now.' Britain, Trenchard still believed, had missed a unique opportunity to finish the Third Reich with a single devastating blow from the air at the heart of Germany. Even after eight months of war, the powers and limitations of air forces remained an enigma to the 'father of the RAF', to most of the British public and to their politicians.

On 10 May 1940 the German invasion of France and the Low Countries swept away the Phoney War. The overture was ended. The realities of air power were about to reveal themselves.

2 82 Squadron, Norfolk, 1940–41

With broken wing they limped across the sky,
Caught in late sunlight with their gunner dead,
One engine gone – the type was out of date –
Blood on the fuselage turning brown from red . . .

So two men waited, saw the third dead face,
And wondered when the wind would let them die.
John Bayliss, *Reported Missing*

Strolling out on to the tarmac at Watton and scanning the sky
early on the morning of 17 May 1940, Wing-Commander the
Earl of Bandon was beginning to wonder where his squadron had
got to. At 4.50 a.m., twelve Blenheims of 82 Squadron had taken
off for Gembloux in central Belgium to attack a German armoured column. On this clear, beautiful summer's day, they should
have been home for breakfast.

The Battle of France was already a week old, but so far 82
Squadron had escaped astonishingly lightly. In the desperate
flurry of anti-shipping strikes that had been ordered throughout
April to impede the German invasion of Norway, they had sunk
nothing but lost only one aircraft. The Blenheims had not been
called upon to take part in the airfield attacks by 3 and 5 Groups
which cost Bomber Command most of the thirty-one aircraft
lost over Scandinavia, and which achieved little even after the
Air Ministry withdrew its initial restriction ordering RAF aircraft to attack only with machine-guns, rather than bombs, to
protect innocent bystanders. Since the German onslaught in the
west began on 10 May, 82 Squadron had operated only once,
against the Maastricht bridges on 12 May, where they saw for the
first time the incredible power of German light flak, but somehow came home to tell the tale. They missed the terrible battle of
14 May, when Barratt's Advanced Air Striking Force lost forty

out of seventy-one Battles, attempting to break the German bridgehead at Sedan. The same evening, Wing-Commander Basil Embry lost seven of the twenty-eight 2 Group Blenheims he led in the desperate effort to stem the tide with support from England.

On 17 May, Paddy Bandon was not himself leading 82 Squadron because his navigator was away in London being interviewed for a commission. In any event, although Bandon often flew, he was modest enough usually to let one of his experienced flight commanders lead the formation, for he was conscious of his own imperfections as a Blenheim pilot. He had spent the year before the war at the Air Staff College, hearing 'Ugly' Barratt lecture on the 'great fist' of air power, Ludlow-Hewitt argue the superiority of the offensive over the defensive, Group-Captain Robert Saundby declaring the importance of economy of force, of not 'wasting' fighters as bomber escorts. Even in 1938 the students learnt nothing of radar, although there was much discussion of such theories as the invincibility of the Lysander Army Co-Operation aircraft, which was thought to be too slow for modern fighters to engage – a year later, the surviving Lysander pilots cast convincing doubts on the validity of this concept. After Staff College, he was posted to the Air Ministry, and at the outbreak of war angled for command of a fighter squadron. But at thirty-six he was too old. Instead, although he had never dropped a bomb or flown a Blenheim in his life, in the predictable manner of service bureaucracies Bandon was sent to 82 Squadron, one of 2 Group's seven Blenheim units, stationed at Watton in Norfolk, only a few miles from 37 Squadron's Wellingtons at Feltwell.

Like most other pre-war squadrons, 82 was a family in arms, a group of men scarcely changed since 1937. Like most of his service colleagues, they fell in love with Paddy at first sight. There was something rather stylish about having an Irish earl as Squadron CO. When he had the charm of Paddy Bandon, the effect was irresistible. He was a mischievous extrovert with a boundless talent for enjoying life, at the front line of every party, finest shot at the squadron partridge shoots with which they passed the winter of 1939–40, chain-smoking compulsively, racing round the airfield in his little black Morgan two-seater with his uncontrollable spaniel Fluff and his flamboyant black moustache, to the impotent fury of Vincent, the station commander, who had already reprimanded him for scruffiness. The week before Gembloux, an 82 Squadron pilot named Charlie Breese forgot to put down the wheels of his Blenheim before landing, and was at once put under open arrest by the station commander for needlessly wrecking an aircraft. He was confined to his quarters with another disgraced pilot, 'Atty' Atkinson, and allowed out only to fly operations. At last the two were summoned to appear before the group commander. Paddy Bandon drove them to headquarters in Huntingdon himself, and stood behind the AOC while he delivered a fierce reprimand, making faces at the hapless Atkinson and Breese in the hope of reducing them to hysterics. Paddy Bandon's popularity was instantly understandable – the only matter that caused general astonishment was that he eventually retired from the RAF as an air chief marshal.

At 8.20 a.m. that 17 May, the handful of aircrew who were not flying and the ground crews waiting for the return of their charges wandered out into the sunlight when they heard a distant aircraft on the circuit. As the Blenheim approached, they could detect the erratic beat of its single remaining engine. A red Very light lanced into the sky from the cockpit. The ambulance and fire tenders bumped hastily across the grass towards the runway. The aircraft wobbled down, bounced, then coasted along the ground until the propeller abruptly stopped. The pilot, Sergeant Morrison, climbed stiffly down from the hatch with his observer and gunner. They sank down on the grass.

'Where's everybody else, Morrison?' asked Paddy Bandon.

Shortly before lunch, three crews who had been on another mission that morning arrived over Watton, puzzled by the curious emptiness of the field beneath them. The pilots – Atkinson, Breese and Hunt – had been guiding three fighter squadrons to France (with written orders that 'There is to be no fighting on the way', but no proposals about what to do if the Luftwaffe thought otherwise). Now, returning from Lille with their Blenheims loaded with looted champagne, they landed to be ordered to report at once to the CO's office. There was a groan at the prospect of trouble from Shoreham Customs about their cargo.

They walked into Paddy Bandon's office to find him sitting at his desk, the sparkle of his eyes for once quite dead. 'Well, chaps,' he said. 'We're now 82 Squadron. Yes, just us.' The formation of Blenheims had missed their rendezvous with a hastily organized fighter escort, and pressed on alone. They had been opened up to face the flak approaching Gembloux when they were attacked by fifteen Me109s from the vast air umbrella covering the German advance. Sergeant Morrison was the only pilot to bring his aircraft home. Before lunch that day orders came from Group to disband the squadron. It was only after a fierce struggle that Paddy Bandon had the order rescinded, and they began to rebuild the wreckage of 82.

In the days that followed, as the German armies swept across France, and Britain entered her season of unbroken disaster, half-trained crews were sent to them from the Operational Training Units with 200 or 300 hours' flying experience against the 600 that would become a minimum later in the war. Atkinson began to teach them the rudiments of formation flying. A few survivors of Gembloux trickled back from France. Paddy Bandon was touched when his own navigator and two others returned from London with the promise of their commissions, but at once offered to forgo them and stay at Watton to keep 82 Squadron alive. An Irish gunner who had gone to the glasshouse for desertion was released at the end of his sentence and asked to be allowed to return to flying duties. He too came back, to be killed like so many others in the weeks that followed.

The so-called heavy aircraft with which the RAF entered the war – the Hampden, Whitley and Wellington – were adequate night-bombers of their generation, chiefly deficient in navigation equipment and crew comfort. But the 'mediums' – the Battle and the Blenheim – were suicidally ill-fitted for their role as daylight tactical bombers. Cruising at 180 mph, the Blenheim was almost 200 mph slower than the fighters whom it must inevitably encounter. Armed with a single .303 in its rear turret, a fixed rearward-firing gun in the port engine nacelle designed solely as a 'frightener' and a clumsy rear-firing gun under the cockpit, it was quite incapable of surviving an efficient fighter attack. Lightly built, it could stand little punishment. It packed a negligible 1,000-lb punch in its bomb bay, and could achieve less than half the rate of climb of a German fighter. Under attack, a Blenheim's only chance of survival was to find cloud or to attempt a hedge-level escape. Quite unknown to the survivors of 82 Squadron and the bewildered young trainees who arrived at Watton to fill the vacuum after Gembloux, Portal as C-in-C of Bomber Command had been fighting a losing battle with the Air Ministry, since the day before the German invasion of the west began, about the employment of the Blenheims.

I am convinced [he wrote on 8 May] that the proposed use of these units is fundamentally unsound, and that if it is persisted in, it is likely to have disastrous consequences on the future of the war in the air . . . It can scarcely be disputed that at the enemy's chosen moment for advance the area concerned will be literally swarming with enemy fighters, and we shall be lucky if we see again as many as half the aircraft we send out each time. Really accurate bombing under the conditions I visualize is not to be expected, and I feel justified in expressing serious doubts whether the attacks of 50 Blenheims based on information necessarily some hours out of date are likely to make as much difference to the ultimate course of the war as to justify the losses I expect.

The Air Staff could not rationally dispute Portal's judgement. But even after the Wilhelmshaven raids, it was unthinkable to admit that the RAF possessed no bomber capable of operating in daylight with acceptable losses. For the remainder of the Battle of France, Portal ceased to have any effective voice as C-in-C of Bomber Command. He became merely the fireman, struggling to meet the minute-by-minute demands of the British Government and the Air Ministry. It had long ago been decided that the RAF should seek to support the army by attacking German communications rather than forward positions. Whether or not this policy made any sense from the outset, within days of 9 May most of Barratt's Battles, which had been intended to execute it, had been wiped out by the brilliantly deployed Luft-waffe screen of flak and fighters covering every key position. The Air Ministry sought as far as possible to reserve the night bombers for operations against German installations and com-munications far behind the lines. In reality, it was quite un-important what targets were chosen, since it rapidly became clear that Bomber Command was incapable of hitting any pinpoint accurately in the hours of darkness, and was unable to break through the defences in daylight.

Only 2 Group's Blenheims, however tragically inadequate, could be risked on daylight ground-support operations in the face of the Luftwaffe. No ground-to-air communications existed to make their strikes effective. Efforts to provide them with fighter cover were only spasmodically successful. But they were all that there was. 82 Squadron were much bewildered at morning parade on 21 May. Beside their ordered ranks, a handful of scarecrows fell in, dressed in fragments of uniforms, bandages, tin helmets. They were the survivors of 18 Squadron, newly evacuated from France. Their commanding officer requested that his three remaining aircraft be attached to 82 for operations that day. They flew with fighter escort to attack a reported Panzer division laagered in a French wood. Instead they found a British Red Cross column. Somehow they came home intact, except for one 18 Squadron Blenheim, whose unusual camouflage markings were mistaken by a nervous Hurricane pilot for those of a Ju88. It was shot down without survivors. On the 22nd Atkinson led them against German armour at Samar near Boulogne, losing one aircraft. There was then another momentary lull after a further intervention by Portal, who pointed out that operations in France were 'draining away the Blenheim crews at the rate of between one and two squadrons per week . . . It is the height of unwisdom to throw the Blenheims away in an attempt to do the work of artillery. . .'

But the supreme crisis of Dunkirk swept away all reservations. 2 Group were once again flung into the battle. The great pall of black smoke hanging a thousand feet high over the beaches made it impossible to pinpoint the German batteries accurately before attack, but it did give them vital cover when they dived away from the pursuing Messerschmitts. Again and again, they escaped home clinging to the waves, holed from nose to tail, desperately seeking to sidestep the German fighters. Basil Embry, who would escape to become a legendary 2 Group commander later in the war, was among scores of Blenheim pilots shot down in these days. 6 June was a bleak day for 82 Squadron, when they came home with an aircraft missing and most of the others holed, a gunner draped dead in his turret. The crane that drew up along-side the wreck at Watton to winch the corpse out of his position remained one of their grimmest memories of that summer. Honry and Mackenzie went on 8 June. On 13 June they went to strafe a tank laager at Le Gault. They had just opened bomb doors when the Me109s fell on them. Within minutes they had lost Charlie Breese, Williams and Merritt. They were all carrying the standard bombload of two 250-lb, nine 40-lb and a can of incendiaries. One of Breese's 40-lb bombs was still hung up when his aircraft crashed, and exploded on impact.

A few days later a new crew crashed on take-off, and an Me109 poured fire into Atkinson's Blenheim as he bombed. His observer threw himself to the floor to bring the ventral gun to bear, meeting a burst that lashed through the aircraft and himself, lifting him bodily into the air. French flak hit them in the bomb bay as they hedgehopped home, flying low so that the great columns of refugees could see the RAF roundels and escape being obliged to dive into the ditches. Somehow they got back to Watton.

There were days when they flew in formations drawn from the whole of 2 Group. 'Mac' McFarlane had joined the RAF as a Direct Entry Observer in 1938, and now at twenty was the most experienced on 82 Squadron. Three of his pre-war training course survived the war. One morning his Blenheim was in the midst of a long train of thirty-six aircraft, in vics at 8,000 feet, attacking an airfield near Bethune. To his astonishment and dismay, the formation leader took them over the airfield once without bomb-ing, and began a long, slow turn for a second run over the target. The Me109s and 110s were already scrambling. Wellings, Mc-Farlane's pilot, went into a vertical dive as an Me110 flashed by so close that they saw the crews' white faces staring up at them. McFarlane was struck by the fire axe at the stern of the aircraft breaking loose and falling upon him. The compass dial cracked and the air speed indicator reached a mad, screaming 350 mph. A line of holes stitched across the port wing, and there was a sudden explosion as black smoke poured from the engine. The pilot struggled to force back the yoke with McFarlane's assis-tance. They pulled out of the dive over a wood. In a series of jolting concussions, they lost the ventral gun nacelle, the bomb doors, the trailing aerial and the tailwheel in the tree tops. But the fire was out and the Messerschmitt had vanished. They went home across the fields, sending an old Frenchman diving from his tractor into the corn as they roared over him, then over the coast and skimming the waves of the Channel. Their hydraulics were gone, and over Watton they fired a red Very light. On their second attempt, they made a successful belly landing and walked away from the wreckage.

The German bombing of Rotterdam, although it killed a thousand Dutch civilians rather than the 30,000 reported across the world at the time, seemed a convincing moment for the Royal Air Force to lift some of its restrictions on bombing military targets inside Germany. On 15 May Bomber Command was authorized to attack rail and oil installations east of the Rhine. As the summer of 1940 melted into autumn, Bomber Command's attentions were divided between German airfields in France and the Low Countries, the gathering concentration of invasion barges in the coastal ports, and the oil installations which Portal had become convinced were the key to striking at the German war machine. While 3, 4 and 5 Groups flew night after night over Germany accomplishing little but also losing very few aircraft, 82 Squadron, like the rest of 2 Group, was called upon to fight by day and night.

The results of their efforts were indecisive. 'Object of strike: Attack 1 (a) (ii) 28a Mannheim Rhenonia Oil Works', reads a characteristic photographic intelligence report of the period, for an attack on 25 June 1940. 'Photograph does not appear to show all the target, but no evidence of damage is visible.' Their losses were also predictably crushing. Under the terms of their new orders, they were not required to press on with a daylight attack unless there was cloud cover en route, but it was left to each pilot to make his own decision, and more and more often they flew on missions independently rather than in formation. On 2 July twelve 82 squadron aircraft took off. Ten turned back for lack of cloud cover, but of the two which went on, one was lost. The figures were the same for 7 July and 11 July. Three aircraft had thus been lost for six sorties completed. On the 13th, nine Blenheims took off and two more were lost. On the 18th, only two aircraft attacked of the twelve which took off.

On 29 July, Bill Keighley was the pilot of one of four aircraft which were sent in daylight to attack oil refineries at Hamburg. A psychologist had just come down to study 82 Squadron's morale, and reported that he was astonished to find it so buoyant. If he had talked to Flight-Lieutenant Keighley, the young officer would have told him that he did not expect to last the course. At that time, indeed, nobody on 82 seemed to know when a tour of operations was supposed to finish, because no one had ever completed one. Keighley had arrived at the squadron on 20 June and had noticed that the crews who fared best were those who allowed themselves to think least. On this, his ninth and last operation with Bomber Command, he set course conscious of ill omen because he had taken off through a covey of Norfolk's ubiquitous partridges, downing them all. A man who disliked killing things, he felt that they were in for a bad day.

He had been an engineer in his father's business in Darlington until 1936, when on his third application he was accepted for a short-service commission. He flew the RAF's full range of obsolete medium bombers before the war, the Fairey Gordon, the Wellesley, the Battle and finally the Blenheim, but he reached 82 with very little experience of flying with a full bombload. Like other pilots, he had developed a healthy respect for the Blenheim's alarming accident rate. Banking before adequate airspeed had been obtained on take-off killed scores of novices. There had always been a deep-seated RAF belief that an uncomfortable pilot – indeed preferably a pilot in an open cockpit – remained a wide-awake pilot. There was no danger of falling asleep in a Blenheim, with a generator too weak to support a proper heating system, and crews in winter reduced to flying encased in water-filled 'Ever-Hot' bags to escape freezing. The Blenheim's windscreen was of unstressed glass that could and did shatter under the impact of a passing pigeon. It was not an aircraft to give confidence to the inexperienced.

After flying eastwards across the North Sea, Keighley turned south on the dogleg approach to Hamburg. The clouds had evaporated and the sky ahead was completely clear. Only one of his colleagues risked an attack on 29 July, closing in to bomb, missing the target, then narrowly escaping the pursuing gaggle of Messerschmitts. Keighley decided to divert to their secondary target, Leuwarden airfield in northern Holland. They attacked from 2,000 feet and had turned across the coast for home when the gunner reported two Me110s closing fast. Pulling the 9-lb boost lever that gave the engines a burst of extra power at the cost of very rapid fuel consumption, Keighley drove the Blenheim at its 265 mph maximum speed towards a friendly peninsula of cloud. It was quickly clear that he would lose the race. Still minutes short of safety, the first bursts of fire began to clatter through the fuselage, and as Keighley pushed the aircraft into a steep dive for the sea, he heard the gunner's agonized cry: 'I'm hit! I can't see!' The turret never fired and there was sudden silence on the intercom. The German fighters swung in again. Keighley felt as if he was in a corrugated iron shed with someone bouncing dried peas on the roof. The cannon fire rippled into the fuselage. The windscreen shattered, the engine nacelles were riddled.

Then suddenly they were in cloud, and oblivious of the splinters in his leg and back Keighley muttered exultantly: 'We've made it!' In the crowded five minutes of the action, the observer, apparently paralysed, had hung over the ventral gun without firing a shot. The aircraft broke from the cloud bank to find itself alone in the peaceful sky, and for a moment Keighley sank back, exhausted with relief. Then the propeller sheared from the port engine and spun glittering away towards the sea. The oil pressure on the starboard engine began to drop rapidly as oil poured from a fractured line. 'There's no future in this,' thought Keighley, and swung resignedly back towards the German coast. He saw the Texel ahead, and threw out his maps and the radio frequency list while they were still losing height over the sea. They crash-landed in a cornfield, where they found the gunner dead. Keighley and his observer were taken away in a German ambulance, having been inspected by the very cocky young Luftwaffe Me110 pilot who had brought them down. Keighley spent six weeks in hospital before being transferred to wait out the next five years in a prison camp.

In the autumn of 1940, as the threat of invasion hung over England, 82 Squadron's aircrews were pushed through a punishing cycle of operations against barges and oil installations, interspersed with long, dreary Invasion Stand-By duties. The Blenheims had been moved to the satellite airfield of Bodney, leaving 21 Squadron in sole possession of Watton, and the crews were now living in a nearby mansion requisitioned by the RAF, Claremont Hall. The house had been taken over complete with furniture and fittings, and the young men revelled in the unaccustomed elegance, whenever they were allowed to enjoy it. Every night the stand-by crews had to sleep in their aircraft, with one officer dossing down alone in the woodman's cottage by the flarepath that served as a Flight Office. They carried revolvers on the ground and in the air.

When they were stood down for a few hours, they hired a coach to go to a dance hall, or made for The George in Fakenham or the Samson and Hercules in Norwich, 2 Group's unofficial headquarters. Meeting crews from other squadrons was a grim business: 'How's old so-and-so?' 'Oh, didn't you know? He bought it on Thursday. . .' Girls were passed from dead pilots to their successors with the fatalism that became part of the harsh legend of Bomber Command. They always seemed to know the targets, and at this time when Fifth Column mania was rife, more than one pilot began to study the blonde beside him at the bar with the most extravagant suspicions.

Bodney itself was alive with game, and the autumn days became hideous with reckless gunfire as pilots and ground crews emptied pistols and rifles at hares, rabbits, partridges and pheasants, narrowly missing the Church Army canteen van parked beside the trees that lined the field. The airmen commuted to and fro between Watton and Claremont Hall on trucks that often went home with the spoils of battle hung ready skinned or plucked over the tailgate. Even after Gembloux, even after the deadly stream of losses throughout the summer, 'Mac' McFarlane was surprised how he and many of the others could still treat everything that happened to them as a great lark, glorified 'cops and robbers': 'To us kids, it was all a marvellous game at first.'

But the squadron's spirits slipped when Paddy Bandon vanished to 2 Group headquarters staff, and in his place came a chilly, ruthless officer who feared nothing himself and had no sympathy for others who obviously did. The new CO was given to cutting remarks about his pilots in the mess, muttering as he watched through the window a Blenheim taking off for an operation: 'Well, I suppose *he'll* find some excuse to creep back before he's half way across the Channel.' One day the CO came back from a strike with the underside of his Blenheim scarred with shrapnel from the explosion of his own bombs beneath him. He called out all the crews to gaze at it: '*That* is the way I expect crews to bomb, and *that* is the height at which I expect them to attack!' he announced furiously. The squadron shrugged its shoulders. Even when crews were being lost faster then they could unpack, they did not shrink from doing the job. But they shared no enthusiasm for a man who was obviously indifferent to his own survival. When he went missing soon afterwards, he was unregretted.

In his place came 'Black Mac', sent down from 4 Group to pull the squadron together, no mean task when it was being decimated weekly, when some crews went so rapidly that the Squadron Office did not bother to enter their names in the operational record book. They were not so much demoralized as brutally fatalistic. 'Where are my quarters, please?' asked a big, red-headed former Church of England parson who arrived in the sergeants' mess one afternoon having put aside his dog collar to become an air gunner. 'I wouldn't worry if I was you,' said Bill Magrath blithely, a hardened young veteran of twenty. 'You won't be here a week.'

The planning of operations was a cottage industry. McFarlane, first into the Briefing Room one evening, was summoned to the big map by Vincent, the station commander. He pointed to the flags stuck at intervals across northern Europe: 'Well, you're first. Take your pick.' McFarlane settled for a German aerodrome. In the event, they found it empty, and on their own initiative searched for something better. They unloaded their bombs on a steelworks close to the Dutch border, took a photograph, and came home to show it to the Intelligence Officer. He was horrified: 'Good God, you might have killed women and children.' With the insane irony of the times, they were taken off operations for three days in punishment.

The short, savage encounters with the enemy lasting perhaps two or three hours seemed to create a quite different atmosphere from that of the night bomber stations later in the war, when crews were flying over Germany for eight, nine, ten hours or longer. Bodney in 1940 was more akin to a Royal Flying Corps field in France in the First World War, with its frightful losses and carefully contrived callousness. All these men were pre-war regulars or reservists or auxiliaries, not yet the wartime volunteers from every corner of civilian life. Afterwards, it was the very squandering of these relatively experienced crews in the first year of war that would give some men bitter memories. But at the time they gave themselves willingly enough. There was still a dogged amateurishness about their approach to war that would not survive many more months. It was 'not done' to think too much about personal safety, and dinghy drill always developed into a party. For a long time parachutes were seldom worn because they were uncomfortable, and the use of oxygen was thought rather 'sissy' until a crew passed out at 20,000 feet. There was only one neurosis common to aircrew throughout the war. Rather sheepishly, some met it by installing a piece of armour plate under their seat; others by putting a steel helmet beneath themselves as they approached the target. There is no evidence that this ever saved life or manhood, but it made them feel better.

On the ground, 'Uncle Duggie', the adjutant, was their confidant. A greying veteran of the Royal Flying Corps twenty-five years before, he worried about their fortunes far more than they did themselves, and felt the pain far more deeply when losses mounted. The adjutant of a neighbouring squadron had already cracked under the strain, and spent his time writing poetry and drinking a bottle of whisky a day. At Bodney, the villagers counted the aircraft taking off and coming home each day, and profoundly pitied the aircrew. The landlord of The Flying Fish at Watton gave a party one night for the NCOs (who still lived rigidly segregated from their officers). He played his favourite Caruso records for them, and was a little disappointed by their indifference. They preferred to sing their own songs: 'Craven A', 'Moriarty', 'Eskimo Nell', or the simple ditties they made up for themselves round the mess piano:

Keep the home fires burning,
    While the props are turning,
Keep the beacon flashing bright
    Till the boys come home.

Then when ops are over,
  We shall be in clover,
Keep old Duggie up all night,
  Till the boys come home . . .

One night one would see a face, and the next day it was gone, and somebody would ask: 'Who on earth was that?' There was Gadsby, who arrived and was shot down within twenty-four hours. Spencer came with his crew, saw his observer volunteer to fill in for a sick man that afternoon, and vanish for ever before unpacking. One officer terrified his crew by flying with a Bible open in his lap, and on the ground sought to convert his colleagues before it was too late. The pilot's father wrote to the CO and said that he was beginning to think that his son was unsuited to operational flying. The CO agreed. The boy disappeared. 'Mac' McFarlane, who had been with the squadron since October 1939, had at twenty developed a chronic tic on the side of his face. The squadron landed after an operation and walked to the 'Green Goddess' aircrew bus past a Blenheim whose gunner stood slumped against the fuselage, sobbing helplessly. One pilot was remembered as 'Ten Minute' Brady, because he came to the squadron, took off on his first operation, and was dead within ten minutes of crossing the Belgian coast. A few men went on month after month, apparently untouched and apparently invulnerable like the gentle, red-haired Rusty Wardell, who was studying medicine in his spare time. But Wardell would not see August out.

The transition from the prejudices of peace to the harshness, the intrinsic vulgarity, of war was taking a long time. When the first WAAF was posted to the Operations Room at Watton, the station commander felt compelled to make a blushing apology for the language of his staff. 'Oh, that's nothing,' she replied indifferently. 'Before I was here I worked in a racing stable.' 'Atty' Atkinson was sent to instruct at the Blenheim Operational Training Unit at Upwood. He devoted himself to trying to winkle out some of the most dedicated instructors with immense flying experience, who had made it clear that they had no intention of venturing anywhere near an operational squadron if they could avoid it. Word had already gone round that a posting to 2 Group was close to a sentence of death. At the OTUs, the routines of peace went unchanged. The day came when senior staff were asked for recommendations for decorations. Atkinson put in a name. Station headquarters threw up their hands in dismay: 'Oh, you can't possibly ask for a "gong" for him! He's got one already!' The list was rewritten on the time-honoured principle of Buggins's Turn.

August 1940 at Bodney started badly, with a succession of aborted operations in the face of cloudless skies, while over southern England Fighter Command fought for its life against the massed assaults of the Luftwaffe. On the 8th, three crews were detailed 'to make a photographic reconnaissance of the Dutch and Belgian and French coasts with or without the assistance of cloud cover'. Two of them were lost. Another aircraft was shot down on the 10th. On the morning of the 13th – the Luftwaffe's 'Eagle Day' – the squadron was ordered to mount a 'maximum effort' formation attack on the German airfield at Aalborg in northern Denmark.

It remains a mystery why the Blenheims were ordered to carry out this operation known to be suicidal, with negligible prospects of inflicting significant damage. As far back as 24 April, Portal had minuted the Air Ministry in the most forceful terms about the hazards of attacking the Scandinavian airfields: 'It seems to me the height of folly to throw away the experienced ... crews on the bombing of aerodromes which, I think you will agree, shows the least result for loss of equipment expended on it.' 82 Squadron would be operating at the very limit of their endurance. They were warned not to try to get back to Bodney, but to put down wherever they could in northern England. But they knew that if they used 9-lb boost for even a few minutes under battle conditions, they would be quite unable to reach the English coast. More seriously, the navigator of the leading aircraft was an inexperienced newcomer.

'Mac' McFarlane and his crew were disgusted that after so many months of operations they were ordered to fly again on an outing such as this. But by one of those freaks of remission sometimes granted by the gods, as they were in the very act of running up their engines for take-off a mechanic ran out waving his arms in the 'Wash Out' signal. They had been stood down from operations and transferred to instructing duties. Another crew took their aircraft. In the radio hut beside one of the hangars, the wireless operators invariably tuned to Lord Haw-Haw's German news broadcasts in English. Later that day McFarlane was in the hut when the bulletin came through: 'This morning eleven aircraft of the Blenheim type approached Aalborg in Denmark. Six were shot down by anti-aircraft fire and five by fighters.' The airmen burst into noisy laughter. It was only towards tea, when the empty airfield still lay in silence, that the terrible reality sank home to them.

Bill Magrath, the young cynic who had warned a new arrival not to bother about his quarters, was navigating for Sergeant Donald Blair that morning. Magrath was a country solicitor's son from Northern Ireland who had joined the RAF in August 1939. Like all the other young men given immediate NCO rank in the air force at this time, he had to suffer the fierce hostility of the old sweats in the sergeants' mess, whose attitude was ultimately responsible for the creation of separate Aircrew NCOs' messes on so many stations. When Magrath first walked in and ordered whisky, there was a dead silence. Then a senior warrant officer announced witheringly: 'We don't serve whisky to boys.' New NCOs who were foolish enough to take off their jackets to play table tennis were ruthlessly crushed for their impropriety. For some months, NCO aircrew were still obliged to ask to be excused ground duties by the senior warrant officer before taking off on operations. One station CO in 2 Group was so enraged when an NCO pilot arrived late for briefing that he sent him out of the room and refused to let him take part in the operation.

By 13 August, Magrath had completed six sorties – three against invasion barges – the usual targets for 'freshmen' – and three against oil installations. On one of the latter night trips, over Amsterdam, anti-aircraft fire turned the Blenheim on its back and blew a hole in the perspex through which all their navigation equipment was sucked out. Somehow they regained control and found their way home through the balloon barrage up the Thames estuary. On the morning of the 13th, Magrath was called for operations in the spacious former married quarters at Watton where he had been living alone since his room-mate was killed the previous week. In the operations room each of them was handed the usual buff envelope containing details of their target and the relevant maps. They took off into a cloudless sky, although at briefing it had been stressed that if there was less than five-tenths cloud the operation would be aborted. They took up station in the midst of the formation of four stacked vics of three aircraft, and set out across the North Sea, towards that very killing ground which had proved so fatal to 3 Group eight months before.

They were approaching the Danish coast when Greenwood, in the rear turret, said: 'Hello, he's off again.' A sergeant pilot had suddenly dropped his aircraft out of the formation and was turning for home. It had been noticed on previous operations that this man's aircraft was jinxed by repeated problems requiring his return to base. On this occasion, he would claim at his subsequent court martial that he discovered he had insufficient fuel to complete the operation and get home, and he would be acquitted. The remaining eleven aircraft cruised on. Magrath perceived to his consternation that his fears about the navigator of the leading aircraft had been justified – he had brought them across the North Sea on a course that crossed the southern rather than the northern coast of Denmark. They were now faced with a run up the length of the country to attack.

They crossed the shoreline at 8,000 feet in clear sunshine, and flew steadily northwards. They were still twenty miles short of Aalborg when the first Me109s attacked. The fighters raked the formation continuously until they broke away to allow the flak to open fire as they neared the airfield. Half the Blenheims jettisoned their bombs as soon as the fighters engaged. Don Blair dived for the ground with an Me109 on his tail, and levelled out over the sea with one engine on fire. Bill Magrath was knocked unconscious by the shock of their ditching, and woke to find himself floating in the North Sea in his Mae West. Greenwood, their gunner, had three bullet wounds in his legs. Blair had vanished. They were picked up by a Danish fishing boat. Every single aircraft in the formation was shot down. For once Lord Haw-Haw had reported the literal truth. Nine aircrew out of thirty-three survived as prisoners, one of whom, Sergeant Johnnie Oates, almost died of his wounds. Oates had been hedgehopping to escape the fighters after bombing when his port wingtip touched a fence post and the Blenheim cart-wheeled into the ground. His navigator was thrown clear with shock and a broken wrist. When the ambulance came, Oates insisted that the navigator be put on a stretcher. He himself sat on the floor. Only at the hospital did he learn that his own back was broken.

Bill Magrath had a smashed hip, a broken shoulder, a broken leg and was blind in one eye. Yet on 20 November 1941 he escaped from a transit camp in Rouen where he had just learned that plans for his medical repatriation had been cancelled, and began an extraordinary journey across France via Paris and Marseilles, to the Pyrenees. Still as lame as he would remain for the rest of his life, he walked across the freezing January cold of the mountains into Spain and thus home to England. He was awarded the Military Medal for his escape, but he also discovered that having been passed 'unfit for further aircrew duties', he was automatically reduced to sergeant's rank, and lost the warrant officer's pay he would have retained for the rest of the war had he remained in a POW camp. He remained a sergeant until he was later commissioned as an Air Traffic Control Officer.

The Aalborg operation had been a disaster reflecting almost Crimean stupidity on the part of those at Bomber Command and Group who ordered it. At last, however, the staff were being compelled to accept the hopelessness of daylight deep penetrations beyond the range of fighter cover. For 82 Squadron, the Aalborg raid did not signal the end of daylight operations, but a change in the pace of their war that lasted most of that winter. The losses had been too savage for any force to continue on its course unchecked. Night after night, aircraft flew against the barge concentrations along 'Blackpool front', the invasion coast west of Dunkirk. Even after the Germans began to disperse their fleet on 20 September, following the indefinite postponement of *Sealion*, the attacks went on. Bomber Command flew southwards across the Channel while their counterparts of the Luftwaffe droned north towards London. Some nights, 82 Squadron had to provide crews for the oddly-named 'Cheadles', nuisance raids on a triangular course against selected Luftwaffe airfields in France. They dropped empty beerbottles, for like most of the

RAF for the rest of the war, they thought these made a noise that upset bystanders beneath. They shot up any target they could see, and came home frequently a good deal more shaken than the Junkers and Dornier crews in their billets below.

New faces came to replace the ghosts of Aalborg: Sam El-worthy, a polished, brilliant New Zealand-born barrister and graduate of Trinity, Cambridge, to command 'A' Flight with instant distinction; 'Messy' Messervy, an Australian who took over 'B' and enlivened mess parties by setting fire to his long fair hair and then pouring beer over it. Messervy would later be transferred abruptly to Photographic Reconnaissance – where he would die – when it was discovered that he had no night vision. John McMichael, a coal merchant's son from Bedford who had joined the RAF during the Slump, was not amused to notice, as more and more crews ditched in the sea, that it was still left to personal initiative to supply dinghy rations. After an 82 Squadron crew came down beside a convoy off Yarmouth and floated impotent in their dinghy while their gunner, with a broken arm, drifted away to drown, McMichael wrote to the Air Ministry suggesting that every dinghy should be equipped with a quoit on a rope that could be tossed to a drifting man. A civil servant wrote back to say that this was impossible, since it would cost the service 12s 6d for every aircraft dinghy.

The even tenor and less dangerous atmosphere of the squadron's winter operations were shattered abruptly on the night of 4 December, when they were sent in appalling weather to attack Essen steelworks. At briefing it was suggested jovially that if the fog continued to close in, on their return crews could bale out as a last resort. In the event, Messervy force-landed at Mildenhall, grazing the mess chimney. Two crews crashed in the fog, killing everybody aboard. One crew was lost without trace in the North Sea. McMichael baled out over King's Lynn, having the disconcerting experience of descending with his own abandoned aircraft circling round him. His gunner came down on Marham cookhouse, where for some moments he was thought to be a mine. One sergeant pilot had sufficient fuel to circle until dawn, when he landed safely at Bodney.

It would be difficult to exaggerate the dedication with which most crews strove to complete these impossible operations. Sergeant Ted Inman and his observer, Ken Collins, spent New Year's Day 1941 circling Ostend for an hour in a snowstorm in a vain effort to locate their target. Peter Tallis in a few weeks on 82 Squadron developed an extraordinary reputation for completing attacks when everybody else had abandoned them, pressing on to the Dutch coast in broad daylight when others had returned for lack of cloud cover. One day early in January, Tallis was halfway across the Channel when his Blenheim suffered an electrical failure. He simply went home and immediately set off again in a spare aircraft. A few men, not surprisingly, cracked. On one trip a cannon shell took off the head of an observer. The gunner crawled forward to drag the body down the fuselage so that the pilot would not be compelled to sit behind a headless corpse all the way home, but it was to no purpose. The pilot never flew an operation again. The steady drain of losses continued. Moller crashed on take-off, one of several pilots who suffered the fatal consequences of oiling-up their idling engines during the interminable wait on the flarepath for the take-off signal. One night Ju88s followed 21 Squadron home to Watton next door, and shot up a succession of Blenheims as they landed. Those of 82's aircrew who survived a few weeks became accustomed to duty with burial parties: 'You soon got the knack.'

The spring of 1941 brought the onset of the most horrific phase of 2 Group's operations, the anti-shipping strikes in the North Sea and the Channel. At a moment when Britain stood passive on almost every front, the Prime Minister was determined that she should assert herself at the very gates of the 'island fortress'. The Royal Navy sent out its torpedo boats night after night, and fought convoys through the eastern Channel Narrows at terrible cost not because it was the only possible route for British shipping, but because it had become a matter of national prestige to keep the way open. Bomber Command's Hampdens took off every night to mine the approaches to Germany's harbours – 'gardening', as it was called, would become one of the undisputed successes of the RAF's war. Finally, it fell to 2 Group's Blenheims to attack enemy shipping in daylight wherever and whenever it could be found. In the spring and summer of 1941, at terrible cost, the Blenheims did so.

Day after day, sometimes in formation and sometimes in pairs,

82 Squadron took off in search of German convoys, invariably bristling with light flak and guarded by a screen of flakships. The Blenheims came down in a slow dive from 5,000 feet, through the flickering hail of fire to the very tips of the waves. As the ship raced up before them, the pilot called: 'Now!' to his observer in the nose. Away went the aircraft's 250-lb bombs with five-second delay fuses. The Blenheim lunged upwards to avoid the ship's masts and climbed for home. This at least was the theory. In reality, again and again the attacking aircraft never recovered from the dive, but plunged into the sea streaming smoke from a score of cannon hits. Sea-level attack was not a figure of speech. Blenheims were known to come home with propeller tips and even the entire airframe bent by contact with the water. One 82 Squadron pilot misjudged his run and smashed into the mast of a German ship, ripping open the perspex nose of his aircraft and the body of his observer who had been staring though it. Another was so appalled by the spectacle of his wingman diving through the barrage to bomb that when the time came for him to follow, he froze at the controls and circled, paralysed. Eventually he came home, never to fly an operation again.

2 Group's squadrons were detailed in rotation for the notorious 'Channel Stop' duties, attacking German coastal convoys. On average, a unit lasted a fortnight before being replaced, decimated. As the shipping strikes intensified, the usual crop of passengers from Bodney who flew on occasional operations died away abruptly. The orderly room clerk was joyriding in one aircraft that vanished into the sea. When Ken Collins asked Caesar, the engineering officer, if he would like to come on a trip one day. Caesar shook his head decisively: 'All my previous chauffeurs have gone for a burton . . .'

One day in April the squadron was attacking a convoy off the German coast in formation, led by Sam Elworthy, who had now become CO. He and a sergeant pilot hit two 3,000-ton tankers before the Me109s swept in, slashing at the Blenheim of a new pilot on his first operation. Somehow they escaped, but the novice was nursed home by Elworthy with his gunner dead, having had the unnerving experience of watching one of his propellers fall off. In the middle of April, the squadron was suddenly transferred to the RAF station at Lossiemouth on the north-east coast of Scotland, to attack shipping off Norway. They took off in formation and then as they approached the enemy coast broke off in pairs, each sweeping a sector of sea for a few dangerous minutes before turning hastily for home whether they had bombed or not, in the hope of anticipating the scrambling Messerschmitts. A crew which ditched on these operations knew that their slender hope of survival in the Channel had dwindled to nothing off Norway. It was on one of these sorties that the dedicated Tallis, on his last operation with the squadron, vanished without trace and defied all their efforts to find him. Elworthy was especially depressed by his loss. A few days later Ian Spencer, on his first trip with the squadron, came home hours late with his aircraft shot to pieces and somehow dragged the Blenheim into a belly landing at Lossiemouth. As he sat exhausted in his cockpit in the midst of the runway, the station commander's staff car raced up. The furious group captain jumped out and began berating Spencer for making a mess of his airfield. Sam Elworthy arrived at this moment, and did not mince words about the station commander's sense of priorities. Only when Spencer checked the aircraft later did he find that one 250-lb bomb was still hung up in the bomb bay, and the aileron was held on only by the Bristol Aeroplane Company's name tag.

One day, under the leadership of a somewhat reckless flight commander, the squadron strayed hopelessly off course on a daylight operation and missed Norway altogether. Fumbling their way home, they broke cloud a few feet above the Firth of Forth, rapidly approaching the Forth Bridge. As they blundered into the balloon barrage around Edinburgh the formation broke up, every man for himself. They landed all over eastern Scotland, on airfields or farms according to where their fuel ran out. Around Lossiemouth snowstorms were common, and more than one crew became detached from formation, and were obliged to feel their way home, sheepish and lonely.

In May 82 Squadron returned to Bodney. Elworthy was promoted to a staff appointment at Group headquarters, where he continued his efforts to persuade Air Vice-Marshal Donald Stevenson, AOC of 2 Group, that his command was being slaughtered to no purpose on the anti-shipping operations. Many wartime Bomber Command officers attracted controversy, but few such universal dislike as Stevenson. He was christened 'Butcher', not with the rueful affection with which the name was later attached to Harris, but with bitter resentment. An arrogant, ruthless man with no apparent interest in the practical problems facing his crews, Stevenson seemed to regard 2 Group's operations solely in the light of their value to his own advancement. 'A ship hit is a ship sunk!' he declared emphatically, as he compiled wilfully and grossly exaggerated statistics of his Group's achievements. Losses did not disconcert him at all. When Paddy Bandon tried to convince him that morale was suffering severely from the futile attrition over the Channel, Stevenson seized an inkwell and hurled it at the wall, 'Churchill wants it!' he declared incontrovertibly.

Yet for all his commitment to the struggle, the Prime Minister was greatly disturbed by 2 Group's losses. In August 1941, for example, of 77 Blenheims that attacked shipping, 23 were lost. In a total of 480 sorties, 36 aircraft were gone in a month. In one of a series of 'Action This Day' minutes to the Chief of Air Staff on Bomber Command casualties, Churchill wrote on 29 August:

The loss of seven Blenheims out of seventeen in the daylight attack on merchant shipping and docks at Rotterdam is most severe. Such losses might be accepted in attacking *Scharnhorst*, *Gneisenau* or *Tirpitz*, or a southbound Tripoli convoy, because, apart from the damage done, a first-class strategic object is served. But they seem disproportionate to an attack on merchant shipping not engaged in vital supply work . . . While I greatly admire the bravery of the pilots, I do not want them pressed too hard.

The next day Churchill drafted a message to the crews: 'The devotion of the attacks on Rotterdam and other objectives are beyond all praise. The Charge of the Light Brigade at Balaclava is eclipsed in brightness by these almost daily deeds of fame.' From the pen of a man with the Prime Minister's profound sense of history, it could have been no accident that he compared 2 Group's achievements with another futile British sacrifice. Yet Stevenson was unshakeable. One day while Elworthy was still commanding 82 Squadron, he was appalled to be ordered by the AOC to prepare them for a daylight attack on Krupps of Essen. It was the only occasion of the war on which Elworthy wrote a

'Last Letter' to his wife. He felt compelled to make one further effort to remonstrate with Stevenson. 'Oh well, if you feel that strongly about it, you needn't feel you have to fly yourself,' replied the group commander blithely. To Elworthy's overwhelming relief, the operation was later cancelled on higher authority. To Bomber Command's overwhelming relief, in December 1941 Stevenson would at last be replaced as AOC of 2 Group.

On 9 May, 82 Squadron flew down to St Eval in Cornwall. They were briefed that evening for a dawn attack on La Rochelle. As darkness fell, the crews were dismayed to see all the ground crews quit the airfield. 'Where are we going? God, you wouldn't catch us here at night if you paid us. Didn't you know? The Stukas never miss this place.' The Blenheim crews wrote it off as a 'lineshoot' and were sleeping soundly when the pandemonium of an air raid alarm descended. They were in the shelter when a voice called down: 'Any 82 pilots here? You're wanted to disperse the aircraft.' Amidst the hail of falling bombs, nobody moved. The Blenheims were neatly lined up beside the hangars for the German bomb-aimers. At dawn there were four serviceable aircraft to go to La Rochelle. The rest of the crews went home by train.

They were back in the West Country only two days later, at Portreath this time, for a low-level daylight attack on U-boats alleged to be tied up alongside the quays at St Nazaire. That morning of 13 May they passed over a German convoy minutes before they reached the French coast. Their spirits sank, for they knew that now they would be expected. They were not mistaken. King, their new CO, flew into the curtain of flak and dived straight into the sea before they reached the docks. He was not leading the formation because he was still gaining Blenheim experience. He had been with them barely a week. From all over the harbour light flak hosed up. Sergeant Dusty Miller suddenly found holes appearing all over his Blenheim. He pulled up over the cranes with his port engine on fire, released his bombs over the ships tied up alongside the quays, then bellylanded in a field just outside St Nazaire. He and his crew set fire to the remains of the Blenheim, then started walking. They were on the road for three weeks, until they reached unoccupied Vichy France. There they were rash enough to assume that they would be given help, and gave themselves up. They were imprisoned in St Hippolyte fort near Nimes for their pains, and it was from here that Miller and his gunner made successful escapes and walked across the Pyrenees into Spain. They were back in England within two months of being shot down.

On 24 August, 82 Squadron's new CO, Wing-Commander Lascelles, a cousin of the Royal Family, led six aircraft on an operation towards the Heligoland Bight. Finding no cloud cover, he prudently turned back. On returning to Bodney, according to one of his pilots, Lascelles was telephoned by Stevenson the Group commander and threatened with a charge of cowardice. At 10.30 a.m. on the 26th, Lascelles set out once again at the head of a formation of six aircraft. One turned back with engine trouble. The other five were shot down. That evening, the Prime Minister telephoned Watton personally to confirm that Lascelles was missing. At last, Stevenson had overreached himself intolerably. 2 Group's daylight anti-shipping strikes were drastically curtailed. Lascelles was 82 Squadron's seventh commanding officer in eleven months, and the third to be killed.

'Atty' Atkinson, back on operations, took over 82 with orders for Malta. Ken Collins, the observer who had been with 82 since Christmas Eve 1940, looked around at the ghosts of all those who had gone in those five months and said in astonishment to Ted Inman, his pilot: 'We're invincible!' But Inman shook his head: 'I'm surprised we've lasted as long as we have. We've got to go some time.' Less than a week after arriving in Malta. Collins said 'Bombs gone!' over an Italian convoy, and the next thing that he remembered was awakening on the deck of an enemy destroyer. His aircraft and crew had exploded in mid-air. It was his thirty-ninth operation. He had always said that he did not mind being killed, but dreaded capture or the loss of a limb. Now, he had a leg amputated in Tripoli Hospital. He was just twenty.

'Atty' Atkinson went on to become a legend in 2 Group, the only man to survive two anti-shipping tours from Malta. When he came home at the end of the year, the seventeen survivors of his command fitted comfortably into a single Catalina. Dusty Miller, after his escape from Spain, boarded a merchant ship at Gibraltar to find that it was carrying 82 Squadron ground crews on their way back from the Mediterranean.

'How's the old squadron, then?' he asked eagerly.

'The old squadron? There's only one left, and he's been sent home "Lacking moral fibre"....'

It had been a futile, ghastly year for 2 Group, unredeemed by any sense of technical advance, or strategic success. The Blenheims had been thrown into the battle because they were there, not even because they were expected to win, but because it seemed vital that Britain be seen to be continuing the fight with every instrument at her command, however feeble. For the most part, the crews went extraordinarily uncomplainingly. One of Atkinson's pilots wrote to him from a German prison camp:

Dear Atty,

I'm sorry I failed to return on the 26th, but a destroyer picked me off going in to attack, and the merchantman got my second engine, which complicated matters a little. This left me no choice but to fall in the drink about three miles from the convoy ...

Much has been said and written about Fighter Command in 1940. Yet the losses of Bomber Command aircrew far eclipsed those of the fighter pilots, throughout the period of the Battle of Britain and for the rest of the war. The sacrifice of 2 Group in 1940–41 was a legend as dramatic, if not as glamorous, as anything endured by The Few.

3 10 Squadron, Yorkshire, 1940–41

'I wish Jim had joined the RAF,' said Mrs Leonard. 'I'm sure it could have been managed. You know where you are with them. You just settle down at an RAF station as though it was business with regular hours and a nice crowd. Of course I shouldn't let Jim fly, but there's plenty of jobs like my brother's got.'

'Ground staff is all right in war-time,' said Sarum-Smith. 'It won't sound so good afterwards. One's got to think of peace . . .'
Evelyn Waugh, *Men at Arms*

Bomber Command launched its first attack of the war against a land target on the night of 19 March 1940, when twenty Hampdens from 5 Group and thirty Whitleys of 4 Group attacked the German seaplane base of Hornum, on the island of Sylt, a few miles west of the German–Danish coast.

Seven of the Whitleys came from 10 Squadron at Dishforth in Yorkshire, led by their flamboyant squadron commander, Bill Staton. The crews were full of excitement and apprehension to be carrying a live bombload at last. There had been so many months of dreary 'nickelling' – dropping propaganda leaflets over Germany, an exercise which they heartily agreed with Arthur Harris had done no more than 'provide the enemy with five years free supply of lavatory paper'. They might grudgingly have admitted that it had also provided Bomber Command with an insight into the difficulties of navigating at night over blacked-out Europe, without great hazard to themselves. They had lost one crew. In the mood of the day, these men had been commemorated by the unveiling of an oak plaque in the station church at Dishforth. Henceforward, they would be expected to do their dying with rather less ceremony. But in those first months 10 Squadron were allowed to adjust themselves very gently to war.

'Bombs my foot!' said Good King Wence, 'them be leaflets, Stephen!'

– as *Punch* put it that Christmas of 1939. For the night bombers, there were no Gembloux or Aalborg operations, no sudden slaughters or sunlit dramas. Instead, there was only the beginning of the long, painfully slow escalation of the bombing war to its terrible crescendo in 1944 and 1945. It was the Whitleys, the Wellingtons and the Hampdens, blundering blindly through the night skies over Germany in 1940 and 1941, who were the pathfinders for all that followed, for good or ill.

The only pilot in 10 Squadron with any notion of the reality of war was their CO, Bill Staton. A huge, burly rhino of a man, still indecently fit at forty-two, he had flown Bristol Fighters with the Royal Flying Corps in the First World War, become an ace and won the Military Cross, and still bore the great scar across his head where a chair had been broken over it at a mess party in 1917. Everything about Staton was larger than life. The squadron called him 'King Kong' because of his size. He had been destined for a brewer's engineer if the First War had not intervened, but for more than twenty years now the RAF had been his life, and he threw himself into it heart and soul. A former captain of the air force shooting team, he spent his off-duty hours combing the hills for pheasants and grouse for the mess. He scoured the country houses of the area borrowing portraits and furniture to make the officers' quarters the best appointed in 4 Group. Muscular Christianity personified, he presided every morning at a ten-minute voluntary service outside the hangars. Pipe between his teeth and black labrador Sam at his heels, he loped inexhaustibly from squadron offices to dispersals, mess binges to aircrew funerals.

Above all, this enormous, bombastic figure seemed to his crews to regard the war as a marvellous entertainment laid on for his benefit. He flew at every possible opportunity. He seemed to have no understanding of the meaning of fear. After so many months of 'nickelling', he was first into the air on take-off for Sylt at 7.30 that evening of 19 March 1940, equipped as usual for every contingency, a canvas bucket beside his seat filled with shaving tackle and his private escape kit.

As his Whitley approached the target, the German flak began to hose into the sky, red, yellow and white – even the 'Flaming Onions' Staton remembered so well from the First War, wads of wire-linked phosphorus. His novice crew hung tense in their seats as Staton cruised blithely into the barrage. There had been a rumour that the Germans possessed a beam capable of cutting the magnetos of British aircraft, and Staton had made up his mind to test this theory by circling for fifteen minutes to see what happened. Scorning evasive action, he drove the Whitley bucketing through the gunfire over Sylt with its terrified crew. Donaldson, the navigator, shouted to his CO after one burst: 'Can't get the rear gunner to answer, sir!'

'He's probably dead!' said Staton cheerfully. At last, to the other men's relief, they dropped their bombs and turned for home. On the ground they found that 10 Squadron and its commander were heroes. The Press had been summoned to Dishforth and the next day's *Daily Mirror* told the story of 'Crack 'Em' Staton and his leadership of the raid on Sylt. In the squadron record book it was recorded confidently that 'From Captains' reports it is very evident that considerable damage has been done to Hornum.' A day later a Whitley from 77 Squadron at Driffield flew over Dishforth and inundated the station with leaflets: 'Congratulations to CRACK'EM AND CO (the heroes, and leaders, of Sylt) – from an admiring Driffield.' The four other squadrons which had sent aircraft to Hornum were somewhat put out by the epidemic of publicity that had descended on Dishforth.

Yet in the days that followed, Bomber Command was compelled to assess the reality of the raid on Sylt. Of the fifty aircraft which took part forty-one, including all those from 10 Squadron, claimed to have bombed the target, and only one had been lost. Many pilots at debriefing had given circumstantial details of hits on slipways, hangars and workshops. Yet the two photographic reconnaissance Blenheims from 82 Squadron that examined Hornum with the utmost thoroughness after the raid were unable to find evidence of any damage whatever to the base installations. The staff at Bomber Command considered every possibility, including that of the Germans having done an astonishing overnight repair job. But on 10 April the Command report on the Sylt raid concluded with stilted but inescapable dismay: 'The operation does not confirm that as a general rule, the average crews of our heavy bombers can identify targets at night, even under the best conditions, nor does it prove that the average crew can bomb industrial or other enemy targets at night. . .' An untruthful communiqué was issued to the Press, announcing that the reconnaissance photographs of Sylt were of too poor quality for proper damage assessment,.

Neither the Air Staff nor Bomber Command had any ready answers to the very serious problems revealed by the Sylt raid. Instead as the tide of war rushed over them in the weeks that followed, they were compelled to launch their forces where they could, as best they could. In April, 10 Squadron were sent to attack the Norwegian airfields which few of them proved able to find, and fewer still to bomb effectively. In May they were thrust into the Battle of France, seeking railway junctions and bridges behind the lines with negligible success. Then the order came to commence bombing Germany itself – the oil installations and marshalling yards whose names like Gelsenkirchen and Hamm became bywords and eventually wry jokes in that first year of the bomber offensive. In the morning the crews who had felt their way through the German sky in the darkness awoke and turned on the radio in their huts to listen to the urbane voice of the BBC reporting that 'Last night, aircraft of Bomber Command . . .' and they were touchingly delighted to hear themselves spoken of. If the BBC said that they had attacked the marshalling yards at Hamm, well, they couldn't be making quite such a mess of it as they sometimes thought.

Bomber Command possessed seventeen squadrons of aircraft suitable for use as night bombers in September 1939: this slowly expanding force of Wellingtons, Whitleys and Hampdens would constitute the backbone of the bomber offensive until well into 1942. The Hampden was the most urgent candidate for replacement: cruising at only 155 mph, 10 mph slower than the other two, this grotesque-looking flying glasshouse could stand little punishment, lacked power-operated turrets, and could carry only a 4,000-lb maximum bombload. The Wellington, with a 4,500-lb bombload, would never carry the weight to compare with the later heavy bombers, but after modifications to improve its speed and ceiling, it continued as a sturdy makeweight with Bomber Command until 1943. Both the Wellington and the Whitley were exceptionally strong aircraft – later wartime design would sacrifice structural strength to load and performance. Early in May 1940, 10 Squadron had thankfully exchanged their Whitley IVs – equipped with the grossly inadequate Tiger radial engine – for the Whitley V, powered by the excellent Rolls-Royce Merlin. The new model cruised to Germany at 165 mph and could carry 8,000-lb over short distances, but coming home against the prevailing westerly wind often took longer than the loaded outward trip. The Whitley looked for all the world like a rather pedantic middle-aged pipe-smoker, with its jutting chin mounting a single Vickers K gun, and its extraordinary tail-high attitude in flight.

On its début in 1937, *Flight* magazine wrote: 'The Whitley is as kind to its crew as it is likely to be unkind to any enemy down below.' Yet the essential weakness of all Bomber Command's early wartime aircraft was their mass of inadequate ancillary equipment prone to technical failure and their lack of basic comfort for men compelled to live in them for eight hours at a stretch. Each aircraft carried a crew of five:* two pilots; a navigator (the old classification of observer was abolished and by the end of 1940 a bomber navigator was recognized as one of, if not the, most important member of every crew); a wireless operator, who usually spent much of the trip with his 1155 set in pieces in front of him, or struggling to coax more power out of the Whitley's inadequate generators; and a rear gunner, who nursed his four Brownings in a power-operated turret mounted between the twin fins of the tail. The cold was appalling. They flew layered in silk, wool and leather, yet still their sandwiches and coffee froze solid as they ate and drank, vital systems jammed, limbs seized, wings iced-up for lack of de-icing gear. The navigator gave the pilot a course on take-off, and then relied absolutely on being able to establish pinpoints from the ground below at intervals in the six- or seven-hour flight – 'groping', Staton called it. On a clear night it was possible to shoot the stars with a sextant if the pilot was willing or able to fly straight and level for long enough.

---

*In British bombers throughout the war the senior pilot was captain of the aircraft whatever his rank, unlike the Luftwaffe, where the navigator, who was also a qualified pilot, was captain. British squadrons were invariably commanded by pilots except in 4 Group later in the war, where a number of navigators and even gunners became squadron COs.

It was sometimes possible for a skilled wireless operator to pick up a loop bearing from England, but a novice could put an aircraft on a 180-degree reciprocal course if he misjudged the signal, and the Germans frequently jammed the wavelengths. On rare occasions the weather report before take-off was accurate, and it was possible to allow for the wind strength when navigating in the air. More often, the predictions were quite wrong, and the winds were blowing the aircraft off course and speed. Checking drift by dropping a flare or incendiary was a chancy business, and impossible in cloud.

In these nursery days of the offensive, efforts were made to send out the bombers in moonlight, to assist navigation and bombing. In the event, cloud often blanketed the ground for part or all of the operation. Approaching a target wreathed in cloud, there were only two possibilities: to descend to recklessly low level to seek visual identification – which cost many crews their lives – or to bomb on ETA – Estimated Time of Arrival over the target, judged from the last pinpoint, perhaps hundreds of miles back. This was the commonest course among mediocre crews, who had their own saying: 'He who bombs on ETA lives to fly another day.' It was a practice that created errors not of yards, or even miles, but of scores and hundreds of miles. ETA attack was the subject of a savage Bomber Command memorandum to all Groups on 14 June 1940, reiterating that 'bombs are not to be dropped indiscriminately'. But again and again at this period, Germany was genuinely unaware that Bomber Command had been attempting to attack a specific target or even a specific region. There was merely a litter of explosives on farms, homes, lakes, forests and – occasionally – on factories and installations from end to end of the Reich.

Peter Donaldson, the navigator who had been flying with Bill Staton on the night of the Sylt raid, took off at 8.30 p.m. on the evening of 27 May to attack a German aerodrome in Holland. His pilot was a 10 Squadron officer named Warren. They were on course, flying steadily across the North Sea, when they encountered a sudden magnetic storm. Flashes of lightning danced on the wings. The aircraft rocked and bucketed as the pilots struggled to maintain control. After a few minutes Warren asked Donaldson for a new course to escape the weather. The last light had gone now, and as their ETA at the Dutch coast came and went, they began to search the sea below for a pinpoint. At last, they saw the Rhine estuary. Flak curled up towards them. They tracked steadily up the thread of the river, then turned to starboard and began to search for the airfield that was their target. Suddenly Rattigan, the second pilot, called from the nose: 'This is it! I've got it!' The Whitley lifted as the bombs fell away. 'Give me a course for base,' said Warren.

At first light as their ETA Dishforth approached, they dropped through the cloud. They saw below them a city, and the sea beyond. They were obviously on the west coast of England. Two Spitfires wheeled curiously across them. They identified the port of Liverpool below. Warren turned to the crew and said flatly: 'According to my calculations, we can only have bombed something inside England. Christ, what are we going to do?' They flew miserably home to Yorkshire. Their magnetic compass had been thrown out of true by the storm. They had picked up the Thames estuary in place of the Rhine, and dropped a stick of bombs with unusual precision across the runway of Fighter Command's station at Bassingbourn in Cambridgeshire. Their Captain was demoted to second pilot, and known to the mess for ever after as Baron Von Warren. The ordnance experts were dismayed to discover that a stick of Bomber Command bombs had done scarcely any damage at all to Bassingbourn, and thus presumably would have done little more to Germany. Two Spitfires flew over Dishforth and dropped Iron Crosses. It had been a comic episode that might easily have been a tragedy, yet in the context of those days and the equipment with which they were operating, it was astonishing that it did not happen more often.

Beyond navigation problems, they were increasingly aware of the imperfections of their bomb-aiming. During an attack on oil installations at Bremen, Bill Staton organized one of the first attempts to mark a target with flares and Very lights in the hands of his best crews. He himself made six runs over the city at less than a thousand feet, while one of his sergeant pilots tried to decoy the searchlights. Staton's aircraft was riddled. As the battered Whitley crossed the North Sea, he offered his crew the option of ditching rather than attempting a forced landing. When they somehow reached the end of the runway at Dishforth, they counted 700 holes in the aircraft.

They were still deeply concerned about the risk of hitting civilians. The Government's 'Revised Instruction' to the Air Ministry in June 1940 insisted that 'the attack must be made with reasonable care to avoid undue loss of civil life in the vicinity of the target'. Their orders emphatically stated that if they could not identify their target they were to come home with their bombs. Crew after crew crashed attempting the difficult landing with an explosive load aboard, and it was months before they introduced the concept of 'last resort' targets – those bizarre creatures SEMO and MOPA, 'Self-Evident Military Objective' and 'Military Objective Previously Attacked', to be bombed if the primary and secondary targets could not be located. One of 10's pilots, Pete Whitby, found a bomb hung up over an oil plant they were attacking one autumn night. It freed itself a few moments later to fall in the midst of Hanover. He and his crew flew home deeply worried by the thought that it might have landed on women and children. One night over Coblenz, a flight commander named Pat Hanafin made four runs and then called to his second pilot to drop the bombs. 'No, no, we're too near the hospital,' the man shouted from the nose. In these days when only a fraction of the crews could find a given city, hospitals were still individually marked on every navigator's maps.

That idyllic summer of 1940 they were driven out relentlessly night after night, orders and bombloads being changed at a moment's notice, briefings and cancellations falling over each other as crisis followed crisis. In the wake of Dunkirk, relations between the British army and the RAF plumbed bitter depths. Two of Pat Hanafin's crew rash enough to walk into a Harrogate pub full of soldiers fell out again shortly afterwards, badly beaten up. The incident was repeated everywhere that soldiers and airmen met. The weather mocked their confusion. 'Temperature 85 degrees. Another glorious summer's day,' recorded the squadron operations book on 9 June. The next day Italy declared war, and Bomber Command was ordered forth in the hope of making Mussolini regret his decision. 3 Group's Wellingtons, attacking from staging points in France, were eliminated from the operation when the French drove lorries across the runway to prevent them from taking off – they feared Italian reprisals. 10 Squadron flew from Guernsey in the Channel Islands, to bring Turin just within range.

Pat Hanafin was a Cranwell-trained regular RAF officer who had asked to be posted from his staff job to operations when the invasion of Norway began. He requested Group to send him anywhere but to 10 Squadron, because his bull terrier had once savaged Staton's labrador Sam, and he did not think Staton was the sort of man to forget it. But to his surprise, Staton requested him as a flight commander. The trip to Turin was his seventeenth in less than two months. The cold was murderous. They were fired on by French flak. A few miles short of the Alps, they flew headlong into black cumulus clouds. The lightning eddied around them until suddenly there was a great flash which ripped through the Whitley. It blew the rear gunner backwards out of his turret into the fuselage with the left side of his body paralysed. It burned the wireless operator's hands, cut both engines, and put the aircraft into a vertical dive, laden with ice. Somehow Hanafin regained control before they reached the ground, but they lacked the fuel to climb the Alps once more, even if they still possessed the will. They turned back for Guernsey.

Those of 10 Squadron who reached Italy that night looked down at the great pale ghosts of the Alps in the moonlight with wonderment that would strike so many Bomber Command crews following their course in the next four years. Most were numbed by the relentless cold, for they had little experience of the hazards above 10,000 feet. The Whitley's oxygen supply was inadequate for long flights at high altitude. The exactor controls, which enabled the pilot to vary the engine pitch, were chronically prone to freezing, leaving the engines trapped in fine pitch and the aircraft unable to climb. When the lines froze, the fluid inside them began to leak through pinpoint holes until pressure was gone. Crews learned to unscrew the exactor system and refill it with coffee, urine – anything to restore pressure. Only a handful of pilots claimed to have found Turin that night, despite the indifferent Italian blackout. One aircraft failed to return. The others had strawberries and cream for breakfast in the summer sunshine of Guernsey, then flew home, a little thawed, to Yorkshire.

They were now operating from the new station of Leeming, although until its buildings and tarmac runways were completed they were obliged to fly before each operation to nearby Topcliffe or Linton for briefing and bombing-up. Shortly after the fall of France, Sid Bufton arrived to become their commanding officer. Bufton had been transferred from a staff job at the Air Ministry to the Advanced Air Striking Component a few weeks after the outbreak of war. One May morning he was having a haircut in a French barber's shop when the Luftwaffe appeared overhead and began to rain bombs upon them. He escaped from France on 17 June at the final French collapse, and came home looking for command of a fighter squadron. Instead he was sent to Leeming, where he astonished the adjutant by making his first appearance crawling through the hangar window, having been unable to find the door. He was a former Vickers engineering pupil who had learnt to fly with the RAF in Egypt in 1927. A quiet, earnest, thoughtful man, he inherited Bill Staton's preoccupation with the problem of marking targets at night, which would become the major concern of his war.

The strain of constant operations was telling on them all. Night after night they forged out into the blackness, over the flakships off the Dutch coast where they knew that the German night fighters had begun to fly standing patrols, on towards the empty darkness of Germany. Each captain chose his own route. In the moonlight they could sometimes see the silver thread of a river, and on clear nights the finest ground detail. Once Peter Donaldson picked out a German riding a bicycle. His new pilot, Ffrench-Mullen, was one of those who often flew the outward leg at a thousand feet or less, in his determination to find the target. The searchlights would flick on suddenly: first one, two, three, then perhaps a dozen until the night sky was cut open by a tent of light visible for miles. These were mere gestures compared with the great cones of seventy or eighty lights defending the cities of Germany two years later, but they were quite frightening enough. The flak would start to come up, in all the colours of the rainbow. Cold-blooded captains stooged around the target area until they saw another aircraft pinned by the lights and gunfire, then made their run, but this was too callous for most. Some pilots, like Pat Hanafin, fired recognition cartridges in the hope of bluffing the defences into silence. Peter Donaldson would man the forward Vickers K gun and crouch behind the perspex screen in the nose, blasting off pan after pan of ammunition at the lights or simply at the German countryside to relieve the tension. The smell of cordite filling the cockpit made the crew feel that at least they were hitting back. Some pilots made run after run over the target before bombing, or like Sid Bufton dropped only part of their load on each run. There was a vogue for making a silent approach, gliding in with the engines cut from 10,000 to 5,000 feet, but most crews were too nervous about being unable to start up again to risk it. Some, hazy about their position, bombed the blazes below in the hope that their predecessors had been on target. In reality, these were usually the decoy fires that the Germans were already setting nightly.

10 Squadron's operations that autumn took on outlandish overtones at the behest of Bomber Command. In August, for the first time, the Whitleys carried in addition to their bombload a clutch of 'Razzles', phosphorus-coated strips that they dropped on the fields of Germany, allegedly to set fire to the ripening crops and summer-dry woods under the terms of Western Air Plan 11. 'Razzles' had to be transported in milk churns of water in the fuselage to avoid spontaneous combustion in the aircraft, then released down the flare chute at suitable moments. 'Razzling' ended abruptly after a few weeks when there had been no great blazes in the fields of Germany, but Whitleys had repeatedly come home damaged by 'Razzles' which had lodged in their tails and caught fire. The next extravagance was the 'W' mine, a small explosive device which was also carried in a milk churn, this time to be dropped in Germany's rivers, to drift down and explode against locks and small craft. 'W' mines were also short-lived. Instead, for some months aircraft carried quantities of tea bags, to be thrown out over Holland as a propaganda exercise to demonstrate that beleaguered Britain still possessed sufficient comforts to be generous with them.

Bomber Command's losses were still less than 2 per cent of sorties dispatched, perhaps one aircraft every two or three nights of operations from 10 Squadron, a fraction of those that would become commonplace in 1942 and 1943. But as the old sense of a familiar and well-loved flying club faded, as each squadron saw its pre-war personality vanish and die, the pain was acute. A pilot from 10's sister unit at Dishforth, 51 Squadron, wrote to a former colleague in July:

I'm afraid you wouldn't know 51 if you went back now. Of the pilots at the beginning of the war, only Gillchrist, Otterley and Murray are left in A Flight and Bill Emery in B. Baskerville, Fennell, Gould, Birch and Johnny Crampton are missing – have been for months. Turner, Peach, Milne, Hayward and Johnny Bowles are prisoners. Teddy Cotton is in dock with a compound fracture of the thigh, having run out of petrol and hit the Pennines coming back from Oslo in dirty weather. Marvin is at Torquay recovering from a broken leg acquired by baling out two nights later, also out of petrol coming back from Oslo. But I expect you have been watching the casualty lists . . .

It was the same at 10 Squadron. The excitement of flying over Germany in the innocent days of 'nickelling' had been overtaken by new sensations: fatalism, callousness, reluctant intimacy with the mingled smell of burning paint, fabric, rubber, petrol and human flesh from a crashed aircraft. Above all they had learnt the reality of fear.

In a matter of seconds we were in a box barrage, the first warning of which was a heavy thump underneath our tail. [Wrote a Whitley pilot after a winter night of 1940 over Kiel.[1]] Almost instantaneously black puffs of smoke materialized around us. Plainly visible, like clenched fists against the faint light of the night sky, they crowded in upon the aeroplane from all sides. I just had time to think that this was how the hero comes in to bomb on the films, before fear broke its dams and swept over me in an almost irresistible flood. Concentrating all my energies, I forced myself to sit motionless in my seat next to the pilot, fighting back an insane impulse to run, despite the fact that in an aircraft you cannot run because there is nowhere you can run to, unless you can take it with you. As the gunfire got heavier, light flak joined in and I gazed fascinated, as if at a deadly snake, when a stream of incendiary shells came up in a lazy red arc which rapidly increased speed as it got nearer and at last flashed past a few inches above the wing on my side, two feet from the window. As the shells went by, they seemed to be deflected by the air flow over the wing and to curve round it, describing a fiery red line round its upper contour. By now the aircraft was becoming filled with fumes of cordite from the bursting flak shells. It seemed each second must be our last, and that we must surely disintegrate in a blinding flash at any moment, or come tumbling down flaming from a direct hit. We sat the aircraft in that box barrage for ten minutes, and did not get out of it until we had flown out of range . . .

Some men cracked, and were treated much more generously than their successors a year or two later. Three able and experienced pilots who had been with the squadron since before the war proved thoroughly unhappy on operations and were quietly transferred to instructing duties elsewhere. One or two members of ground crew, who had volunteered for aircrew duties before the war, applied to remuster in their original earthbound trades. Tom Sawyer, one of the flight commanders, found his navigator literally frozen with fear one night over the target, unable to move a muscle or speak a word for more than an hour.

Every trip was fraught with some kind of incident. Pat Hanafin's Whitley was peppered with holes from the rifles of nervous Home Guards as he crossed the English coast on the way home from Turin early one morning. He was then beaten up by Hurricanes, to whom he could not identify himself because 4 Group had run out of two-star recognition cartridges that were the colours of the day. Hanafin decided to forced-land at White Waltham, a little Berkshire airstrip that he knew well. But as he made his approach, he found the runway blocked with derelict cars to forestall a German landing. He eventually got down with his fuel tanks all but dry. Others were less lucky, Smith crashed in Norfolk on his way back from Amsterdam. Parsons ditched in the sea off Lympne, and only three of his crew were picked up. Cairns overshot the runway at Leeming on the way back from Ostend and crashed in the middle of the Great North Road. He was pulled from the burning wreck by his wireless operator. A few nights later he climbed out of his aircraft after a trip to Hamburg and turned cheerfully to Sid Bufton: 'Well, sir, that was my thirtieth "op" and I'm nineteen tomorrow!'

They were very young and they took their fortunes very lightly. Few were drunken neurotics, most were rather conscientious boys striving to fulfil that eternal maxim of the English public school: achievement must be apparently effortless. It is a crime to be *seen* to *try*. That autumn, Sid Bufton's 23-year-old brother wrote a letter to his girlfriend from Scampton, where he was flying Hampdens with 83 Squadron. It is worth quoting at length, because it reflects so perfectly the mood of so many young men of Bomber Command, that first year of the strategic offensive. 'Jenny darling,' wrote John Bufton,

At last, a spot of time to sit back and answer your last two letters! I can hardly read one of them 'cos I was reading it in the bath after a hard day's work on Friday and I was so tired that it fell in the water and got badly smudged!

I wonder if you were very disappointed at getting my telegram and letter about the weekend? I was mad at having to send them, but there was no way out. Maybe we'll have better luck next weekend. Trouble with us here is that weekends are precisely the same as any other time now.

Poor Jenny, I'm so sorry you were so upset by my last letter. Perhaps I shouldn't have been so blunt in what I wrote, but I only wanted to put things to you as fairly as I could. You've got such wonderful faith, dear, in my chances and I mustn't upset you by being pessimistic. Anyway, I'm not pessimistic – I've rarely felt happier and more set on a job in my life, and my chances are as good as anyone else's. But I'm not ass enough to assume *I'm* going to be okay and everyone else will be unlucky, as it's a sheer gamble in the game, but damn good fun while it lasts.

Way back, Jen, my idea of the future was pretty idealistic. We've talked about it so often in peace time, and were agreed on what we wanted out of life, and it was a grand outlook. But now it seems such a myth! Like one of those dreams that can't possibly come true. We'll get married and be awfully happy – I know you'll do everything to make it seem what we both want – but there'll be a cloud over it all for both of us, dear, a cloud that we can't hope to brush aside. For you, it will be the realization that you've given everything in your life to give me a fleeting happiness, and that in accepting it I'm condemning you tó great unhappiness ahead, when you could have been *almost* as happy elsewhere, otherwise, with a future both safe and bright.

If the chances were very good, I wouldn't dream of writing like this, but I'm no dreamer, Jen, and the facts are that immediately ahead is the winter, with all the danger that filthy weather invariably brings to flying (your pullover will help immensely there!). Despite this, our bombers are bound to become even more active than they have been in the summer months, and we'll hit harder and wider and more often than ever before. We're the only active force operating against Germany and as it's the only way of striking directly we'll be exploited more and more, especially as the force grows. The RAF, fighters and bombers combined, will undoubtedly win this war in time, but the end isn't nearly in sight yet, and before it's all over the losses will be enormous. I wonder how many people ever wonder what the average flier's outlook on life is in these times? In most cases it's vastly different from what it was a few months ago. It's almost entirely fatalistic. There seems no point in making any plans about the future. The present is all that matters, and in this day-to-day existence there are three things that occupy one's energies most of all:

(1) Intensive attention to one's machine and equipment, ready for the next trip, so that nothing is left to chance.

(2) Getting enough sleep and exercise.

(3) Getting 'social glow' in the Saracen's Head and keeping mentally fresh!

Doesn't sound very ambitious, but I'll bet anything that 95 per cent of the RAF take these as their guiding principles, because only by doing so can they have the most chance of hitting the target and getting back OK . . .

Why am I writing all this, Jen? Well, it's the answer to what you asked in your letter: you say 'Do I really want to marry you?' Yes darling, 'course I do, and we'll go through with it in that spell of leave that may come through when I've done enough trips to qualify. But I don't feel much of a man taking you up on such a bad bargain, lovely tho' it'll be for me. In the meanwhile, darling, you'll make me easier in mind if you'll promise this – until we're married, if I should be unlucky enough to go up as 'missing', don't wait too long . . . If I could only be sure, Jen, that your future was assured I'd be content, whatever happens.

If anything happens to me, I'll want you to go and have a perm, do up the face, put the hat on and carry on – it'll take a lot of guts but I know you'll tackle it in the right way. And remember that I'd be wanting you to get happily married as soon as you could. And don't worry for me these nights more than you can help. It may buck you up to know that I'm feeling bung full of confidence in my own ability, but if I'm to be unlucky, well, I'm prepared for anything. Over the last three months I've got used to the idea of sudden accidents – they've happened so often to friends and acquaintances that the idea doesn't startle one much now. Realizing fully what one is up against helps one along a lot. I'm not really windy about anything now. Anyway, there's too much to do to get windy. I'm longing to see you again, Jenny, and we must make it soon! Keep writing, and when you come up, wear your hat, please, and the smile that cheers me up!

John Bufton was never married, for he was killed a month later.

At 10 Squadron, Peter Donaldson, the navigator who had survived Sylt and the bombing of Bassingbourn, was shot down in the sea and taken prisoner with the rest of Ffrench-Mullen's crew on 9 July. The steady drain of casualties continued. On 16 August they were sent to the Zeiss works at Jena. 'This place has never heard the sound of gunfire since the Napoleonic War,' declared Staton in his usual ringing tones at briefing – he was now station commander at Leeming. 'Make sure it hears it tonight. I don't want to see anybody back who bombs above 4,000 feet!' Pete Whitby was flying as a second pilot. His Whitley was approaching Jena at 6,000 feet when the searchlights seized it. They broke away amidst intensive flak, and turned to try again. On their second run at 10,000 feet, shortly after midnight, they had just bombed when their port engine was hit and burst into flames. The fire died, but so did the engine. They settled down to a long struggle home against the headwind, throwing out everything ditchable down to the guns and ammunition.

Tall, fair, lazily good-looking, Whitby had worked in the wool trade in Europe until at the age of twenty he decided to go into the RAF. He was over-age for a short-service commission, but his father wrote to their local MP, Winston Churchill. Whitby got his commission. Since he joined Bomber Command, he had divided his energies between flying and horses, which he loved. He kept an old steeplechaser at Thirsk to ride in off-duty moments in the occasional point-to-point race, and a mare named Myrtle Green at Catterick.

Their ailing Whitley was hit again by flak as they staggered towards the Dutch coast. The wing caught fire and they jettisoned the hatches and leaned out into the slipstream, struggling to beat out the flames. At 3 a.m. they crashlanded in a field just west of Breda. After walking and hiding from German patrols for twenty-four hours, they were taken prisoner. Pete Whitby's father received a telegram, then a note from 10 Squadron:

Ref 105/6/41/Air

Dear Mr Whitby,
It is my unhappy duty to inform you that your son, F/O Whitby, is missing. The aircraft of which he was Second Pilot failed to return from operations over enemy territory on the night of 16th/17th August.
S.O. Bufton

Pete Whitby remained a prisoner for the duration, and came home in 1945 to find that his mare Myrtle Green had bred him four foals and run up a bill for £600 for fodder while he was the guest of the Third Reich.

One was attuned to getting the chop [said Bufton²]. You were resigned to dying every night. You looked round your room before you went out, at the golf clubs in the corner, the books on the shelves, the nice little radio set, the letter to one's parents propped on the table . . .

One night I saw a Whitley coned by dozens of searchlights on the way back from Cologne, and then shot down in flames. I came back and found that Sergeant Hoare was missing. He was the only 4 Group casualty that night, so I knew that it must have been him that I had seen go. But all that night I kept thinking that I heard the beat of his engines approaching the airfield.

Then I realized that it was only the hot-water pipes in the hut . . .

On 12 December 1940, 10 Squadron sent ten aircraft among 134 from Bomber Command to attack Mannheim. It was a clear night, and most of them came home to report that they had found the target without difficulty. Yet the significance of 'Operation Rachel', as the raid was codenamed, lay in the fact that this was the first occasion on which an entire city was the deliberate target of an attack. It was planned on the direct orders of the Prime Minister as a reprisal for the formidable German raid on Coventry a month earlier that had laid waste the centre of the city. The Mannheim operation was an isolated episode that winter, but it was a foretaste of much that was to come.

The Battle of Britain and the German blitz on British cities had changed the mood of the war in the air. To the fighter pilots on both sides, it might sometimes have seemed a chivalrous 'duel of eagles'. To those below on the ground it was the very rain of sudden death and terror that they had awaited and feared for so long. Both sides had accidentally bombed each other's city centres on several occasions since September 1939, and sought to make maximum propaganda capital out of their sufferings, but now it was no longer a matter of accidents. After the first bombs fell on central London on 24 August, the Prime Minister ordered Bomber Command to Berlin on the night of the 25th. In November the Luftwaffe's Kampfgruppe 100 had marked Coventry for devastation using the *X-Gerat* beam system more than two years in advance of any comparable British technique. 400 German aircraft followed in the main wave. Their attack totally destroyed 20,000 houses, killed almost 600 people and injured a thousand more.

At Leeming, Staton pinned photographs of blitzed London, Coventry and Southampton on the wall of the operations room and stabbed a finger at them as he briefed the crews: 'Go now and do likewise to the Hun!' The night after the 14 November attack he turned to the crews and asked who lived in Coventry. Bob Dodd put up a hand. He was invited to choose his own target from the four the squadron were detailed to attack that night. Instead of Hamburg or Cologne, however, young Dodd chose Eindhoven aerodrome in Holland, simply because he thought it would be the cushiest. For the most part, these were boys who flew out over Europe, pressing the bomb release as they were ordered without anger, and with little thought for what lay far beneath in the darkness. But as the rage of the Press mounted, and with it the conviction of the Government that the British public demanded vengeance, so Bomber Command's anxiety about the avoidance of civilian targets in Germany diminished.

Sir Charles Portal, the C-in-C, had been one of the earliest and most important advocates of Bomber Command's offensive against the synthetic oil plants on which Germany was over-whelmingly dependent. In twentieth-century war, cutting off a nation from its fuel supplies would clearly be a decisive blow, and this had long been recognized in Western Air Plan 5(c). But as the nights of 1940 went by and the results of Bomber Command's sorties were examined, Portal's doubts about the feasibility of 'precision' bombing mounted.

All through the summer of 1940 there had been a surge of directives from the Air Ministry, each overtaking the last with bewildering speed as the Government and the Chiefs of Staff sought to hold back the floodgates of strategic disaster. The first reports from Germany on the effects of British bombing were absurdly optimistic, but warmly welcomed in Whitehall. The Air Ministry directive of 4 June 1940 ordered Portal to press on with the oil attacks. On dark nights when this was impracticable he was instructed to hit targets which would contribute to the 'continuous interruption and dislocation of German war industry', particularly in areas where the German aircraft industry was concentrated, notably Hamburg, Bremen, Frankfurt and the Ruhr. In the next paragraph, however, the directive stated emphatically: 'In no circumstances should night bombing be allowed to degenerate into mere indiscriminate action, which is contrary to the policy of His Majesty's Government.'

The next directive, on 20 June, relegated oil targets to third priority, below attacks on the German aircraft industry aimed at 'reducing the scale of air attack on this country', and below attacks on communications between Germany and her army's forward areas. On 4 July, these in turn were displaced by a new priority: attack on German shipping in port and at sea. Then on 13 July the aircraft industry was reinstated as the primary target, with oil as the secondary. Portal was told to concentrate the attacks of his force on fewer targets 'with a view to complete destruction rather than harassing effect'. To this end, fifteen key installations were listed for priority attention: five aircraft assembly plants, five depots and five oil refineries.

Portal replied to the 13 July directive with a sharp note commenting that of the ten aircraft industry targets, 'only three can be found with any certainty in moonlight by average crews'. He added, in a most significant subordinate clause, that 'since almost all the primary first priority targets are isolated and in sparsely inhabited districts, the very high percentage of bombers which inevitably miss the actual target will hit nothing else important and do no damage'. Portal said that he believed in dispersing attacks over the widest possible area of Germany: 'It largely increases the moral effect of our operations by the alarm and disturbance created over the wider area.'

Here was the seed of the attack on the morale of the German people, of area bombing: a district was to be chosen for bombardment in which was concentrated the highest possible proportion of vital industrial installations. Every hit would be of value, to be sure, but the attack could be launched with the prospect that the very many bombs that missed industrial targets – the overwhelming majority of those dropped – would hit the homes and shops and cinemas and cafés of the industrial workers and their families upon whom the German war effort must depend. In the eighteen months that followed – and for that matter in the next five years – there would be hesitation and fierce debate about the policy of launching bombers wholesale against the cities of Germany. But already, in July 1940, the idea had taken root. As will become apparent, it had the wholehearted support of the Prime Minister, whose natural combativeness craved revenge for the laying waste of Coventry and Southampton, and indeed for the rape of Western Europe. But there is a certain irony that it should have been Portal, the cool, calmly reasoning committee chairman whom some believed lacked the iron resolution that marks great captains, who proved to be Trenchard's first true disciple in the Second World War. It was Portal who suggested, on 1 September 1940, that twenty German towns might be 'proscribed', just as Slessor had proposed earlier – warned by radio that they would be attacked indiscriminately one by one, following each occasion on which a British town was devastated by the Luftwaffe. It was under Portal that a note was circulated to all Bomber Command aircraft captains, reminding them that 'in industrial areas there are invariably a very large number of targets. In view of the indiscriminate nature of the German attacks, and in order to reduce the number of bombs brought back . . . every effort should be made to bomb these.' It was an instruction carrying the obvious inference that it was now preferable to attack anything in Germany than to attack nothing.

The Air Staff was not only surprised and dismayed by Portal's attitude, but determined to resist his proposals. On 5 September the VCAS, Sir Richard Peirse, wrote to Churchill that he thought there was 'little doubt that the reason for the effectiveness of our night bombing is that it is planned; and relentless until the particular target is knocked out or dislocated, whereas German night bombing is sporadic and mainly harassing'. In the Air Ministry's latest directive to Portal on 21 September the priorities for Bomber Command were restated: 'precision' attacks on invasion barges, the German aircraft industry and submarine works, German communications and oil resources would continue. The only comfort for Portal's convictions was a final paragraph authorizing occasional morale attacks on the German capital 'although there are no objectives in the Berlin area of importance to our major plans'.

In the words of Webster and Frankland, the official historians of the British strategic air offensive, there was now general agreement that

if there was to be any strategic bombing at all, civilians would be killed; hospitals, churches and cultural monuments would be hit. The Air Staff, as represented by its Vice Chief, Sir Richard Peirse, believed that what was inevitable was also desirable only in so far as it remained a by-product of the primary intention to hit a military target in the sense of a power station, a marshalling yard or an oil plant. Bomber Command, as represented by its Commander-in-Chief, Sir Charles Portal, now believed that this by-product should become an end-product. He believed that the time had come to launch a direct attack on the German people themselves. He believed that this course had been justified by previous German actions, and that it would be justified as a strategy in the outcome.[3]

Portal's biographer is unable to accept the official historians' interpretation of the C-in-C's attitude:

It seems to carry the suggestion that Portal favoured the deliberate killing and maiming of civilians as a major strategy . . . Portal was not at this time, however, nor did he ever become an advocate of killing civilians. He became, while it was the most practicable policy, an advocate of destroying industrial towns.[4]

Some of the moral issues that are forever entangled in the story of Bomber Command will be discussed in more detail later. Here it is sufficient to say that to his colleagues and contemporaries it seemed that Portal's recommendations amounted to commencing indiscriminate air warfare, and a significant minority opposed them for this very reason. Yet to most of those around him in the RAF, Portal seemed absolutely right and the Air Ministry absolutely wrong. Every morning at High Wycombe they studied the results of the previous night's operations, in which a hundred or more crews had stumbled through the night sky over Germany, searching for an oil plant or a factory which Portal suspected that they seldom reached. After months of this the power of the Third Reich was visibly undiminished. Yet in England the Luftwaffe had bombed recklessly from Birmingham and Coventry to Plymouth and London, and all around lay the ruins and the corpses. No one in England that winter of 1940 cared to suggest aloud that morale was cracking under the

Blitz, and indeed it never did. But deep in his heart, each man knew the terror of hearing the bombs whistling down, the shuddering crump and the roar of falling masonry, the agony of expectation before the explosion. If Englishmen were moved by air bombardment, it seemed reasonable to expect that Germans would be more so. Much of the thinking that led to the mass morale bombing of Germany took place in the silence of men's minds, and was never articulated in minutes or memoranda.

On 4 October 1940, Sir Cyril Newall was retired as Chief of Air Staff and replaced by Sir Charles Portal. Sir Richard Peirse, who had been among the foremost advocates of 'precision' bombing, became C-in-C of Bomber Command. Portal could now unquestionably have secured the launching of an area bombing campaign. Churchill would not only have endorsed such a proposal, but was urging it himself throughout the winter of 1940 and spring of 1941: 'We have seen what inconvenience the attack on the British civilian population has caused us,' he wrote to the Air Ministry on 2 November 1940, 'and there is no reason why the enemy should be freed from all such embarrassments.'

But Portal made no effort immediately to test his faith in area bombing. For the next year he allowed Bomber Command to continue on the course which had been, in May 1940, attempting precision attacks on chosen industrial objectives. Only when this policy was universally agreed to have failed would it finally be abandoned.

From October 1940 until early March 1941 oil remained the first priority of Bomber Command whenever the weather allowed. The attacks on invasion barges continued into the winter. It is unlikely that the loss of an estimated 12 per cent of their fleet played a decisive part in the German cancellation of the invasion of England, but it is important not to underestimate Bomber Command's contribution in constantly reminding Hitler that the RAF still possessed striking power to match the defensive strength of its fighters. There is little doubt that in 1939 the Nazi leaders had believed that Goering's Luftwaffe could prevent any enemy aircraft from attacking the Reich. Bomber Command's incursions into Germany in 1940 and 1941 may have been erratic and materially ineffectual. But they played a real part in asserting the fact of Britain's survival in the minds of the German people.

Portal's concern with attacking German morale was embodied only as a secondary priority in the Air Ministry directive to Peirse of 30 October 1940, ordering him to attack Berlin and other German towns

with such regularity as you may find practicable . . . As many heavy bombers as possible should be detailed for the attack, carrying high-explosive, incendiary and delay-action bombs with perhaps an occasional mine. The aim of the first sorties should be to cause fires, either on or in the vicinity of the targets so that they should carry a high proportion of incendiary bombs . . . The objectives considered most suitable for these concentrated attacks are the sources of power, such as electricity generating stations and gas plants, and centres of communication; but where primary targets such as the oil and aircraft industry objectives are suitably placed in the centres of the towns of populated districts, they also might be selected.

Portal always suffered from a measure of intelligent indecision and now he was divided between his hopes that the attack on German oil would provide a 'quick death clinch' with Germany, as he put it, and his doubts about Bomber Command's ability to bring this about. He was still undecided in December 1940 when the Lloyd Committee on German oil resources made their remarkable report, asserting that Bomber Command had already achieved a 15 per cent cut in enemy fuel availability. This had allegedly been achieved by the dropping of only 539 tons of bombs, 6.7 per cent of Bomber Command's effort since the summer.

Since in reality the Germans were scarcely aware that their oil resources were supposed to have been the object of a systematic British assault, it is a measure of the inadequacy of British economic Intelligence that the Lloyd Committee could reach these conclusions. It is even more remarkable that Portal and the airmen allowed themselves to accept them. Yet not only did they do so but they allowed the report to become the basis for Bomber Command's continued attack on oil throughout the spring of 1941, despite the Prime Minister's scepticism. They were simply desperate for good news of bombing, and when it came they received it uncritically. To have allowed themselves to believe the truth would have been the negation of scores of careers dedicated to the fulfilment of the Trenchard doctrine.

It is often suggested that in August 1941 Bomber Command received a quite unexpected thunderbolt when it was learnt that only a tiny proportion of crews were bombing within miles of their targets. Yet throughout the winter of 1940 there were few grounds for illusions at High Wycombe about what was taking place over Germany. As early as October Peirse, the urbane advocate of British 'planned' bombing, reckoned that somewhere around one in five of his crews found their primary target on a given night. Calculations for the success of the oil offensive required at least 50 per cent of sorties on target. Arthur Harris at 5 Group, perpetually sanguine, continued to assert his faith in his crews' navigation. But Coningham at 4 Group, who only a few months earlier had been saying that he expected the same precision from night bombing as from day, now admitted that 'for my part, I have little idea of what the Whitleys do, and it causes me considerable anxiety'. Most significant, however, were the results of the first careful analysis of target photographs. Gelsenkirchen oil refineries, the objects of repeated attacks, appeared virtually undamaged. Mannheim, to which 10 Squadron and so many others had been dispatched for the Coventry retaliation attack of 16 December, was scarcely scarred. It was concluded that it had become a matter of urgency to equip aircraft with night cameras, so that it was at once apparent who had and had not reached his target. Yet in the face of the overwhelming evidence of their inability to achieve success, Bomber Command was launched once more upon the oil offensive. Peirse's squadrons continued to struggle in futility over Germany – now receiving much increased oil imports from Rumania – all that winter and through the spring of 1941.

It was the escalation of the Battle of the Atlantic which diverted Bomber Command from the oil offensive. In the face of the mounting U-boat successes and the threat posed by German capital ships, on 9 March 1941 Peirse received a new directive from the Air Ministry, ordering him to concentrate all his resources on supporting the Royal Navy in the war at sea, by attacking the U-boat bases at St Nazaire, Bordeaux and Lorient in France, by mining the German approaches, and by bombing the ports and construction yards. Portal's letter to Peirse on the new policy, dated 1 March 1941, was a sad throwback to the worst traditions of the RAF and it may have masked the depths of his own disappointment at the failure of Bomber Command: 'A very high proportion of bomber effort will inevitably be required to pull the Admiralty out of the mess they have got into . . .' That summer, it would have been more pertinent to inquire whether Bomber Command, at the existing point of its fortunes, was capable of affording the Admiralty any useful support at all in its struggle to save Britain from starvation.

We attacked Lorient from the north [wrote a novice Whitley pilot, Denis Hornsey[5]]. Having taken over the controls just beforehand I throttled back the engines and began a glide towards the target at 12,000 feet. My intention was to drop the bombs at 8,000 feet. Richards, who had gone forward to map read, guided me in to the target, the rough position of which I could detect myself from a cone of searchlights and a smattering of light flak immediately ahead. Nearby the Germans were shooting at some parachute flares dropped by previous visitors, and somewhere underneath lay our objective, four submarines reputedly lying close together in the dry docks.

'Steady, steady,' came Richards's voice. 'Keep as you are going, Skipper,' he added, dropping the official bombing patter in his excitement. 'The docks are right ahead.'

'OK,' I said. Then remembering my duty, I called up the rear gunner. 'Skipper calling rear gunner. Skipper calling rear gunner. Keep your eye open for fighters.'

'OK, Skipper,' the rear gunner replied. 'There's some searchlights after us,' he went on laconically. 'Bang on our tail.'

He had no sooner said this than the searchlights were upon us and the inside of the cabin was suddenly illuminated as by an arc lamp. I sat motionless at the controls for a moment, wondering whether they would flick over us or not, and while I did so Richards's voice came through again.

'Running up! Running up!' he was saying imperturbably. 'Bomb doors open! Bomb doors open!'

I repeated the patter and concentrated on the bombing approach. I had opened the bomb doors as directed and was now gliding the aircraft at a steady speed down to our bombing height of 8,000 feet. The search-lights were still on us, and it could not be long before we received attention from fighters or anti-aircraft guns if we remained in them.

'Drop the bombs in one stick,' I ordered Richards. 'We're still in the searchlights.'

The last statement was redundant, for Richards could scarcely be unaware that we were now coned by about twenty beams with others swinging across the sky to join in. It was high time we took evasive action.

'Skipper calling bomb-aimer. We'll have to let the bombs go. Can't hold out much longer,' I said breathlessly, feeling more and more apprehensive as the seconds ticked by.

'OK, skip, we're coming on the target now.'

'Let the bloody things go then,' I said.

'OK. Bombs gone,' Richards replied.

I thankfully closed the bomb doors and opening up the engines, pulled hard back on the stick to go into a steep climb. Climbing steadily for a few minutes, minutes which seemed like an age, I felt as naked in that bright light as if I was standing unclothed in the middle of Piccadilly. Then I tried some diving and climbing turns to left and right, but we were still held relentlessly in the beams as if impaled by twenty or thirty silver lances. All this having availed nothing, it was essential to get out of the searchlights with no more delay, for every second increased the risk of being shot down. Certain that our course and height must have now been accurately plotted by the enemy, I put the aircraft into a dive. I did this automatically and instinctively, without conscious thought, but as the needle of the air speed indicator crept round its dial I watched it without comprehension. I was in a muck sweat and almost exhausted by my efforts.

'Shall I fire at the searchlights, skipper?' came Richards's voice.

'Yes, have a go. You too, rear gunner.'

'No, no,' cried Barney, 'you'll give away our position.'

The noise of the guns came over the intercom.

'Got one,' said Richards triumphantly, ignoring the wireless operator's protest.

My intense concentration during these manoeuvres was interrupted by Franklin tapping my shoulder. He leaned over me from behind and pointed to the altimeter, which was showing only 3,000 feet. We were still going down fast in a steep dive at 260 mph, very fast indeed for a Whitley. I had become so engrossed in trying to get out of the search-lights that I had forgotten how near we must be getting to the ground. Nodding as if to indicate that I was fully aware of our position and that everything was going to plan – I was enough of a Captain to remember such necessities – I pulled hard back on the stick to flatten out of the dive. We shot out of the beams like an orange pip squeezed from one's fingers, into blessed darkness and relative safety. My unintentional dive had taken us across the headland north of Lorient and out over the sea.

'Hurrah!' said Richards. 'We're out!'

Night after night that spring and summer of 1941, 10 Squadron and the rest of Bomber Command poured their bombloads into the smokescreens shielding 'Salmon' and 'Gluck' – the *Scharnhorst* and the *Gneisenau* at Brest – and the U-boats at Lorient and Bordeaux from the eyes of their bomb-aimers. Peirse protested to Portal that they were wasting hundred of tons of explosives on a task for which they had never been intended and were not trained or equipped. Yet air attack on enemy warships had always been an obvious, vital strategic role for Bomber Command. If this, too, was beyond their capabilities, to what were they suited? For what were they equipped and prepared?

10 Squadron spent the early spring bombing Germany in the occasional breaks in the weather and standing-by for hours, acutely bored. By the end of February there had been only two nights on which the sky was clear enough to attack oil targets – only 221 sorties had taken place of the 3,400 estimated to be necessary to have decisive effect on German oil supplies. Often aircraft taxiing out from the dispersals had to weave a path through a sea of mud, becoming bogged down and having to be towed out at predictable cost in temper and tiredness. One day in March an 'oil expert' came down from Group to lecture at Leeming on the importance of what they were doing. His talk merged into the haze of information and misinformation that was crowded into their idle hours: lectures on escaping, on evasive action in the air, on searchlights and the growing defensive belt reaching down across northern Germany into Holland, on the significance of the appearance of the first radar-equipped night-fighters over Holland. One day Trenchard came, a charming, paternal old gentleman, who endeared himself to them at once. Listening to him lecturing them all in a great semi-circle outside a hangar was like hearing Moses himself, after so many

years in which they had learned to think of him as the exalted prophet of bombing.*

Most operations were very monotonous. But difficult though it may be to grasp today, many aircrew still very much enjoyed the business of flying an aircraft, and managed to gain great pleasure from what they were doing in these months before the odds against their own survival became overwhelming. Pilots revelled in the occasional clear, bright night when they sat in their cockpits watching the shooting stars, with an overwhelming sense of the vastness of the universe. They knew nothing of the intense debates that were taking place at Group and at High Wycombe. They would have been very dismayed if they had, for they believed that they were doing a good job. It had taken eighteen months of war for Bomber Command to grasp a simple but remarkable truth about night bomber operations, that the airmen themselves were the last people to know what they had or had not achieved. They were not wantonly dishonest – perhaps sometimes a little optimistic, but generally gauchely frank about their own efforts. In a memorandum to the Air Ministry at about this time, Trenchard made the point that the level of debriefing was still abysmal, in the hands of staff officers who had no idea how to ask the right questions, and who invariably overstated crews' claims. In the years to come, skilled interpretation of night photos and improved debriefing would enable the Command to form a more accurate image of what had taken place on operations. But throughout the war, part of the unique character of the bomber offensive was that the men who carried it out were totally dependent on their commanders for information about the success or failure of what they were doing. An infantry platoon commander, over a period of weeks or months, could achieve some notion of his army's gains or losses by noticing

*Even among conscript aircrew later in the war, the old man cast a powerful spell. Visiting 76 Squadron in 1942, he walked into the mess tent set for lunch in his honour, sidestepped his intended place among the 'Brass', and sat down instead with the young pilots below the salt. He noticed one man wearing the single ribbon of the DFC, and glanced down at his own vastly decorated chest: 'Don't worry, my boy,' he boomed. 'Once you've got one, they grow on you like measles.' They loved him.

whether he himself was moving forwards or backwards. A convoy escort officer could judge a great deal from the rate of sinkings around him. But the bomber pilot, with rare exceptions such as the great firestorms of Hamburg and Dresden, had to wait for the next bulletin from High Wycombe to learn whether his colleagues were dying to good purpose or in vain. It was utterly necessary for him to believe that his commanders' view of the bomber offensive was accurate. For if it was not, then he was flying out each night to risk his life and those of his crew for nothing.

The men who survived those primitive operations of 1940 and 1941 would look back on them afterwards as almost lunatic in their crudeness compared with what came later. The little clusters of boys around the Whitleys and Hampdens in the photographs still look like young Sapper heroes, hair plastered down, radiating health and willingness and energy. The superb propaganda films made about Bomber Command at this time had perhaps captured their imagination as well as that of Britain. They themselves were secretly rather impressed by *F for Freddie* and *Target for Tonight*. At briefing, they were given their targets, perhaps a post office or power station, and solemnly handed street maps of the relevant city to guide their way. They drew their flying rations and parachutes and boarded the truck for the dispersals. Two airmen waited with the battery cart. For fifteen minutes they ran up the Merlins, then began the long bumpy journey to the taxi lamp at the end of the runway, among the seagulls in the dusk. They waited for the green flash from the control caravan then rumbled away down the runway. The undercarriage came up and the wireless operator signalled briefly: 'G-George on course', then lapsed into silence. They picked up Flamborough Head below them, and settled back for the long haul across the North Sea to the Zuider Zee. Bob Dodd of 10 Squadron described a not untypical night:[6]

The weather was ten-tenths cloud and we had navigated on Dead Reckoning to ETA target. We broke cloud (*hoping* there was no high ground) so as not to waste the trip, and found a river. After following it for a while we decided we had found our position on the southern border of Germany. We bombed a small town and our incendiaries set fire to the church, which appeared to have a wooden spire and burned fiercely. Houses were also burning. Since we had come down to about 1,000 feet, we had a clear view. When we returned to base and were able to evaluate the wind direction and speed, we calculated that we had attacked Epinalle in Vichy France. This was later confirmed by our Intelligence Officer. Our Dead Reckoning position with no wireless fix was so far out that we were attacked by flak over Birmingham. Our Dead Reckoning position was over the North Sea. I entered in the log: 'Base-Mannheim-Base. Village bombed ten miles south of Epinalle'.

One night in March 1941, in his Whitley high over the North Sea, a navigator named George Carter settled down to pass the trip writing a letter to his girlfriend on sheets torn from the log. 'Dear Nicole', he wrote, putting '2020 hours' in brackets after her name, then 'Bound for Berlin':

As you can see from the address, I am on the job. It is the first time I have been to the 'Big City' and as I have nobody else to tell the great news, I tell you. We are at present sixty-four miles off the English coast, a lovely night, moon as near as dammit full. We are punching the old kite along at about 8,000 feet to get full benefit of a favourable wind over this long sea crossing (three hours) and I have not a lot to do. I started to write this note in ink but the reduced pressure up here has forced it all out and the pen won't work, so I'm reduced to pencil now.

I shall have to break off for a while now as I have to work out some wireless bearings and switch on one of the auxiliary tanks, and check our drift by flame float. It's getting cold – 0° on the clock now, and a cold white moon lighting up the plane . . .

2137. Here I am again after getting drift, about two dozen loop bearings and three sights on astro (I think my sight must be wrong, it gave our position about 180 miles south of where we ought to be, maybe dropping it last night had something to do with it).

I hope we knock the blazes out of the target (which incidentally is the post office in the centre of the city). Before, I have always felt sorry for the people down below, but the other night I came over Portsmouth on the way home and saw it afire. I saw an explosion about 2,000 feet high. So now I feel different about it, and I shall not be too careful to hit the post office. I have got one bottle, one brick and one piece of concrete to throw out with some personal messages to the Hun.

0120. Well, that was Berlin that was. Their AA was mustard – shook me rigid. We appear to be doubtful about our position so some work must be done . . .

0330. I managed to get back on track and now we're in the middle of the North Sea going home. The wind changed from the met forecast and I found myself well to the south of my track, and with a bit of wangling we are OK, touch wood! You see, we have only just enough juice to get us to Berlin and back . . .

The flak over Berlin was very accurate and the searchlights held us at 18,000, AA going off all around us – I bet we're full of holes. The shells keep bursting in front of us, and me being in front with the bomb sight, kept getting the smoke in my eyes. Was I scared? I'll say I was scared! I let our bombs go in the middle of the city. I hope they helped our war effort. I could not see where they landed . . .

It was still the stone age of bombing, but this would now be elevated to Britain's principal weapon of war.

4 Crisis of confidence, 1941–42

'Then shall the right aiming thunderbolts go abroad; and from the clouds, as from a well-drawn bow, shall they fly to the mark' Wisdom v.21.
From the Air Ministry handbook *Bomber Command*, 1941

What took place in the mind of Winston Churchill to cause the man who had written in 1917 'it is improbable that any terrorization of the civil population which could be achieved by air attack would compel the Government of a great nation to surrender', to become, by the end of 1941, the foremost political advocate of area bombing? 'The bombers alone provide the means of victory,' he wrote on 3 September 1940. From the outset Churchill was doubtful of the efficacy of the Air Staff's 'precision' attacks on oil and communications. He demanded retaliation for the blitz on Britain, an attack on German morale that was no more than a euphemism for bombing the cities of Germany. On 20 October 1940, in the midst of the Luftwaffe's night attacks on Britain, he minuted the Air Minister Sir Archibald Sinclair:

I am deeply concerned with the non-expansion, and indeed contraction of our bomber force which must be expected between now and April or May next, according to present policy. Surely an effort should be made to increase our bomb-dropping capacity during this period . . . Is it not possible to organize a second-line bomber force which, especially in the dark of the moon, would discharge bombs from a considerable and safe height upon the nearest large built-up area of Germany, which contains military targets in abundance? The Ruhr, of course, is obviously indicated . . . I ask that a whole-hearted effort shall be made to cart a large number of bombs into Germany by a second-line organization such as I have suggested, and under conditions in which admittedly no special accuracy could be obtained.

Most men found during the course of the war that whatever moments of rage and passion they suffered at the sight of a blitzed building or in the heat of battle, as the months and years went by it was impossible to sustain a white-hot hatred for the enemy. War became a job, a routine of its own, as much as peace. But Winston Churchill never for a moment lost his passion. The force of his hatred for the German people and their leaders contributed immensely to his triumph as a war leader. His determination that Britain should survive and destroy the nation that had brought such misery upon the world never faltered. It would not have occurred to him to permit the maltreatment of a prisoner, or to tolerate excess in the government of captured German territory. Once Germans ceased to be enemies in arms, he had no further interest in them. But as he gazed out across the map of Europe at the Third Reich during the six years of war, he sought to bring fire and slaughter without scruple upon the German people. It is doubtful whether at any time after the fall of France he debated whether killing German civilians was a moral exercise. He was concerned only with what was strategically desirable and tactically possible. After the war, in a note to a former staff officer of Bomber Command, Churchill scribbled: 'We should never allow ourselves to apologize for what we did to Germany.'[1] Whatever he may have written elsewhere for public consumption, there is no reason to suppose that Churchill ever suffered a moment's private misgiving about the course and consequences of the strategic air offensive.

It is important to dwell on Churchill's personal attitude to the bombing of Germany, because it will be necessary to emphasize the extent to which the elevation of Bomber Command to its prime place in the British war effort was his personal decision, in the face of intense and important opposition. The bomber offensive would consume a lion's share of Britain's industrial resources – the exact proportion will never be known, but Mr A. J. P. Taylor suggests more than one-third.[2] Alternative claims on production were pressed with fierce determination. To give some impression of the debate that took place, it is helpful to take certain events out of order, and to consider as an entity discussions that took place between August 1941 and the spring of 1942. In these months the future of the strategic bomber offensive was decided. Once the great Allied commitment had been decided, it has been insufficiently recognized to what extent the Chiefs of Staff in 1944 and 1945, in greatly changed circumstances, were the prisoners of the vast investment in industrial effort and national prestige which had already been made in the strategic bomber forces. By early 1942 the destruction of Germany's cities was still years away, but their ultimate fate had already been decided.

Throughout the winter of 1940–41 and into the spring, the Prime Minister had followed closely the progress of the bomber offensive – the raid on Mannheim, the attacks on the *Scharnhorst* and the *Gneisenau*, the debate between Portal and the Air Ministry and subsequently between Peirse and Portal about bombing policy. He was aware of shortcomings in the results that had been achieved. He was disturbed by 2 Group's losses in the RAF's continuing effort to maintain some sort of daylight bomber effort, and by the inability of Bomber Command to do decisive damage even against the invasion barge concentrations, whose photographs he studied personally. But it is doubtful whether he understood the full extent of the failure: the near-farce of many sorties; the overwhelming majority of crews who never came within miles of the target; the repeated attempts to bomb on ETA; the paltry fruits of the immense effort against the oil plants. Then one morning in August 1941 he was presented with a report by Mr D. M. Butt of the Cabinet secretariat on the current performance of Bomber Command against targets in France and Germany. Its conclusions seem to have been a great shock to him, and had decisive repercussions on the future of the bomber offensive.

Mr Butt had been directed to carry out his independent investigation by Lord Cherwell, the Prime Minister's personal scientific adviser and the most powerful *eminence grise* in Downing Street. Cherwell had been doubtful for some time about the results being achieved by British bombing, and Mr Butt's conclusions exceeded his worst fears. On any given night of operations, it was already understood that around a third of all aircraft returned without claiming to have attacked their primary target. So Mr Butt analysed only the target photographs and reports relating to the remaining two-thirds of crews who had allegedly bombed their targets, during the preceding two months of June and July 1941. He reported that of these, only one-third had come within five miles of the aiming point. Against the Ruhr this proportion fell to one-tenth. At a moment when perceptive airmen already foresaw an end of moonlit bombing operations as German night-fighter activity intensified, Mr Butt found that moonlight was indispensable to the crews of Bomber Command: two crews in five came within five miles of their target on full-moon nights; this ratio fell to one in fifteen on moonless ones.

The Royal Air Force was not disposed to make much of the Butt Report. Sir Richard Peirse, who had already achieved a reputation for almost arrogant overconfidence about the work of his Command, found its conclusions incompatible with the degree of damage alleged to have been done to Germany, and thus simply unacceptable. Air Vice-Marshal Carr, now AOC of 4 Group, argued that 'lack of a photograph of the precise target should not be regarded as conclusive proof that the aircraft failed to attack its proper objective'. Air Vice-Marshal Saundby, SASO at High Wycombe, noted that the weather had been especially bad in the months studied by Butt, and also suggested rather improbably that squadron commanders tended to give cameras to those crews in whom they had least confidence. All this reflected a natural exasperation on the part of the airmen, who found themselves being reminded of a situation of which they had been tacitly aware for many months by a Whitehall civil servant.

But however thoroughly Bomber Command's doings were understood within the Royal Air Force, Butt came as a major revelation to one man: the Prime Minister. On 3 September 1941 he dispatched a personal note to the Chief of Air Staff with a copy of the report: 'This is a very serious paper, and seems to require your most urgent attention. I await your proposals for action.'

The submission of the Butt Report signalled the low-water mark of the fortunes of Bomber Command. Since September 1939 its crews had sought to attack warships in harbour and at sea, oil installations and factories, power stations and airfields, by day and by night. In almost all these things, they were now being asked to accept, they had failed. The *Scharnhorst* and the *Gneisenau* had been slightly damaged. One brave pilot's efforts had won him the Victoria Cross and closed the Dortmund–Ems canal for ten days in 1940. 100,000 tons of coastal shipping had been sunk by air-dropped mines. A wide variety of industrial plants had been slightly damaged. The Focke–Wulf aircraft works in Bremen and a number of other important factories had begun to disperse their operations, more in anticipation of the future than because of the damage of the past. A few thousand German civilians had been killed, and immense labour was being diverted to the construction of air raid shelters. Flak and searchlight defences were being greatly strengthened. Some oil plants had been temporarily shut down by bomb damage, but at no cost to the German war economy.

It was fortunate for the airmen that they did not know more than this; of the huge slack capacity in the German economy, the single-shift working that still prevailed in most major factories. Far fewer women were employed than in England. Germans had more to eat (and would continue to have almost until the end of the war), could buy a far wider range of consumer goods and possessed vastly more machine tools than the British. What the German armed forces lacked in equipment was the result of maladministration and not of any shortage of manufacturing capacity or raw materials. The German economy had been geared for a short war, and had scarcely even begun to exert itself. It has been said that if Britain had understood in 1941 how powerful and how effortless was the German industrial machine, what enormous untapped potential it possessed, how widely its resources were dispersed, no one could have contemplated the overwhelming task of attempting to crush it by bombing. But the Air Ministry and the Ministry of Economic Warfare did not know this. They believed that Germany was under immense strain. Perhaps most important of all, the airmen were still imbued with the mystic faith that had sustained them through the inter-war years, that the mere act of bombing was having effects upon the enemy out of all proportion to any hits achieved on economic objectives. The chronic lack of clear thinking that had dogged bombing policy since the end of the First World War persisted even in the face of the most convincing evidence. When the airmen pressed their case for the bomber assault upon the German nation, they believed that they were battering a door already loose upon its hinges.

But even if the exact realities of the situation in Germany and the failure of initial bomber offensive were not known, before the Butt Report reached Whitehall, Bomber Command and the massive industrial commitment to heavy bombers were already being assailed in powerful quarters. The Americans in particular, with their own observers in Germany, were sceptical. Their military attaché in London, General Raymond Lee, recorded in his diary a meeting that August of 1941:

I lunched at the Dorchester as the guest of Colonel Larner, who had Moore-Brabazon, the [junior] Air Minister, and four Air Marshals, together with Royce and myself . . . As soon as the coffee was served, Moore-Brabazon began to talk about how essential it was that the British should have hundreds and hundreds, if not thousands, more long-range bombers with which to bring Germany down. Finally, he turned to me and asked me what my opinion was. I told him that I was no expert, but so far as my observation went, the British had no proof yet that their bombing had been any more effective than the German bombing of England, and that I thought they were asking the United States for a good deal when they wanted it to divest itself of all its bombers, and devote a lot of production capacity to the construction of more bombers, thereby committing the United States to the policy of reducing Germany by bombing, without affording sufficient proof that this was possible. I pointed out that the Luftwaffe under the most favourable conditions had failed to paralyse the British or reduce this country to impotence in over a year of attack, at very short range, and when its energies were not engaged elsewhere. So why, I asked, should the RAF believe they could bring down Germany at a greater range and with its targets very much more dispersed than those in England and protected by very much better anti-aircraft defences now than the British had here last year. I built on absolutely sure ground here because I have had a little time to study the statistics on the damage done to Britain in the seven months between 1 June and 31 December 1940, and it is really surprisingly small . . .[3]

It was the American air attaché in London who reported to Washington as late as April 1942: 'The British public have an erroneous belief, which has been fostered by effective RAF publicity, that the German war machine can be destroyed and the nation defeated by intensive bombing.'

Throughout the war the Royal Navy waged an unceasing battle against the Air Ministry not only for a larger share of industrial resources, but for the services of the greatest possible numbers of the long-range aircraft being built, for anti-submarine operations and reconnaissance. Both sides in the dispute stooped to unseemly depths in the pursuit of their case, and the Royal Navy greatly diminished its own credibility as a judge of the effective use of air forces by insisting that Bomber Command waste so much effort first on the abortive bombing of the *Scharnhorst* and the *Gneisenau*, and subsequently on the impenetrable concrete-encased U-boat pens of the French ports. 'Our fight with the Air Ministry becomes more and more fierce as the war proceeds,' wrote Admiral Whitworth at the height of the controversy. 'It is a much more savage one than our war with the Huns, which is very unsatisfactory and such a waste of effort.'[4] Some shrewd and able naval officers, fighting impossible odds in the far corners of the world, understandably deplored the immense concentration of resources in Bomber Command.

'It certainly gives us furiously to think when we see that over 200 heavy bombers attacked one town in Germany,' wrote Admiral Willis, second-in-command of the Eastern Fleet, to Admiral Cunningham in the Mediterranean, a few months after the Japanese entered the war. 'If only some of the hundreds of bombers who fly over Germany (and often fail to do anything because of the weather) had been torpedo aircraft and dive-bombers the old Empire would be in better condition than it is now...'[5]

Professor Pat Blackett did not impress airmen, because he was an adviser to the Admiralty. But he was also one of the most distinguished defence scientists of his generation. Blackett pointed out that in 1941 British bombers had been killing Germans no faster than the German defences had been killing highly trained British aircrew. Computing brutal realities, he concluded that the future British bomber offensive could not expect to kill more than one German for every five tons of bombs dropped.

I say emphatically [he wrote on 18 February 1942] that a calm dispassionate review of the facts will reveal that the present policy of bombing Germany is wrong; that we must put our maximum effort first into destroying the enemy's sea communications and preserving our own; that we can only do so by operating aircraft over the sea on a very much larger scale than we have done hitherto, and that we shall be forced to use much longer range aircraft. The only advantage that I see in bombing Germany is that it does force the enemy to lock up a good deal of his effort on home defence . . . The heavy scale of bombing will only be justified in the concluding stages of the war when (or if) we are fortunate enough to have defeated the enemy at sea and to have command of it.

But it was not only the Admiralty and its advisers who questioned the bomber offensive. Few men could claim a more intimate knowledge of air technology than A. V. Hill, one of the founding fathers of British radar, and also Independent Conservative Member of Parliament for Cambridge University. Hill felt sufficiently strongly about the great error that he believed was being made in concentrating resources on Bomber Command that on 22 February 1942 he took the unpopular course of denouncing in the House of Commons 'the brave adjectives about big and beautiful bombs, and the fate which will await Berlin next year – it is always next year – from them'. He went on:

Such adjectives do not impress the enemy at all. He quietly does some simple arithmetic and smiles . . . Past controversies about the independence of the Royal Air Force have had one most unfortunate result, the exaggeration of the importance of bombing an enemy country. Against an ill-defended enemy bombing, no doubt, can quickly produce disastrous results, but so can other forms of offensive action – against an ill-defended enemy. In the present struggle none of the protagonists is ill-defended now against attack from the air . . . The idea of bombing a well-defended enemy into submission or seriously affecting his morale – of even doing substantial damage to him – is an illusion. We know that most of the bombs we drop hit nothing of importance. The disaster of this policy is not only that it is futile, but it is extremely wasteful, and will become increasingly wasteful as time goes on.

A few months earlier the House of Commons had aired an agony of protests about the news that Professor Solly Zuckerman and a team of biologists had been carrying out experiments about the effects of explosives on live animals. The House was less moved by Hill's speech. Flight-Lieutenant Boothby MP rose to say that 'in Bomber Command we have fashioned a most formidable weapon of offence'. He deplored statements that might erode confidence in bombing: 'It is tough to ask these chaps to undergo great dangers and perils, which they do cheerfully and bravely, unless they are convinced, as they are at present, that it is worth doing...'

In the Cabinet criticism of the bomber offensive was muted by a mixture of deference on a matter so close to the Prime Minister's heart, and inability to suggest any alternative strategy. The Air Minister, Sir Archibald Sinclair, argued in October 1940 that

our small bomber force could, by accurate bombing, do very great damage to the enemy's war effort, but could not gain a decision against Germany by bombing the civil population ... Unless we get a decision we achieve nothing by promiscuous bombing. Except when he uses mines, it is uncertain to what extent the enemy is deliberately choosing to bomb the civil population when he might hit military targets. When he cannot see to hit the latter he bombs centres of population, and we are now doing the same ... In so far as the Germans may have been led away by their theories of total war into attacking our civilian population instead of concentrating upon our aircraft and air engineering factories, it is very lucky for us.

Yet when bombing policy changed, Sinclair changed with it. He was a man in deep personal thrall to the Prime Minister – 'Head of school's fag', as he was sometimes unkindly described in political circles – and as Air Minister he was always the RAF's political representative rather than master. As will become apparent, he was to be an assiduous public apologist for area bombing, whatever his earlier private misgivings.

Yet at this low point of the bomber offensive in the winter of 1941–2 there would have been deep dismay at the Air Ministry if it had been known that Captain Harold Balfour, Sinclair's Parliamentary Under-Secretary and a man of wide personal experience of air policy, had become sceptical about Bomber Command. On 24 January 1942, in a confidential memorandum to Sinclair that is unmentioned in any of the official histories, Balfour reviewed past hopes for British bombing:

The fact is that this plan has not been fulfilled ... Night defences have, on both sides, increased in quantity and efficiency. As regards accuracy, I believe we calculate that only some 10 per cent of bombs fall in the target area.

The public are more and more questioning the effectiveness of bombing policy and beginning to wonder whether bombs can bring Germany's effort to a standstill and thus be a deciding factor in winning the war.

Balfour was convinced that as Britain faced crisis in the Middle and Far East, bombers must be diverted from the assault on Germany: 'It may be that the believers in bombing Germany to destruction – though right if war were confined to the Western battlefield only – are wrong having regard to the war in the East which has to be won and may continue long after victory in the West if the deteriorating position cannot be checked before then.'

Balfour kept his misgivings to himself. But Sir Stafford Cripps, Lord Privy Seal and Leader of the House of Commons, made a speech in the House of Commons in the spring of 1942 which caused widespread astonishment, interpreted as a vote of no confidence in British bombing:

Another question which has been raised by a great number of members is the question of policy as to the continued use of heavy bombers and the bombing of Germany. A number of hon. members have questioned whether, in the existing circumstances, the continued devotion of a considerable part of our effort to the building up of this bombing force is the best use that we can make of our resources. It is obviously a matter which it is almost impossible to debate in public, but if I may, I would remind the House that this policy was initiated at a time when we were fighting alone against the combined forces of Germany and Italy and it then seemed that this was the most effective way in which we, acting alone, could take the initiative against the enemy. Since that time we have had an enormous access of support from the Russian armies . . . and also from the great potential strength of the United States. Naturally, in such circumstances, the original policy has come under review. I can assure the House that the Government are fully aware of the other uses to which our resources can be put, and the moment they arrive at a decision that the circumstances warrant a change, a change in policy will be made.

Cripps' statement caused momentary alarm at the Air Ministry and in America, where at that very moment a British delegation was labouring to ensure that the USAAF joined Bomber Command in mounting an even more ambitious combined offensive against Germany. But in reality, while Cripps had made his own scepticism clear, for all his grandiose titles he had no influence on the vital decisions, and no information from the Prime Minister that could possibly have justified his hopes.

Another impotent critic was Lord Beaverbrook. Not in the least afraid of speaking his mind to Churchill, after a relatively brief period of real power as Minister of Aircraft Production, by the end of 1941 his influence had waned greatly. His fierce comments on the bomber offensive, like Cripps' remarks, are important because they were made, not because they influenced policy.

The events of the past eight months [wrote Beaverbrook on 7 February 1942] have shown that the achievements of our powerful and growing bomber force have been in no way commensurate with its potentialities, with the man hours and materials expended on its expansion, nor with the losses it has sustained . . . The aircraft in these operations could have been performing vital services in other theatres of war . . . The policy of bombing Germany, which in any event can yield no decisive results within any measurable period of time, should no longer be regarded as of primary importance. Bomber squadrons should be flown forthwith to the Middle and Far East.[6]

Beaverbrook, who had been at the heart of air warfare policy-making (and at loggerheads with the Air Ministry) since 1940, was better informed than most of his Cabinet colleagues about the reality of the bomber offensive. Many ministers knew little or nothing about the struggle taking place over Germany beyond what they read in the newspapers. Ordinary members of the House of Commons and the British public knew scarcely anything. It will become apparent below that real debate about the nature of the bomber offensive did not develop even in well-informed circles until long after area bombing began, because so few people had any knowledge of it. Very early on, it was agreed by the War Cabinet that there should be no admission of changes in bombing policy. At a meeting on 24 March 1941,

Several ministers reported that many people in the country believed that although the enemy was attacking the civil population . . . we were still deliberately refraining from attacks on the German civilian population. No minister suggested that we should alter our policy to the extent of ceasing to attack military objectives. But it might be wise to take steps to bring home to our people that attacks such as those which we have carried out on Mannheim and Hannover had already resulted in inflicting grave injury on the civilian population of those towns: and that as the strength of our bomber force increased, the civilian population of Germany would increasingly feel the weight of our air attack.

The general view of the War Cabinet was that it was better that acts should speak louder than words in this matter . . .

Therefore although the making of war policy remained in Britain a much more open business than in any Axis state, the debate about the future of the bomber offensive was conducted almost entirely within a very small circle headed by the Prime Minister. Politicians such as Captain Balfour, even those with Cabinet rank such as Cripps and Beaverbrook, were entirely eclipsed by the power of the service chiefs in deciding the course of the war. Even the Chiefs of Staff often became no more than a rubber stamp for decisions already taken in Downing Street, in consultation with the Air Ministry. Major-General Sir John Kennedy, the Director of Military Operations, noted without pleasure that 'the bombing policy of the Air Staff was settled almost entirely by the Prime Minister himself in consultation with Portal, and was not controlled by the Chiefs of Staff'.[7]

The purpose of all the foregoing has been to show that in the critical months of decision for the bomber offensive there was a formidable body of dissent in the service departments and in Whitehall which held that strategic bombing had proved a failure, and that, as the war widened and Britain's sources were stretched more tightly around the world, it was a grave error to reinforce the huge commitment to Bomber Command. Yet none of this made any impact on the decisive debate: between the Chief of the Air Staff and the Prime Minister himself.

In the months that followed the fall of France in 1940, there is no dispute about the emphasis thrust upon Bomber Command. Britain possessed no other means of taking the war to Germany. The campaign in North Africa was, and would remain, at best a sideshow and at worst a strategic irrelevance. The Royal Navy had embarked upon the long struggle to keep the Atlantic sea lanes open. But although this would be one of the decisive battles of the Second World War, it was also a defensive one. The war could not be won without victory in the Atlantic, but victory in the Atlantic alone could not win the war. Churchill, with his boundless belligerence, perceived this clearly. He sought to attack Germany with whatever means were at Britain's command. 'In the fierce light of the present emergency,' he wrote to Beaverbrook at the Ministry of Aircraft Production on 8 July 1940:

the fighter is the need, and the output of fighters must be the prime consideration till we have broken the enemy's attack. But when I look around to see how we can win the war I see that there is only one sure path. We have no Continental Army which can defeat the German military power. The blockade is broken and Hitler has Asia and probably Africa to draw from. Should he be repulsed here or not try invasion, he will recoil eastward, and we have nothing to stop him. But there is one thing that will bring him back and bring him down, and that is an absolutely devastating exterminating attack by very heavy bombers from this country upon the Nazi homeland. We must be able to overwhelm him by this means, *without which I do not see a way through.**

This is one of Churchill's most moving papers, because it reveals so clearly his knowledge of his own unreason. Reason dictated that Germany must triumph, that there was no means by which the enemy could possibly be defeated. Britain stood alone and impotent. Bomber Command was the sole remaining tool for offensive action. All Churchill's earlier and later writings suggest that he never rationally believed that the bomber alone could win the war. Yet in July 1940, if he did not make himself believe this, he could advocate nothing but surrender. He chose to commit himself totally to galvanizing ministers and mobilizing industry, goading air marshals and sweeping aside army and naval protest, to create the most powerful possible bomber offensive with the utmost expedition. The moment that the first, vital fighter priorities had been met, the best brains and the greatest factories in Britain were directed towards the bomber campaign. He chafed constantly at the delay between decision and production:

Prime Minister to the Air Minister, Minister of Aircraft Production and Chief of Air Staff:
30 December 1940
   I am deeply concerned at the stagnant condition of our bomber force

*Author's italics.

137

. . . I consider the rapid expansion of the bomber force one of the greatest military objectives now before us . . .

While the Prime Minister pressed the claims of the bomber offensive with all his remorseless energy, a kind of euphoria gripped the Royal Air Force, which never entirely died for the rest of the war. In the wake of the Battle of Britain, with the nightly operations of Bomber Command in the papers and on every newsreel, with the guidance of the Air Ministry's large and energetic public relations department, the airmen had achieved a public and political recognition beyond the wildest dreams of the pre-war years. They had gained a priority in production capacity and a primacy in strategic debate little short of intoxicating to senior RAF officers who had grown up amidst the real and imagined snubs of the army and the Royal Navy. By mid-1941 the first of the new heavy bombers, the Stirlings and Halifaxes with their five-ton bombloads to the Ruhr and 200-mph cruising speed, were coming into squadron service. The Air Staff now advanced the plan that was to remain a touchstone among bomber enthusiasts for the remainder of the war. They proposed the creation of a force of 4,000 heavy aircraft to bomb Germany, against the existing daily availability of something less than 500 of all types.

It was, in effect, a demand that the Royal Air Force be permitted to take over the British war economy, of which it was already appropriating such an enormous share. Each Halifax required 76,000 man-hours to build, compared with 52,000 for a Whitley and 15,200 for a Spitfire. Even this figure took no account of the sophisticated radar technology that would soon be in service. There was no possibility of creating a force of 4,000 heavy bombers from Britain's industrial resources alone – it was doubtful whether it could be done even with large-scale support from American factories. But the Air Ministry had now embarked on the earliest of a series of increasingly fantastic statistical calculations about the weight of explosives that it was necessary to drop upon the Third Reich in order to bring it to its knees, and the 4,000-bomber plan was the first fruit of these. To the airmen it was also the sweetest, a scheme on a scale of which they never lost sight even when all hope of Britain fulfilling it had gone.

From the beginning, the 4,000-bomber plan was greeted with a kind of fascinated awe in Whitehall. Sinclair minuted Portal on 16 June 1941, explaining something of the consternation it had caused among those who might be called upon to find the resources to transform it into reality. Ministers were 'reluctant to commit themselves to so big a concentration of effort upon one means of winning the war'. But it is an indication of the Prime Minister's unshakeable determination to persevere with the bomber offensive that on 7 September, only days after the Butt Report reached his desk, he wrote:

In order to achieve a first-line strength of 4,000 heavy and medium bombers, the RAF require 22,000 to be made between July 1941 and July 1943, of which 5,500 may be expected to reach us from American production. The latest forecasts show that of the remaining 16,500, only 11,000 will be got from our own factories. If we are going to win the war, we cannot accept this position . . .

Since no man knew better than the Prime Minister that bomber production forecasts invariably failed to be met,* it is unnecessary to take this note too literally, or to regard it as evidence of Churchill's commitment to the 4,000-bomber plan. It was one of the innumerable galvanizing memoranda that he wrote to drive the production departments to greater efforts. There is much to suggest that by September 1941 he had already set aside the concept of winning the war by bombing alone. The desperate circumstances of 1940 had forced him to grasp at desperate expedients, but now the whole pattern of the war was changing out of recognition. England was safe from invasion for the foreseeable future, left to stagnate in her backwater by the conquerors of Europe. The Wehrmacht had 'recoiled eastward' as Churchill had anticipated, and was now deep in Russia. It was too early to anticipate the scale of Germany's Napoleonic disaster in the east, but any man with Churchill's sense of history must have cherished

*Heavy bomber production was delayed at several periods by industrial action. For those who believe that the war was a halcyon era of British unity, it is worth recalling that wartime production lost by strikes in the metal, engineering and shipbuilding industries alone rose from a low of 163,000 days in 1940 to a high of 1,048,000 days in 1944. See the *Manpower* volume of the official history of wartime production for details.

hopes that mounted with every day of winter. The Prime Minister feared as deeply as any of his generation the prospect of sending a new British army to the Continent to engage in a prolonged struggle to the death with Germany, which could inflict casualties to make the Somme a pleasant memory. Historically, England had always striven to avoid committing major land armies to the Continent, and had sought instead to win her wars by blockade, naval action, and moral and financial support to her allies. In the winter of 1941, it became increasingly apparent that even if the Russians could not defeat the German army, the titanic struggles in the east must seriously weaken it. The likelihood of America entering the war was growing rapidly.

Yet even if she did so, it was evident that the Allies would be compelled to adopt an indirect strategy for many months to come. Churchill wrote towards the end of 1942:

In the days when we were fighting alone, we answered the question 'How are you going to win the war?' by saying, 'We will shatter Germany by bombing.' Since then the enormous injuries inflicted on the German army and manpower by the Russians, and the accession of the manpower and munitions of the United States, have rendered other possibilities open ... We look forward to mass invasion of the Continent by the liberating armies, and general revolt of the populations against the Hitler tyranny. All the same, it would be a mistake to cast aside our original thought – which, it may be mentioned, is also strong in American minds, namely, that the severe, ruthless bombing of Germany on an ever-increasing scale will not only cripple her war effort, including U-boat and aircraft production, but will also create conditions intolerable to the mass of German population ... We must regard the bomber offensive against Germany at least as a feature in breaking her war-will second only to the largest military operations which can be conducted on the Continent until that war-will is broken ... [8]

Churchill conceived the bomber offensive battering Germany like the siege artillery of old, until the crumbling walls and the starvation, squalor and weariness within made it much easier for the assaulting armies to try the breach. It was precisely because some of the RAF's bomber enthusiasts understood this intention – that they should be the long-range guns of the army until the invasion of Europe could begin – that they fought so fiercely to elevate their campaign into something more, indeed into a battle to destroy Germany by bombing alone, to reduce the invasion to the mere disembarkation of the Allied armies of occupation. The American official historians wrote of the USAAF in the war that it was

young, aggressive, and conscious of its growing power. It was guided by the sense of a special mission to perform. It had to justify the expenditure of billions of dollars and the use of almost a third of the army's manpower. It sought for itself, therefore, both as free a hand as possible to prosecute the air war in accordance with its own ideas and the, maximum credit for its performance.[9]

These words apply with equal force to the RAF and to Bomber Command. Seldom in history have men been so devoted to justification of a strategic theory in the midst of war. Only in the unique circumstances of the Grand Alliance from 1941 to 1944, when the bulk of its armies were idle or preparing for the future, when such Allied land operations as took place were the merest sideshow to the great struggle taking place in Russia, could the airmen have achieved and maintained such independence of action in the face of the hostility and disbelief of the generals and admirals.

At the end of September 1941, Portal sent Churchill a paper which 'seeks to show that judging from our own experience of German attacks, the strength required to obtain decisive results against German morale may be estimated at 4,000 heavy bombers and that the time taken would be about six months'. Churchill dealt brusquely with this formidable assertion:

It is very disputable whether bombing by itself will be a decisive factor in the present war. On the contrary, all that we have learnt since the war began shows that its effects, both physical and moral, are greatly exaggerated ... The most that we can say is that it will be a heavy and I trust a seriously increasing annoyance.

Churchill's apparent ambivalence to bombing was to confuse and irk the airmen until the end of the war. At one moment he seemed to be offering them his utmost support, at the next to be damning their pretensions. Yet, in his turn, the Prime Minister was exasperated by the airmen's attempts to transform a pragmatic decision to throw the largest possible weight of explosives at the German people into a scientific theory of war. He was always mistrustful of statistics and mathematical forecasts, from whatever source. In reading his flood of minutes and letters, it is essential to bear in mind the context in which they were written. Each day, he dictated an enormous correspondence. Much of it was unreasoned and unreasonable – barbed questions and comments to service departments on a huge range of strategic, tactical and technical issues. Churchill sought to urge, to provoke, to test argument. His energy in searching out the darkest corners of bureaucracy was part of his genius as a war leader. It is significant that unlike Hitler, who shared his interest in minutiae, Churchill rarely allowed his own moments of crankiness to divert the war effort. A core of common sense sustained him even at the height of his own extravagances, and it was this which was offended by the special pleading of the service departments. The following year, when Admiral Tovey dispatched a paper to the Admiralty condemning the bombing of Germany as 'a luxury not a necessity', Churchill dismissed him as curtly as ever he handled the airmen, remarking shortly that the paper 'damns itself'.[10]

But Portal was nettled by Churchill's rebuff in September 1941, and by its apparent inconsistency. He reminded the Prime Minister that only weeks before he had approved a review of strategy by the Chiefs of Staff which stated that 'it is in bombing on a scale undreamt of in the last war that we find the new weapon on which we must principally depend for the destruction of economic life and morale'. On 7 October 1941 the Prime Minister answered Portal at length:

We all hope that the air offensive against Germany will realize the expectations of the Air Staff. Everything is being done to create the bombing force on the largest possible scale, and there is no intention of changing this policy. I deprecate, however, placing unbounded confidence in one means of attack, and still more expressing that confidence in terms of arithmetic. It is the most potent method of impairing the enemy's morale we can use at the present time. If the United States enters the war it would have to be supplemented in 1943 by simultaneous attacks by armoured forces in many of the conquered countries which were ripe for revolt. Only in this way could a decision certainly be achieved. Even if all the towns of Germany were rendered largely uninhabitable, it does not follow that the military control would be weakened or even that war industry could not be carried on . . . The Air

Staff would make a mistake to put their claims too high ... It may well be that German morale will crack, and that our bombing will play a very important part in bringing the result about. But all things are always on the move simultaneously, and it is quite possible that the Nazi war-making power in 1943 will be so widely spread throughout Europe as to be ʒo a large extent independent of the actual buildings in the homeland ... One has to do the best one can, but he is an unwise man who thinks there is any *certain* method of winning this war, or indeed any other war between equals in strength. The only plan is to persevere ...

This was a brilliant commentary on the reality of war, perhaps much more so than its contemporary readers perceived. Churchill was not withdrawing his support from the bomber offensive, indeed he would confirm the commitment of great resources to it in the months that followed. He was serving notice of the moderation of his own expectations.

But what now was Bomber Command to seek to achieve? Since the autumn of 1940, the Air Staff had tacitly conceded that daylight operations against Germany were not a feasible proposition, although many airmen nourished long-term hopes of their resumption. There might be occasional precision attacks by night when opportunity arose and when certain targets demanded urgent attention, but the Butt Report had conclusively demonstrated that the majority of Bomber Command's crews could not find and hit a precise target at night.

For the first time in air force history [wrote the official historians] the first and paramount problem of night operations was seen at the highest level to be not merely a question of bomb aiming, though that difficulty remained, but of navigation. While the bombers were still not within five miles of the aiming-point, it was a matter of academic interest as to whether a bomb could be aimed with an error of 300, 600, or 1,000 yards.

Left to themselves, it is reasonable to suppose that the airmen would have continued to dispatch bombers to attack precise targets in Germany, maintaining their private conviction that even if these missed their targets by miles, air bombardment would somehow cause Germany to crumble. But now they had been compelled to face the Butt Report and the illogic of bombing strategy. A new policy had become inevitable.

5 The coming of area bombing, 1942

'Moderation in war is imbecility.'
Admiral of the Fleet Lord Fisher

The decision that was taken at the end of 1941 was that, since a city was the highest common factor which British aircrews crews could hit on a given night under average conditions, Bomber Command would abandon its efforts to hit precise targets and address itself simply to attacking the urban areas of Germany. Although spasmodic precision attacks would take place for the rest of the war, of the total tonnage of bombs dropped by Bomber Command throughout its campaign, three-quarters fell on area targets. The area attack was thus by far the most significant of Bomber Command's war.

The Prime Minister had always been doubtful about the RAF's alleged 'precision' offensive, the search for vital economic arteries, what Harris would later scornfully call 'panacea' targets. The concept of attacking whole cities rather than individual installations held no moral terrors for Churchill although, as the War Cabinet had agreed in March 1941, there was no need to announce publicly any change in policy. Portal had been one of the earliest advocates of attacking German morale, and in the wake of the Butt Report he required no convincing that the way to do this was to launch the heaviest possible attack on urban areas.

In fact throughout 1941 this process had been getting under way. Although specific aiming-points had been given to every crew, it was tacitly understood that most were merely carting explosives to the surrounding city areas. Now this reality would be recognized and the campaign greatly intensified. The only lingering division of opinion within the Royal Air Force lay between those who accepted the need to embark on area bombing merely as a necessary tactical expedient until the means to undertake a new precision attack became available, and those who regarded the policy as an end in itself. Much more will be heard from both these factions.

As far as it is possible to discover, there was no moral debate in Downing Street or the Air Ministry about the launching of the offensive on the cities. No one acquainted with the reality of war had ever believed that it was possible to conduct a bombing campaign without incidental civilian casualties. Whether it was morally any different to kill civilians incidentally, as Bomber Command had done hitherto, or deliberately as they would now begin to do, was a very nice question indeed. Churchill himself in his 1917 memorandum had argued that the killing of civilians should remain an unavoidable side-effect rather a deliberate policy. The Americans were to justify their bombing policy in these terms throughout the war, even when the civilian death toll from their attacks reached extravagant heights. The British official historians have little patience with this sort of moral hair-splitting:

There was, for example, a school of thought which maintained that, although it was morally permissible to attack specific targets such as factories, oil plants and railway centres even at an incidental risk to life and property, it was immoral to attack that life and property. In other words, the implication was that targets in or near towns could be attacked but that towns themselves could not . . . It was, indeed, an argument which was generally put forward without operational factors in mind or even in sight . . .[1]

This seems facile, for it suggests that in warfare moral debate is irrelevant when operational requirements are at stake. Civilized nations, including the western Allies in the Second World War, have customarily waged war by a code which assumes that while all war corrupts, total war corrupts totally. They have tried to modify the worst excesses of the slaughter, especially by avoiding the deliberate killing of non-combatants. The airmen of the Second World War argued that the Royal Navy's blockade in the First World War had killed civilians by starvation as surely as did their own bombs a generation later. Likewise, coastal bombardment by naval squadrons inflicted severe civilian casualties, but had always been a feature of war. Extreme apostles of air war-fare such as Mr J. M. Spaight in his book *Bombing Vindicated*, published in 1944, argued that 'The justification of air bombard-ment is that it is essentially *defensive* in purpose. You kill and destroy to save yourself from being killed or destroyed . . . it would be a suicide, normally, for a bomber formation to approach its target at a height at which precision of aim would be certain.' Yet a significant number of people felt that by embarking on a systematic attack on cities occupied largely by non-combatants in the traditional sense, the Allies sacrificed something of their own moral case and that they contributed substantially to the terrible moral collapse that took place in the Second World War, most especially in the treatment of prisoners and civilians. More of this will be heard later, in 1942 and 1943, when the nature of the Allied air offensive slowly became clear to the public in Britain and America.

The official historians dismiss the moral question overhanging area bombing with the simple assertion that by the winter of 1941 the only choice offered to the Royal Air Force was between area bombing and no bombing at all. Yet there was a third choice – to persist, in the face of whatever difficulties, in attempting to hit precision targets, supported by the growing range of radio and radar navigational and bomb-aiming devices that were already in the pipeline. There was also a fourth, and more realistic alter-native: faced by the fact that Britain's bombers were incapable of a precision campaign, there was no compulsion upon the Govern-ment to authorize the huge strategic offensive that was now to be undertaken. Aircraft could have been transferred to the Battle of the Atlantic and the Middle and Far East where they were so urgently needed, and many British strategists would have whole-heartedly approved the decision to move them. There was a genuine moral and strategic dilemma facing the Government in the winter of 1941. There were alternatives to the area campaign, albeit at great cost to the *amour propre* of the RAF.

But in those icy months of debate, when Britain lay scarred by the Luftwaffe's blitz, labouring amidst the trauma of almost total catastrophe on every front, conscious of the appalling suffering that Nazi Germany was inflicting upon the world, the directors of the Allied war effort could scarcely be expected to perceive all these issues quite as clearly as they appeared to a generation of liberals thirty years later. The moral opposition to area bombing came from a small, if articulate, minority. The people of Britain might not be crying aloud for vengeance upon the women and children of Germany with quite the fervour that some British politicians supposed, but it is most unlikely that they would have opposed area bombing if they had been allowed to vote on it. Mr Geoffrey Shakespeare, Liberal MP for Norwich, wrote to Sir Archibald Sinclair in May 1942: 'Incidentally I am all for the bombing of working class areas of German cities. I am Cromwellian – I believe in "slaying in the name of the Lord", because I do not believe you will ever bring home to the civil population of Germany the horrors of war until they have been tested in this way.'

Whatever reaction Shakespeare's remarks may inspire today, they would have been perfectly acceptable at any but the most radical cocktail party in 1941 and 1942. The enthusiastic publicity accorded to the bomber offensive was to play an important role in keeping hope alive among the British people until at least June 1944.

Between the delivery of the Butt Report and the beginning of the concentrated attack on Germany's cities in the early spring of 1942, there was a pause. At the very moment when the Air Staff were brought face to face with the failure of their efforts, Bomber Command's casualties began to rise alarmingly. In the first eighteen nights of August 1941, 107 aircraft were lost. In September, 76 aircraft were missing and another 62 crashed inside England, out of 2,621 dispatched. In October, 68 were missing and 40 crashed out of 2,501 dispatched. On the night of 7 November, 37 aircraft were lost out of 400 dispatched. 12.5 per cent of those sent to Berlin, 13 per cent of those sent to Mannheim and 21 per cent of those sent to the Ruhr failed to return. Only those sent to targets in France came home relatively unscathed.

Including those aircraft which had crashed inside England, the entire front line of Bomber Command had been statistically wiped out in less than four months. Throughout 1941, an aircraft had been lost for every ten tons of bombs dropped. Bomber Command would suffer far more severely in 1943, but by then the context of the war had changed enormously. In 1941 it was unthinkable to accept this rate of attrition when the Butt Report made it clear that no significant results were being achieved. There was also a lack of confidence in Sir Richard Peirse's direction of Bomber Command. He seemed to have little grasp of operational realities, and he was a convenient scapegoat. On 13 November 1941 the Air Ministry instructed him to curtail drastically the scale of sorties against Germany, especially in bad weather. The War Cabinet, stated the directive, 'have stressed the necessity for conserving our resources in order to build a strong force to be available by the spring of next year'. That winter, the most significant of Bomber Command's operations were again launched against the *Scharnhorst* and the *Gneisenau*, to little effect, but with a dramatic fall in loss rates. The bomb figures fell from 4,242 tons dropped by Bomber Command in August 1941 to 1,011 tons in February 1942.

It is true that the strength of Bomber Command gained little on paper from this respite, because there was a constant drain of squadrons to Coastal Command to support the Battle of the Atlantic, and to prop up Britain's ailing fortunes in the Middle and Far East. There was also the abrupt loss of the expected American contribution to British bomber strength, when the United States entered the war and at once appropriated almost all domestic aircraft production for her own needs. But in these months the Whitleys and Blenheims were being rapidly phased out, and the new generation of 'heavies' was beginning to arrive. American Venturas and Bostons were replacing the unlamented Blenheims. Later there would be the Mosquito, Geoffrey De Havilland's superb all-plywood light bomber and night fighter which the Air Ministry had spurned in their enthusiasm for all-metal airframes, but which De Havillands developed on their own initiative into a two-seat aircraft capable of carrying a 4,000-lb bomb to Berlin at 265 mph. It was already apparent that the twin-engined Avro Manchester was a disappointment, but Avro's designer Roy Chadwick had conceived the notion of solving its lack of power problems by stretching the wings and adding two more engines to the same fuselage. The result was the Avro Lancaster, one of the outstanding successes of wartime aircraft design when it came into service. The new four-engined Short

Stirlings and Handley-Page Halifaxes would look inadequate in 1943 and 1944 – the Stirling's pathetic 16,500-foot ceiling was quite inadequate for operations over Germany – but in 1941 and 1942 they were a vast improvement on what had gone before.

The spring of 1942, for which the air marshals were delaying, promised not only better weather and the first substantial deliveries of four-engined bombers from the factories, but above all the means to navigate with improved accuracy over Germany. The scientists had devised a radio-pulse system, codenamed *Gee*, by which the navigator of an aircraft could fix his position by reference to three transmitting stations in England. *Gee* had been tested over Germany in 1941, dangerously if satisfactorily, since one set had already been lost with an aircraft, compromising its security. The scientists believed that when *Gee* was issued in quantity to Bomber Command early in 1942 it would take the Germans six months to devise effective jamming methods, and by the autumn they hoped to introduce still more advanced British devices. At this early stage, some scientists and airmen hoped that *Gee* would prove accurate enough to become a blind-bombing device. Even if it did not, for the first time crews would have the means to find their way to Germany whatever the cloud which masked pinpoint landmarks. Now that the immense technological needs of the air war had been identified, the scientists of the Telecommunications Research Establishment were giving birth to a range of equipment that by the end of the war would make Bomber Command overwhelmingly the most technically complex weapon in the hands of the Allies. Even now, at the end of 1941, with *Gee* in prospect the airmen could wait for the spring without impatience.

They possessed a new policy – the destruction of Germany's industrial cities by fire. They had been promised the means to undertake this. They lacked only a basis by which they might measure their achievements. In March 1942 the Prime Minister's Scientific Adviser, Lord Cherwell, provided it. His paper was not the blueprint for the bomber offensive – the critical decisions that were to influence British strategy so profoundly for the remainder of the war had already been taken and immense industrial resources had been committed. But Cherwell's report provided the final rationalization for the programme Bomber Command was undertaking, and it would henceforth be permanently paper-clipped to the plans of the bomber offensive.

The following [Cherwell wrote to the Prime Minister on 30 March 1942] seems a simple method of estimating what we could do by bombing Germany.

Careful analysis of the effects of raids on Birmingham, Hull and else-where have shown that, on the average, one ton of bombs dropped on a built-up area demolishes 20–40 dwellings and turns 100–200 people out of house and home.

We know from our experience that we can count on nearly 14 operational sorties per bomber produced. The average lift of the bombers we are going to produce over the next fifteen months will be about three tons. It follows that each of these bombers will in its lifetime drop about forty tons of bombs. If these are dropped on built-up areas they will make 4,000–8,000 people homeless.

In 1938 over 22 million Germans lived in fifty-eight towns of over 100,000 inhabitants, which, with modern equipment, should be easy to find and hit. Our forecast output of heavy bombers (including Wellingtons) between now and the middle of 1943 is about 10,000. If even half the total load of 10,000 bombers were dropped on the built-up areas of these fifty-eight German towns the great majority of their inhabitants (about one-third of the German population) would be turned out of house and home.

Investigation seems to show that having one's house demolished is most damaging to morale. People seem to mind it more than having their friends or even relatives killed. At Hull signs of strain were evident, though only one-tenth of the houses were demolished. On the above figures we should be able to do ten times as much harm to each of the fifty-eight principal German towns. There seems little doubt that this would break the spirit of the people.

Our calculation assumes, of course, that we really get one-half of our bombs into built-up areas. On the other hand, no account is taken of the large promised American production (6,000 heavy bombers in the period in question). Nor has regard been paid to the inevitable damage to factories, communications, etc., in these towns and the damage by fire, probably accentuated by breakdown of public services.

Sir Charles Portal and Sir Archibald Sinclair reported that they found Lord Cherwell's paper 'simple, clear and convincing', although they noted that for his projections to be fulfilled, bomber production forecasts would have to be met, 50 per cent of sorties would have to be effective, the loss-rate would have to remain within reasonable proportions, and strategic diversions would have to be avoided. These were large reservations. But the airmen were not about to quarrel with the Prime Minister's scientific adviser when he offered his energetic support to the bomber offensive, whatever their private uncertainties about some of his reasoning. 'Lord Cherwell's minute', in the words of the official historians, 'had done no more and no less than to acknowledge a "design and theme" for the air offensive.'[2]

Cherwell, the erstwhile Professor Lindemann, had been close to the Prime Minister throughout his years in the wilderness in the 1930s, and his fertile mind had provided Churchill with many scientific defence ideas with which to belabour supine pre-war governments. Unfortunately, however, Lindemann concentrated his attention on air defence, almost the only area of military preparation in which, under the guidance of Sir Henry Tizard, great strides were being made. Churchill induced the Government to give Lindemann a seat on the Committee for the Study of Aerial Defence, where he at once made himself insufferable. Tizard and his colleagues had concluded after much heart-searching that they must risk pouring all the resources at their command into the development of radar. Lindemann's fatal weakness was that he rarely found it possible to believe in an idea unless he had been at least a midwife at its delivery. 'He suffered from the didactic approach that he himself knew everything worth knowing, and that anything outside his field of knowledge must be wrong', said Barnes Wallis.[3] Within weeks of his appointment to the Committee, he had caused chaos and dismay by insisting that the priority given to radar be set aside, and that the Government instead concentrate on two brain-children of his own, aerial mines to be cast in the path of oncoming bombers and infra-red beams. His interference was intolerable. Tizard and the others resolved the situation in the classic civil service manner, by dissolving the Committee of Aerial Defence and forming another almost identical body without Lindemann on it. Momentarily, 'The Prof' was eclipsed. But at the outbreak of war he was foremost among those who shared the rewards of personal loyalty to Churchill. He followed his master first into an office at the Admiralty, then into

151

Downing Street with a peerage and in 1942 a seat in the Cabinet sa Paymaster-General. He never lost Churchill's confidence, and wielded immense power for the remainder of the war.

Cherwell was a man of arrogance and wealth, at ease in the company of the mighty all his life, full of charm when he chose to exercise it. He demonstrated his personal courage by his experiments with spinning aircraft in the First World War. He was a clever man, but had never been quite in the top flight of scientists, and certainly lacked that superlative brilliance which alone can justify sublime conceit in pursuit of one's own prejudices. Above all, Cherwell was personally vengeful. He never forgot a defeat. Sir Henry Tizard was a doomed man from the day that Cherwell achieved power. The outstanding scientific civil servant of his generation had inflicted on Cherwell the most humiliating reverse of his career, and he had never been forgiven.

In the winter of 1940 Tizard delivered himself into Cherwell's hand. He made a serious error of judgement in declining to accept the existence of the navigational beams by which the Luftwaffe was bombing Britain with alarming accuracy. He was never allowed to forget it, and by the spring of 1942 his influence was waning fast. But in one of his last important interventions in the direction of the war,* he felt compelled to express his deep misgivings about Cherwell's 'de-housing' paper.

Tizard had already shown his scepticism about the weight of resources being devoted to bombing in a memorandum to the Ministry of Aircraft Production dated 12 December 1941, commenting on heavy aircraft plans: 'The war is not going to be won by night bombing,' he said. 'This programme assumes that it is.' Now, on 15 April 1942, he wrote to Lindemann: 'I am afraid that I think that the way you put the facts as they appear to you is extremely misleading and may lead to entirely wrong decisions being reached, with a consequent disastrous effect on the war. I think, too, that you have got your facts wrong. . .'

Tizard went on to say that he feared that while the RAF's proposed massive bomber force was being assembled the war might be lost elsewhere for lack of sufficient defensive weapons. He was thinking especially of the Battle of the Atlantic. He also

*Tizard left Whitehall to become President of Magdalen College, Oxford.

mistrusted Cherwell's sums. He reckoned that Bomber Command could only hope for 7,000 bombers by mid-1943, not Cherwell's 10,000. He questioned the crews' ability to find and hit Cherwell's fifty-eight towns. He doubted (correctly) that the next generation of radar navigation and bombing aids would be available much before the spring of 1943. He thought that it was unreasonable to expect more than 25 per cent of bombs lifted to reach their target. All this, he recognized, 'would certainly be most damaging, but would not be decisive unless in the intervening period Germany was either defeated in the field by Russia, or at least prevented from any substantial further advance'.

I conclude therefore

(a) that a policy of bombing German towns wholesale in order to destroy dwellings cannot have a decisive effect by the middle of 1943, even if all heavy bombers and the great majority of Wellingtons produced are used primarily for this purpose.

(b) That such a policy can only have a decisive effect if carried out on a much bigger scale than is envisaged in [Cherwell's paper].

Cherwell crushed his critic with considerable scorn. 'My dear Tizard,' he wrote, 'many thanks for your note. I would be interested to hear what you think wrong with my simple calculation, which seemed to be fairly self-evident. . . My paper was intended to show that we really can do a lot of damage by bombing built-up areas with the sort of air force which should be available.'

His own estimates had not been made for statistical analysis, but 'partly to save the Prime Minister the trouble of making arithmetical calculations'. Whatever disparities there might be between his figures and reality, if Bomber Command concentrated its utmost efforts on Germany's cities, the effects would be 'catastrophic'.

Here was the very heart of the debate about the efficacy of area bombing. No one could reasonably argue that Bomber Command could pour explosives on to Germany over a period of years without doing terrible damage. No one with the slightest experience of bombing could deny that it is a terrifying business to endure it. The reasoned critics of the bomber offensive did not dispute that Bomber Command could raze to the ground areas of Germany – they questioned what contribution this would make to final victory, as against applying similiar resources to other sectors of the war effort. Every pound of explosives carried to Germany by Bomber Command cost at least a pound sterling to deliver. No one by this stage of the war disputed that tactical air superiority and tactical bombing were critical in the execution of any naval or military operation, and every aircraft that could be produced was vitally needed.

Tizard was a man who hated headlong confrontation, which ran against a lifetime's habit of academic circumspection. 'I should like to make it clear', he wrote mildly and probably insincerely[4] to Cherwell, 'that I don't disagree fundamentally with the bombing policy.' He merely doubted whether it could be effective unless carried out on a scale beyond Britain's means. He might have expressed himself more forcefully had he known the full extent of the misinformation on which Cherwell founded his original paper. The basis for Cherwell's projection of the effects of the bombing of England on to Germany's cities was a report, to be known as 'The Hull and Birmingham Survey', then being compiled by two scientists, Professor Bernal and Professor Zuckerman. Throughout their investigations, Bernal and Zuckerman had been answering a stream of questions from Cherwell's office, and feeding him on request with fragments of data. But the impression Cherwell gave in his paper that he had founded his conclusions on a study of Bernal and Zuckerman's completed investigations was false. Their report did not appear until 8 April 1942, ten days after Cherwell submitted his paper. Professor (now Lord) Zuckerman has described[5] his astonishment when he first saw Cherwell's minute, years after the war, and found that it drew on 'Hull and Birmingham' to argue directly opposed conclusions to those which the surveyors had reached. Zuckerman and Bernal wrote: 'In neither town was there any evidence of panic resulting either from a series of raids or from a single raid . . . In both towns actual raids were, of course, associated with a degree of alarm and anxiety, which cannot in the circumstances be regarded as abnormal, and which in no instance was sufficient to provoke mass anti-social behaviour. There was no measurable effect on the health of either town.'

But Zuckerman and Bernal did not have the ear of the Prime Minister, and nor did Tizard, Blackett or other distinguished scientists who opposed the bomber offensive. Lord Cherwell, always a devoted advocate of levelling Germany, retained his influence until the end of the war. Measurement of acres of built-up area demolished would become the standard method of computing the progress of the bomber offensive.

It is important to emphasize, however, that although all the principals were now in agreement about launching a major air attack on Germany's cities, there was still great unspoken confusion about the results to be sought from doing so. Lord Cherwell hoped to create a nation of refugees, and no doubt also a good many corpses under the rubble, although he was too genteel to say so. The airmen's aims were less coherent. In a paper of 19 September 1941 justifying the 4,000-bomber plan, the Air Ministry's Directorate of Bomber Operations said that 'It must be realized that attack on morale is not a matter of pure killing ... It is an adaptation, though on a greatly magnified scale, of Air Control.' Presumably, therefore, DB Ops hoped that after a dose of mass destruction there would be a moral collapse in Germany in fear of worse to come, perhaps on the lines suggested by Liddell Hart a generation earlier, with mobs of starved and crazed civilians roaming the streets demanding peace. Sir Charles Portal probably shared this long-term aspiration, but hoped in the short term for drastic reductions in German war production caused by absenteeism and flight from the cities, compounded by direct destruction of industrial plant. Sir Norman Bottomley, Deputy Chief of Air Staff, had composed a long memorandum in his days as SASO at High Wycombe in September 1940, in which he urged that Bomber Command's aim must be 'primarily to destroy the enemy's will to win the war, leaving the destruction of his means to win the war as an incidental or indirect task'.

Sir Arthur Harris, who would shortly become the man charged with executing the area bombing policy, claimed in his post-war memoirs that he always regarded morale as a subordinate target. He says that he chiefly sought the direct destruction of German ability to produce. He was convinced by evidence suggesting a direct correlation between acres of urban devastation and lost industrial man-hours: 'The destruction of factories, which was nevertheless on an enormous scale, could be regarded as a bonus. The aiming-points were usually right in the centre of the town.'[6]

If all this leaves some confusion in the mind of the reader, it also suggests extraordinary vagueness on the part of the airmen. The concept of a Trenchardian thunderbolt fascinated them. But as far as it is possible to discover, they never recorded a common assent about the exact nature of what they hoped to achieve by area bombing, beyond the destruction of punitively large areas of German real estate. The importance of this lack of rigorous thinking, the absence of a definable and measurable goal for the bomber offensive, cannot be overstated. If a precise definition of success was not arrived at, nor was a yardstick of failure. Admirals could be sacked for failing to sink or save ships, generals for failing to win or hold ground. But nowhere was it suggested in the winter of 1941–2 that if Germany failed to collapse by a given date in the face of air attack, then the bomber offensive would have to be judged a failure. Even in Cherwell's 'de-housing' paper, there was no definition of a precise number of refugees that it was necessary to create to achieve decisive results. For all the talk about morale, no one tried to sketch a realistic political scenario for the overthrow of the Nazi leadership and crumbling of the German armies in the field.

After the war some airmen argued that they had failed to achieve decisive success because they had been denied the 4,000 bombers they had demanded to defeat Germany. Yet in 1942 they never made the undertaking of the area offensive conditional on being given such forces. At the end of the day, Britain's huge area-bombing offensive was launched on the basis of no more reasoned expectation – on the part of the air marshals, at any rate: the Prime Minister's view will be considered below – than that if a large enough weight of bombs was poured on to Germany, something vital must give somewhere.

The Air Ministry directive issued to Bomber Command on 14 February, St Valentine's Day 1942, was the blueprint for the attack on Germany's cities, and removed all constraints on targeting. The winter injunction to conserve forces was withdrawn. 'You are accordingly authorized to employ your forces without restriction.' wrote Bottomley, Deputy Chief of Air Staff. Annex A, appended to the directive, listed Bomber Command's new targets. Under the heading 'Primary Industrial Areas' came Essen, Duisburg, Düsseldorf and Cologne. 'Alternative Industrial Areas' included Lübeck and Rostock, Bremen and Kiel, Hanover, Frankfurt, Mannheim, Stuttgart and Schweinfurt. The directive ordered continuing harassing attacks on Berlin 'to maintain the fear of attack over the city and to impose ARP measures'. Above all, the directive stressed that during the six months' expected life of *Gee* – TR 1335, as it was referred to – Bomber Command must seek to concentrate the weight and density of its attack as never before. Operations 'should now be focused on the morale of the enemy civil population and in particular, of industrial workers'. It had been recognized for some months that incendiary bombs – 4-lb thermite sticks – had a special part to play as fire-raising weapons. Essen was suggested for the earliest bombardment. The remainder of the cities on the list would follow. Lest there be any confusion about objectives, Portal wrote to Bottomley on 15 February: 'Ref the new bombing directive: I suppose it is clear that the aiming-points are to be the built-up areas, not, for instance, the dockyards or aircraft factories. . . This must be made quite clear if it is not already understood.'

The Air Ministry directive was addressed to Air Vice-Marshal Baldwin, acting C-in-C at High Wycombe. Peirse had gone. He had inspired little sympathy or affection among his subordinates at Bomber Command, and little faith in his judgement in high places. He also paid the price for having been the man in command at the lowest ebb of Bomber Command's fortunes. There was now a new policy, new equipment. It was concluded that it would be best to find a new C-in-C, untarnished by the failures of the past.

One evening in December 1941, during the first great Washington conference between the leaders of the British and American war efforts, Sir Charles Portal sought out Air Marshal Arthur Harris, head of the permanent RAF delegation in the United States and asked him to take over Bomber Command. Harris accepted. Portal said: 'Splendid! I'll go and tell Winston at once.'[7] On 22 February 1942, a week after the issue of the Air Ministry directive unveiling area bombing, Harris became Air Officer Commanding-in-Chief at Bomber Command headquarters, High Wycombe. He was just short of fifty and he remained in the post until the end of the war. In the thirty months of war that had already passed, Bomber Command had lost 7,448 aircrew killed in action and accidents or taken prisoner. By May 1945 this figure would have reached 72,350. The bomber war had scarcely begun when Harris became C-in-C. Henceforth, his name would be indelibly associated with its fortunes.

Arthur Travers Harris was the son of a member of the Indian Civil Service, conventionally privately-educated in England until he fell out with his parents over their wish that he should enter the army. He then took the usual path of disgruntled young Edwardian Englishmen, and departed for the Colonies. At the age of sixteen he arrived in Rhodesia with five pounds in his pocket. In the six years that followed, he tried his hand at farming, gold mining and driving horse teams. Rhodesia was kind to him, and he returned her welcome with lifelong affection. At the outbreak of war in 1914, he joined the Rhodesia Regiment as a boy bugler and fought through the fierce hardships of the German South-West African campaign. When this ended in 1915, he found his way back to England, determined that he had had enough of footslogging. He joined the Royal Flying Corps and was posted to France. He finished the war as a major, with the Air Force Cross. In the next twenty years he commanded bomber squadrons exercising Trenchard's Air Control scheme in the further outposts of the Empire, and served from 1933 to 1937 in staff posts at the Air Ministry. Unlike Portal or Ludlow-Hewitt, he was not regarded as an obvious high-flier, destined for the highest ranks. But he advanced steadily to command of 4 Group in 1937, to head the RAF Purchasing Mission in America in 1938, then to command the crack 5 Group in the early days of the war. It was here that he made a reputation as a forceful director of bomber operations.

Sir Arthur Harris, as he now became, had something of the earthy, swaggering ruthlessness of an Elizabethan buccaneer. A broad man of medium height, his piercing eye gave him immediate presence in any company. 'There are a lot of people who say that bombing cannot win the war,' he declared to a newsreel interviewer a few weeks after taking over at High Wycombe, in the crisp, clipped tones that cowed so many havering staff officers.

'My reply to that is that it has never been tried yet. We shall see.'
He gave no sign of fearing God or man, and in Washington his
outbursts of frankness had left behind a trail of savaged American
military sensitivities. He had been an early convert to the concept
of strategic bombing, and ranked among Trenchard's most
dedicated disciples. He had devoted much energy between the
wars to means of improving bomb-aiming and target-marking.

His dry, cutting, often vulgar wit was legendary throughout
the RAF, as was his hatred of the British army and the Royal
Navy. He was fond of saying that the army would never understand the value of tanks until they could be modified to 'eat hay
and shit'. A man of boundless energy, he spent much of the war
racing his Bentley at breakneck speed between High Wycombe
and the Air Ministry, and was the bane of motor-cycle policemen
on the London road. 'You might have killed somebody, sir,' said
a reproachful constable who stopped him late one night.

'Young man, I kill thousands of people every night!' snapped
Harris. He seemed to like the ogre-ish role that fortune had cast
for him. His contemporaries called him 'Bert', but his crews
called him 'Butcher', 'Butch' for short. His subordinates at High
Wycombe were deeply in awe of him, and there was little scope
for dissent at his councils. He was a man of startling directness,
and his temper cannot have been improved by the ulcers from
which he suffered throughout the war. Saundby, his SASO, once
sent him a memorandum, painstakingly describing ten alternative methods of attacking a target. Harris returned it with a
scrawled endorsement :'TRY FERRETS'.

From the beginning of the war, he had been convinced that
given the vast shortcomings of Britain's armed forces compared
with those of Germany, a bomber offensive was inevitable:

I could . . . see only one possible way of bringing pressure to bear on
the Boche, and certainly only one way of defeating him; that was by air
bombardment. It consequently looked as if it was going to be a
straight fight between our own and the enemy's production of heavy
bombers. . .

If we could keep ahead of the Germans, I was convinced, having
watched the bombing of London, that a bomber offensive of adequate
weight and the right kind of bombs would, if continued for long enough,

be something that no country in the world could endure.

It was, of course, anybody's guess what effort would be required and over what period the offensive would have to be continued.[8]

Harris had naturally been an ardent advocate of the 4,000-bomber plan, which it was apparent would never be fulfilled. Some compromise with the Royal Navy's demands for heavy aircraft and the insistent needs of other theatres had to be made. Harris would have nothing like the resources he hoped for until at least 1943. But he would fight until the last day of the war to ensure that Bomber Command achieved the utmost possible strength, and the 1,600 heavy bombers that he commanded in his operational squadrons by April 1945 were a personal tribute to his determination and force of personality. Area bombing was not his creation, but he applied himself to executing the policy with an energy and single-mindedness that persisted long after less committed airmen had turned their minds to other strategies.

At the time that he became C-in-C, Harris knew Churchill scarcely at all. Once in 1940, when he was commanding 5 Group, he had been summoned to the Prime Minister's occasional retreat at Ditchley, but had been granted only a few words. Now, however, an apparent intimacy between Harris and Churchill began to attract widespread attention and jealousy, not least among the admirals, who were enraged to hear of the airman being invited to drive the few miles from High Wycombe to Chequers for dinner and presumably a great deal of special pleading for his Command. The precise relationship between the C-in-C and the Prime Minister remained a matter of curiosity and controversy throughout the war and afterwards. General Paget, C-in-C Home Forces, thought that 'Bert Harris was the sort of buccaneer whom Churchill particularly liked. . .'[9] But Major Desmond Morton, the Secret Service officer who had been one of Churchill's intimate circle since before the war, believed quite otherwise:

Curiously enough, I think he *never* cared for Harris as a person. I do not know why not, though I know why *I* did not . . . My own distaste . . . was based on what I thought, rightly or wrongly, of his personality. He seemed to me to be a bit of a boor (not bore) with little or any sort of fine thoughts or sign of anything distinguished in his mind or person.

I am always attracted by anyone who seems to be, or to be trying to be, and behave like a gentleman in any way. I found nothing of this sort in Harris. I do not condemn Harris absolutely. He did many great things doubtless. It is not easy (if possible) to become a Marshal of the Royal Air Force without doing many notable things well. But in my opinion many of the things he did and said and did well, were done and said in a manner lacking refinement'.[10]

Whatever the admirals' fears about Churchill's relations with Harris, the airman never gained the Prime Minister's confidence for his grand vision of victory by air bombardment alone. And whatever the truth of Morton's suspicions about the Prime Minister's personal attitude, there is no doubt that many of those in high places reacted to Bomber Command's C-in-C like the fastidious Major.

Yet Harris's style, the stories about his rudeness and extravagance, contributed immensely to his popularity with his overwhelmingly lower middle-class bomber crews. They endeared him to them, though they never saw him, with a warmth that a more distant, patrician figure such as Portal could never have achieved. Harris was a real leader. From beginning to end, he succeeded in seeming to identify himself totally with the interests of his men.

Yet for all his bluntness, it is impossible to accept that Harris was a realist about operational difficulties. From the beginning of the war, he had refused to accept the inadequacy of Bomber Command's navigation, even when most of his contemporaries had done so. He was foremost among the self-deluded about the early achievements of bombing. In October 1940 one of the most fanciful Intelligence reports quoted 'Well-informed industrialists' assessments that 25 per cent of Germany's productive capacity had been affected by bombing'. Harris wrote to Peirse expressing his delight about 'the accuracy with which our aircraft hit military objectives as opposed to merely browning towns. . . These summaries serve to impress upon one . . . the by now patent fact that the Air Ministry Publicity department is half-witted.'

Harris complained, as he was to do repeatedly when he became C-in-C, that the Press gave inadequate recognition to Bomber Command's achievements:

What a riot of publicity would attend such results had they been secured by the Army, and what a catastrophic spate of words if the Navy had succeeded in doing a thousandth as much! Yet when the bombers begin to win the war – and we are the only people that can win it, and we are winning it – what happens? Nix!

Harris suggested that the only possible explanation for the Publicity Department's passivity was that its staff 'are all long since dead, and nobody's noticed it! Naturally enough, nobody would!'

On 1 February 1941, when the Air Ministry was deeply concerned about Scientific Intelligence's discovery that the Germans were bomb-aiming by radio beam, Harris as Deputy Chief of the Air Staff wrote crossly:

Are we not tending to lose our sense of proportion over these German beams? . . . We use no beams ourselves but we bomb just as successfully as the Germans bomb, deep into Germany . . . I do not agree that the beams are in fact a serious menace to this country, or that they have proved to be in the past. They are simply aids to navigation, and it is within our experience that such aids are not indispensable to the successful prosecution of bombing expeditions. I could go further and say that they are not even really useful . . . Long may the Boche beam upon us!

This was the man who was now called upon to direct Bomber Command's first major operations under the influence of *Gee*, who would resist to the utmost the creation of the Pathfinder Force, who would fight every attempt to transfer the attentions of Bomber Command from area to precision bombing, and who in 1944 professed his astonishment, when he had been overruled and compelled to dispatch his aircraft on precision operations, on finding that they were brilliantly capable of carrying them out.

Harris was an inflexible man, chronically resistant to negotiation and compromise, who treated those who disagreed with him as mortal enemies. He seemed driven, in the words of one historian,[11] by an 'elemental tenacity of purpose'. This was a quality that would earn him many enemies and abrupt dismissal at the end of the war. But it was also a characteristic that, in the midst of war, has much value. Harris was a nerveless commander of great forces, and the history of warfare shows that such men are rare. His very insensitivity rendered him proof against shocks and disappointments. He possessed the considerable gifts of clarity of speech and purpose, and from the moment that he became C-in-C at High Wycombe, he infused these into his entire Command. He was never afraid of taking decisions. He made his officers at every level feel that they were now part of a great design instead of merely running a ramshackle air freight service exporting bombs to Germany. If his superiors ever lost confidence in him, or considered that he was failing to meet their hopes or wishes, it was their business to replace him, as so many wartime C-in-Cs were replaced.

When Harris took command, there had been twenty-two directives from the Air Ministry to Bomber Command since the outbreak of war, endless changes of policy as the planners groped in the darkness for Germany's economic jugular. Harris was determined that there should be no more of this, no more 'panacea targets' such as oil plants or aircraft factories. He believed that there were no short cuts to defeating Germany from the air. It was necessary to concentrate all available forces for the progressive, systematic destruction of the urban areas of the Reich, city block by city block, factory by factory, until the enemy became a nation of troglodytes, scratching in the ruins. This conviction would become his obsession. Given time and technique – and at the beginning of 1942 it was plain that he could expect years – he would demonstrate to the world the force of properly handled strategic air power, and the unique place of the Royal Air Force in the Allied war effort.

Thus Bomber Command became committed to area bombing, and the Government committed to Bomber Command an industrial capacity eventually equal to that devoted to the entire British army, along with the cream of Britain's wartime high technology.

It remains only to emphasize that the Prime Minister, while he endorsed the strategic offensive, shared few of the airmen's extravagant expectations for it. In 1940 he had supported Bomber Command from necessity. Yet now, with the German army mired in Russia and with America not only an ally but committed to a policy of 'Germany first', why did he persist with a bomber attack in which he had limited strategic faith? The need to sustain the morale of the British people by visible action is a partial answer.

But by far the most convincing reason is that the Prime Minister had already become determined to postpone the opening of a second front in Europe until the last possible hour. There was no longer any doubt that the Allies would ultimately win the war. The questions were how soon, and at what cost? Already the Americans with their military innocence and huge resources were pressing for an early invasion of northern Europe to get to grips with the enemy. The Prime Minister was resisting this notion with all the force at his command. He thwarted first proposals for an invasion in 1942, then others for 1943. He was determined that when the Allies landed in France, it should be under conditions of overwhelming advantage. There must be no great campaign of attrition, such as would be inevitable against an unbroken German army.

Churchill never shared the airmen's faith that the bomber offensive could eliminate the need for a land campaign to defeat the enemy. But the bombers could enable the western Allies to delay aggressively, while Russia fought out the huge battles that broke the Wehrmacht, that caused Hitler by June 1944 to deploy 156 divisions in the East against 50 in France and the Low Countries. Neither the Russians nor the Americans could flatly be told that the British proposed to fight no campaign in Europe for years to come. If the bomber offensive, fuelled by publicity and boosted with American support, met with even moderate destructive success, this would be convincing evidence of Britain's commitment to the struggle at tolerable cost in British lives. Bomber Command's 56,000 killed would represent, at the end, the lowest possible stake that Britain could be seen to throw on the tables of Europe, when the Russians were counting their dead in millions. In this sense, the bomber offensive was the greatest panacea of all. Yet if this was indeed in Churchill's mind when he authorized the area campaign at the beginning of 1942, then Bomber Command would fulfil his hopes in the next two years far more satisfactorily than those of the Royal Air Force.

6 50 Squadron, Lincolnshire, 1942

Across the road the homesick Romans made,
The ground-mist thickens to a milky shroud;
Through flat, damp fields call sheep, mourning their dead
In cracked and timeless voices, unutterably sad,
Suffering for all the world, in Lincolnshire.

And I wonder how the Romans liked it here;
Flat fields, no sun, the muddy misty dawn,
And always, above all, the mad rain dripping down,
Rusting sword and helmet, wetting the feet
And soaking to the bone, down to the very heart . . .
Henry Treece, *Lincolnshire Bomber Station*

Harris conducts an overture

1942 was the pivotal year for the Allies in almost every theatre of
war. The tide turned at Stalingrad; the Japanese were defeated
at Midway; the North African diversion was at last brought
within sight of ending by the defeat of the Afrika Korps; the
Atlantic lifelines were held open in the face of horrifying losses.
At this critical time, when the Allies were not yet prepared to
confront the Germans in Western Europe, the strategic air offensive might have made a central contribution had it been ready to
do so. But Bomber Command was still hesitantly gathering its
strength. In June, its most effective month, only 6,485 tons of
bombs were dropped against the 15,271 that would fall in the same
month of 1943 and the 57,267 tons of June 1944. Thirteen of the
squadrons mustered and equipped with such exertions were
detached to Coastal Command and the Middle East, leaving
only thirty (with an establishment of sixteen aircraft each) in
Harris's front line. He strained credibility when he claimed to the
War Cabinet that he controlled only 11 per cent of the RAF and

Fleet Air Arm's front line, for this ignored the vast resources needed to produce and operate heavy aircraft compared with fighters. But bomber production was lagging. Stirling and Halifax output had been delayed by repeated teething troubles, and the twin-engined Manchester was proving grossly underpowered. Only the Lancaster showed signs of fulfilling the hopes of the pre-war visionaries of heavy bombers.

Yet in 1942 the mould of the offensive was formed, the image in which Bomber Command would fight and send so many men to die and in which it would be etched into history. With hindsight, it is possible to see that there were two wars between 1939 and 1945. The first was the last war of a past generation. The second was the first of the new era. Technology was coming of age: radar and the atomic bomb, the jeep and the high-performance aircraft. Somehow even the faces in the photographs look different. A Bomber Command group from, say, Honington in 1939 merges imperceptibly into the sepia shades of Camels and 'Archie' and the old Royal Flying Corps. But then study the faces of the Lancaster crews of Harris's Bomber Command (ironically, for he himself was anything but a modern man): so many of the faces are already those of the knowing, professional young technocrats of the post-war era, children who have lost their innocence thirty times over Germany, who will vote for the Welfare State in 1945, who are the most highly trained front-line fighters in the history of warfare.

By 1942 most of the pre-war generation of regular aircrew had been killed off, promoted to non-operational posts, or left languishing behind German barbed wire. Now, in the spirit of Kitchener's New Armies of 1915, the first flower of the volunteers of 1939 were reaching the squadrons. These were the excited young idealists, almost to a man aspiring fighter pilots, many of them the colonials who would make such an enormous contribution to Bomber Command – New Zealanders, Australians, Canadians. They had trained all over the world for two years or more – some in America, others in Canada, Rhodesia, South Africa.[1] The pilots and navigators represented the highest skills – most of the latter had been eliminated from pilot training courses. Bomb-aiming had at last been recognized as a specialist trade for which men were specifically trained. Gunners,wireless operators and flight engineers were taught what they needed to know to operate their equipment, and little more.

At the Operational Training Units in England they were brought together. There was no more arbitrary assembling of men for odd operations: it was clearly understood that the fate of Bomber Command hung on the integrity and mutual confidence of the operational crews, and every possible step was taken to allow like-minded souls to fit together. In the first few days at OTU, a milling herd of assorted aircrew were left to crew up by natural selection:

'I hear you want a gunner? Can you fly a Wimpey without making me throw up?'

'We're looking for a wireless operator and you're the only bloke here who doesn't look as if he's got DTs...'

'Our driver flew into a hill this morning so we wondered if you might do us for a new one...'

The accident rate at OTUs was appalling.* Some courses lost as many as 25 per cent of their trainees before graduation four or five months after arrival. Tour-expired aircrew posted to instruct rapidly learned that flying pupils in tired and often under-maintained bombers was anything but a rest-cure. But at least men were learning new tactical and technical skills at OTU that a year before they were compelled to teach themselves over Germany.

At the end of their training, these rather bewildered but intensely willing young men went to their stations. Little huddles of blue-clad humanity clutching their gas-masks and kitbags stood on some East Anglian railway platform to be collected by a nonchalant MT driver in a three-quarter-ton truck. If they were destined for 5 Group, they fetched up at Newark or the old garrison town of Lincoln. If they were going to 50 Squadron early in 1942, they found themselves driving down the Fosse Way, the old Roman road south-west from Lincoln to Swinderby, the big pre-war station from which 50's ageing Hampdens took off for Germany. Here, amidst the flat, rich fields of East Anglia, something more than half of them would be making their final homes.

*5,327 officers and men were killed and a further 3,113 injured in RAF train-in accidents 1939–45.

5 Group had always been considered – not least by 5 Group – Bomber Command's crack division. 50 was one of its outstanding squadrons. In 1941 they had been commanded by one of the legendary leaders of Bomber Command, Gus Walker. By early 1942 Walker had been succeeded by Wing-Commander 'Beetle' Oxley, a rather more pedestrian figure. The corpulent Oxley was an excellent and forceful administrator, but flew only a minimum of operations himself. At his briefings, crews would sometimes shout that half-serious, half-mocking taunt at groundlings: 'Get some in!' Oxley would say. 'Piece of cake tonight, chaps. Last time I was over Mannheim it was only defended by two men and a dog', which caused a good deal of derisive laughter, since everybody knew that he was harking back to some primeval date in 1940. But Oxley knew how to drive men, and he detested the enemy. Every new crew at 50 Squadron was given a CO's peptalk on 'the need to work up Hun-hate'. Oxley's passionate dedication to the business of killing Germans had become a sort of legend in 5 Group, and not only there. A 50 Squadron gunner shot down early in 1942 was astonished by one of the first questions put to him by a fascinated German interrogator at Dulag Luft: 'Who is this man Oxley?'

50 Squadron in 1942 bred a long succession of outstanding pilots and crews, including many who went to form the Dambusters a year later. Henry Maudslay, the quiet, gentle Old Etonian son of a rich West Country family, was a former Coastal Command 'Kipper Fleet' pilot. Like his 50 Squadron colleague 'Hoppy' Hopgood, he would die over the Mohne Dam. Les Knight, a little Australian, completed his tour with 50 and burst the Eder dam before his luck ran out over the Dortmund–Ems canal one night in 1943. The rumbustious 'Trev' Trevor-Roper, with his Oxford accent and Billingsgate vocabulary, was a sergeant gunner at Swinderby before he was commissioned and became Guy Gibson's rear gunner.

Micky Martin, who with Gibson and Leonard Cheshire would be regarded as one of the three great British bomber pilots of the war, transferred to 50 from the Australian 455 Squadron when 455 were posted to Coastal Command. The son of a well-established Australian medical family, Martin had been sent to England early in 1939 to sow his wild oats before settling down to train as a doctor. Single-minded in anything he attempted, he managed to get through a thousand pre-war pounds in eight weeks, much of it on horses – he had ridden in amateur races himself. He then applied to join the RAF as a fighter pilot, and after some bureaucratic problems he was accepted and abandoned his flat in Mayfair for initial flying training. By early 1942 he had completed part of a tour of operations in 455 with his all-Australian crew. Foxlee and Simpson, his gunners, Bob Hay, his bomb-aimer, and Jack Leggo, his navigator, eventually became almost as famous as Martin himself. Aweing English colleagues with their reckless tastes on the ground, they had already made a reputation for brilliance and utter determination in the air. In 1942 Martin was one of a select band of like-minded spirits. By 1945 this wild man was a unique phenomenon. He lived.

Like every squadron in the RAF, 50 also had its private celebrities, known to every man on the station but few outside it, and mostly destined for unmarked graves in Germany. There was Charlie Stone, the tough, flippant former architectural student who was their tame cartoonist; Drew Wymess, married to an enviably beautiful model; Jock Abercrombie, who once flew Ed Murrow to Berlin and brought him home a shaken reporter; Paul Crampton, who suffered every possible mishap and near-disaster as he lurched through his tour; Flash Southgate; Micky Moores; Hughie Everitt, with his unnaturally flawless uniform and crisp salute; the three American gunners in Canadian uniforms who each earned more in a week than 'Beetle' Oxley – Swinderby knew them all intimately.

It is important to stress the extraordinarily high calibre of the human material that came to Bomber Command. The majority had matriculated and would have been at university or working for a bank or insurance company if they were not in the RAF. Their imaginations had recoiled from the prospect of trudging through the war in the infantry, and they had been captured by the vision of flying, the glamour that only faded from the blue uniform as they climbed into their lonely cockpits at dusk.

Ken Owen was a 50 Squadron navigator, one of almost half his sixth form at Pontypridd Grammar School who volunteered for the RAF at the outbreak of war: 'We tended to be the gilded youth of our generation; we belonged to the local tennis and

cricket clubs, and our fathers knew the local bank manager. . .'²
Owen reached Swinderby after the usual tortuous paperchase
through service bureaucracy. He left university at the end of his
first year when he was summoned to attend an aircrew selection
board at Penarth, outside Cardiff. There was a prolonged, searching medical examination which eliminated many of the queue
on the first day as colour-blind, slightly deaf or slow-reflexed.
The next day they sat an intelligence test which emphasized
spatial judgement. In the afternoon they went before an interview
board. A few days later, Owen was among the successful candi-
dates who found themselves summoned by letter to St John's
Wood reception centre in north London. Here, like so many RAF
volunteers through the war, he spent a dreary fortnight among
men falling asleep in rows at lectures on cricket and similar
time-fillers until they were packed off to Elementary Flying
Training School near Carlisle. Owen was washed out of pilot
training within a fortnight, and posted to learn to be a navigator.
At an OTU in Shropshire, he joined a crew and graduated on the
old Blenheim. They reached Swinderby bursting with enthusiasm to get into the air, and were deeply crestfallen when the
flight commander said offhandedly: 'Oh, nobody's going to let
you near an operational aircraft yet', and made them fly day and
night training exercises for a fortnight before they took off on a
trip to Germany.

They flew their first operation to Kassel in a curious daze,
almost euphoric in their sense of unreality. It was bright moonlight and the flak was intense, but their excitement somehow
numbed their fear. It was only afterwards, remembering, looking
ahead to the next time and knowing what was to come, that fear
began to seep in. Over the North Sea their feet froze while they
sweated profusely under their arms. A few trips later, over the
Dortmund–Ems canal, their rear gunner Jackie Smith suddenly
shouted: 'Corkscrew port!' and the aircraft shook as the cannon
shells hammered home from the German fighter. When they
pulled out of the dive and found themselves alone, there was still
silence from the rear gunner. Owen felt his way aft. Jackie Smith
with his curly hair and big black eyes lay hunched over his guns,
dead.

For the rest of the crew, there was no more excitement in flying operations, only the grim sense of a job to be done from which there was no honourable escape. The early weeks of 1942 passed in a round of mining sorties, blind groping over Germany in impossible weather, and the abortive efforts to find and sink the *Scharnhorst* and *Gneisenau* in the Channel on their break-out from Brest on 12 February. It was a routine of its own with no sense of the days of the week or any punctuation beyond the next leave or the end of the tour. To a post-war generation, the bomber offensive may conjure up images of terrified German women and children huddled in their shelters as distant British aircraft rained down death from above. To the crews of Bomber Command, Germany was not a place of innocent *gasthausen* and beer cellars where buxom girls smiled and drinkers stamped their feet to the accordion music, but a terrifyingly hostile environment where British airmen died in scores every night. If they thought at all about what lay far beneath them, they imagined the flak gunners and searchlight crews in their coalscuttle helmets pumping up 88 mm shells and those deadly beams of light that made a man feel 'as if reproving fingers were pointing at him, as if he himself were a naughty boy suddenly discovered in the dark of a larder'. Even the most sensitive young Englishman found that 'he felt no guilt or dismay at dropping bombs, simply because his fear entirely submerged any more noble or humane emotion'.[3] A fascinating anonymous report in the Air Ministry files dated 21 June 1942 analysed aircrews' letters opened by the censors: 'They illustrate the effect of airmen's remoteness from their attacks on human beings. Expressions of satisfaction that the Germans are having to undergo the punishment they have hitherto meted out to others are found in almost all letters, but there is an absence of vindictiveness or fanaticism in the phrases used. . .'

Their own nation's propaganda had been perfectly effective in making them visualize the Germany below them as the arsenal of Nazi Europe, the cradle of the Gestapo and the Luftwaffe's pioneer *blitzkriegs*, of Hitler himself and his millions of hysterical arm-raising followers. The opening of Bomber Command's area offensive came at a moment when 30,000 people in Britain had already been killed by German bombing, when vast areas of the City of London, of Coventry and Southampton and a score of other towns lay in ruins. The crews of Bomber Command were very young, and sprung from a generation accustomed to defer to authority. They had been trained and ordered to fly to Germany and release their bombload at a given point. They were told that by doing so they were making a vital contribution to the war effort. With great fear in most of their hearts, they went out each night to do no more and no less than they had been ordered. The notion of killing German civilians severally or in bulk troubled only a tiny handful.

One of the first proposals to reach Sir Arthur Harris in the days after he took up his post at High Wycombe in February 1942 came from the Foreign Office. They wished to revive the old idea of proscription: to name publicly, on the radio, twenty German towns that would be subjected to saturation attack by Bomber Command, and hope for panic among the population, a mass exodus of refugees, and a rising tide of terror across the Third Reich. But whatever Harris's long-term plans for Germany's cities, he understood that Bomber Command as yet possessed quite inadequate resources for the sort of wholesale destruction that the Foreign Office wanted. He needed time, and he had no intention of encouraging the Germans to concentrate their defences around preordained targets. In the months to come, the most effective contribution that Bomber Command could make would be to divert resources from Germany's offensive war effort to the defence of her own cities. To provoke this, Harris proposed to skirmish across the widest possible front.

But as Bomber Command fought off its critics, and most especially the demands of the Royal Navy for transfers of aircraft that would have caused its virtual dissolution, Harris also knew that his forces needed some spectacular successes. In his early months at High Wycombe, he stage-managed a succession of operations which, whatever their strategic shortcomings, were brilliantly successful public relations efforts for the bomber offensive. On 9 March he sent 235 aircraft to hit the Renault works at Billancourt, producing 14,000 trucks a year for the *Wehrmacht*. They attacked in a new pattern, led by a wave of flare-droppers, followed by a wave of bombers carrying maximum incendiary loads to fire the centre of the target, followed in turn by the main force with high-explosives. It was another step on the path towards evolving a target-making routine, that would shortly be followed by a development codenamed *Shaker*, which sought tó exploit *Gee* as a blind-marking aid in the leading aircraft. 470 tons of bombs were dropped on Billancourt. When the photographs of the Renault works came in the next morning, they were hailed as a triumph. 'All aircraft bombed the primary,' exulted 50 Squadron record book. The concentration of bombs around the aiming-point was judged exceptional. Immediate post-raid euphoria was dampened somewhat when the final damage assessments were in a few weeks later, suggesting that the plant had lost less than two months' production. But by then Harris's forces had moved on to greater things.

On 28 March, 234 aircraft attacked the old north German Hanse town of Lübeck. In the weeks following his arrival at High Wycombe, while Harris sent his aircraft to grope through the haze over Essen and other cities of the Ruhr in obedience to the February Air Ministry directive, he had been searching for an area target that they could find, strike and utterly destroy. 'I wanted my crews to be well "blooded", as they say in foxhunting, to have a taste of success for a change,'[4] he said. Lübeck was on the coast and thus a relatively simple navigation problem. It was lightly defended and had not even been incorporated in the major German civil defence schemes because it seemed an unimportant target. But it was on the Air Ministry's February list. Above all, as had been pointed out by Bomber Command's town-planning advisers, it was an old, closely-packed medieval town that would burn far better than the spacious avenues of any modern metropolis. Lübeck was built 'more like a fire-lighter than a human habitation', to quote Harris. 'The inclusion of such a relatively unimportant place as Lübeck, which happened to be especially inflammable, in the target lists', remark the official historians, 'showed the extent . . . to which a town might become a target mainly because it was operationally vulnerable.'[5] Lübeck, then, did not attract the attention of the bombers because it was important, but became important because it could be bombed.

The attack was led by ten Wellingtons equipped with *Gee*,

which laid flares over the city. They were succeeded by a wave of forty fire-raising aircraft loaded with incendiaries. Then came the main force, armed with incendiaries and the huge 4,000-lb high-explosive 'cookies' that were to become the central weapon of the new generation of heavy bombers. They struck at very low level, in clear skies. The raid was an overwhelming success. The *Gee* aircraft found the target, the incendiaries created huge fires, and the old town of Lübeck was no more. 1,425 houses were totally destroyed and 1,976 badly damaged, 312 people were killed. 12 aircraft were lost of 191 that claimed to have attacked. Of the six aircraft that took part from 50 Squadron, apart from one which returned early with technical trouble, the squadron record book noted almost unprecedentedly that 'all aircraft were successful in the task'. The Ministry of Economic Warfare in London estimated that Lübeck would take six or seven weeks to resume full industrial production. The bombers' achievement was hailed as a personal victory for the leadership of Sir Arthur Harris.

Bomber Command had begun to establish the emphasis on concentration that was to dominate the offensive – aircraft seeking to bomb within the shortest possible space of each other, saturating the German defences and fire-fighting system. Timing over the target had become vital. Routeing across the North Sea to surprise the night-fighters was developing into an art. The days of individual attack 'by guess and by God' were ending. But it was still difficult to assess the full potential of *Gee*, because the hundred or so crews who were now equipped with the device were taking time to learn to use it effectively. The navigator operated the set from a receiver mounted to the right of his table behind the pilot. By timing the radio pulses received from three English ground stations whose signals appeared as lines on a cathode ray tube, he could determine the aircraft's position on charts marked with special *Gee* grids. Accuracy depended heavily on individual proficiency and it was clear from the continuing attacks on the Ruhr that the device was not in fact precise enough to become a blind-bombing system. But *Gee* was a vast improvement on Dead Reckoning, and added greatly to the confidence of the crews.

At Swinderby that spring, however, enthusiasm for the delights of the new navigational aid was qualified by dismay at exchanging their Hampdens for Manchesters. Initially, everybody was excited by the prospect of the new aircraft with its vastly more sophisticated equipment and seven-man crew – two pilots, navigator, bomb-aimer, wireless-operator, mid-upper and rear gunners. Then the first reports seeped in of the unreliability and lack of power in the Vulture engines, the poor rate of climb and lack of ceiling. The Manchester could not, in fact, reach the Hampden's fully loaded maximum height of 20,000 feet. Tolley Taylor, one of 50's sergeant pilots, took his new aircraft for a spin and came back to report that it was 'ideal for going out to lunch': comfortable, properly heated at last after the icy Hampden, pleasant to fly. But apart from lack of performance, its weak undercarriage punished heavy landings by instant collapse. Under each engine nacelle ran a Y-shaped coolant pipe that proved lethally vulnerable to local shrapnel bursts. The squadron's aircraft serviceability rate fell dramatically. But until the new Lancaster reached them later in the year, the Manchester was all that there was. They set themselves to learn how to get the best out of it.

After the usual assortment of 'Gardening' operations and desultory raids on the Ruhr and some of the less dangerously defended German cities, towards the end of April they were committed to the second of Harris's devastating eradication attacks, on the north German coastal town of Rostock. The ingredients were the same as for Lübeck: a lightly defended tinderbox old city. It was a seven-hour round trip, well beyond *Gee* range. The force was divided, part being directed to attack the city itself, others the Heinkel aircraft factory beyond the southern suburbs.

This time the attack was continued over four nights. On the first two, 23 and 24 April, results were disappointing. But the third and fourth raids, by 128 and 107 aircraft respectively, were greeted at High Wycombe as triumphs to match the destruction of Lübeck. The centre of Rostock was left ablaze. 50 Squadron were among the contingent from 3 and 5 Groups briefed to attack the Heinkel works at low level. Oxley assured them at briefing that they were due for another walkover against negligible defences. In reality, the Germans had brought up every flak gun they could muster from the length of north Germany by the third night. The defences were fierce. But when the photographs were analysed the next day, the crews were informed that they had staged one of the most accurate precision attacks of the war. Goebbels declared almost hysterically: 'Community life in Rostock is almost at an end.' The Ministry of Economic Warfare reported: 'It seems little exaggeration to say that Rostock has for the time being ceased to exist as a going concern.' Thousands of people fled in panic from the blazing ruins, public buildings were levelled. The surrounding towns and villages became vast temporary refugee camps.

At 50 Squadron, there was another verse for the intelligence officer's long epic poem, set to the tune of Noel Coward's 'Mad Dogs and Englishmen':

When the sirens moan to awake Cologne
  They shiver in their shoes;
In the Berlin street they're white as sheets
  With a tinge of Prussian blues;
In Rostock the Wardens knock and yell 'Put Out That Light'
  When Hampdens from Swinderby go out in the moonlight, out in the
    moonlight, out on a moonlight night.[6]

'Thus, by the end of April 1942,' wrote the official historian, 'Bomber Command, under the vigorous leadership of Air Marshal Harris, had shown, not only to Britain's Allies, but also to her enemies the tremendous potential power of the long-range heavy bomber force.'[7]

But they add immediately, almost in contradiction, that Bomber Command 'had yet to win a major victory against a major target'. German production in both Lübeck and Rostock returned to normal with astonishing speed. Far from losing the six to seven weeks' output estimated by the Ministry of Economic Warfare, Lübeck was operating at between 80 and 90 per cent of normal within days, and even the severely damaged Heinkel factory made a miraculous recovery within weeks. If the destruction of the two Hanse towns had been a test of Bomber Command's technique for firing cities, it had also been a forewarning – albeit unknown in London or High Wycombe – of the extraordinary resistance of industrial plant to bombardment. Only the medieval hearts of Lübeck and Rostock lay irrevocably dead and still, rotting in their own remains.

But Sir Arthur Harris exploited publicity brilliantly to further his policies. The attacks on Lübeck and Rostock had been blazoned across Britain. Now, in May 1942, Harris conceived a further, extraordinarily imaginative stroke: a force of one thousand British bombers, the greatest concentration of air power in the history of the world, would attack a single German city in a single night.

There was, of course, no military magic about the figure of a thousand aircraft. It was the potential effect on popular imagination, on the politicians and the Americans and Russians, that fascinated Whitehall. Portal grasped the beauty of 'The 1,000 Plan' at once, and gave Harris his full support to muster this enormous force, double the strength of Bomber Command's front-line squadrons. The Prime Minister, with his great sense of theatre, was won over immediately. Only the Admiralty, in the midst of the Battle of the Atlantic, were exasperated by such gimmicky enterprises as they struggled to fight their convoys through. The First Sea Lord absolutely refused to allow Coastal Command aircraft to be diverted to the operation. Harris was compelled to raise his force almost entirely from his own squadrons at maximum effort, and from his Operational Training Units. It was a remarkable logistical achievement that, on the night of 30 May 1942, 1,046 Bomber Command aircraft took off for Cologne. They had been crowded on to the stations of eastern England, where ground crews worked around the clock to bring the training aircraft to operational standard and staff briefed OTU pupils and instructors. Only at the last moment did the weather determine that Cologne rather than Hamburg was the target. At his headquarters at High Wycombe, Harris had listened to the forecast in silence. Then, with his unerring eye for drama, his gave his orders:

The C-in-C moved at last. Slowly he pulled an American cigarette carton from his pocket, and, flicking the bottom with his thumb, selected the protruding Lucky Strike . . . He continued to stare at the charts and then slowly his forefinger moved across the continent of Europe and came to rest on a town in Germany . . . He turned to the SASO, his face still expressionless:

'The 1,000 Plan tonight.'

His finger was pressing on Cologne.[8]

50 Squadron put up seventeen aircraft that night. At briefing, when the CO announced that there would be more than a thousand aircraft over the target, there was a moment of awed silence. They were alarmed by the prospect of collision, but they were told that Bomber Command's operational research scientists had computed that statistically there should be no more than two aircraft colliding in the target area. Somebody piped up: 'That's fine – but do they know which two?' and the gale of tense laughter passed into the legend of the bomber offensive. Then they walked out into the dusk of a beautiful summer evening, and took off through clear skies for Cologne.

They attacked in three waves, led by the Wellingtons of 3 Group. Almost uniquely, 3 Group's AOC, Air Vice-Marshal 'Jackie' Baldwin, whom we last saw writing the post-mortem report on the Wilhelmshaven raid two and a half years earlier, flew in person as a passenger in one of his own aircraft. Senior officers were generally forbidden to fly on 'ops' for common-sense security reasons, although this dangerously increased their isolation from the realities of war over Germany. Behind 3 Group came the Stirlings, and last of all the Manchesters and Lancasters of 5 Group, for in these days the 'heavies' were usually left to bring up the rear on the theory that they were best able to withstand punishment over the thoroughly awakened defences. But on the night of 30 May, crews in the later waves crossed northern Germany, skirting the heavy flak around München-Gladbach, unable to accept the reality of the vast red glow in the sky ahead of them. Some crews thought that a great forest or heath must have caught fire, others that the Germans had created an enormous dummy fire to draw the bombers. Only as they drew near did they perceive the incredible truth, that this was the city of Cologne, apparently ablaze from end to end.

Micky Martin was due over the target forty-five minutes after

H-Hour. From miles away, he could see the huge fires lighting the sky ahead, dwarfing the pathetic flicker of flak and searchlights. Martin came in low at 4,000 feet, his crew gazing on the glowing red core of the city, broken by the silver thread of the Rhine, the shimmering white spangles of blazing incendiaries, the great silhouette of the cathedral, its twin towers still lingering amidst the miles of rubble around the Rhine bridge. Many of the flak batteries had run out of ammunition, for transport could no longer cross the city from the dumps to the guns. Searchlights were meandering wildly like drunken men. Some pilots felt as if their own aircraft were on fire with the city, as the red glow danced up and down on their wings. Three times Martin swung over Cologne awed, like so many airmen that night, by the devastation below. They had never seen anything remotely like it. Between 0047 and 0225 that morning, 3,330 houses were utterly destroyed, more than 2,000 badly damaged, more than 7,000 partly damaged. 12,000 fires raged among the breached water mains, severed power cables, exploded gas mains and wrecked telephone system. 36 factories had been totally destroyed, 70 more badly damaged, more than 200 partially damaged. The docks and railway system had been savaged, the tram system put totally out of action for a week and dislocated for months to come. 85 soldiers and members of civil-defence teams had been killed along with 384 civilians. Almost 5,000 people required first aid. 45,000 people had lost their homes.

It was a mere token of the destruction Bomber Command would achieve in 1943 and 1944, indeed the real damage to Cologne proved astonishingly slight in relation to the forces employed. But in 1942 it seemed to the airmen that Britain had achieved the power to unleash Armageddon. Micky Martin hesitated before deciding where it was still worth dropping bombs, and finally let them fall across the battered railway station. The crew chattered excitedly on the intercom. They would see many such urban funeral pyres in the next three years, but no man who was there ever forgot this baptism at Cologne.

Tolley Taylor's was one of the few aircraft which had the ill luck to be hit that night. Running in to bomb at 12,000 feet, shrapnel struck the starboard engine, setting it on fire. He pressed the feathering button to shut off power, and after a frightening half-minute falling steeply through the sky, the fire went out and he regained control at around 9,000 feet. 'Stand by to bale out,' he ordered. The gunners slipped out of their turrets, the hatches plummeted away from the aircraft and a rush of air swept through the fuselage. As they turned out of the target, Taylor peered at his gauges. They were losing height and could cruise at barely 110 mph. But they were still flying. They might make it. He ordered the crew to free every ounce of spare weight. They began to hurl out guns, ammunition, armour plate, the Elsan portable toilet – anything movable whirled away into the slip-stream as they staggered painfully across the Channel. After more than six hours in the air they forced landed at Tempsford, the base of the Special Duties squadrons who operated the cloak-and-dagger flights to occupied Europe. Taylor pushed his way into the debriefing room, full of unaccustomed cubicles and unfamiliar blackened faces. 'Terrific prang! Weren't the fires great?' he said eagerly to the pilot beside him. 'There weren't any fires where I've been,' said the other young man bleakly. Taylor and his crew flew home to Swinderby the next day in a Whitley, in time for the general celebrations.

'OVER 1,000 BOMBERS RAID COLOGNE,' proclaimed *The Times*. 'Biggest Air Attack Of the War. 2,000 Tons of Bombs in 40 Minutes.'

Bomber Command had lost only forty aircraft on the Cologne operation, an acceptable 3.8 per cent of those dispatched, all the more astonishing in view of the number of OTU crews involved. 50 Squadron had lost two Manchesters, one of them piloted by a quiet, diffident young man named Leslie Manser. His aircraft had been badly damaged over the target, and he faced a long, difficult struggle to bring it home. At last it became clear that he could no longer keep it in the air, and he ordered the crew to bale out, waving away the parachute his flight engineer offered him as he fought to hold the Manchester steady while they jumped. He was killed with the aircraft, but was awarded the Victoria Cross for his sacrifice, which was in no way diminished by the fact that it was so frequently required from the pilots of Bomber Command aircraft.

Harris staged two further massive raids, on Essen and Bremen, before it became necessary to dismantle his '1,000' force to avoid serious damage to the training and logistics of the Command. Neither was a significant success. The weather frustrated the Essen raid by 956 aircraft on 1 June – an experiment with the *Shaker* marking technique. German radio did not even recognize Essen as the target, and reported 'widespread raids over western Germany'. 31 aircraft, or 3.2 per cent, were lost. On 25 June, 904 aircraft attacked Bremen, doing some damage to the Focke–Wulf plant at the cost of 44 aircraft, or 4.9 per cent missing, and a further 65 more or less seriously damaged.

Bomber Command settled to spend the remainder of the summer pounding Germany on a wide front, at less spectacular intensity and with results that could not compare with the dramatic devastation of Cologne. But Harris could bide his time now. In four months as Commander-in-Chief, he had established his own reputation; delighted the Prime Minister whose sense of drama matched his own; and made an immense contribution to British propaganda at a time when the nation's fortunes in the Middle and Far East were at their lowest ebb. The British public and their politicians had been generally awed by the scale and vision of power presented by the '1,000' raids. The Prime Minister proclaimed after the bombing of Cologne: 'Proof of the growing power of the British bomber force is also the herald of what Germany will receive city by city from now on.' Harris said: 'We are going to scourge the Third Reich from end to end. We are bombing Germany city by city and ever more terribly in order to make it impossible for her to go on with the war. That is our object; we shall pursue it relentlessly.'

Amidst the terrible scars of the Luftwaffe's blitz on Britain, there is no doubt that the nation derived deep satisfaction from Harris's words and deeds. Unlike some of his service and political masters, he was never a dissembler or a hypocrite. He gave unequivocal notice of his intentions. Whatever criticism may be made of the strategic substance of Harris's campaign, it is essential not to underestimate the power and value to England of his remarkable military showmanship at this, one of the grimmest phases of the war for the Grand Alliance.

Operations

In July 1942, to the relief of 50 Squadron, the Manchesters were retired after their brief and alarming months in service. In their place came the four-engined Avro Lancaster, indisputably the great heavy night-bomber of the Second World War. Pilots have a saying about aircraft: 'If it looks right, it is right.' The Lancaster looked superb, its cockpit towering more than nineteen feet above the tarmac, the sweep of its wings broken by the four Rolls-Royce Merlin engines with their throaty roar like a battery of gigantic lawnmowers. The green and brown earth shadings of the upper surfaces gave way to matt black flanks and undersides, the Perspex blisters glittering from the ceaseless polishing of the ground crews. The pilot sat high in his great greenhouse of a cockpit, the flight engineer beside him – second pilots were scrapped in the spring of 1942 to economize on aircrew. Behind them sat the navigator, bent over his curtained-off table in almost permanent purdah in flight, his work lit by a pinpoint Anglepoise lamp. Behind him sat the wireless operator, his back to the bulk of the main spar between the wings, a waist-high barrier in the midst of the fuselage. The space beyond, in the rear of the aircraft, was clear and roomy when the aircraft left the production line, but as the electronic war intensified, the interior became more and more crowded with equipment: the big, squat case of the *Gee* receiver, linked to the screen beside the navigator; the Distant Reading Compass, wired to a repeater on the pilot's windscreen; the Air Position Indicator gear; the flare chute; the rest bed for a wounded man; the 'tramlines' carrying the long linked belts of machine-gun ammunition to the rear gunner's four Brownings and the two in the mid-upper turret; the Elsan toilet which crews used with acute caution after a 50 Squadron gunner left most of the skin of his backside attached to the frozen seat one icy night over Germany. Beneath the fuselage, the bomb bay lay long and shallow. In the nose, the bomb-aimer stretched behind the perspex blister searching for pinpoints to assist the navigator until they approached the target, or occasionally manned the twin front guns to frighten the light flak gunners on low-level operations. Gunners trained the power-operated Brownings to right and left with a twist of the grips to which their triggers were fitted. The British hydraulic turret was one of the outstanding design successes of the bomber war* although tragically it was fitted with the quite inadequate .303 machine-gun. The last hopes of equipping Bomber Command with .5s, as Harris had demanded for so long, vanished when America entered the war and her own needs eclipsed British hopes of .5 imports from American factories.

The Lancaster inspired affection unmatched by any other British heavy bomber. The Stirling was easier to fly – a gentleman's aircraft, according to Stirling pilots. But its lamentable ceiling made it the first target of every German gunner and night-fighter pilot, provoking the callous cheers of the more fortunate Lancaster crews when they heard at briefings that the clumsy, angular Stirlings would be beneath them. The Halifax was a workhorse of no breeding and alarming vices in the air. The British never took to the American Flying Fortress, although Bomber Command experimented with a handful in 1941 and 1942; its virtues would only become apparent in the hands of the Americans with their lavish supplies of aircraft and men, when the day-bombing offensive came into its own at the beginning of 1944.

But the Lancaster, cruising at 216 mph, intensely durable and resistant to punishment by the standards of the lightly armoured night-bombers, beautiful to the eye and carrying the bombload of two Flying Fortresses at a ceiling of 20,000 feet, ranks with the Mosquito and the Mustang among the great design successes of the war. 50 Squadron, like the rest of Bomber Command, took to it at once. Throughout 1942, while the numerical strength of Harris's forces expanded scarcely at all, the effectiveness of his

*In 1944 the distinguished scientist Freeman Dyson, now at the Princeton Institute for Advanced Studies, was working in the Operational Research Section of Bomber Command. He argued strongly that gun turrets should be abandoned altogether, adding 50 mph to the Lancaster's speed. Dyson was deeply impressed by his own research, which he claimed showed that, contrary to popular myth, experienced crews had no better chance of surviving an operation than novices. It was a matter of pure chance which aircraft were shot down. The basis of his powerful indictment of Bomber Command, published in 1979 in the *New Yorker* magazine, is that the leaders of the RAF showed no interest in this or any other evidence of operational realities that conflicted with air force doctrine.

aircraft and equipment was being steadily transformed. In May 1942 there were 214 Wellingtons, 62 Halifaxes and 29 Lancasters among the front line of 417 aircraft. By January 1943 there were only 128 Wellingtons left, and 104 Halifaxes and 178 Lancasters among the total of 515 first-line aircraft. In the interval the bomb-carrying capacity of the Command had increased by more than a third.

The mood of this new Bomber Command was utterly different from that of 1939. Most squadrons were no longer billeted amidst the solid brick comforts of the pre-war airfields, but were learning to live with Nissen huts and chronic mud, to fly from hastily concreted strips now carpeting eastern England, as the island was transformed into a gigantic aircraft-carrier. The old spirit of the officers' mess as home, the idea of the squadron as a family, had been replaced by that of a human conveyor belt, a magic lantern show of changing faces. Bomber Command had dickered briefly with committing crews to tours of 200 operational hours, but this stopped abruptly when it was found that some men flew home with their wheels down in order to prolong 'ops' to their limit. Now there was a thirty-trip standard before men were posted to notionally less dangerous instructing jobs. Aircrew might operate seven or eight times a month, weather permitting. A first-class CO could create a squadron spirit, but the aircrew had become passing three- or four-month guests on their own stations, leading a parallel yet utterly different life from that of the huge permanent ground-support staff, who might remain at one base year after year, drinking in the same pubs and servicing aircraft in the same hangars.

The aircrew, as befitted men who were statistically not long for this world, spent their last months fattened with whatever comfort wartime England could provide for them, unheard-of luxuries such as extra milk, fruit juice, sugar and real eggs. They were warmed by sun-ray lamps in the medical quarters, dosed with halibut-oil capsules and protected from all but the most essential duties when not flying. The former pressure on non-commissioned aircrew had been lifted. Now they usually occupied their own mess separate from that of non-flying NCOs, and enjoyed much the same comforts and privileges as their commissioned counterparts. Crews drank, womanized, often even went on leave together as a close-knit entity, regardless of individual rank. A commissioned navigator called his sergeant-pilot 'Skipper' in the air without a hint of resentment. They were all too close to death to dicker with formalities over Germany now. Throughout 1942, the loss-rate, including fatal crashes in England, seldom fell much below 5 per cent, one aircraft in twenty on every operation. A crew faced thirty trips. It needed no wizard of odds to read the chances of their mortality, even if each man deep in his heart believed that it would be another's turn until the instant that he plunged headlong from the night sky.

But unlike the days in France a generation earlier, when these men's fathers queued below the red lamps before they went over the top, brothels seldom flourished around the bomber stations. Many aircrew preferred to relax with drink and each other rather than with women. For those who craved female company, local girls, lonely soldiers' wives and station WAAFs found it difficult to refuse boys who were likely to be dead within a month. It was chiefly remarkable, in the almost frenzied celebrations that accompanied a 'stand-down' or a 'good prang' or the end of a crew's tour or somebody getting a 'gong', that so many aircrew went to their fate as innocent as they had emerged from the cradle. A nineteen-year-old who was given his opportunity by a sentimental WAAF still blushes to recall that he turned her down because he had been warned by the medical officer to keep his strength up for operations. A survivor from the crew of a pilot who was awarded a posthumous Victoria Cross for his efforts to save his aircraft over France never forgot that on their last night together, the boy admitted sheepishly that he had never kissed a girl in his life.

By that summer of 1942 the strange inverted timetable of night-bomber operations had become a routine. The crews awoke in their huts as the Lincolnshire ground mists slowly cleared from the runways, and wandered across to the mess for a late breakfast in the patchy sunshine. By 11 a.m., they were playing cricket or lounging on the grass around the flight offices, waiting to hear if operations were 'On' for that night. Some days – the good days – they were at once 'stood down'. They dashed for a bus to Nottingham or piled into their cars, illicitly fuelled with 100-octane aviation spirit. Often – very often – they were ordered to prepare for an 'op' that was cancelled at five, six, seven o'clock after they had dressed and been briefed and their aircraft bombed-up. This they hated most of all, because by evening they had been fighting the battle against fear and anticipation all day, and they had overcome the worst. 'Ops scrubbed' was only an illusory reprieve, because if they did not fly their first or fifth or twentieth trip that night, it would only be waiting for them tomorrow. More often than not, it was the prospect of bad weather over England in the early hours that caused cancellations. There had already been some appalling nights when aircraft crashed all over East Anglia in impossible visibility, and exhausted crews were compelled to abandon their aircraft and bale out over their own bases rather than risk descending to ground level.

If 'ops' were 'on', the armourers began the long, painstaking routine of bombing-up the aircraft. Knowing their fuel and bombload in the morning, crews could quickly assess the rough distance and perhaps the nature of their target. That summer, Harris was still unwilling to commit his force headlong against Berlin or the Ruhr amidst the stiffening German defences. As he waited for more aircraft and the new generation of navigation and bomb-aiming devices, he advanced with caution. 50 Squadron and the rest of Bomber Command made spasmodic trips to Duisburg, Düsseldorf and other Ruhr targets, but generally bombed less perilous and more easily located ones: Bremen, Osnabrück, Kassel, Nuremberg. They were burning thousands of houses and not a few factories, but Harris was biding his time for the punishing attacks on the industrial heart of Germany.

After taking their aircraft for a brief air test before lunch, gazing down at the chequer board of airfields visible in every direction around them in the naked light of day, some crews tried to sleep on the afternoon of an 'op'. Many never succeeded. It was these hours of preparation and expectation that ate into men's courage and nerves as much as anything that was done to them in the air. Many felt that it was the contrast between the rural peace of afternoon England and the fiery horror of early morning Germany that imposed greater strain on bomber crews than the even tenor of discomfort and fear on a warship or in a tank. They had time to remember vividly each earlier trip. They gazed around them at the familiar hangars; the 'erks' – the ground crews – pedalling their bicycles round the perimeter track to the dispersals; the fuel bowsers beside the distant aircraft, silhouetted against the flat horizon. The panorama took on a strange unreality. They were called upon to fly over Germany in the midnight hours when human enterprise and resistance is naturally at its lowest ebb. The very young, under twenty, and the older men over thirty seemed to suffer most, although the latter were often invaluable ballast in a crew. Those in their early twenties seemed able to summon up remarkable reserves of resilience.

After the traditional bacon and eggs in the mess, they went to briefing. The old informality of Hampden days, when a cluster of pilots and navigators assembled around the central table in the Ops Room, had vanished with the coming of the 'heavies'. Now each specialist was independently briefed by his respective squadron chief: signals leader, navigation leader and so on. Then they gathered together, more than a hundred young men, arrayed crew by crew on the bench seats of the Briefing Room facing the central stage, the map still hidden by a curtain until the heart-stopping moment when the CO walked forward and pulled it away to reveal the target. 'Funf', the Swinderby 'Met' man, talked to them about the weather. The Intelligence Officer briefed them about the importance of the target from notes sent down to him by High Wycombe. He gave them the latest information on the German defences. The 'Kammhuber line', named by the British after the German general who had created it, now reached the length of north Germany, Holland and Belgium. It was almost impossible for a British bomber to avoid. But within its network of interlocking radar-controlled night-fighter and searchlight zones, each 'box' could control only one fighter to one interception at a time. Bomber Command's constantly intensifying 'streaming' technique, pushing the British aircraft along a single course through the defences in the shortest possible time, sought to defeat this outer line of German defences by saturating them. Little was yet known about the new *Lichtenstein* radar mounted in the fighters themselves, although Scientific Intelligence at the Air Ministry was working towards an astonishingly comprehensive picture.

The station commander stood up to wish them luck, and strode out trailing his attendant staff officers. The crews shuffled to their feet, chattering and gathering up maps and notes.

They were a queer conglomeration, these men – some educated and sensitive, some rough-haired and burly, and drawn from all parts of the Empire, Great Britain, Canada, New Zealand and Australia . . . Some of them were humming, some were singing, some were laughing, and others were standing serious and thoughtful. It looked like the dressing room where the jockeys sit waiting before a great steeple chase . . .[9]

They stripped themselves of personal possessions and gathered up parachutes, escape kits, mascots. Swinderby's station commander chatted easily to them as they prepared. Sam Patch was a popular 'station master', at his relaxed best talking to crews, never above stopping his car to offer a crowd of NCOs a lift as they walked back from the local pub on a stand-down night. Waiting for transport to the dispersal was among the worst moments of the night. Stan Gawler, one of the rear gunners, was always loaded down with dolls and charms with which he decorated his turret. One night he forgot them, and his crew had a nightmare hour over Hamburg. Peggy Grizel, a young WAAF Intelligence Officer, never failed to be moved by the way in which each man fought down his fear. Henry Mossop, a Lincolnshire farm boy, lay calmly on the grass looking out into the dusk, smoking his pipe. A young New Zealander sat down with anybody who would listen and talked about his home. Macfarlane, one of 'Beetle' Oxley's successors as CO, insisted on having 'The Shrine of St Cecilia' played on the mess gramophone, and after the record was broken one afternoon, dashed into Lincoln to buy another copy before operating that night.

At the dispersals, they lay smoking on the grass until the time came to swing themselves up into the fuselage. There was a familiar stink of kerosene, with which the erks washed out the dirt of every trip. As the sky darkened around them, the pilot and flight engineer ran up the great Merlins one by one. The pilot slid back his window and gave 'thumbs up' to the ground crew by the battery cart. Port-outer: Contact. He lifted the cover from the starter button and pressed it down, waiting for the puff of grey smoke shot with flame, the cough and roar as it fired. At last, with all four engines running, he checked the oil pressure and tested the throttles, checked revolutions and magneto drop. The navigator spread his maps. The gunners crammed themselves into the turrets they could not leave for the next six or seven hours.

The rear gunner faced the loneliest and coldest night of all. Gazing back into the darkness behind the aircraft, he often felt that he inhabited another planet from the tight little cluster of aircrew so far forward around the cockpit. Even after electrically heated suits were introduced, they often broke down. Some gunners cut away their turret doors to dispel the nightmare of being trapped when the aircraft was hit – they were wedged impossibly tightly in their flying gear. It was difficult even to move far enough to clear jammed guns with their rubber hammers. There was no chance of wearing a parachute – it was stowed beside them. Some carried a hatchet for a forlorn chance of hacking their way out of a wreck. The cold was intensified by the removal of a square of perspex to provide a central 'clear view panel' to the night sky, an idea pioneered by Micky Martin's gunner, Tammy Simpson, among others. Further forward in the aircraft a powerful heater system had been installed, but there was a perpetual war in most crews about the level at which it was maintained, the wireless operator by the hot-air outlet being roasted, the navigator shivering amidst the draughts further forward.

At the dispersals, the flight-sergeant fitter handed his pilot Form 700 on his clipboard, to sign for the aircraft, then slipped away to the ground. The flight engineer reported: 'Engineer to pilot. Rear hatch closed and secure. OK to taxi.' The pilot signalled to the ground crew to slip the chocks, and closed his window. The wireless operator made a test signal to the Watch Office. 'Receiving you loud and clear. Strength Niner.' All over the airfield in the dusk, the Lancasters broke into movement. Twenty tons of aircraft, perhaps five tons of fuel and five more of bombs, bumped slowly round the perimeter to the end of the runway.

The control officer flashed a green ray for a split second, which was the signal that this plane was designated for take-off [wrote an American spectator as he watched for the first time a Bomber Command take-off for Germany]. Its roaring grew louder and louder as it dragged its heavy tail towards the starting point like a slow, nearly helpless monster. About twenty yards away we could just discern a vast dinosaurish shape; after a moment, as if stopping to make up its mind . . . it lumbered forward, raising its tail just as it passed us, and turning from something very heavy and clumsy into a lightly poised shape, rushing through the night like a pterodactyl. At this instant, a white light was flashed upon it and a Canadian boy from Vancouver who was standing beside me, put down its number and the moment of departure. It vanished from sight at once and we stood staring down the field, where in a few seconds a flashing green light announced that it had left the ground . . .

A great calm settled over the place as the last droning motors faded out in the distance and we all drove back to the control room where a staff hang onto the instruments on a long night vigil . . . I went to sleep thinking of the . . . youngsters I had seen, all now one hundred and fifty miles away, straining their eyes through a blackness relieved only by the star-spangled vault above them.[10]

A critical measure of a squadron's efficiency was its rate of 'Early Returns', aircraft which turned back over the North Sea with technical trouble. It was always a matter of nice judgement whether pressing on with a jammed turret or malfunctioning oxygen equipment represented courage or foolhardiness. Every crew could expect an Early Return once in a tour. To abort more often suggested accident-proneness or something worse. 50 Squadron had a tradition of pressing on: one night, for instance, an aircraft hit a servicing gantry on take-off. At Swinderby control, they waited for him to request permission to land. Instead there was silence. He simply flew on to complete the trip. Some captains took a vote among the crew whether to turn back. Bill Russell, Oxley's successor as CO, had no patience with the hesitant. One night a sergeant pilot reported from dispersal that he was suffering magneto drop on one engine and could not take off. It was the man's third attack of 'mag drop' in a month. Russell ran down the control tower steps, drove furiously to the Lancaster, and ordered the pilot out. He flew the aircraft to Cologne himself, in his shirtsleeves. The pilot was court-martialled and dismissed from the service.

Every night over the North Sea, after the gunners had fired their test bursts and they had climbed slowly to cruising height and synchronized their engines, the crew would hear the immortal cliché of Bomber Command down the intercom: 'Enemy coast ahead.' The flight engineer checked the aircraft black-out. Henceforth, each man became only a shape in the darkness, each part of the aircraft only recognizable by touch or momentary flash of a penlight torch. The instruments glowed softly. The engines roared distantly through the helmet earpieces. Stale air pumped through the constricting oxygen masks. They watched the gunfire lacing the sky from the flakships off the Dutch coast, the brief flicker of explosions and the pencil cones of searchlights sweeping the darkness. From here to Germany, each pilot had his own conviction how best to survive. Some captains on 50, like Jock Abercrombie, flew straight and level all the way to the target. Some changed their throttle settings constantly or desynchronized their engines. Others, like Micky Martin, weaved or changed course constantly every moment that they were within range of the defences.

To fly a heavy bomber called for quite different skills from those of a fighter pilot. Airmen say that contrary to popular belief, there was no special temperament that equipped one man to fly a Spitfire and another a Lancaster: the job made the man. Pilot trainees who showed outstanding virtuosity in handling an aircraft were generally sent to Fighter Command. Only a handful of men in Bomber Command could throw a four-engined bomber through the sky with absolute assurance, or indeed wished to. Most wartime pilots, even after two years' training found it a strain coping with the technical problems of taking off, flying and landing a heavy aircraft in one piece, before they began to come to terms with the enemy. It is essential to understand that flying a bomber required a good measure of brute physical strength. Hundreds of aircraft were lost in mishaps in which the enemy played no part: freak weather, collision, bombs falling on friendly aircraft below, botched landings by tired young men. The first six trips accounted for a disproportionate share of casualties. Those who survived that long became statistically slightly more at risk again only in mid-tour, when they began to think that they knew it all, and on their last trips when they had grown tired and stale.

To survive, brilliant flying was less important than an immense capacity for taking pains, avoiding unnecessary risks, and maintaining rigid discipline in the air. Canadians were highly regarded as individual aircrew, but incurred intense criticism as complete crews, as squadrons, as (eventually) their own No. 6 Group, because they were thought to lack the vital sense of discipline. A 50 Squadron gunner who was sent one night as a replacement with an all-Canadian crew came home terrified after circling the target while they sang 'Happy Birthday To You' down the intercom to their 21-year-old pilot. Later in the war, 6 Group became notorious for indifference to radio-telephone instructions from the Master Bomber over the target.

A pilot such as Micky Martin was daring in the air, but also very careful. He and his crew checked every detail of their own aircraft before take-off, far more meticulously than routine demanded. Martin personally polished every inch of perspex on his cockpit canopy. At 10,000 feet over Germany at night, a fighter was no more than a smear at the corner of a man's eye until it fired. Martin studied the techniques for improving his own vision, moving his head backwards and forwards constantly, to distinguish between the reality and the optical illusion beyond the windscreen. He taxied the aircraft to the butts before each trip so that his gunners could realign their Brownings. Every man who survived Bomber Command agrees that luck was critical: however brilliant a flier, he was vulnerable to the Russian roulette of a predicted flak barrage. But a careful crew could increase their chance of survival a hundred per cent.

It was difficult for so many young men who flew perhaps a dozen trips without a glimpse of a fighter, without being struck by flak, without becoming lost: operations began to take on the tedium of an eternal drive on a darkened motorway. Reflexes numbed, vigilance flagged, because this is human nature. Careful pilots banked gently every few moments to enable their gunners to search the sky beneath the aircraft. No good captain tolerated chatter on the intercom: it was sacred, reserved for the paralysing second when the rear gunner shouted: 'Fighter port! Corkscrew port – now!' Then they would heel into the mad, stomach-churning routine of fighter evasion, the gunner who could see the enemy directing the pilot who could not, the aircraft screaming in torment, the smell of vomit so often wafting up from a navigator or bomb-aimer overcome by fear and the violence of their movement, the fuselage shuddering as the gunners fired. The first seconds were critical: so often, if the fighter was observed he would break away to seek easier meat. A pilot's confidence in throwing his aircraft through the sky was vital. Some, in their fear of causing the bomber to break up, banked cautiously and died. Others – the ones who lived – recognized that the danger of a wing breaking off was nothing to that of a fighter's cannon. Steep bank to port, full left rudder, fall sideways for a thousand feet, wrench the aileron controls to starboard, soar into a climbing turn to the right, then opposite aileron and dive again...

Anyone who had not done plenty of practice flying by instruments might well have been terrified by the result of all this. The speed varied between 200 and 90 mph, the altimeter lost and regained 1,000 feet, the rate of descent and ascent varied between 1,000 and 2,000 feet a minute, the horizon level just went mad and the rate of turn and skid needles varied from a maximum to port to a maximum to starboard every half minute. The physical exertion for each pull at the bottom of each dive was about equal to pulling on a pair of oars in a boat race.[11]

Micky Martin and other highly skilled pilots almost cartwheeled their Lancasters, banking savagely on to one wingtip as they raced the upper engines and cut the lower. They knew that the bomber's gunners had precious little chance of shooting down a well-armoured German fighter, that almost their only hope of survival lay in escape. Some crews believed that it was best not to fire their own guns until they were certain the fighter had seen them, lest they betray their position. The true value of the gunners was as look-outs. If they saw the German first, they could survive. If they did not, they were probably dead men. Gunners smeared lanolin on their necks to fight the aches and soreness of constantly scanning the sky. They were taught never to gaze into the flames of a target, which destroyed their night vision. They took caffeine tablets to stay awake and faced instant dismissal from most crews if they were caught dozing. Yet boredom, monotony, the corrosion of cold and fatigue were deadly enemies. Again and again, a bomber was surprised.

One night in December 1942, 50 Squadron were on a harassing raid over north Germany, part of a drive to force the Germans to spread their defences more thinly by launching pinprick attacks on scores of small towns, an assignment which uncharacteristically troubled some crews. Norman Goldsmith's crew were armed to the teeth – the flight engineer was carrying a Thompson gun – because they had been ordered to go in low and beat up anything in sight. 'Mitch' Mitchell, the wireless operator, was playing the new game of *Tinsel* – tuning to German night-fighter frequencies and then blasting the ether with engine noise from a microphone specially fitted in one of the Lancaster's nacelles. He was bent over his headphones enjoying the rage of the German controller when he was hammered on the shoulder by the mid-upper gunner. He looked out of the astrodome to see the starboard wing on fire. A German fighter had slid up beneath the fuselage and fired one deadly burst, badly wounding the rear gunner and injuring the mid, mortally damaging the aircraft, 'Bale out,' ordered Goldsmith. Mitchell and Jim Farrell, the Australian navigator, were the only survivors who reached the sodden fields of north Holland alive.

As they cruised across Europe, most pilots worked to gain height, bouncing the aircraft upwards in precious thermals, winning every foot of sky they could put between themselves and the enemy, so often invisible far below the cloud layers. Martin was exceptional in that he preferred to go in low, skimming the waves so that his Lancaster came home coated in salt spray and dirt, running along roads and railway lines to dodge the enemy balloon barrage, although on one notable night he flew home from Kassel with a balloon cable streaming from his wing. Little Toby Foxlee blazed the front guns at German flak the moment the enemy opened fire; his belts were loaded with continuous tracer instead of the usual one in five, as a simple 'frightener' to throw the gunners' nerve. Martin liked to operate at around 4,000 feet, because this was just beyond the height at which German light flak was effective, and yet low for the heavier 88-mms. He would climb to bomb, then slip back to deck level for the long run home. For most crews, however, height represented safety, and they valued every foot of it. They had learned that it was vital to stay in the stream. If they were a minute or two early approaching the target, they flew a dogleg to lose time. If they were late, they pushed up their revs as much as they dared. A lone aircraft was instantly vulnerable.

Every pilot responded differently to sudden crisis. Martin found that he became ice-cold. He and his crew had achieved an almost telepathic mutual understanding and instinct for danger. Others were less fortunate. Tolley Taylor had a flight engineer who became literally paralysed with fear on his first trip to Essen, and clung motionless to the window-catch from the enemy coast to touch-down, compelling Taylor to cope with the fuel system as well as flying the aircraft. Stewart Harris, a navigator, fought down his terror during a bad flak barrage over Wilhelmshaven by gobbling his flying rations; the following night he collapsed, in delayed reaction, at a pub in Lincoln, although he operated again the night after. 'Are you hurt, Philips?' 'King' Cole asked his flight engineer, as the man sat pale beside him after a near-miss. 'No, sir, but I'm very frightened. . .' Even some pilots were known to become numbed into momentary paralysis by a night-fighter attack. Every good captain checked his crew every few minutes of every trip: 'Rear gunner OK?' 'Yes, skip.' 'Mid-upper OK? 'OK, skipper', and so on. But there were many bad captains and bad crews, and they died still ignorant of the follies of omission that had killed them.

At the climax of every trip came the long run-up to bomb, through the dazzling web of lights, the flicker of flak, the curling, twisting pattern of tracer, the glow of fires and incendiaries in all the colours of the rainbow. The bomb-aimer lay in the nose over his Mark XIV bombsight, wired to the primitive grey computer box beside him. The navigator and wireless operator frequently abandoned their cubby-holes to join the gunners searching the sky for fighters at this most vulnerable moment of all. The whole crew held their breath as the bomb-aimer called off 'Left . . . left . . . right a bit . . . steady.' Then there was the sudden 'twang' from beneath them, and 'Bombs gone' from the nose. 'Was this fighting?' V. M. Yeates had asked himself as he released his bombs over the German lines in France a quarter of a century before. 'There was no anger, no red lust, no struggle, no straining muscles and sobbing breath; only the slight movement of levers and the rattle of machine-guns. . .'[12] For a few seconds they held course until the photo-flash fell from the aircraft and exploded to light the sky for their aiming-point picture, without which the trip could not count towards their tour. Then they swung away from the glowing, spitting shambles below and thanked God once more, unless there had been some heart-stopping hang-up, the bomb-aimer had been dazzled at a critical moment, or they had been compelled to bank sharply to avoid a converging aircraft. Then they would hear an unhappy voice announce: 'We're going round again.' With the exception of a few phenomena like Martin, no man circled a target more than once in 1942 unless from dire necessity. By that summer, one crew in three was bombing within three miles of the aiming-point. It was not enough, yet it was a vast improvement on 1941.

1942 was the year in which the dominant threat to a bomber over Germany became the night-fighter rather than the flak gun. The British computed that there were now 12,000 heavy anti-aircraft guns and 3,276 searchlights defending Germany. The Luftwaffe's flak units had almost doubled their strength from 255,000 men in 1940 to 439,000 in 1942. Flak damaged many aircraft and drove the bombers to fly high, but it destroyed few. Fighters, on the other hand, seldom sent a damaged victim home. The overwhelming majority of British bombers attacked were shot down. In 1942, German night-fighter strength rose from 162 to 349 aircraft, almost all Ju88s and Me110s. Over the target the bomber crews had learned to welcome heavy flak, for it indicated that the fighters were elsewhere. Creeping fear grew on the nights when the target was lit by scores of searchlights, yet the guns were silent. On these nights, the British knew that somewhere in the darkness fighters were searching the sky for a hapless Lancaster, or tuning the *Lichtenstein* radar sets to catch them in their grasp.

Crews suffered some strange illusions about means of saving themselves. One was that switching on their IFF – Identification Friend or Foe transmitter, controlled by a six-position dial above the wireless operator's head and designed to provide a recognition blip for British radar on the way home – somehow jammed the German searchlight control system if they were coned. Since late 1941, Dr R. V. Jones and his colleagues of Scientific Intelligence had been urging Bomber Command that not only was IFF profitless over Germany, but that like all transmissions that could be monitored by the enemy, its use represented a positive threat to bombers' safety. Yet High Wycombe remained unconvinced, arguing that if pilots believed that IFF benefited them, their illusions should be cherished for the sake of morale. 50 Squadron's signals leader was still teaching the technique in 1942, and most of the squadron's aircrew accepted it implicitly. It was the same with 'Scarecrows', the shells the crews believed that the Germans fired to frighten them, resembling an exploding bomber. There were no such projectiles as 'Scarecrows'.What the crews saw were indeed exploding British aircraft. But to this day many aircrew will not accept this.

The crew of a stricken aircraft had a one-in-five chance of escaping alive. Fighting the G-forces of a diving or spiralling, uncontrollable descent, they had to ditch the hatches, reach their parachutes and somehow struggle clear before the bomber struck the ground. They tried desperately to avoid baling out in the immediate target area, for they had heard too many stories of bomber crews killed by enraged civilians or soldiers, a fate not unknown to Luftwaffe airmen in the London blitz. Luftwaffe men on the ground in Germany often showed astonishing fellow-feeling for baled-out RAF crews, saving them from mobs, treating them with intense kindness. When Stewart Harris of 50 Squadron became a prisoner, he was forced to travel through Düsseldorf with the three men of his Luftwaffe escort. The city had suffered appallingly at the hands of Bomber Command. The mother of one of the escort came to meet them at the station. Her own home and the factory in which she worked had already been destroyed. Yet she brought four packed lunches.

It was not unknown for Bomber Command crews to take occasional passengers on operations. Some were authorized – station commanders or reporters. Others were quite illicit – members of ground crew and in extremely isolated cases, WAAfs. The Germans sought to make propaganda capital out of an episode early in 1942 when they claimed to have found a dead WAAF in a shot-down Stirling.[13] It was often far more frightening to be a passenger, without the pressure of duty to suppress fear, than to be one of a crew. One night Micky Martin took Group-Captain Sam Patch, Swinderby's station commander, on a trip to the Ruhr. Patch stood behind Martin's seat. Crossing the Belgian coast, Martin scented night-fighters – the searchlights were wavering uncertainly, a sure sign that they were seeking to avoid their own aircraft. He saw a line of tracer curving across the sky to port. 'If you turn round and look now, you'll probably see an aircraft blow up,' he said to Patch. Sure enough, on the German's third burst a few seconds later, a Wellington exploded. Every crew became hardened to seeing others go down, and felt that guilty surge of gratitude that it was another man's turn to die. Martin changed course to fly south of Liege and avoid the night-fighters. The diversion brought them late over the target, which was already burning fiercely. Martin circled three times at his customary 4,000 feet, terrifying yet fascinating Patch. When they came home, he said that he had never before understood how a crew could be frivolous, drunken, apparently irresponsible on the ground, yet utterly close-knit and professional in the air.

In those days, they still came home by their own route, instead of being locked into the stream all the way out and back, as they were a year later. Crews were tired now, aching and stiff and stale. They drank their coffee and ate their flying rations, but those who wished to remain alive did not relax in their cockpit or turrets. If the pilot could not resist the urge to urinate, he did so into the tin below his seat – he could never leave the controls. The wireless operator, in his shirtsleeves by the heater, might read a book or filter music from his radio down the intercom if the captain allowed, but the navigator was still checking fixes and peering into his *Gee* scope, which from August 1942 began to flicker with the green 'grass' of German jamming as soon as the aircraft crossed the enemy coast. The flight engineer juggled the fuel tanks, computing consumption constantly to check the notoriously inaccurate petrol gauges. Some captains allowed crews to smoke, puffing out of the edge of their oxygen masks: Tolley Taylor got through a steady forty cigarettes on every outward trip, twenty more coming home. Most pilots rigidly discouraged the practice, and rear gunners who dragged surreptitiously to ease their lonely vigil came home with their boots stuffed with fag-ends to conceal the evidence.

By now, approaching the Channel homewards, some pilots were nursing damaged engines or flak-torn controls, losing height over France and struggling to get across the sea before forced landing at Manston or Woodbridge, the bombers' emergency strips. In some aircraft, in the darkness of the fuselage a bomb-aimer or wireless operator stooped over the body of a wounded gunner on the rest-bed, doing their pathetic best to repair terrible wounds made by shrapnel or cannon fire with morphia and sulphanilamide, by the feeble light of a torch. Others had thrown out everything movable, yet were still drifting helplessly downwards towards the North Sea or the Channel. They had a good chance of surviving ditching, a fair chance of being spotted if their navigator could still take a fix and their wireless operator still tap out a Ditching signal. But often they could not give their position, and lingered for hours or days in their dinghy before rescue or death over took them.

The lucky crews, those whose aircraft were still unwounded, glimpsed other bombers going home, and thought about the girls with whom they might be drinking that night, at the Black Bull or the Baron of Beef. They droned on towards Lincolnshire, hoping that for once they would not be stacked waiting to land for half an hour or more, or diverted because a damaged aircraft had collapsed on the runway. An aircraft that crashed in England was never included in Bomber Command's published casualty figures, however many of its crew were killed or wounded, and these added at least 10 per cent to official losses for most of the war.

Their hearts rose at the red wink of the airfield beacon. They heard the comforting thump as the undercarriage locked home, and prayed that no unseen joint in the aircraft's structure had been fatally damaged, to crumple as they landed. Then they were in the circuit, losing height and power as they slipped on to the runway, bumping heavily as their tired pilot let them down with a moment's imprecision, then idling along the black rubber-streaked concrete, switching open the bomb doors and gathering up their equipment. After an interminable night's flying to La Spezia and back, Stewart Harris clambered out of the fuselage and opened his flybuttons with boundless gratitude above the tailwheel. 'God, this is good!' he exclaimed deeply to the shadowy figures beside him in the darkness.

'Nice to see you back, too, Harris,' chuckled Sam Patch, stepping aside to reveal the Group commander behind him. The trucks bore them to the headquarters building for debriefing. They climbed wearily out, inhaling the blessed fresh air, then walked into the brightly-lit room with the blinking, dazed look of men woken at the wrong moment of the morning. A young WAAF scribbled her industrious notes about the trip as they lit their cigarettes and drank their tea. A cluster of brass – the station commander, a handful of staff officers, the padre and the doctor – hovered in the background. A WAAF chalked their landing time on the long, wide crew blackboard on the wall of the Ops Room. They had survived. Tomorrow night, or perhaps the one after, they would do it all again.

7 Protest and policy, 1942–43

Dissent

On 12 October 1942, a memorandum from the Assistant Chief of Air Staff (Policy) was circulated to Command and Group AOCs throughout the RAF. It was a commonplace document in the paperchase of wartime instructions, but it sought to clarify and codify the reality of what had been taking place over Europe for many months:

1. The following rules govern our bombardment policy in British, Allied or Neutral territory occupied by the enemy:
   Bombardment is to be confined to military objectives, and must be subject to the following general principles:
   (1) The intentional bombardment of civilian populations, as such, is forbidden.
   (2) It must be possible to identify the objective.
   (3) The attack must be made with reasonable care to avoid undue loss of civilian life in the vicinity of the target.
2. German, Italian and Japanese territory:
   Consequent upon the enemy's adoption of a campaign of unrestricted air warfare, the Cabinet have authorized a bombing policy which includes the attack of enemy morale. The foregoing rules do not, therefore, apply to our conduct of air warfare against German, Italian and Japanese territory.

Behind the circumlocutions, therefore, Britain was also pursuing a policy of unrestricted air warfare. On operational grounds alone, the Prime Minister and the senior officers of the RAF felt no doubt about its advisability, and to the majority of the British people the crimes of the Nazi regime across Europe justified the most terrible counter-offensive. Harris, to his credit, was always in favour of telling the British public exactly what he was seeking to do to the Germans, and no one who read his statements in the course of the campaign had much cause to plead ignorance about area bombing. But the Government was more squeamish. From beginning to end of the war, ministers prevaricated – indeed, lied flatly again and again – about the nature of the bomber offensive.

'Have instructions been given on any occasion to British airmen to engage in area bombing rather than limit their attentions to purely military targets?' Richard Stokes MP asked the Air Minister in the House of Commons on 31 March 1943.

'The targets of Bomber Command are always military, but night-bombing of military objectives necessarily involves bombing the area in which they are situated,' replied Sir Archibald Sinclair.

'Is the Right Hon. Member aware that a growing volume of opinion in this country considers indiscriminate bombing of civilian centres both morally wrong and strategic lunacy?' Stokes asked the Deputy Prime Minister on 27 May 1943.

'No, there is no indiscriminate bombing,' replied Mr Clement Attlee, amidst rousing cheers. 'As has been repeatedly stated in the House, the bombing is of those targets which are most effective from the military point of view.'

In the wake of the blitz on Britain, the Government could have made a powerful and popular case for the area bombing of Germany had they chosen to do so, but by taking refuge in deceit they were contributing mightily to the post-war controversy about the bomber offensive. If ministers in 1942 were embarrassed about what they were doing, so the argument would go, they must indeed have had something to be ashamed of. But during the war itself, while service departments and scientists mounted a fierce campaign against Bomber Command on strategic and practical grounds, the civilian opponents of bombing represented only a tiny, articulate minority.

In the House of Commons, Richard Stokes, the Labour MP for Ipswich, was the most determined. His own background was anything but that of an armchair pacifist. A barrister's son, he was educated at Downside and Trinity College, Cambridge, and won the Military Cross and Croix de Guerre as a gunner major in the First War. Stokes never questioned the necessity for tactical bombing in support of military operations, but, from 1942 to

1945 he was a constant thorn in the Government's flesh on the matter of the area bombing of cities:

'Will the Secretary of State say whether the policy of limiting the objectives of Bomber Command to targets of military importance has, or has not, been changed to the bombing of towns and wide areas in which military targets are situated?' he demanded of the Air Minister in the House of Commons on 1 December 1943.

Sir Archibald Sinclair: 'I would refer the Hon. Member to the answer which I gave him to a similar question on 31 March. There has been no change of policy.'

Stokes: 'Within what area in square miles was it estimated that the 350 blockbusters recently dropped on Berlin fell?'

Sinclair: 'The answer to that question would be of value to the enemy.'

Stokes: 'Would not the proper answer be that the Government does not dare give it? Does not my Right Hon. Friend admit by his answer that the Government are now resorting to indiscriminate bombing including residential areas?'

Sinclair: 'The Hon. Gentleman is incorrigible. I have indicated a series of vitally important military objectives.'

Sinclair was rescued from further bombardment on this occasion by a succession of loyal members who asked when there could be more bombing raids on Germany. The House passed on to a question about why airmen were forbidden to send pyjamas to service laundries. The Commons was overwhelmingly hostile to the handful of critics who returned again and again to sniping attacks on the deeds of the Royal Air Force. When Mr McGovern asked the Air Minister on 6 May 1942 'whether instructions to the RAF who raided Lübeck and Rostock included instructions to impede and disorganize the German effort by the destruction of workmen's dwellings?' Sinclair set his mind at rest:

The objectives of our bomber offensive in Germany are to destroy the capacity of Germany to make war and to relieve the pressure of the German air force and armies on our Russian allies. No instruction has been given to destroy dwelling houses rather than armament factories, but it is impossible to distinguish in night-bombing between the factories and the dwellings which surround them.

203

Even among diehard Tories, there was a sense of regret about the destruction of so much beauty and culture in Germany in the course of the bomber offensive. One of the most interesting letters in Sir Archibald Sinclair's personal correspondence files came on 26 November 1943 from the Marquess of Salisbury, head of the great Cecil family which had played so large a part in English public life for four centuries. It was handwritten, and marked 'Confidential':

My dear Sinclair,
Forgive a somewhat critical note. Your praise of the valour and skill of the air force in their attack on Berlin is abundantly deserved. They are splendid. But Sir Arthur Harris's reply gives one a shake. These attacks are to go on 'until the heart of Nazi Germany ceases to beat'. This would seem to bring us up short against the repeated Government declarations that we are bombing only military and industrial targets. Perhaps that is all that Harris contemplates, and I shall be delighted if you tell me so. But there is a great deal of evidence that makes some of us afraid that we are losing moral superiority to the Germans, and if Harris means not merely that incidental casualties to women and children cannot be avoided, but also that the residential heart of Berlin is to cease to beat, then a good many people will feel that they have been let down – though in writing this I speak in the name of no committee. Of course the Germans began it, but we do not take the devil as our example. Of course all these criticisms may be groundless, but if not, issue fresh confidential orders, I *hope*.
Yours Very Sincerely
    SALISBURY

Please remember that we can say nothing in public for obvious reasons.

This was a difficult letter for Sinclair. Salisbury could scarcely be fobbed off with the usual platitudes about 'hoping for an early end of the war to end this regrettable destruction'. His eldest son Lord Cranborne was Lord Privy Seal in the Government. Sinclair passed the letter to Sir Norman Bottomley, the Deputy Chief of Air Staff, for comment.

To be strictly accurate [suggested Bottomley], our primary object is the progressive destruction and dislocation of the German military, industrial and economic system and *the undermining of the morale of the*

*German people.** There is no need to inform Lord Salisbury of the underlined phrase, since it follows on success of the first part of the stated aim.

Thus Sinclair replied to Lord Salisbury on 29 November 1943:

Our aim is the progressive dislocation of the German military, industrial and economic system. I have never pretended that it is possible to pursue this aim without inflicting terrible casualties on the civilian population of Germany. But neither I, nor any responsible spokesman on behalf of the Government, has ever gloated over the destruction of German homes.

We have resisted a policy of reprisals ... although there were those who wanted us to select certain small German towns and villages for deliberate destruction ... we refused, and adhered fully to the principle that we would attack none but military targets.

Most of the British Press supported the bomber offensive with gusto. 'These first blasts of the whirlwind that Hitler, who sowed the wind at Warsaw and Rotterdam, has now to reap have raised the spirits of the fighters for freedom everywhere,' proclaimed a *Times* leader after the 1,000 Raid on Cologne. On 11 March 1943 Harold Balfour declared emphatically that Britain was bombing only military targets: 'I can give the assurance that we are not bombing the women and children of Germany wantonly.' The *Sunday Dispatch* attacked this statement as weak-kneed: 'It is right that the German population should "smell death at close quarters". Now they are getting the stench of it.' To the satisfaction of the Air Ministry, the influential American *Time* magazine was calling for a growing air attack on Germany. Some commentators exceeded even the apostolic enthusiasm of the airmen for bombing Germany. The *Sunday Express* criticized the Air Staff when the weight of bombing seemed to be flagging. Peter Masefield, air correspondent of the *Sunday Times*, argued on 6 June 1943 that 'If the present bomber offensive could be multiplied by four, her war production would be completely halted. That conclusion emerges from a deliberately conservative examination of the damage done by the big bombers.' The Director of Bomber Operations noted drily on his copy of the cutting: 'I consider

*Bottomley's emphasis.

rather a rosy picture is painted, as it assumes that every load falls on the target and does fresh damage.'

Propaganda and public relations had begun to loom large in the minds of the directors of the war. The airmen, even more than the other two services, monitored public opinion intently. A report was sent to the Air Ministry analysing a sample of civilian letters opened by the censor in the wake of the 1,000 Raid on Cologne: 'There are those who are pleased, and those who regret that so much suffering should have to be inflicted. There are those who fear reprisals. Many of the letters contain two or more of these elements. Predominant is satisfaction, but many women express regret . . .' A tiny lobby group calling themselves The Bombing Restriction Committee distributed leaflets on the streets headed 'STOP BOMBING CIVILIANS!' Their purpose, they declared, was 'to urge the Government to stop violating their declared policy of bombing only military objectives and particularly to cease causing the deaths of many thousands of civilians in their homes'. Much more typical of popular opinion was Brigadier Cecil Aspinall-Oglander's distaste for the media's raucous delight in the achievements of the bomber offensive.

Britain and her Allies and well-wishers must all be devoutly thankful that the RAF is at last able to repay Germany in her own coin [the Brigadier wrote to *The Times* on 1 May 1942] and to inflict upon her cities the same devastation that she has inflicted on ours. But it must offend the sensibilities of a large mass of the British population that our official broadcasts, when reporting these acts of just retribution, should exult at and gloat over the suffering which our raids necessitate . . . Let us at least preserve the decencies of English taste. An Englishman does not exult when a criminal is condemned to the scaffold, nor gloat over his sufferings at the time of his execution.

At the end of 1943, Portal produced a subtle proposal: rather than proscribe German cities for destruction, Britain might now declare certain cities immune from attack, in the hope of provoking a panic-stricken flight of refugees towards them. Sinclair was enthusiastic, for his own reasons:

There might . . . be cities which would remain on the list because they contain no industries of war importance, but possess buildings or works of art of exceptional historic or aesthetic value. This would appeal to an important section of public opinion which is concerned about the destruction of such monuments in the bomber offensive.

The Air Staff eventually rejected this idea, chiefly on the grounds that it was impossible to ensure that the listed cities would not be bombed by mistake. It is significant that Sinclair was so eager to appease the cultural critics. The airmen were far more concerned about attacks on their strategy.

What are we doing to try and educate *The Times*? [Slessor, as Assistant Chief of Air Staff, minuted Bottomley on 9 September 1942]. The policy of the paper seems to be, while giving the inevitable lip-service to the exploits of the Air Force, to carefully cut them down as being of no value apart from their contribution to land and sea operations. Fortunately the *Daily Telegraph* continues to champion the cause of Air Power . . .

It was not only the effect of newspaper criticism on politicians and the public that the airmen feared, but a faltering of morale on the bomber stations if crews began to believe that they were being sent to their deaths to no purpose. A 1942 issue of the Russian propaganda paper *Soviet War News*, normally distributed free to service establishments, was banned from all RAF stations when it was found to contain an article entitled 'Air bombing cannot decide the war'.

Britain's most distinguished military thinkers of the pre-war era, Major-General J. F. C. Fuller and Captain Basil Liddell Hart mounted one of the most significant offensives against Bomber Command. Both men had long since turned away from their uncritical worship of air power in the 1920s. They had been the outstanding theoreticians of the art of *blitzkrieg*, mobile warfare spearheaded by tanks and tactical aircraft, and Germany's Panzer leaders shared faith in this gospel. Yet now both these men perceived an overwhelming flaw in the concept of a strategic bomber offensive intended to break the enemy's will to fight, when viewed against the background of the Allied doctrine of Unconditional Surrender, promulgated in January 1943. To what purpose could one terrorize the enemy's population into demanding peace from its leaders, if there were no terms to be made? Fuller was appalled by the rising tide of systematic destruction. In August 1943, for example, he drafted an article for the London *EveningStandard*, edited by the alleged radical socialist Michael Foot, in which he heaped insult upon insult against the instigators of the bomber offensive: 'the worst devastations of the Goths, Vandals, Huns, Seljuks and Mongols pale into insignificance when compared to the material and moral damage now wrought'.

Foot wrote to Fuller to say that he lacked the nerve to publish the article.[1]

Basil Liddell Hart drafted a private 'Reflection' in the summer of 1942, in the wake of the 1,000 Raid on Cologne:

It will be ironical if the defenders of civilization depend for victory upon the most barbaric, and unskilled, way of winning a war that the modern world has seen . . . We are now counting for victory on success in the way of degrading it to a new low level – as represented by indiscriminate (night) bombing and indiscriminate starvation . . . If our pounding of German cities, by massed night-bombing, proves the decisive factor, it should be a sobering thought that but for Hitler's folly in attacking Russia (and consequently using up his bomber force there, as well as diverting his resources mainly into other weapons) we *and* the Germans would now be 'Cologning' each other's cities with the advantage on Germany's side, in this mad competition in mutual devastation . . .

Liddell Hart attacked the bomber offensive in newspaper articles and in his books of the period, but like Fuller he was quite without political influence. Fuller had been discredited in English public life by an eccentric flirtation with the Italian Fascists in the 1930s. Liddell Hart was almost obsessively personally hostile to Churchill. In his papers he noted a conversation with General Sir Frederick Pile, Britain's flak defence chief, in which Pile allegedly told him that 'Winston is pinning all his faith to the bombing offensive now. The devastation it causes suits his temperament, and he would be disappointed at a less destructive ending to the war. . .' Liddell Hart's own brother-in-law Barry Sullivan was serving with the RAF in Malta, and wrote from the island expressing the fear that the Government 'has become Frankenstein, dominated by its own creation – the monster of Bomber Command'.[2]

Liddell Hart's opponents would have argued that he was living in a fantasy world in which warfare could still be conducted as an academic chess-game, rather than the reality, in which the Allies were fighting to the death for the survival of freedom. No member of Churchill's government would accord Liddell Hart or Fuller any more respect than was due to disgruntled pundits without posts or power. Until the end of the war, they cried in the wilderness.

Most of Britain's churchmen supported the strategic offensive, for much the same reasons that Dr Garbett, the Archbishop of York, advanced for refusing to join protests against area bombing in 1943: 'Often in life', he said, 'there is no clear choice between absolute right and wrong; frequently the choice has to be made of the lesser of two evils, and it is a lesser evil to bomb a war-loving Germany than to sacrifice the lives of our fellow-countrymen who long for peace, and to delay delivering millions now held in slavery...'

George Bell, Bishop of Chichester, was unable to accept this compromise. Throughout the war, he was the most persistent and the most articulate critic of the bomber offensive, to the impotent fury of the British Government. He supported the struggle against Nazi Germany and tactical bombing operations, but he was unrelentingly hostile to area bombing:

I desire to challenge the Government [he told the House of Lords on 9 February 1944 in a characteristic speech] on the policy which directs the bombing of enemy towns on the present scale, especially with reference to civilians who are non-combatants, and non-military and non-industrial objectives...

I fully realize that in attacks on centres of war industry and transport the killing of civilians when it is the result of bona fide military activity is inevitable. But there must be a fair balance between the means employed and the purpose achieved. To obliterate a whole town because certain portions contain military and industrial establishments is to reject the balance...

The Allies stand for something greater than power. The chief name inscribed on our banner is 'Law'. It is of supreme importance that we, who, with our Allies, are the Liberators of Europe should so use power that it is always under control of law. It is because the bombing of enemy towns – this area bombing – raises this issue of bombing unlimited and exclusive that such immense importance is bound to attach to the policy and action of His Majesty's Government...

Bell was the most prominent moral critic of the bomber offensive. It is widely held that his campaign later cost him the archbishopric of Canterbury. But in the midst of war, as Britain's leaders struggled with their enemies and their Allies and their own exhaustion and dwindling resources, it seemed to them intolerable to be assailed by the darts and pinpricks of men who shared no part of their enormous responsibilities. At no time after the fall of France did the Allied warlords consider restricting the bomber offensive for moral reasons. At no time did the offensive's moral critics extend beyond a tiny minority of English men and women. It may be argued that it is a tribute to the survival of democracy in wartime that they were able to speak as freely as they did in attacking Bomber Command. Harris believed that the Government made a major error in failing to answer them more frankly: 'In the House of Commons he [Sinclair] should have been far more forthright than he was. . . There was nothing to be ashamed of, except in the sense that everybody might be ashamed of the sort of thing that has to be done in every war . . .'[3]

Sinclair himself told the House of Commons on 4 March 1942: 'The talk about the futility of bombing is dangerous. . . Well armed, highly trained and inflexibly determined, they are the only force upon which we can call in this year, 1942, to strike deadly blows at the heart of Germany.'

Casablanca – the airmen victorious

It is ironic that just as Harris's '1,000 Raids' were thrilling and aweing the British public, a worm of doubt about area bombing was beginning to gnaw the minds of some powerful officials of the Air Ministry. Sir Wilfred Freeman, the Vice-Chief of Air Staff, was especially irked by the gulf between Bomber Command's real achievements and the publicity given to them, and submitted a memorandum to Portal on the subject on 16 September 1942.

There is an increasing tendency among Commanders-in-Chief to compete for publicity [wrote Freeman]. This is in itself contrary to the best traditions of the service. More serious, however, is the fact that in their efforts to attract the limelight they sometimes exaggerate and even falsify facts. The worst offender is C-in-C Bomber Command . . . This is not the first occasion on which there have been complaints of the way in which Bomber Command exaggerates its achievements.

Harris could have claimed that the fastidious Freeman entirely missed the point about the value of the bomber offensive in 1942. Bomber Command's principal task and principal achievement had been to impress the British people and their Allies, rather than to damage the enemy. But as U-boat sinkings rose in the Battle of the Atlantic, as calls for heavy aircraft intensified from every theatre of war, was this still enough to justify Bomber Command's huge claim on the war effort?

The airmen resisted the navy's demands for more heavy aircraft, partly on the spurious grounds that it would take months to convert bombers to an anti-submarine role, and fit them with ASV radar. Likewise, when H2S centimetric radar was introduced – one of the decisive technological breakthroughs of the war – the Admiralty lost its fight for first priority to Bomber Command, and Scientific Intelligence were overruled when they suggested that Coastal Command should be equipped first, because H2S sets lost at sea would be in no danger of capture. Thus, one of the first H2S sets fitted to a bomber was indeed captured by the Germans, and the secrets of its cavity magnetron revealed.

Harris's argument against the diversion of heavy aircraft to the Atlantic battle was put forward in his long paper of 28 June 1942 to the War Cabinet, reviewing the work of Bomber Command.

While it takes approximately some 7,000 hours of flying to destroy one submarine at sea, that was approximately the amount of flying necessary to destroy one third of Cologne . . . The purely defensive use of air power is grossly wasteful. The naval employment of aircraft consists of picking at the fringes of enemy power, of waiting for opportunities that may never occur, and indeed probably never will occur, of looking for needles in a haystack . . .

He was a master of rhetoric. Why search for submarines over hundreds of thousands of square miles of ocean, he urged, when Bomber Command could destroy the very factories in which they were built? The admirals could never match his force in debate. Yet it is only necessary to study a single convoy battle in 1942 or 1943 to perceive the extraordinary influence that a heavy aircraft could exert. It was not the submarines that were sunk, but the mere appearance of an aircraft that forced U-boats to dive and frequently thwarted a major wolfpack attack. Adequate numbers of long-range aircraft in 1942 could have turned the tide in the Battle of the Atlantic months earlier. But to spirits such as Lord Cherwell, who supported Harris vigorously, the distant splash of plummeting depth-charges held none of the magic of firing the heart of Germany:

It is difficult to compare quantitatively the damage done to any of the forty-odd big German cities in a 1,000-ton raid with the advantages of sinking one U-boat out of 400 and saving three or four ships out of 5,500 [Cherwell wrote to Churchill on 28 March 1943]. But it will surely be held in Russia as well as here that the bomber offensive must have more immediate effect on the course of the war in 1943 ...

The importance of keeping Russia in the war dominated Allied thinking. No one had forgotten the near-catastrophe that followed the Bolsheviks' negotiated peace with Germany in 1917. In 1942 and 1943 the War Cabinet cherished the conviction that the Russians needed to be and could be persuaded of British sincerity, of British support for the Russian struggle. The Russians were understandably contemptuous of the fuss the British made about their Arctic convoy losses when the Soviet armies were losing hundreds of thousands of men in a single battle. From 1942 onwards, Stalin was perfectly clear that only by opening the second front in northern Europe could the Allies make a real impact on the war in the east. Instead, Churchill offered him the bomber offensive. 'I am deeply conscious of the giant burden borne by the Russian armies and their unequalled contribution to the common cause,' the Prime Minister wrote to Stalin on 6 April 1943. 'I must emphasize that our bombing of Germany will increase in scale month by month. . .' Throughout the war, Stalin was sent updated copies of Harris's celebrated 'Blue Books', the C-in-C's personal photograph albums of the wrecked cities of Germany. Beyond a few platitudes congratulating Churchill on the bombing of Berlin, the Russian never seemed much impressed. But the need to support Russia remained a constant chord in the theme of those in Britain and America arguing the case for intensifying the bombing of Germany.

On 3 November 1942, Sir Charles Portal submitted a paper to the Chiefs of Staff on the prospects for the bomber offensive.

I am convinced [he wrote] that an Anglo-American bomber force based in the United Kingdom and building up to a peak of 4,000 to 6,000 heavy bombers by 1944 would be capable of reducing the German war potential well below the level at which an Anglo-American invasion of the continent would become practicable.

With such a force at their command, Portal promised, six million German homes could be destroyed, 'with a proportionate destruction of industrial buildings, sources of power, means of transportation and public utilities'. 25 million Germans would be made homeless. There would be 'civilian casualties estimated at about 900,000 killed and 1,000,000 seriously injured'. If, as Portal's biographer argues, his purpose in mounting the bomber offensive was never to kill German civilians as such, then he was now hoping to achieve the most dramatic by-product in the history of strategy.

Sir Alan Brooke, the Chief of the Imperial General Staff, was openly sceptical about Bomber Command's ability to fulfil these promises: 'Experience had shown that built-up areas could stand much more knocking about than had been anticipated,' he said. The First Sea Lord was never less than scathing about the bomber offensive. Yet on 31 December 1942 the British Chiefs of Staff jointly endorsed Portal's proposals, and recommended that 'we should aim at a force of 3,000 British and American heavy and medium bombers operating from the United Kingdom by the end of 1943.'

Portal had unveiled his plan weeks before the great Allied conference at Casablanca. Whatever strategic proposals the service chiefs were considering at this time, Winston Churchill approached Casablanca with one overriding priority: to dissuade the Americans from launching a second front in northern Europe in 1943. The British could scarcely suggest to the Americans, still in their first flush of idealism for the liberation of the world, that infinite delay provided infinite time for the Russian army and the Wehrmacht to destroy each other. But the concept of using 1943 to wage a great bomber offensive specifically intended to pave the way for the second front gave purpose to prevarication.

It was for this reason that the British Chiefs of Staff supported Portal's paper, and for this reason that the bomber offensive remained at the forefront of the British war effort in 1943.

The British went to Casablanca with the knowledge that they would have powerful support for their indirect strategy: from the American airmen. Since 1939 the Americans had been studying British bombing with intense interest. The United States Army Air Force envied the RAF's independent status, and cherished hopes of establishing its own place as a third force, separate but equal, alongside the army and navy. The American airmen's commitment to air power – and specifically to strategic bombing – matched that of the British.

But they had entirely their own methods for doing so. Unmoved by Bomber Command's failures in 1939 and 1940, they believed that the B-17 Flying Fortress was uniquely capable of carrying out an unescorted daylight offensive against Germany: cruising at 260 mph, heavily armed, heavily armoured, and with a 33,000-foot ceiling. More important still, they believed that the Norden bombsight gave them the tool to carry out a precision-bombing campaign against the key elements of the German economy. The Americans rejected the concept of area bombing, of attacking enemy morale, not least because they believed that it had proved ineffective. In 1942, Major Alexander Seversky, one of the foremost American proponents of air power, was already writing:

Another vital lesson – one that has taken even air specialists by surprise – relates to the behaviour of civilian populations under air punishment. It had been generally assumed that aerial bombardment would quickly shatter popular morale, causing deep civilian reactions . . . The progress of this war has tended to indicate that this expectation was unfounded . . .

These facts are significant beyond their psychological interest. They mean that haphazard destruction of cities – sheer blows at morale – are costly and wasteful in relation to the tactical results achieved. Attacks will increasingly be concentrated on military rather than on random human targets. Unplanned vandalism from the air must give way, more and more, to planned, predetermined destruction. More than ever the principal objectives will be the critical aggregates of electric power, aviation industries, dock facilities, essential public utilities and the like.[4]

Americans believed that the German blitz on Britain might have succeeded had it been properly planned. They argued throughout the war, and indeed through Vietnam a generation later, that incidental civilian casualties in the course of precision bombing were acceptable in a way that deliberate slaughter was not. The 8th Air Force flew its first mission to Rouen marshalling yards on 17 August 1942. From then until the end of the year, they flew a further twenty-six operations over Europe, losing only thirty-two aircraft in 1,547 sorties, a missing rate of under 2 per cent. American gunners began to submit a flood of claims for enemy fighters destroyed, surpassing even the wild estimates of the RAF early in the war. On 27 August 1942, Ira Eaker, commanding the 8th Air Force, was already predicting that 40 per cent of his Fortresses' bombs could be dropped within five hundred yards of the aiming-point. He believed that ten bomber groups in 1942 reinforced by a further ten by June 1943 would be adequate 'coupled with the British night-bombing effort, completely to dislocate German industry and commerce and to remove from the enemy the means for waging successful warfare'. General Carl 'Tooey' Spaatz endorsed Eaker's enthusiasm. The USAAF's great bubble of optimism, mirroring that of the RAF two years earlier, was airborne. It would be a year before it was brutally exploded.

An uncommitted observer would quickly have perceived that no sweeping conclusions could be drawn from American bomber operations in the autumn of 1942. The formation attacks had done some damage to their targets, but they had also scattered bombs among the French civilian population in an alarming manner. The Norden sight, so impressive in clear American summer skies, became useless in overcast European ones. From October 1942 to January 1943 almost half of all American bomber sorties were uncompleted. Above all, not a single 8th Air Force aircraft crossed the border of Germany. The Americans had operated during this working-up period entirely against short-range targets under Spitfire escort, which the British had advised the Americans was essential. The build-up of the 8th Air Force was also being persistently delayed. Throughout the autumn and winter of 1942, as fast as bomber groups could be equipped and assembled in England, they were transferred to support Allied operations in North Africa. By January 1943, Eaker could muster scarcely eighty bombers.

Yet by the coming of the Casablanca Conference, the British airmen were as eager as the Americans to make common cause of their enthusiasm for the 8th Air Force's slender achievements. A number of British airmen, including Sir Arthur Harris himself, had been so impressed by the American experience that they had begun a renewed flirtation with the concept of daylight bombing. On 11 December 1942 Harris wrote to the AOC of 4 Group:

I think everybody is much too apprehensive about daylight operations . . . I have never been apprehensive about the ability of the heavy bomber to look after itself in daylight *vis-à-vis* the fighter . . . I want daylight operations started as soon as you are ready against lightly defended targets . . . There is not the least doubt in my mind that if we and all the available Americans started daylight attacks against the less heavily defended targets in Germany by big formations of heavy bombers now, we should knock the German fighter force out of the sky in two or three months, by the simple process of shooting them down . . . It has all along been our experience that whenever the rear gunner, even at night, sees the enemy fighter first, he either destroys it or the fighter refuses to come in and attack.[5]

While this note severely damages Harris's claims to be a realistic judge of the operational facts of life over Germany, it also indicates the mood that prevailed among some British airmen after the early American sorties. The British fell over themselves to be complimentary. The notes survive for a public speech of Sir Archibald Sinclair, delivered on 12 October 1942. He eulogized 'the prodigies of' – the word 'accurate' is here crossed out, and 'daylight' substituted – 'daylight bombing which the US Bomber Air Force have already begun to achieve'. On 17 October, eight squadrons of Lancasters staged a daring daylight attack on the Schneider Armament Works at Le Creusot, and returned with the loss of only one aircraft. Bomber Command was now equipped and trained for night operations, and no abrupt change of policy was possible. But some British airmen were thinking furiously.

The Americans, for their part, were indifferent to what Bomber Command did or did not do over Germany, provided that the USAAF had its chance to win the war by a precision-bombing offensive before Allied armies landed in France. Spaatz and Eaker might have no faith in area bombing, but they had no intention of saying anything publicly that might endanger the solid front presented by Allied airmen to their naval and military counterparts. General 'Hap' Arnold, Commanding General of the USAAF, was to display growing concern and indeed anger about the lack of co-ordination between Bomber Command and the 8th Air Force, but Spaatz and Eaker were at pains to take no controversial part in a debate on issues so close to the hearts of British airmen. Throughout the war, the two generals enjoyed almost continuously harmonious relations with the British. They understood each other's difficulties perfectly. Harris's struggle with the Royal Navy was mirrored by the USAAF's difficulties with Admiral King, the Chief of Naval Operations, who was fighting for priority for the Pacific. As early as July 1942, Eisenhower was indicating that he hoped to use the 8th Air Force to support ground operations, a prospect totally at odds with the ambitions of the American airmen.

Harris sought to support the American airmen in their inter-service struggles with as much loyalty as they offered him in his difficulties with British colleagues and with Arnold in Washington. In the file of Harris's correspondence with the Prime Minister there is an undated memorandum from the winter of 1942–3 headed 'Most Secret and Strictly Personal', in which Harris urges Churchill to support Eaker and Spaatz in their difficulties with the US Navy and Army. 'My American air friends are despondent,' he wrote. Among his fellow airmen, Harris laboured constantly for a united front: 'We can defeat the enemy if we are not defeated by our friends,' he wrote to Arnold in August 1942.

Thus the Allied airmen came to Casablanca in January 1943 united in their determination to fight for a mandate for the growth of the bomber offensive. In the event it did not prove necessary to do so. Once the British had got their way about the major strategic decision taken at the conference, the postponement until 1944 of Operation *Overlord* – the invasion of northern Europe – in favour of Operation *Husky* – a step-by-step advance through Sicily and Italy – it was apparent that the Allies must continue the bombing campaign as the only major offensive against Germany. Churchill withdrew his objections to the

American daylight attack, which he personally believed was doomed, after an appeal by Ira Eaker. It was agreed that the goal of the Combined Bomber Offensive, as it would henceforth be known, should be 'to weaken Germany's war-making capacity to the point to which invasion would become possible'.

In reality, of course, this was the airmen's phrase: the soldiers would never have acknowledged the implication that invasion could not take place until strategic bombing had achieved some definable and decisive effect on Germany; the armies would be launched upon the invasion when the generals and statesmen saw fit, and their only major concern was that tactical air supremacy should be maintained around the battlefield. If Sir Charles Portal had ever believed that the war could be won by bombing alone, he no longer did so. At Casablanca he said emphatically that it was necessary 'to exert the maximum pressure on Germany by land operations; air bombardment alone was not sufficient'.

The Casablanca Directive – CCS 166/I/D from the Combined Chiefs of Staff to Air Marshal Harris and General Eaker – ordered them to embark on the demolition of a range of German target systems as essential preliminaries to D-Day. First on the list, with the Battle of the Atlantic still foremost in the Allies' concerns, came submarine yards and bases. Then followed the German air force, its factories and depots. After these, ball-bearings, of which it was thought that Germany could be deprived with limited bomber effort against a handful of vital targets; oil; synthetic rubber and tyres; and military transport. The opening phrase of the directive reflected the intended marriage of British and American bombing policies:

Your primary aim will be the progressive destruction and dislocation of the German military, industrial and economic system, and the undermining of the morale of the German people to a point where their capacity for armed resistance is fatally weakened . . .

After the preamble, most of the detailed thinking in the directive about the German economy was American. It had been essential for the British to defer to the Americans' precision-bombing ambitions in order to gain their main objectives at Casablanca. In the months following the conference, an Operational Committee produced what became known as the Eaker Plan, intended to transform the Casablanca Directive into realistic orders for Bomber Command and the 8th Air Force. The Eaker Plan reflected some of that general's astonishingly vivid projections. If the 8th Air Force could be built up to a strength of 1,746 aircraft by 1 January 1944, and 2,702 aircraft by 1 April 1944, Eaker promised that German submarine construction could be reduced by 89 per cent; fighter construction by 43 per cent; bomber construction by 65 per cent; ball-bearings by 76 per cent; synthetic rubber production by 50 per cent. 'These figures', he added, 'are conservative and can be absolutely relied upon.'

The plan drawn up by the Operational Committee was endorsed by Portal and Harris in April 1943, with only minor reservations about the prominence given to the submarine bases on the French coast, which had already proved virtually invulnerable to bombing.

This plan [said its authors] does not attempt to prescribe the major effort of the RAF Bomber Command. It simply recognizes the fact that when precision targets are bombed by the Eighth Air Force in daylight, the effort should be completed and complemented by RAF bombing attacks against the surrounding industrial area at night. Fortunately the industrial areas to be attacked are in most cases identical with the industrial areas which the British Bomber Command has selected for mass destruction anyway . . .

Harris wrote to Eaker on 15 April 1943:

I am in complete agreement with the policy recommended. The effect of linking up precision bombing of selected targets in daylight by an adequate force of the VIII Bomber Command with intensified night-bombing by the RAF will unquestionably cause damage to *matériel* and morale on a scale which the enemy will be unable to sustain.

As regards the detailed presentation, there are naturally some points on which I would lay slightly varied emphasis if I were presenting the case to my own Chief of Staff, but these are of no consequence compared with the major aim, which is to build up the bomber forces in Britain at the maximum pace, and to the size necessary to achieve our common purpose.

At Casablanca it had been decided that the Chiefs of Staffs' authority for the conduct of the Combined Bomber Offensive should be nominally vested in Sir Charles Portal. The allocation of targets and 'the effective coordination of the forces involved' was to be ensured 'by frequent consultation between the Commanders in Chief'. General Arnold in Washington was thoroughly uneasy about this cosy arrangement. On 22 April 1943 he wrote to Portal:

It occurs to me that the time has arrived for the establishment of somewhat more than formalized machinery for the closest possible coordination, or rather integration of the two bomber efforts. The increasing complexity of their operations would appear to me as soon to be beyond the capabilities of the commanders, in person, to coordinate.

To the British, Arnold's note and many others that would follow it represented the very Trojan horse that they were utterly determined to keep from their gates. Harris, with his experience of America as head of the RAF delegation in Washington, was one of the first to foresee and prepare to repel American attempts to incorporate Bomber Command in some joint Allied command structure. On land it was inevitable that the Americans would overwhelmingly dominate the war effort. At sea the British still played the principal part in the Mediterranean and were equal co-partners in the Atlantic only because the US navy was so heavily committed in the Pacific. In the air, in each month of 1943 America would build an average of 801 heavy bombers against Britain's 380, 787 twin-engined aircraft against Britain's 464, 866 single-engined fighters against Britain's 679. Even to achieve their own existing levels of aircraft production, the British were compelled to rely entirely on America for transport aircraft, and very heavily for tanks, ammunition and landing-craft. In 1944, American dominance would be even more dramatic.

Bomber Command was Britain's last entirely independent contribution to the Allied war effort, gripping the imagination of the British people and much of Occupied Europe. As the enormous build-up of American air power developed in 1943 and 1944, the British were determined to ensure that Harris's forces were not submerged. High Wycombe had always regarded the Casablanca Directive as a general mandate for the bomber offensive, rather than as a specific instruction to be strictly obeyed. A number of staff officers at the Air Ministry were already impressed by the

American concept of precision bombing, and would seek to press their views upon Portal and Harris. But Harris and his staff considered Casablanca merely an authorization to continue what they were doing already, and at this stage Sir Charles Portal made no attempt to make them think otherwise.

Arnold's proposals for integrating the British and American bomber offensives were rejected. Perhaps at Harris's instigation,[6] certain phrases in the draft directive for the Combined Bomber Offensive which was now being refined from the Casablanca Directive were altered, to make an already vaguely worded document woollier still. It was a measure of Churchill's waning emphasis on the bomber offensive that when the final proposals based on Casablanca and the Eaker Plan, and now christened *Pointblank*, came before the Washington summit of May 1943 for approval, the Prime Minister nodded them through with the brief assertion that it was unnecessary further to discuss bombing policy, since there was virtual British and American agreement. On 10 June 1943 the *Pointblank* Directive was formally issued to Bomber Command and the 8th Air Force. It was to be the basis of the strategic bomber offensive – at least in the minds of the Chiefs of Staff – until the invasion.

The American airmen had got what they wanted: orders to develop their precision-bombing offensive. From the beginning of 1943, 8th Air Force strength had grown steadily from a daily average of 73 heavy bombers available in February to the 279 dispatched on a single operation in May. The Americans' hopes and ambitions for the destruction of German industry were based on the same blend of ignorance, optimism and astonishing statistical projections as those of the British, unrelieved by the RAF's additional hopes for damaging enemy morale. The Americans' first priority was to destroy the German air force in production. With unbounded courage and hope they addressed themselves to their task.

But just as the Americans would ignore the phrases about attacking German morale embodied in *Pointblank*, so Sir Arthur Harris proposed to ignore the implication which the directive's creators certainly intended, that Bomber Command address itself specifically to areas in which the key German target systems were found. Long before Casablanca or even before Cologne, Harris had conceived his campaign for the systematic laying-waste of Germany's cities, and he never had the slightest intention of being deflected from it. In *Pointblank* 'he was able to discover a mandate for pursuing the policy upon which he was in any case resolved. . . For most of 1943 there was no combined offensive, but, on the contrary, a bombing competition.'[7] Harris was in many ways a much more shrewd political animal than has been recognized. Although he sometimes damaged his own cause by his appalling exaggerations, he understood one prime principle of diplomatic manoeuvre: that by agreeing to a course of action loudly and often enough in public, it is possible in reality to do something entirely different. Harris's letters to Eaker were almost effusive in their expressions of common purpose. Harris was certainly sincere in wanting to see a large American strategic bomber force committed to the assault on Germany. But beyond this, he treated the *Pointblank* Directive as a harmless plaything for the Ministry of Economic Warfare and the Air Staff.

In 1943 he would have a devastating strike force at his command. He would use it to hit the cities of Germany. His only concession to *Pointblank* was that when his aircraft attacked an urban centre, he was at pains to catalogue for the Air Ministry and for the Americans the aircraft factories or aero-engine plants or oil refineries which it contained, and which were duly scheduled for destruction in *Pointblank*.

There was one more essential dimension of the Combined Bomber Offensive in 1943: while the soldiers regarded the strategic air offensive at best as subordinate, at worst as irrelevant to grand strategy, both Harris and Spaatz still believed that in the year left to them before D-Day, their forces could defeat Germany without a land campaign. To both men and to many of their subordinates, the role allotted to them in *Pointblank* as mere harbingers of the invasion forces fell far short of their hopes. The only lasting significance of Casablanca and of *Pointblank* was that they confirmed the air forces' claims on a huge share of their nations' resources for the bomber offensive. Now Harris and Spaatz, each in his own way, set out to prove that by air power alone they could bring Germany to her knees.

The tools of darkness

In Winston Churchill's *History of the Second World War*, it is remarkable that even long after the event, he retained his contempt for the techniques of the Luftwaffe in 1940, and especially for the German *Knickebein* navigational beams:

With their logical minds and deliberate large-scale planning [he wrote] the German Air Command staked their fortunes in this sphere on a device which . . . they thought would do us in. Therefore they did not trouble to train the ordinary bomber pilots, as ours had been trained, in the difficult art of navigation. A far simpler and surer method, lending itself to drill and large numbers producing results wholesale by irresistible science, attracted alike their minds and their nature. The German pilots followed the beam as the German people followed the Führer. They had nothing else to follow.[8]

Yet the techniques of which Churchill wrote with such scorn, *Knickebein* and *X-Gerat* and the 'pathfinder' concept of Kampfgruppe 100 of the Luftwaffe, were precisely those which Bomber Command sought in vain to match throughout 1940 and 1941. Only in 1942 did *Gee* come into service, and by August it was being jammed by the Germans everywhere beyond the coastline of Occupied Europe. Only at the beginning of 1943 was Bomber Command at last equipped with the new generation of radio and radar aids that made it possible to strike with real force at Germany, to bring the bomber offensive out of its cottage-industry phase into the age of automated mass destruction.

It might be thought that once area bombing had been introduced, 'browning' a city became a relatively simple exercise. But until the last day of the war it remained a very difficult test of navigating and bomb-aiming skill. A modern British historian argues that 'the one gleaming lesson of twentieth-century warfare is that strategy follows, and does not precede, the scientist and the technician'.[9] It is true that the bomber proved unable to play a decisive part in war until armed with a devastating scientific weapon in the atomic bomb, yet one may also claim that the strategic air offensive proves the reverse of the argument. So many of the new tools that became available in 1943 only did so because Bomber Command's needs had belatedly been identified, just as those of Fighter Command had been in 1936. The scientists at the

Telecommunications Research Establishment at Malvern applied themselves to solve the proven operational problems of 1940 and 1941. The fruits of their labours were a triumph for British technology – until the end of the war the Americans were almost totally dependent on British electronic devices to wage their own air offensive.

It was Harris's good luck that at the beginning of 1943 he could take advantage of the new generation of equipment just as his force of heavy bombers began its major expansion. In the words of the official historians: 'The air attack on Germany in 1943 increased so much in weight and efficiency that it became something quite different from anything that had preceded it.'[10] Harris himself acknowledged that in 1942 he had merely scratched at the roof of Germany: 'So ended a year of preparation', he wrote in his memoirs, 'in which very little material damage had been done to the enemy which he could not repair from his own resources, but in which we had obtained or had in near prospect what was required to strike him to the ground, and learned how to use it.'[11]

The first vital innovation to match the techniques of the Luftwaffe had been introduced in August 1942: the Pathfinder Force was born. Henceforth, on almost every operation of the offensive, the 'Main Force' squadrons of Bomber Command were preceded to their target by PFF, dropping aerial route markers to guide the stream across Germany, then marking the target by a range of increasingly sophisticated techniques, some visual, some 'blind' by radar.

The creation of the Pathfinders followed one of the most bad-tempered debates of the war between the Air Ministry and Harris. He had nursed a contempt for staff officers since his days as Deputy Chief of Air Staff early in the war. He believed emphatically that subordinates should know their place, which was executing the orders of their superiors:

My first impression on arriving at the Air Ministry was that the staff of every department was fantastically bloated. Junior officers were to my mind quite needlessly named directors of this and that, and they all imagined themselves as commanders in the field of the commands they were supposed to direct – a very nice job, too, because they thought – mistakenly – that they were running the show without having to take the responsibility for the results.

I looked upon C-in-Cs in the field as responsible people who were not to be bothered by the trumpery opinions of young Jacks-in-office . . .[13]

Harris reserved his most virulent disdain for the Air Ministry's Directorate of Bomber Operations, whose staff acted as the Chief of Air Staff's personal advisers and agents in all matters relating to bombing policy. The Director in 1942 was Air Commodore J. W. Baker, shortly to be succeeded by his then deputy, Group-Captain S. O. Bufton, whom we last met commanding 10 Squadron at Leeming in 1940. Ever since his nights over Germany in a Whitley, and subsequently commanding 76 Halifax Squadron, Bufton had been preoccupied by the problems of target location and marking. Back in 1941 he had asked for barometrically fused flares to ignite above the target. He and his crews had experimented with such desperate gambits as firing coded Very cartridges when an aircraft positively identified the target. Now, at the Air Ministry, Bufton had become convinced that Bomber Command must have a specially trained 'Target-Finding Force' to lead them across Germany. It is significant that Bufton was dedicated to the concept of precision bombing, and had the gravest doubts about the value of area attack. He enjoyed close relations with the American 8th Air Force, perhaps not least because of his faith in their objectives, if not their tactics. He was prominent among those at the Air Ministry who regarded area attack as a necessary last resort only until the techniques became available to make Bomber Command a precision-bombing force. It was partly because the creation of a 'Target-Finding Force' might bring this day closer that Bufton advocated it so passionately. It was perhaps for the same reasons that Harris fought the proposal tooth and nail. He had no intention of opening the door an inch to 'panacea merchants'.

Harris's stated reason for opposing Bufton was that morale would suffer throughout Bomber Command if an *élite* force was created within it:

I wanted six Pathfinder forces – one in every group. Having only one, we were told to send all the best crews to it. Imagine the feelings of squadron commanders on being told to hand them over! Portal had no right to overrule me on the advice of a junior staff officer whose only qualification was that he had dropped a few leaflets on Europe at the beginning of the war.[13]

'I don't think that the formation of a First XV at a school makes the small boys play rugger any less enthusiastically,' remarked Sir Henry Tizard, in answer to Harris's objections. Throughout the early summer of 1942 there was a series of acrimonious meettings at High Wycombe. Harris and his group commanders were hostile, but, as Bufton pointed out, not one of them had operational experience over Germany. It was a new and entirely unwelcome experience for the C-in-C, who kept dissent at High Wycombe to a minimum, to be thus harried by a junior officer. The morning after one fierce conference, as Bufton walked up the steps of the Air Ministry in King Charles Street, Harris's Bentley drew up at its usual relentless rush, and the C-in-C sprang out, noticing the staff officer without enthusiasm as he passed: 'Morning, Bufton. And what are you going to do to me today?'

Harris began to lose the battle when the file was passed to Freeman, the Vice-Chief of Air Staff. A consensus clearly emerged at the Air Ministry that whatever the problems of a 'Target-Finding Force', it offered better prospects than the existing system of 'Raid Leaders' evolved in the spring, using arbitrarily selected line squadrons to mark for the Main Force with incendiaries. In July 1942 Harris learnt that he had lost his case.

But there were still some rearguard actions that the C-in-C could win. First, he would not have the new Group called a 'Target-Finding Force'. They would be considered primarily as route guides, 'Pathfinders'. When a proposal was put forward that they should be commanded by the dashing spirit of 2 Group, Basil Embry, Harris would have none of it. His critics said that it was because he feared that Embry would prove as self-willed as himself. In any event, Harris's choice for the command of PFF – No. 8 Group, as it became – was a young Australian group captain named Donald Bennett. Bennett had served under Harris in flying-boats before the war, left the RAF to fly for Imperial Airways, and created a reputation as one of the most brilliant technical airmen of his generation: an outstanding pilot, a superb navigator who was also capable of stripping a wireless set or overhauling an engine, Bennett had spent the early months of the war as one of the directors of the transatlantic ferry, flying aircraft from America to Britain. After his return to the RAF he commanded a Halifax squadron until he was shot down attacking the *Tirpitz* in a Norwegian fjord, and made a successful escape through Sweden. He was still only thirty-two, twenty years younger than his fellow group commanders. The important reservations about Bennett were that he had no large-scale administrative experience, yet he would be immediately responsible for a hundred aircraft and their huge supporting organization, ultimately for nineteen squadrons. He was a difficult and arrogant 'loner' who gained respect but little personal affection everywhere that he went. He made no secret of his opinion that his appointment represented the eclipse of the 'gentlemen' and the arrival of the 'players'. Yet Harris overcame widespread service objections to get Bennett his job, and kept him in it until the end of the war. In a letter to the Prime Minister soon after 8 Group was formed, Harris described its new commander as 'one of the most efficient and finest youngsters I have ever come across in the Service'.

PFF would never get all the resources that it believed it needed. According to Bennett himself,[14] 4 and 6 Groups loyally sent him the best crews they could muster, but the other Group AOCs were half hearted, to say the least, in providing their share of men for secondment to PFF. Bennett and Harris fought a tough battle with the Treasury and the Air Ministry to gain some special recognition for PFF crews, who it was decided should do forty-five trips instead of the usual thirty in a tour, to make the most of their experience. In the end, in addition to the Pathfinder badge which was always genuinely coveted by aircrew, Pathfinders were granted a step-up in rank and pay for as long as they were on 'ops', to be dropped when they finished their tours. They did not, however, get the pick of the aircraft. The five squadrons of Pathfinders that were operational by the beginning of 1943 flew the general Bomber Command mixture of Stirlings, Halifaxes, Lancasters and the new Mosquitoes.

In the last months of 1942 the concentration of bombs dropped by Harris's forces improved marginally with the introduction of the Pathfinders, despite appalling operating weather. A few Main Force crews still ignored the PFF markers and sought their own identification of the target as a matter of pride and genuine conviction that their own judgement was better; but the vast majority were immensely relieved to see the Target Indicators glowing at the heart of a city, marking the aiming-point. Inevitably now, when PFF marked the wrong place, the whole of Bomber Command likewise went awry. There was an embarrassing night when they were sent to Saarbrücken, but the Pathfinders marked nearby Saarlouis in error, and the unfortunate town was duly devastated, while Saarbrücken scarcely received a bomb. The Pathfinder Force developed and was trained to mark for the area offensive and not – as Bufton and others had hoped – to pave the way towards precision bombing. There would be many nights of scattered marking and thus scattered bombing; blind-marking techniques through cloud never became satisfactory even with the new generation of radar aids. But the Pathfinders contributed immensely to the enhanced capability of Bomber Command in 1943.

By far the most important arrivals at the turn of 1942–3 were two new radar aids, H2S and *Oboe*. H2S was the first airborne radar set that could paint a shadowy image of the ground below on a cathode ray tube for its operator in an aircraft above. It held out the prospect of identifying targets through cloud, although like *Gee* – and as Tizard emphatically warned – it would never prove the talisman, the precision blind-bombing aid which the airmen always sought. H2S sets came into use gradually through 1943, and were issued initially to Pathfinder units. They suffered considerable teething trouble, and always performed best in the vicinity of bodies of water which showed up clearly on their screens. But, unlike *Gee*, they operated on a 10-cm waveband that could not be jammed by the German defences.

The second device was indeed a vital blind-bombing aid. *Oboe* was a brilliantly sophisticated variation of the system by which the Germans had bombed England in 1940. An aircraft flew at the end of a beam laid by a ground station, like a conker on a string whirled around a child's head. Its bombs or markers were released at the exact point of intersection with another beam from a second ground station. There was no scope for visual error. The device proved accurate to 600 yards on tests over Lorient and St Nazaire in December 1942. *Oboe* suffered just two limitations: Bomber Command possessed only two sets of ground stations, and could thus control only twelve *Oboe* aircraft an hour over the target. It was necessary to have Pathfinder heavy bombers constantly available to 'back up' the *Oboe* markers if there was any lapse in the visibility of these during the Main Force attack. The second difficulty was more serious: owing to the curvature of the earth, *Oboe* beams could only reach aircraft at limited range from their English ground stations. They could get to the Ruhr, but not much further. Until the Allied advance into Europe in 1944, British attacks on more distant targets had to rely on *Gee*, H2S and pilot judgement for their success. As will become apparent, these were not enough.

But beyond *Oboe*, Harris was now being equipped with the perfect aircraft to carry it, the twin-engined De Havilland Mosquito, which could mark from 28,000 feet to get the utmost range from the device. Since the prototype Mosquito showed its 350 mph promise, rival Commands of the RAF had been struggling fiercely for priority on supplies. It became the best night-fighter of the war, and it could also take a 4,000-lb bomb to Berlin while giving conventional German fighters only the flimsiest chance of catching it. Mosquito casualties over Germany were negligible, a fraction of those suffered by the 'heavies'. The aircraft was a delight to fly. In its bomber role it carried no armament, relying solely on speed for survival. From 1943, it became a vital element in Bomber Command operations, first spearheading the Pathfinder force, later carrying out diversionary raids and Intruder operations against German fighter airfields.

The winter of 1942–3 saw other, less dramatic innovations in tactics and equipment. It had at last been recognized that bright moonlight made bombers too vulnerable to fighters, and now the 'Met' men sought broken cloud and dark nights for operations. For the first time, the Pathfinders were given specially designed Target Indicators, varicoloured projectiles that were big enough and bright enough to be seen from great height amidst the smoke and haze of a burning city. The 'plate rack' principle of sending aircraft in to attack at varying heights had come into general use. The 'streaming' policy for concentrating aircraft over the target had been intensified. Bombers were being fitted with *Boozer* to give early warning of gun and searchlight radar, and with *Monica*, which detected other aircraft closing in. The first of the immense range of radio counter-measures against the German defences was being employed by Group-Captain Addison's 80 Wing, which would ultimately flower into a fully-fledged Group – No. 100.

Now, at the beginning of 1943, Harris wrote: 'At long last we were ready and equipped.'[15] He identified the start of his true strategic offensive as the night of 5 March 1943, when 443 aircraft of Bomber Command attacked Essen under *Oboe* marking laid by the Pathfinder Force. The winter months of sporadic skirmishing against Berlin, and the impenetrable U-boat pens at Lorient and St Nazaire were over. He was free to launch the three great 'battles' which made 1943 the most celebrated and the bloodiest year of the British bomber offensive: the Ruhr, Hamburg and Berlin. These would represent the central thrusts of his campaign, his attempt to bring a devastating concentration of force to bear on selected regions of Germany. March 1943 to March 1944 would be Harris's year of astonishing independence and personal power.

8 76 Squadron, Yorkshire, 1943

'If you live on the brink of death yourself, it is as if those who have gone
have merely caught an earlier train to the same destination, and whatever that destination is, you will be sharing it soon, since you will almost
certainly be catching the next one.'
F/Lt Denis Hornsey, 76 Squadron, 1943

The Ruhr

Although history now remembers the Ruhr as one of Harris's
three great 'battles' of 1943, the crews of Bomber Command
which carried out its forty-three major attacks between 5 March
and 12 July had no such privilege of hindsight. They only knew
that they flew night after night to the most heavily defended
targets in Germany. Several of these – Stettin, Berlin, Munich,
Stuttgart – were not even in the Ruhr. The campaign was by its
nature incapable of yielding any visible proof of victory. The
American official historians have written:

The heavy bomber offensive was an impersonal sort of war, and monotonous in its own peculiar way ... Rarely was a single mission or series
of missions decisive; whatever earlier they had taught of sudden paralysis of a nation by strategic bombardment, in actual practice the forces
available in 1942–3 were quite inadequate for such Douhet-like tactics.[1]

To the bomber crews, the only reality was the intensity of the
struggle. In the four and a half months of the Battle of the Ruhr,
Harris lost almost a thousand aircraft missing over Germany and
crashed in England. His men learnt to hate and fear the ferocity
of the defences of 'Happy Valley', most especially the wall of
flak and light surrounding Essen and the great Krupp works.
They were riddled by gunfire and mauled by the German night-
fighter force, now approaching its zenith. They made bomb run
after bomb run struggling to resist the urge to flinch and turn

aside before reaching their aiming-point, the instinct which created a chronic 'creep-back' of bombs falling short or wide on every raid. In the dense mass of heavy aircraft closing on the target, they learned to fear collision, sometimes even to know the terror of seeing another aircraft directly above them with its bomb doors open. They came to take for granted vast conflagrations reaching across the cities of Germany which had seemed the wonder of the age at Cologne a year before.

Yet it was characteristic of the bomber offensive that each squadron, cut off on its lonely airfield somewhere down the length of eastern England, lived in a private world and knew little of what went on outside except from the bulletins of Group and High Wycombe. Bomber Command could have a disastrous night, losing scores of aircraft, yet a squadron came home unaware of anything amiss, having attacked in a wave that missed the night-fighters. Conversely, another night for no definable reason a squadron might lose four, five, six aircraft – far above Bomber Command's average.

76 Squadron, one of 4 Group's Halifax units stationed at Linton-on-Ouse in Yorkshire, lost a steady one and occasionally two aircraft a night throughout the Battle of the Ruhr. In 1943 as a whole, they operated on 104 nights and lost 59 aircraft missing, four times their operating strength. Sometimes weeks went by without a crew successfully completing a tour.

Harris's assault on the Ruhr began where he had skirmished just a year before, when he took command at High Wycombe: Essen. Led by eight Pathfinder *Oboe* Mosquitoes, 443 aircraft began their attack at 9 p.m. on the moonless night of 5 March 1943. 76 Squadron's Halifaxes were among the first wave, attacking from Zero plus two minutes to Zero plus twenty. The Wellingtons and Stirlings followed from $Z+15$ to $Z+25$, and last came the Lancasters, from $Z+20$ to $Z+40$. They carried a bombload of one-third high explosive to two-thirds incendiaries, for by now it was established that fire was a more effective destroyer of towns than blast. The HE was intended only to expose the city, literally to blow open its windows and walls and doors for the fires. At Bomber Command, the attack was considered an extraordinary success. 153 aircraft had bombed within three miles of the aiming-point. 160 acres of Essen had been laid waste for the loss of only fourteen aircraft. But one of the fourteen came from 76 Squadron, and after debriefing WAAF Intelligence officer, Pam Finch, noted in her diary: 'They all seem rather badly shaken up.'

Three nights later, they were over Nuremberg, where the markers went down two minutes late, and as they exploded a great mass of bombs deluged them, as aircraft that had been lingering nervously overhead thankfully unburdened themselves. The night after, they were at Munich. The squadron operational record book noted coolly: 'Opposition not up to usual standard.' Then the losses began to creep up. Flight-Sergeant Gallantry baled out over the English coast on the way home from Stuttgart. An aircraft was lost over Essen and another crashed on landing. Two crews were missing after the raid on Berlin on 29 March, one of them that of Sergeant Cursley, who had been a pre-war 'erk' in Singapore, and was on his twenty-ninth trip. It was a night of heavy rain, icing and low cloud, and only three of eleven crews claimed to have attacked. Just three of Bomber Command's 481 aircraft bombed within three miles of their aiming-point.

On 7 April, Pam Finch, the WAAF Intelligence girl, went to a cocktail party at the house of Linton's station commander with a Canadian pilot named 'Morty' Mortensen. He claimed to be awed by the honour of 'Groupie's' hospitality: 'Now I'm sure to get the chop!' A week later, the squadron went to Pilsen. Pam Finch looked out at the moon and made a wish for 'Morty' to come back. The raid was a failure. The Pathfinders mistook a lunatic asylum for the Skoda works, and a rain of bombs descended on the countryside around it. The 'missing' rate was 11 per cent, the highest of the Battle of the Ruhr. 'Being that the raid was carried out in perfect moonlight, heavy losses were to be expected,' noted the Squadron Record Book. Three new crews failed to return from 76 Squadron. One of them was Mortensen's.

On 10 April, Group-Captain John Whitley, Linton's popular station commander, was shot down on a trip to Frankfurt. It was uncanny how often senior officers were lost when they made their rare sorties as passengers in bombers. Whitley's successor was lost over Mülheim only two months later. But Whitley himself astonished and delighted everybody by reappearing at

233

Linton large as life only weeks after he was 'Posted Missing to No. 1 Depot Uxbridge', as records put it. A prudent man, he always carried a set of civilian clothes with him on operations, and when his aircraft was shot down by a night-fighter over France, he was well-prepared both mentally and physically for the adventure that followed. Many aircrew were understandably dazed and disorientated after being blown from the sky. But if they were fortunate enough to land in Occupied Europe rather than in Germany itself, those with the will and the luck to survive the first hours on the ground uncaptured often made it to England. With the help of the Resistance, Whitley walked and bicycled across France to the Pyrenees, and came home to receive a well-earned DSO.

On 20 April they went to Stettin. It was a test of new tactics. They flew at sea level across the North Sea in the moonlight, then swept across Denmark low enough to see the windows opening as astonished Danes craned to watch the great stream of bombers roar overhead. One aircraft crashed into a windmill on almost the only hill on the route. All 76's Halifaxes came home. But the next trip they lost a crew over Duisburg, and another over Essen on 30 April. This was a chaotic night, demonstrating the havoc that weather and ill-luck could wreak upon schedules. A Halifax became bogged on the runway, and the three aircraft behind were unable to take off in time to reach the target on schedule. Two of those who got airborne returned early, and only six of those dispatched from 76 Squadron claimed to have attacked.

May began with an attack on Dortmund, one of the most severely punished targets of the battle. On the 11th they went to Duisburg again, another highly successful operation. 572 aircraft were dispatched, and 410 bombed within three miles of the aiming-point. All that early summer, Harris's squadrons seldom bombed less than 300 aircraft strong, often 600 or more. By a characteristic twist of fate, all 76's twelve aircraft came home safe from Duisburg that night, yet 78 Squadron with whom they shared Linton lost three Halifaxes. The mid-upper gunner of one aircraft had suddenly parachuted over the target for no evident reason. Pam Finch noted in her diary: 'The Group Captain thinks the man was temporarily insane.'

On 27 May they were bombing on ETA through ten-tenths

cloud over Essen. Two nights later, they went among 719 aircraft to Wuppertal. It was a most effective attack, marked by *Oboe*. Intelligence estimated that 118,000 people had been made homeless. Yet some of 76's crews were unhappy about the trip, because they had been told by their own Intelligence Officer, 'The Colonel', at briefing that part of their purpose was to catch the thousands of refugees believed to have poured into Wuppertal after the Dambusting operation a fortnight earlier had temporarily flooded areas of the Ruhr. Somehow, bombing refugees didn't seem quite what they thought they were there for. But they all went and came home safely except one aircraft which crashed at Watton.

There was a brief respite in June, when they moved from the pre-war comforts of Linton to the wartime austerity and Nissen-hutted mud lakes of Holme-on-Spalding Moor. Their bitterness about the transfer was heightened by the knowledge that it was caused by a political decision to give the most comfortable pre-war North Yorkshire bases to the newly formed Canadian 6 Group. At Holme, the winter cold sometimes induced NCOs to sleep on sofas in the mess rather than in their quarters, and men hoarded coal under their beds in the fierce contest for warmth. It was from Holme that they fought the last actions of the Ruhr battle, flying to Krefeld and Gelsenkirchen, Cologne and Aachen, although this last operation became another fiasco for 76 when a Norwegian pilot crashed on take-off, jamming the runaway and compelling the eleven Halifaxes behind him to return wearily to their dispersals.

76 was an exceptionally international squadron even by the standards of Bomber Command. Its little group of Norwegian aircrew added a distinctive character and an underpinning of fierce determination. They were drawn from the steady trickle of escapees from occupied Norway. They had come to England to fight, and unlike, for instance, some of the Free French, they were single mindedly dedicated to doing so. 'The Norwegians never cared about the economic importance of a target,' said one of 76's COs in 1943,[2] 'they just wanted to know how many Germans per acre. . .' They lived in their own private world not because they were unfriendly, but because their experience set them a dimension apart from their young English colleagues.

The Norwegians were more serious, less playful in the mess. On evasion exercises on the moors, they were always back first, while the others idly allowed themselves to be captured. They flew with Norwegian flags pinned in the cockpits. They clustered together in their strange forage caps, sharing avidly the occasional letter from home. They seldom turned back early from an operation, whatever technical trouble their aircraft developed. Hulthin, one of the Norwegians who was later killed when his aircraft collided with a night-fighter over Kassel on his twenty-sixth trip, was well known for his calm readiness to circle a target until he was certain of his aiming-point.

'Target ahead, skipper,' said his navigator, as they approached Hamburg one night.

'I see it, navigator.'

'Rear gunner here, skip. What's it look like?'

'Remember the last time?'

'Yes, skip.'

'Well, it's ten times worse.'

Three other Norwegians, – Giortz, Lindaas and Bjerke – were known to the squadron as 'Pip', 'Squeak' and 'Wilfred' after the cartoon characters. 'Squeak' – Lindaas – was a charming, fair-haired, blue-eyed 21-year-old. All the Norwegians were immensely rich by RAF standards because they received flying pay of eight shillings per hour operational in addition to their £28 a month salary. Lindaas told his crew when they joined him that since they were all in it together, they would pool his flying pay. They became the richest crew on the squadron.

At twenty-four, Fred Beadle the rear gunner was the oldest man in Lindaas's aircraft. One night they were on their way home from Frankfurt when the cloud thickened dramatically. The aircraft suddenly started to ice up, and within minutes the pilot lost control. Weighed down by their great frozen burden, they fell through the sky. The intercom had iced up, and Beadle knew nothing until he realized that they were plunging steeply for the ground. He pulled himself out of his turret and slid forward to the cockpit. Only Lindaas and the flight engineer were left – the rest of the crew had already baled out. The flight engineer tried to buckle a parachute on Lindaas. The Norwegian pushed it away. Beadle and the other man jumped. Only when they came home after two years in a prison camp did Beadle learn that Lindaas's brother had already been shot by the Gestapo. Lindaas knew that he himself was a dead man if he landed alive in Germany. He preferred to crash with the aircraft.

As the intensity of Bomber Command's raids on the cities of Germany grew, so did the hazards of parachuting over enemy territory. Many men reached prison camp with terrible stories to tell. A gunner who landed near Kassel was held for five days in a pigsty without food or water by a civilian policeman. Another was attacked by a mob in the streets of Frankfurt, and only saved by a Luftwaffe patrol who pulled him into a basement and later smuggled him out in one of their tunics. Fred Beadle was lucky. He landed near Frankfurt in a snowstorm. Feeling that he had no hope of escape, he hid his parachute, walked into a nearby village, and sat on a doorstep in the early morning darkness, watching the flames of his wrecked aircraft in the distance, until a woman emerged from a door opposite. 'Morgen,' he said, straining his knowledge of German. 'Englander!' she shouted in horror, and ran inside, slamming the door. Eventually soldiers appeared and took him to the local civic office. Children had found his parachute. Villagers fingered his fleece-lined flying clothes and the cigarettes and chocolate emptied from his pocket. 'Churchill propaganda!' said a girl scornfully. Later in the afternoon a truck came to take him, none the worse for wear, to Dulag Luft for interrogation and thence to prison camp.

In the opinion of much of 76 Squadron, John Maze should have been an early candidate for 'the chop'. Immensely tall, easy and languid, he proved a remarkable survivor. Night after night he lifted his Halifax, the long-suffering T-Tommy, off the runway with a sudden wrench as if it was a fighter. Then he set his auto-pilot for the long haul across the North Sea, chatting on the intercom, singing 'I like coffee, I like tea' or some such little ditty, until they approached the German flak belt. Maze's greatest problem on operations was his height, crammed into the Halifax cockpit, until he managed to get hold of a high Lancaster seat and had it fitted in his aircraft. Then Hulthin borrowed T-Tommy while Maze was on leave, and wrecked it on take-off for Aachen. Maze flew the rest of his tour in acute dis-comfort, and his chief memory of bomber operations was

237

constant exhaustion. But blessed with that gift of luck which was a pilot's most priceless possession, he lived.

He was the son of the distinguished French-born painter Paul Maze, and indeed his real name was Etienne – he only called himself John in the RAF. He had been educated at Stowe and Oxford, where he joined the Air Squadron. In November 1941 he was sent to America for flying training. Like so many pilots of the period, he found when he came home that nothing he had been taught prepared him for the reality of operations. In Georgia they were drilled and disciplined like Marine Corps recruits, and three of every five trainees were rejected. But they never flew in any but clear skies, and night-flying practice consisted of cruising from one beacon to another. Maze reached Linton and began operations in April 1943.

Rather than weaving constantly on the way to the target, he used his auto-pilot, because he concentrated on flying accurately in the midst of the stream, thus hopefully avoiding exposing his aircraft. He was always experimenting in the air: opening and closing the radiator flaps, increasing speed and losing height coming home. Despite the discomfort, he valued his six foot six inches flying the Halifax, notoriously the most heavy-handed of all the wartime heavy bombers. In an emergency, he had the reach to throw the aircraft fiercely across the sky. The only crisis that Maze encountered in his first twenty trips came when they were coned on the way home from Wuppertal, and his drastic evasive action tore them free.

On their twenty-first trip, a normally cushy run to Milan for which the 'erks' threatened to paint an ice-cream cone on the nose of T-Tommy instead of the usual bomb in the morning, they were crossing the French coast at 20,000 feet when they saw a sudden streak of tracer, and an aircraft fell in flames in front of them.

'Good God! That was a fighter in front,' shouted the astonished Maze. 'Keep a sharp look-out, chaps. Somebody's bought it just ahead. Keep looking down, Rammy' – this to the rear gunner. 'They can see us perfectly in this light.'

Maze was acutely sensitive to the difficulty of seeing another aircraft in darkness. One night when the entire crew were keeping a sharp look-out, he had been horrified to glance up and see another bomber glide across them only feet above the cockpit. The two Halifaxes had been quite oblivious of each other. But on this night he still declined to unlock T-Tommy's auto-pilot. The first that they knew of the fighter attack was a cannon shell bursting in the rear turret, putting the guns out of action. A second smashed into the controls in the tail, a third into the bomb bay. Maze snatched the controls and flung the Halifax into a dive amidst the appalling din in the fuselage. The tracer fell away to starboard, then they were corkscrewing.

'Can you see him, Rammy?' asked Maze urgently.

'Get weaving, skipper, he's coming in from the port,' shouted the rear gunner.

They straightened out at last and Maze ordered the bomb-aimer to jettison their load. 'Give me a course for home, Dave,' he said to the navigator. 'Have a look aft, will you, Willie. The elevator is almost impossible to control.' They had lost the trimming tab control and the rear gunner was lying slightly wounded on the rest bed in the darkness of the fuselage. They were back over the sea now, heading towards England. The flight engineer knotted the dinghy rope round the control column, then he and the bomb-aimer joined Maze's straining efforts to force back the stick and maintain height. The Halifax lurched and bucked across the sky, losing height with every lunge. The rear gunner, slightly cut in the leg, began to apologize down the intercom for failing to spot the fighter more quickly.

'Shut up, Rammy!' snapped the preoccupied Maze. 'I've no time to listen to you now.'

'Is that an aerodrome coming up, Dave?' he asked the navigator, as he hung with fierce concentration to the yoke.

'It could be Ford, skipper.'

Maze began to talk urgently into the R/T: 'Hallo, Ford, hallo, Ford, I am in difficulty, may I have permission to land?'

There was an eternity of silence, then: 'Hallo, hallo. You may land.'

There was no chance of circling to make an approach. Maze merely plunged for the runway. With a final heave on the stick with half the crew straining at the dinghy rope, they lurched on to the tarmac, bounced and steadied. The Halifax's cargo of frightened, exhausted young men stumbled out in the darkness to face an angry Control Officer who berated them for landing without permission. They had touched down not at Ford, but at nearby Thorney Island, miraculously avoiding three training aircraft who were simultaneously practising circuits and bumps.

Maze's crew had one more bad night. They lost an engine over Munich, and for several minutes feared vividly that they could not remain airborne, while Maze put them into a steep dive to extinguish the flames. Sometimes this tactic succeeded, sometimes it bellowed the flames into melting off the wing. Somebody muttered urgently over the intercom: 'Let's bale out and walk home over the Alps.' But Maze said: 'For goodness sake – it's a hell of a lot worse down there than it is up here!' No one baled out. After eleven hours in the air, they came home. John Maze, just twenty-one, became one of the few 76 Squadron pilots to complete a tour in 1943. He was posted to become ADC to Sir Arthur Harris.

At the end of the Battle of the Ruhr, Bomber Command had flown 18,506 sorties, and lost 872 aircraft missing over Germany – 4.7 per cent – plus a further 16 per cent damaged. On some nights, 30 per cent of all aircraft dispatched had come back damaged or failed to return at all. They had poured 58,000 tons of bombs on to Germany, more than the Luftwaffe had dropped on Britain throughout 1940 and 1941, more than Bomber Command had dropped on Germany in the whole of 1942. The photographs of cities that they had attacked revealed thousands of acres of industrial and residential devastation. High Wycombe computed that up to the end of 1942, 400 acres of urban Germany had been razed by bombing. In 1943, this figure would rise to 26,000 acres. Crews were coming faster and faster from the training machine, and aircraft from the production line. Harris's daily availability of bombers rose from 593 in February to 787 in August 1943. Yet who was being punished more severely, Germany or Bomber Command? Who was winning the extraordinary contest between bombs and concrete? The rate of attrition on both sides was becoming awesome, yet the struggle seemed as far as ever from any decisive conclusion.

Hamburg

Holme-on-Spalding Moor was a bleak, unfriendly sort of place. It was widely felt by the aircrew that the village had turned its back on the war. The locals resented the RAF's domination of their bowling alley. Wives and girlfriends who lodged nearby were treated with ill-concealed disdain, scarlet women from the cities. Every six weeks or so, for those aircrew who survived there were seven days' leave. Some men went home, others hastened with their crews to the blacked-out joys of London. They were crestfallen to discover how little they knew about how to be sinful. Most ended their evenings at the RAF Club or the YMCA. On evenings off from Holme, there were cheap taxis to York and the pleasures of Betty's Bar and The Half Moon. In the officers' mess, more often than not they would merely drink a few pints and go quietly to bed after a game of darts. Only a few relentless spirits went to the village every night and drank themselves to oblivion like a gunner, 'The Pommified Aussie', who had to be retrieved with monotonous regularity from the police station. Most men waited until there was some excuse for a binge, and then threw themselves into the traditional excitements of wartime bomber stations: great choruses of 'Do You Know the Muffin Man?' as one by one they tiptoed across the mess floor with a pint of beer on their heads; frenzied games of 'Flarepath', diving across the floor between two lines of human beacons clutching flaming newspapers. But, often in 1943, they were too tired for party games.

In the morning they hung about the Flight Office playing with the station's stray mongrel, 'Flak', or teasing somebody about 'Calamity Kate', the decorative WAAF clerk who was widely believed to be a passport to 'the chop' for any man who took her out.

Then despite a very gloomy picture painted by the Met Office, we learned that the raid was 'on'. Our system for finding this news in advance was for all the pilots to put a penny in a box, the contents of which were given to the Wing Co's confidential clerk. In return for this small consideration, we were given 'the gen' and could make our plans accordingly.

The atmosphere in the Flight Office would be very tense until the news came through. Completely contrary to the popular impression given in books and films, there would be a relieved cheer, loud laughter and a babble of excited talk if we were not to operate that day. If we were due to do so, the pilots would merely make some casual remark and quickly slip away to get themselves, their aircraft and crews ready. Later we would return to learn what the target would be – not without some secret dread in our hearts that it might again be Berlin or the Ruhr.[3]

On the evening of 24 July 1943, 76 Squadron were briefed to take part in the most massive attack of the war by Bomber Command, on Hamburg. They had been to the great north German port before. But this time, they were told, it would be different. First, 791 aircraft would be taking part in 'Operation Gomorrah'. Second, and much more important, this time it would be easy. They were to be equipped with a brilliant scientific device that would fog the radar screens of Germany – guns, night-fighters and all. It was codenamed *Window*, and consisted simply of bundles of narrow metal foil strips, to be pushed down a special chute by the wireless operator and flight engineer at intervals during the run over Germany. It is a measure of the crews' faith in the scientists that they were at once excited and delighted by the vision of chaos among the defences, convinced that they were being given a weapon that would turn the odds dramatically. 'Why haven't we had it before?' asked Bamber, one of the flight commanders. 'Er . . . good question,' said the man from 4 Group Operational Research.

Window had been devised and reported effective by the spring of 1942, but at a meeting to discuss its future, Lord Cherwell made one of his periodic baleful interventions. If it would work against German radar, he pointed out, obviously it would work against our own. What happened if the Germans launched a new blitz against Britain? Cherwell's remarks threw Fighter and Anti-Aircraft Commands and Herbert Morrison's Ministry of Home Security into confusion. They successfully opposed the introduction of *Window* by Bomber Command, despite a belated effort by Tizard, from the wilderness, to have them overruled. But by the autumn of 1942, the Luftwaffe had become a negligible threat to Britain. The official historians remark tartly on the curious failure of Sir Arthur Harris to 'exert himself to secure the introduction of a measure which was expected so greatly to favour the offence at the expense of the defence'.[4] Once again, Harris had been slow to respond to technological possibilities. Only in the summer of 1943, when the losses of his force to radar-directed night-fighters had become intolerable, did he move at last with real urgency to press for the introduction of *Window*.[5] The Prime Minister personally overruled Morrison and Fighter Command's objections. 'Let us open the window!' he declared majestically. On the night of 24 July, Bomber Command did so with remarkable results.

76 Squadron was now a three-flight unit with an establishment of thirty aircraft. On the night of the 24th, twenty-four crews were briefed for Hamburg. Despite the clear night, three returned early. The remaining twenty-one approached the target dazzled by the vision before them. Searchlights wandered lost across the sky like drunken men. The city's fifty-six heavy and thirty-six light flak batteries were firing desperate blind box barrages, helpless in their inability to take radar predictions on the aircraft above. The night-fighters had failed utterly to locate the bomber stream.

It was a brief moment of triumph for the bomber in its duel against the fighter, and the crews savoured it, like the great thrust against Cologne more than a year before. The attack on Hamburg was the most perfectly orchestrated since the war began. Two minutes before zero hour at 1 a.m., twenty Pathfinder aircraft dropped yellow Target Indicators blind on H2S, under ideal conditions since Hamburg's coastline gave the city an exceptionally sharp radar image. They were followed by eight Pathfinders carrying red TIs, which they aimed visually. A further fifty-three Pathfinders backed up visually with green TIs. The Main Force, bombing from Zero + 2 minutes to Zero + 48, were ordered to overshoot the markers by two seconds, in an effort to reduce the 'creepback' which had become such a pronounced feature of recent attacks.

The raid was an overwhelming success. 306 of the 728 aircraft which claimed to have attacked dropped their bombs within three miles of the aiming-point. Vast areas of Hamburg were devastated for the loss of only twelve bombers. The next day, north Germany awoke to find a bewildering array of metal-foil strips littered like errant Christmas decorations over hedges and houses and farmland, being eaten by cows and hung over tele-graph wires. But the Luftwaffe scientists were not puzzled. They had understood the principles of *Duppel*, as they called *Window*, for as long as Bomber Command, but had flinched from employ-ing it for the same reasons. They knew no antidote.

One of the twelve aircraft lost on the night of the 24th came from 76 Squadron, and another piloted by a rather wild young man named Mick Shannon crashed on landing back at Holme. Shannon was having a terrifying tour. The next night, when they went to Essen, his aircraft was hit by flak, shearing off a propeller which spun smashing into the fuselage. In the mid-upper turret was Waterman, a professional poacher in civilian life, and one of the finest shots on the squadron. He normally flew with 'A' flight commander, Bamber, but was filling in for a sick man. Now, Waterman parachuted over Germany before Shannon decided that he could save the aircraft, and staggered home to bellyland at Holme. Such incidents, in which part of a crew baled out in the immediate crisis following an aircraft being hit, were not uncommon. If a man did not jump within seconds, he knew that he might never have the chance to jump at all. Ten days later, Shannon was hit yet again over Mannheim. But this time no one jumped. Neither he nor his crew ever came home.

In daylight on 25 and 26 July, Ira Eaker's 8th Air Force flew 235 sorties to Hamburg to stoke the fires lit by Harris. On the night of the 25th, Mosquitoes staged a nuisance raid on the city, further to exhaust the defenders and the air-raid services.Then, on the 27th, Bomber Command went back. This was an entirely new technique: absolute devastation by repeated attack, saturat-ing the fire services. 787 aircraft were dispatched, by a different route from that taken on the 24th. 722 attacked Hamburg, and of these 325 bombed within three miles. Fires were still blazing from the earlier attacks. Now these were redoubled by the new wave of blast and flame.

But the Luftwaffe responded to *Window* with remarkable speed and flexibility, assisted by their scientists' instant under-standing of the crisis. They knew that, overnight, the ground-controlled interception of individual bombers had been eclipsed. Only weeks before, they had created the first 'Wild Boar' squad-rons, of single-engined fighters which were vectored into the bomber stream over the target by radio running-commentary, as information seeped in from observer posts all over Germany about the bombers' direction and changes of course. Now, these 'freelances' were rapidly reinforced. The 'Wild Boars' became the basis of the Luftwaffe's immediate counter-attack, and formidably effective they proved, although costly in fighter accident losses. British 'spoof' raids by small forces of aircraft *Windowing* in a manner that suggested the Main Force, together with deceptive routeing to the target, would often hold off the fighters until after the bombers had attacked. But then, even amidst their own flak and searchlights, the fighters came in. A handful of Me109s piloted by experts proved capable of shooting down a succession of bombers each in a single night once they had locked into the stream. Until the very end of the war, the Luftwaffe maintained their counter-offensive with all the energy and brilliance that their supplies of fuel and trained pilots allowed. Some airmen argue that in defeating the German radar network with *Window*, Bomber Command showed the Germans the way to a much simpler and deadlier means of controlling fighter defence.

On the night of 29 July, 777 aircraft went to Hamburg again. Thirty of them were lost, including one from 76 Squadron. The casualties were creeping up as the Luftwaffe recovered from *Window*. On the night of 2 August, the fourth and last of Bomber Command's great attacks of the battle, 740 aircraft were dispatched in appalling weather to Hamburg. A further thirty were lost.

Yet Harris had already gained his triumph in the Battle of Hamburg and this last operation was all but redundant. Twenty-two square kilometres of the city had been engulfed in the fantastic firestorm that began on the night of the 27th, the second raid. This was the harbinger of Dresden, Darmstadt and other lesser infernos of 1944 and 1945. As the fires reached incredible temperatures – 1,000 degrees centigrade and more – they sucked in the air and bellowed themselves into hurricanes of flame and smoke that tore through the heart of Hamburg amidst winds of 150 mph. Private hoards of coal and coke in the cellars fuelled the fires from every house. Thousands suffocated, then their bodies were incinerated in the cellars in which they had died.

Air-raid shelters became vast crematoria. 42,000 Germans were estimated to have died. A million refugees fled the city. In one week, Bomber Command had killed more people than the Luftwaffe had achieved in the eight months of the blitz in England in 1940–41. In Hamburg, 40,385 houses, 275,000 flats, 580 factories, 2,632 shops, 277 schools, 24 hospitals, 58 churches, 83 banks, 12 bridges, 76 public buildings and a zoo had been obliterated. Goebbels said that it was 'a catastrophe, the extent of which simply staggers the imagination'. For the first time in the war, Bomber Command had profoundly shaken the Nazi leadership. Since 24 July, Harris's aircraft had flown 3,095 sorties, and poured 9,000 tons of explosives and incendiaries on to Hamburg for the loss of 86 aircraft.

If other cities were pounded as relentlessly at this, the consequences for Germany must have been appalling. No industry, no urban area could stand repeated punishment on this scale. By dawn on 3 August, 1943, Hamburg seemed an empty city, 'sunk in a great silence of death'. But Bomber Command was not to repeat the severity of its attack on Hamburg against the other major cities of Germany until 1945. Harris's staff never appeared to grasp the full significance of their success in July 1943 – that it had been repetition which made possible the climactic destruction. High Wycombe was always nervous about returning again and again to a target in a manner which allowed the Luftwaffe to anticipate them. Hamburg was in north Germany, and thus required a relatively short penetration inside night-fighter range. But those cities which lay deep in enemy territory – above all Berlin – could always put up formidable resistance if the Germans correctly predicted the target or were aided by clear skies. To Harris's staff, it seemed more profitable to strike a target at intervals of some weeks than to return immediately. Barnes Wallis was deeply frustrated that Bomber Command never sent a high-level bombing force to hit the Mohne dam while repairs were being carried out in the weeks after the attack of May 1943. He argued that extreme precision would have been unnecessary – even a few hits by conventional HE bombs would have prevented the Germans from making the rapid repairs that they in fact completed, and thus would have helped to justify the great sacrifice by 617 Squadron.[6] Whether or not this is true, High Wycombe never gave enough attention to the importance of reinforcing the successes of Bomber Command.

From August until the Battle of Berlin in late November, Harris's aircraft embarked upon the series of deepening penetrations that came to be known as 'The Road to Berlin', although many of the targets – Mannheim, Nuremberg, Munich – lay far from the German capital. At the end of August, they went to Berlin itself: from the first day of the bomber offensive to the last, the most terrifying target of all to the crews of Bomber Command.

This was our first raid on Berlin [a 76 Squadron flight engineer named Ferris Newton wrote in his diary]. As we had all heard such stories about the place, we were not at all happy about going. Everyone sat around the kite waiting for start-up time, and nobody hardly spoke a word.

We were first wave in. Berlin's 35-mile area was dotted with light, so that it was hard to distinguish the burst of anti-aircraft shells below from the coloured markers dropped by the Pathfinders. First thing we have to do is fly through a wall of searchlights – hundreds of them in cones and clusters. Behind that all is an even fiercer light. It's glowing red and green and blue, and over that there are myriads of flares hanging in the sky. There is flak coming up at us now. All we see is a quick red glow from the ground – then up it comes on a level – a blinding flash.

There is one comfort, and it's been a comfort to me all the time we have been going over, and that is that it is quite soundless. The roar of your engines drowns everything else. It's like running straight into the most gigantic display of soundless fireworks in the world. The searchlights are coming nearer now all the time. There's one cone split, then it comes together again. They seem to splay out, then stop, then come together again, and as they do there's a Lancaster right in the centre. We start weaving. George puts the nose down and we are pelting away at a furious rate. As we are coming out of the searchlight belt, more flak is coming up from the inner defences.

'Hello, skipper.'

'Hello, navigator.'

'Half a minute to go.'

'OK. Thanks for reminding me.'

'Keep weaving, George, there's quite a lot of light stuff coming up as well – falling off a bit low.'

'Hello, engineer, will you put the revs up?'

'Engineer to pilot. Revs up, skipper.'

'OK. Keep weaving, George. A lot of searchlights and fighter flares left.'

'Hello, bomb-aimer. OK when you are. Bomb doors open.'

'OK, George – right – steady – a little bit longer yet – OK – steady –right a little bit – right – steady – bombs still going . . . OK, bombs gone.'

'Keep weaving, there's some flak coming up. I can actually see ground detail, skipper . . . Oh, it's a wizard sight!'

'OK, Andy, don't get excited – keep your eyes open.'

'Engineer to pilot. Jerry fighter just passed over the top of us port to starboard.'

'OK, engineer, keep your eyes open, gunners.'

'Hello, skipper, will you turn on to Zero 81.'

'Zero 81, right navigator.'

We are out of it and now we are through. I turn and get a glimpse of that furious glowing carpet of light and explosions, that's all I can see of Berlin.

As we approached England we got a diversion message to Catfoss, of all places. Flying time for the trip, 8 hours 50 minutes. This raid had been the heaviest on Berlin to date, at a cost of 58 aircraft out of 700 (this does not include two aircraft which collided on the circuit at Catfoss: damn hard luck, that, all the way to Berlin and back, then get it on your own circuit) . . .

On the night of 18 August, 597 aircraft were sent to Peenemunde on the Baltic, the German V-weapon research establishment. The crews were sobered to be told at briefing that this was a vital 'Radio-location laboratory and aircraft testing site', and that if they failed to destroy it, they would be sent back again and again until they did so. They bombed after a timed run from an off-shore island to the target, and the concentration was exceptional. Widespread damage was done to the workshops and scientists' living quarters. The night-fighters, diverted by a Mosquito 'spoof' raid on Berlin, had been slow to grasp the British intentions, but caught up with the last stages of the attack on Peenemunde. Forty aircraft failed to return. For once, however, 76 Squadron was lucky. Their twenty aircraft had gone in with an early wave, and all returned unscathed except a navigator wounded by a shrapnel fragment. Afterwards, there would be some doubt how seriously the raid had delayed the V-weapon programme, but

Harry Jones of 37 Squadron in a German hospital after being shot down on 18 December 1939

F/Sgt Herbert Ruse *(on the left)* of 37 Squadron being briefed for an operation. On the right is the squadron CO, W/Cdr Joe Fogarty

(above) Marshal of RAF Lord Trenchard
(above right) Sir Edgar Ludlow-Hewitt, C-in-C of Bomber Command 1937–40
(below left) Sir Richard Peirse, C-in-C of Bomber Command 1940–42
(below right) Sir Archibald Sinclair, Secretary of State for Air 1940–45.
He was leader of the Liberal Party until he went to the House of Lords as
Viscount Thurso

A Halifax of Bomber Command sets out for Germany

The face of the enemy: Germany's armament workers continued to produce the tools for the survival of the Third Reich almost until the end, their will unbroken by bombing. Here a factory group is addressed by Albert Speer

Magrath (82 Squadron)

Staton (10)

Donaldson (10)

Lindaas (76)

Maze (76)

Hornsey (76)

Newton (76)

Cheshire (76)

Eclipse: the C-in-C of Bomber Command with his wife and daughter on their
way to South Africa soon after the end of the war. Harris did not share the
honours that fell to other service leaders in the wake of victory, and never
concealed his bitterness that his men were denied their own Campaign Medal

fortunately for the crews, High Wycombe were satisfied. There was no return visit.

Some nights they were fortunate, and were sent to Italy, which was reckoned to be a pushover unless one had a technical failure or very bad luck, and the crews had their awe-struck view of the Alps in darkness. One night over Turin, Group-Captain John Searby presided for the first time as 'Master Bomber', a technique pioneered by Guy Gibson on the Dams raid, guiding the crews by radio-telephone as they approached the target, pointing out the best markers and attempting to concentrate the attack. The Master Bomber never commanded a raid in the fullest sense of being in charge of the huge force of aircraft – Leonard Cheshire was among those who believed that there should have been an airborne commander of every operation, empowered for instance to send everybody home if the weather was hopeless. But the Master Bomber's calm voice across the ether, directing and encouraging aircraft as he circled above them, could be enormously helpful in keeping an attack on course or preventing a fiasco when markers fell in the wrong place.

76 Squadron were still losing a steady one or two aircraft a night against the German targets, and Hanover now inspired almost as deep a fear as Berlin. The behaviour of bereaved families often seemed strange to the men on the stations. Relatives would conduct a long and savage correspondence with a squadron CO about the absence of, say, a fountain-pen from their son's personal effects, returned to them by the RAF Central Depository at Colnbrook. Sometimes a family would become deeply embittered by their son's loss, and seek somehow to attribute blame for it.

Death drifted through the huts and hangars in the most erratic fashion. An aircraft code letter, P-Peter or R-Robert, suddenly became deadly for a succession of crews who flew it. A certain bunk took on the deadly properties of the Black Spot. Alf Kirkham and his crew found that throughout their tour at Holme, the next-door hut was doomed. Every week, new faces arrived to occupy it, and at once vanished.

Kirkham was one of 76 Squadron's stars, a sergeant pilot who completed a distinguished tour on Halifaxes, was commissioned and twice decorated before doing a further tour on Mosquitoes. He was unhappy about 76's enthusiasm for flying operations with the auto-pilot locked in, which he believed was a formula for disaster. Always a 'press-on type', he had gone round three times at Peenemunde as converging aircraft forced him to bank at the critical moment of each bomb-run. On the ground, he cut a swathe through WAAFs, the girls of York and occasional senior officers' daughters. His crew was one of the few to shoot down a night-fighter, apparently a Luftwaffe novice who was so intent on stalking another aircraft that he did not notice Kirkham's Halifax beside him until the gunners blew him apart. But at the end of August, over München-Gladbach, as they turned out of the target a fighter fell on them. It was Kirkham's turn to struggle for his life.

We were hit by cannon shells and tracer immediately. The navigator was badly wounded, a bullet hit me in the right leg, the starboard inner engine was knocked out, the R/T packed up completely and we caught fire. I feathered the damaged engine, but another attack knocked out a lot of my instruments and also my call lights so that I had no communication with the gunners. I took violent evasive action, so much so that if anyone had baled out I wouldn't have blamed them, as they could have thought that we were out of control. The Control column worked well but I had little rudder control, and my right leg did not seem to be much help. By juggling the throttles and using a lot of bank I was able to corkscrew, but maintaining height was out of the question. I remember seeing the engineer being violently sick and using the fire-extinguisher at the same time . . .

The steep dive blew out the flames, but I was getting pretty desperate. Eventually we did a stall turn with a very nearly 90-degree bank, and fell out of the sky. We lost the fighter. We set a rough course for home and checked our damage. I could hold height, but the aircraft was very difficult to fly. The navigator could not possibly bale out, so I decided to crash-land and offer the crew the chance to bale out over England. We encountered flak and searchlights a lot of the time, and at 8,000 feet they were quite accurate.

We eventually hit the coast at Bradwell Bay in Essex, and I saw two searchlights indicating an aerodrome. I found I had fair control at 105 mph, but I couldn't hold the aircraft at speeds below this. There were no flaps available, and the undercarriage didn't work, and it appeared that I would have to fly the plane onto the ground at a very high speed . . . By this time all the crew had vanished to their crash-landing positions behind the main spar, and it seemed very lonely.

As we hit the deck, I throttled back and switched off. We ran along for a long time on our belly, but I was pleasantly surprised to see that there was no sign of fire . . .'

Yet although many crews suffered nights as terrifying as that of Alf Kirkham, there were also a surprising number who went through a tour without any incidents at all. Ferris Newton, the flight engineer who described his first trip to Berlin, was in a crew captained by twenty-year-old Sergeant George Dunn. They had had a series of frightening experiences at OTU, where they were forced to bale out of a doomed Wellington over Scotland, and four crews out of sixteen in their course were killed. But on 76 Squadron their gunners never fired a shot in anger; they were only once hit by a small piece of shrapnel; and only once suffered a mechanical defect – a hydraulic leak on the way home from Peenemunde. This in no way made flying operations less frightening or less difficult, but is an odd aside on the flukes of war.

They were an exceptionally close-knit crew both in the air and on the ground. Ferris Newton himself owned a little pub near Leeds named The Old Ball, run by his wife Catherine, and at every spare moment they piled into his battered Morris 8, with bodies protruding from its sunshine roof, and dashed away to 'The Ancient Knacker' on petrol bought with stockpiled cigarettes. Reg McCadden, the commissioned navigator, was a Northern Irishman who had been dive-bombed on an auxiliary cruiser in August 1940, and decided that henceforth if there was going to be any bombing done around him, he would be doing it. Andy Maitland, their young bomb-aimer, was passionately enthusiastic about bomber operations. He became a compulsive 'hours chaser', one of the few who survived, completing more than ninety trips and ending the war with a permanent commission in Pathfinders.

'I can see the streets! I can see the streets!' he shouted in excitment as he lay over his bombsight on their first trip over Germany.

'F—k the streets, just bomb and let's get out of here,' said a furious and much more typical voice down the intercom.

In October 1943, just before the Halifaxes entered a period of even more appalling losses in the Battle of Berlin, reaching a climax in January and February 1944 when they were losing 11 per cent of aircraft dispatched to Germany, Ferris Newton wrote in his diary:

The target was Kassel with a spoof attack on Hanover . . . This being our last trip, we got a really marvellous send-off by everyone. A whole crowd of people on the officers' mess site waving like mad . . .At the ACP caravan at the end of the runway, S/Ldr Bennett and others all giving us the thumbs-up sign . . .

Needless to say we were first back, for the only time. As we touched down we all gave a loud shout through the intercom, and as George had it on 'Transmit', all and sundry heard what we said, not that anybody cared.

After debriefing I gave Catherine a ring, just to tell her I was back and finished. That was about three o'clock in the morning . . . Back at Holme we were having our second breakfast in the officers' mess kitchen, so we could be with the rest of the crew. There were only three of us who were not commissioned by this time . . .

Completing a tour on Halifaxes in 1943 was a matter for unusual celebration. That early morning of 4 October, as Ferris Newton and his crew rejoiced in their personal victory over the percentages, a WAAF in the operations room at Holme was deleting four missing 76 Squadron crews from the list of nineteen which had taken off a few hours before – twenty-eight more of Harris's men gone. In Kassel, they were counting the bodies of 5,200 people.

Courage

Throughout the war, morale on British bomber stations held up astonishingly well, although there were isolated collapses on certain squadrons at certain periods – for example, during the heavy losses of the Battle of Berlin. Morale never became a major problem, as it did on some 8th Air Force stations during the terrible losses of 1943 and early 1944. An RAF doctor seconded to study aircrew spirit at one American station reported in dismay: 'Aircrew are heard openly saying that they don't intend to fly to Berlin again or do any more difficult sorties. This is not considered a disgrace or dishonourable.' Partly the Americans found the appalling business of watching each other die on daylight sorties more harrowing than the anonymity of night operations. Partly also, they were far from their homes, and many did not feel the personal commitment to the war that was possible for Englishmen.

But most of the crews of Bomber Command fought an unending battle with fear for most of their tours, and some of them lost it. Even today, the Judge-Advocate General of the Forces is implacably unhelpful on inquiries relating to the problems of disciplinary courts martial and 'LMF' – lacking moral fibre – cases among wartime aircrew. I believe that around one man in seven was lost to operational aircrew at some point between OTU and completing his tour for morale or medical causes, merely because among a hundred aircrew whom I have interviewed myself, almost all lost one member of their crew at some time, for some reason. Few of these cases would be classified by any but the most bigoted as simple 'cowardice', for by now the Moran principle that courage is not an absolute human characteristic, but expendable capital every man possesses in varying quantity, has been widely recognized. But in 1943 most men relieved of operational duty for medical or moral reasons were treated by the RAF with considerable harshness. There was great fear at the top of the service that if an honourable path existed to escape operations, many men would take it. 'LMF could go through a squadron like wildfire if it was unchecked,' says one of the most distinguished post-war leaders of the RAF, who in 1943 was commanding a bomber station. 'I made certain that every case before me was punished by court martial, and where applicable by an exemplary prison sentence, whatever the psychiatrists were saying.'[8]

Command was enraged when stories emerged at courts martial of doctors in Glasgow or Manchester who for five pounds would brief a man on the symptoms necessary to get him taken off operations: insomnia, waking screaming in his quarters, bedwetting, headaches, nightmares. Station medical officers became notoriously unsympathetic to aircrew with any but the most obvious symptoms of illness. The Air Staff were in a constant dilemma about the general management of aircrew, who were intensively trained to fly their aircraft, yet for little else. Regular officers were exasperated by the appearance and off-duty behaviour of many temporary officers and NCOs. In their turn, the relentless pursuit of career opportunities by some regular airmen even in the midst of war did not escape the scornful notice of aircrew, especially when this took the form of officers burying themselves in Flying Training Command or in staff jobs rather than flying with operational squadrons.

The Air Ministry considered that morale and disciplinary problems were closely linked. In a 1943 report which attacked the practice of holding All Ranks dances at bomber stations, which noted that Harris's men had the highest rate of venereal disease in the RAF and No. 6 Group's Canadians a rate five times higher than anyone else's, the Inspector-General of the RAF noted with displeasure:

Aircrew are becoming more and more divorced from their legitimate leaders, and their officers are forgetting, if they ever learnt them, their responsibilities to their men. Aircrew personnel must be disabused of the idea that their sole responsibility is to fly . . . and to do this, their leisure hours must be more freely devoted to training and hard work . . .

The Air Ministry never lost its conviction that gentlemen made the best aircrew, and a remarkable staff memorandum of late 1942 expressed concern about the growing proportion of Colonials in Bomber Command and suggested: 'There are indications in a number of directions that we are not getting a reasonable percentage of the young men of the middle and upper classes, who are the backbone of this country, when they leave the public schools.'

When Ferris Newton was interviewed for a commission, the group captain had already noted without enthusiasm that he owned a pub, and inquired whether it catered to the coach trade. Yet the Commonwealth aircrew, especially, believed that it was their very intimacy with their crews, their indifference to rank, that often made them such strong teams in the air. An Australian from 50 Squadron cited the example of a distinguished young English ex-public school pilot who was killed in 1943. This boy, he said, was a classic example of an officer who never achieved complete cohesion with his crew, who won obedience only by the rings on his sleeves and not by force of personality: 'He simply wouldn't have known how to go out screwing with his gunners in Lincoln on a Saturday night.' In his memoirs Harris argues that the English made the best aircrew, because they had the strongest sense of discipline. It was a difference of tradition.

To the men on the stations, the RAF's attitude to their problems often seemed savagely unsympathetic. One day on a cross-country exercise before they began operations, the bomb-aimer of Lindaas's crew at 76 Squadron fell through the forward hatch of the aircraft, which had somehow come loose. The rest of the crew thought at first that he had fallen out completely. Only after several seconds did they realize that he was clinging desperately beneath the aircraft. Only after several more seconds of struggle did they get the dinghy rope around him, and haul him back into the fuselage. When he returned to the ground, he said flatly that he would never fly again. He was pronounced LMF, and vanished from the station. Normally in such cases, an NCO was stripped of his stripes, which had been awarded in recognition of his aircrew status, and posted to ground duties. Only in incontrovertible cases of 'cowardice in the face of the enemy', as at one 5 Group station where one night three members of a crew left their aircraft as it taxied to take-off, was the matter referred to court martial. A further cause of resentment against Permanent Commissioned Officers was that if they wished to escape operations, they could almost invariably arrange a quiet transfer to non-operational duties, because the service was reluctant to instigate the court martial that was always necessary in their case, to strip them of rank.

It was very rare for a case to be open and shut. The navigator of a Whitley in 1941 ran amok and had to be laid out with the pilot's torch over Germany. The man disappeared overnight from the squadron – normal procedure throughout the war, to avoid the risk that he might contaminate others. But the pilot recounting this experience[9] added: 'Don't draw the obvious conclusion. The next time I saw the man's name, he was navigating for one of the Dambusting crews.' Many men had temporary moral collapses in the midst of operational tours. The most fortunate, who were sensitively treated, were sent for a spell at the RAF convalescent home at Matlock in Derbyshire. A post-war medical report argues that many such men sincerely wanted to be rehabilitated and return to operations to save their own self-respect, while genuine LMF cases proved on close study to be men who should never have survived the aircrew selection process.

But the decisive factor in the morale of bomber aircrew, like that of all fighting men, was leadership. At first, it is difficult to understand what impact a leader can have, when in battle his men are flying with only their own crews over Germany, far out of sight and command. Yet a post-war 8 Group medical report stated emphatically: 'The morale of a squadron was almost always in direct proportion to the quality of leadership shown by the squadron commanders, and the fluctuations in this respect were most remarkable.' A good CO's crews pressed home attacks with more determination; suffered at least marginally lower losses; perhaps above all, had a low 'Early Return' rate. Guy Gibson, the leader of the Dambusters, was one kind of legendary Bomber Command CO. Not a cerebral man, he represented the apogee of the pre-war English public schoolboy, the perpetual team captain, of unshakeable courage and dedication to duty, impatient of those who could not meet his exceptional standards. 'He was the kind of boy who would have been head prefect in any school,' said Sir Ralph Cochrane, his commander in 5 Group.[10]

For the first four months of 1943, 76 Squadron was commanded by Leonard Cheshire, another of the great British bomber pilots of the war, of a quite different mould from Gibson, but even more remarkable. Cheshire, the son of a distinguished lawyer, read law at Oxford, then joined the RAF shortly before the outbreak of war. In 1940 he began flying Whitleys over Germany. By 1943, with two brilliant tours already behind him, he was a 26-year-old wing-commander. There was a mystical air about him, as if he somehow inhabited another planet from those around him, yet without affection or pretension. 'Chesh is crackers,' some people on the squadrons said freely in the days before this deceptively gentle, mild man became famous. They were all the more bewildered when he married and brought back from America in 1942 an actress fifteen years older than himself.

Yet Leonard Cheshire contributed perhaps more than any other single pilot to the legend of Bomber Command. He performed extraordinary feats of courage, studied the techniques of bombing with intense perception and intelligence, and later pioneered the finest precision marking of the war as leader of 617 Squadron. At 76 Squadron there was a joke about Cheshire, that 'the moment he walks into a bar, you can see him starting to work out how much explosive it would need to knock it down'. He was possibly not a natural flying genius in an aircraft like Micky Martin, but, by absolute dedication to his craft, he made himself a master. He flew almost every day. If he had been on leave and was due to operate that night, he went up for two hours in the morning to restore his sense of absolute intimacy with his air-craft. He believed that to survive over Germany it was necessary to develop an auto-pilot within himself, which could fly the aircraft quite instinctively, leaving all his concentration free for the target and the enemy. As far back as 1941 he wrote a paper on marking techniques. He had always been an advocate of extreme low-level bombing.

Cheshire himself wrote, 'I loved flying and was a good pilot, because I threw myself heart and soul into the job. I found the dangers of battle exciting and exhilarating, so that war came easily to me.'[11] Most of those he commanded knew themselves to be frailer flesh, and he dedicated himself to teaching them every-thing that he knew. He never forgot that Lofty, his own first pilot on Whitleys, had taught him to know every detail of his aircraft, and he was determined to show others likewise. He lectured 76's crews on Economical Cruising Heights, Escape and Evasion techniques, and methods of improving night vision. They knew that he was devoted to their interests. On a trip to Nuremberg they were detailed to cross the French coast at 2,000 feet. He simply told Group that he would not send them at that height. It would be 200 feet or 20,000. He made his point.

A CO who flew the most dangerous trips himself contributed immensely to morale – some officers were derisively christened 'François' for their habit of picking the easy French targets when they flew. Cheshire did not have his own crew – only Jock Hill, his wireless operator. Instead, he flew as 'Second Dickey' with the new and nervous. Perhaps the chief reason that 'Chesh' inspired such loyalty and respect was that he took the trouble to know and recognize every single man at Linton. It was no mean feat, learning five hundred or more faces which changed every week. Yet the ground crews chorused: 'We are Cheshire cats!' because the CO spent so much of his day driving round the hangars and dispersals chatting to them and remembering exactly who had sciatica. It was the same with the aircrew. A young wireless operator, who had arrived at Linton the previous day, was climbing into the truck for the dispersals when he felt Cheshire's arm round his shoulder. 'Good luck, Wilson.' All the way to the aircraft, the W/Op pondered in bewildered delight: 'How the hell did the CO know my name?' They knew that when Cheshire flew, it was always the most difficult and dangerous operations. He would ask them to do nothing that he had not done himself. It was Cheshire who noticed that very few Halifax pilots were coming home on three engines. He took up an aircraft to discover why. He found that if a Halifax stalled after losing an engine it went into an uncontrollable spin. After a terrifying minute falling out of the sky, Cheshire was skilful and lucky enough to be able to recover the aircraft and land, and report on the problem, which he was convinced was caused by a fault in the rudder design.

Handley Page, the manufacturers, then enraged him by refusing to interrupt production to make a modification. Only when a Polish test-pilot had been killed making further investigations into the problem which Cheshire had exposed was the change at last made. His imagination and courage became part of the folklore of Bomber Command. He left 76 Squadron in April 1943 and later took command of 617, the Dambusters squadron. By the end of the war, with his Victoria Cross, three Distinguished Service Orders, Distinguished Flying Cross and fantastic total of completed operations, he had become a legend.

Cheshire left the squadron in April, to be succeeded by Wing-Commander Don Smith, a regular officer who came to Linton with a log-book which had been endorsed 'exceptional' in every category of airmanship throughout his service career. Smith had flown fifty-eight successful operations in the Middle East while commanding two Blenheim squadrons in Aden in 1940 and 1941. He now began an eventful tour at 76 Squadron, flying the maximum twenty trips, sixteen on German targets. One July night, he and his crew were on the way home from Mont Beliard when unexpected things began to happen. The two starboard engines cut out within five seconds of each other and Red muttered something about 'fifteen gallons left'. Steve looked at Pete, and Pete looked at Steve, and the one thought uppermost in the minds of both of them was just how many seconds the port engines were going to last out. Steve opened the hatch, and Pete went through with no trouble at all . . . They were somewhat shaken by the factory chimneys of Scunthorpe 200 feet below, but fortunately came to earth in the last field before the houses at the edge of the town. Instead of the motley array of pikes and pitch-forks, which they were expecting, they were greeted on arrival by a deputation of Scunthorpe ladies in négligés, all very solicitous and all bearing cups of tea. Inside the aircraft, Red was having a pitched battle with the skipper, who refused to put on his chute and who in any case could not safely leave the controls even had he wanted to. So the skipper neatly hopped a couple of hedges and made another of his renowned belly-landings, this time in a potato field. He and 'Dirts' Ashton went off to search for ham and eggs (and found them), leaving an equally hungry engineer to guard the remains of our third aircraft . . . We never found out just what started it all, but Red, at any rate, was exonerated.

Don Smith remained at Holme until the end of December, when he was awarded a DSO to add to the DFC he had won in May with 76 Squadron, and the Mention in Dispatches awarded to him for operations in the Middle East. He was then posted to instruct at an Operational Training Unit.

Yet whatever the quality of leadership and morale on a squad-ron, there was seldom any Hollywood-type enthusiasm for take-off on a bomber operation. One summer evening at Holme, 76 Squadron's crews were scattered at the dispersals, waiting miser-ably for start-up time before going to Berlin, the most hated target in Germany. The weather forecast was terrible, and the CO had been driving round the pans chatting to crews in an effort to raise spirits. Then, suddenly, a red Very light arched into the sky, signalling a 'wash out'. All over the airfield a great surge of cheering and whistle-blowing erupted.

A 76 Squadron pilot who later completed a second tour on Mosquitoes said that his colleagues on the light bombers 'simply could never understand how awful being on heavies was'. Some men simply found the strain intolerable. There were pilots who found themselves persistently suffering from 'mag drop', so easily achieved by running up an engine with the magnetos switched off, oiling up the plugs. After two or three such incidents preventing take-off, the squadron CO usually intervened. One of the aircrew at 76 Squadron returned from every operation to face persecution from his wife and his mother, both of whom lived locally. 'Haven't you done enough?' the wife asked insistently, often in the hearing of other aircrew. 'Can't you ever think of me?' In the end the man asked to be taken off operations, and was pronounced LMF.

A 76 Squadron wireless operator completed six operations with one of the Norwegian crews before reporting sick with ear trouble. He came up before the CO for a lecture on the need for highly trained and experienced aircrew to continue flying, and was given a few days to consider his position. At a second interview, he told the CO he had thought over what had been said, but he wanted a rest. He felt that having volunteered 'in' for aircrew duties, he could also volunteer 'out'. He was reduced to the ranks, stripped of his flying brevet, posted to the depot at Chessington which dealt with such cases, and spent the rest of the war on ground duties. So did Alf Kirkham's rear gunner:

After our first few trips together, which were very rough indeed [wrote Kirkham[12]], he simply did not like the odds. He decided that he wanted to live, and told me that nothing anyone could do to him would be worse than carrying on with operations. He was determined to see the war out, and as far as I know he was successful.

Marginal LMF suspects, along with disciplinary cases who had broken up the sergeants' mess, had been discovered using high-octane fuel in their cars, or involved in 'avoidable flying accidents', were sent to the 'Aircrew Refresher Centres' at Sheffield, Brighton or Bournemouth. In reality these centres were open-arrest detention barracks, where they spent a few weeks doing PT and attending lectures before being sent back to their stations, or in extreme cases posted to the depot as 'unfit for further aircrew duties'. They were then offered a choice of transferring to the British army, or going to the coal mines. By 1943 the 'Refresher Centres' were handling thousands of aircrew. One 76 Squadron rear gunner went from Sheffield to the Parachute Regiment, and survived the war. His crew were killed over Kassel in October.

F/Lt Denis Hornsey joined 76 Squadron in the autumn of

1943. He was among very many men who spent their war in Bomber Command fighting fear and dread of inadequacy, without ever finally succumbing. At the end of the war Hornsey wrote an almost masochistically honest and hitherto unpublished account of his experiences and feelings.[13] At thirty-three, he was rather older than most aircrew and suffered from poor eyesight – he wore corrected goggles on operations – and almost chronic minor ailments throughout the war. He hated the bureaucracy and lack of privacy in service life, and was completely without confidence in his own ability as a pilot. After flying some Whitley operations in 1941, he was returned to OTU for further training, and his crew was split up. He then spent a relatively happy year as a staff pilot at a navigation school. He felt that he was an adequate flier of single or twin-engined aircraft, and repeatedly requested a transfer to an operational station where he could fly one or the other. But by 1943 it was heavy-aircraft pilots who were needed. Everybody wanted to fly Mosquitoes. Hornsey was posted to Halifaxes. He knew that he was by now being accompanied from station to station by a file of unsatisfactory reports. He began his tour at 76 Squadron with two 'Early Returns', which made him more miserable than ever. Fear of being considered LMF haunted him almost as much as the fear of operations.

Each operation, in my experience, was a worse strain than the last, and I felt sure that I was not far wrong in supposing that every pilot found it the same. It was true that it was possible to get used to the strain, but this did not alter the fact that the tension of each trip was 'banked' and carried forward in part to increase the tension of the next. If this were not so, the authorities would not have thought it necessary to restrict a tour to thirty trips.

There were men who were stronger than Hornsey, even men who enjoyed operational flying, but his conscious frailty was far closer to that of the average pilot than the nerveless brilliance of a Martin or Cheshire. The day after 76 Squadron lost four aircraft over Kassel and George Dunn's crew completed their tour, Hornsey recorded a conversation in the mess:

'What chance has a man got at this rate?' one pilot asked plaintively. 'Damn it all, I don't care how brave a chap is, he likes to think he has a *chance*. This is plain murder.'

'Better tell that to Harris,' someone else suggested.

'You needn't worry,' I said, 'you represent just fourteen bombloads to him. That's economics, you know.'

As it transpired, operations were cancelled at the eleventh hour, when we were all dressed up in our kit ready to fly. It was too late then to go out, so I went to the camp cinema and saw 'Gun for Hire', a mediocre film portraying what I would have once thought was the dangerous life of a gangster. Now, by contrast, it seemed tame.

That night, I found it difficult to settle down. There was much going on inside my mind that I wanted to express. I felt lonely and miserable, apprehensive and resigned, yet rebellious at the thought of being just a mere cog in a machine with no say in how that machine was used.

But I was getting used to such attacks, which I learned to expect at least once in the course of a day, as soon as I found myself at a loose end. As I could now recognize, without fear of it adding to my mental discomfort, they merely signified an onset of operational jitters. So composing myself as best I could, I went to sleep as quickly as I could.

Hornsey's tragedy was that he was acutely imaginative. He pressed the Air Ministry for the introduction of parachutes that could be worn at all times by bomber aircrew, so many of whom never had the chance to put them on after the aircraft was hit. He made his crew practise 'Abandon aircraft' and 'Ditching' drill intensively, and protested violently when he found the remaining armour plate being stripped from his Halifax on Group orders, to increase bombload.

The men who fared best were those who did not allow themselves to think at all. Many crews argued that emotional entanglements were madness, whether inside or outside marriage. They diverted a man from the absolute single-mindedness he needed to survive over Germany. When a pilot was seen brooding over a girl in the mess, he was widely regarded as a candidate for 'the chop list'. Hornsey, with a wife and baby daughter, was giving only part of his attention and very little of his heart to 76 Squadron.

Cheshire argued emphatically that what most men considered a premonition of their own death – of which there were innumerable instances in Bomber Command – was in reality defeatism. A man who believed that he was doomed would collapse or bale out when his aircraft was hit, whereas in Cheshire's view if you could survive the initial fearsome shock of finding your aircraft damaged, you had a chance. Yet by the autumn of 1943, many men on 76 Squadron were talking freely of their own fate. One much-liked officer came fresh from a long stint as an instructor to be a flight commander. 'You'd better tell me about this business, chaps,' he said modestly in the mess. 'I've been away on the prairies too long.' After a few operations, he concluded readily that he had no chance of survival. 'What are you doing for Christmas, Stuart?' somebody asked him in the mess one day. 'Oh, I shan't be alive for Christmas,' he said wistfully, and was gone within a week, leaving a wife and three children.

'The line between the living and the dead was very thin,' wrote Hornsey. 'If you live on the brink of death yourself, it is as if those who have gone have merely caught an earlier train to the same destination. And whatever that destination is, you will be sharing it soon, since you will almost certainly be catching the next one.'

On the night of 3 November 1943, Hornsey's was one of two 76 Squadron aircraft shot down on the way to Düsseldorf. He was on his eighteenth trip with Bomber Command. It is pleasant to record that he survived and made a successful escape across France to England, for which he was awarded a DFC perhaps better deserved and more hardly earned than the Air Ministry ever knew.

9 The other side of the hill: Germany, 1940–44

'Reports . . . from towns recently attacked make one's hair grow grey.'
Josef Goebbels, March 1945[1]

The destruction

Albert Speer became Minister of Armaments in Hitler's government just two weeks before Sir Arthur Harris took command at High Wycombe, in February 1942. Only thirty-six, he proved the outstanding executive appointment of the Nazi regime. It was Harris's misfortune that throughout his campaign, he was confronted by an adversary who had a superb grasp of the German economy and a brilliant talent for improvising. Harris began his offensive just as German industry was awakening from the comfortable routines that had continued into the third year of the war. Thenceforth, the rising tenor of bombing was matched step by step by Speer's ruthless mobilization of the resources of the Third Reich, slave labour not least among them. Only in the last months of the war did precision attacks on synthetic oil plants achieve the Allies' aim of severing the jugular vein of the Reich. By then, it was a matter of fierce debate whether the patient was not already dying from injuries inflicted on the battlefield.

The Allies' major misunderstanding from start to finish was that they saw Hitler's Germany as an armed camp, solely dedicated to the business of making war. They thus assumed that any damage done by bombing represented a net loss to the German effort. In reality, Hitler had in the 1930s created a formidable military machine, but he had never rearmed in depth. Because he regarded war as an instrument of policy to be used and discarded as a matter of short-term expediency, he sought to employ the *minimum* possible economic resources to enable the Wehrmacht and the Luftwaffe to achieve a given objective, whether this was the destruction of Poland or the invasion of Russia. Unlike the British, Hitler in 1940 and 1941 did not see the war as a life-or-death struggle, because the possibility of Germany's utter defeat did not enter his mind. The worst that he then envisaged was the frustration of his immediate goals.

While the Allies saw Germany as a military monolith, Hitler was always intensely nervous about maintaining his domestic political support, much more so than proved necessary. He was determined to preserve standards of living. Until the end of 1941, he tried to provide both guns and butter for the German people, and to a remarkable extent he succeeded. Short-term munitions contracts were placed with German industry in preparation for his great strategic thrusts, then cancelled the moment victory appeared to be in sight. Faced with the Luftwaffe's shortage of bombs in Poland in September 1939, Hitler only reluctantly authorized further bomb production on 12 October.[2] In the late summer of 1941, while Bomber Command was struggling to reduce German munitions production, Hitler was pursuing the same end: he ordered substantial reductions in the scale of arms output, because he believed that victory in Russia was already within sight. The consequences for the German army that winter were privations to match the tragedy of the British army in the Crimea.

Yet at the beginning of 1942, the year of the 1,000 Raid on Cologne, when Britain had been geared to total war and the most stringent rationing for more than two years, German consumer spending was at much the same level as in 1937. Britain had recognized from the beginning that she was fighting for survival, and strained every sinew to tool and arm accordingly. Already by September 1939 she was producing more tanks than Germany. In 1940, the year when the overwhelming strength of the Luftwaffe was pitted against Fighter Command, Britain was building aircraft faster than the Reich. In 1941, German aircraft production was a pitiful 10 per cent higher than in 1940.[3] Vast numbers of British women had been brought into industry, but Hitler resisted pressure to follow suit, because he feared the effects upon the German way of life. Goering's 'Four Year Plan', begun in 1936 allegedly to put the German economy on a war footing, was in reality only a limited programme to reduce the nation's dependence on imported raw materials.

Far-sighted men in the government understood that Hitler's economic policy was fraught with danger. General Georg Thomas, head of the *WiRuAmt*, the 'War Economy and Armaments Branch' of OKW, pleaded in vain for rearmament in depth. When the huge drain of casualties on the eastern front began, the Luftwaffe above all began to feel acute shortages of aircraft and spares. Goering's squadrons lost 3,000 aircraft missing and a further 2,000 damaged in the first ten months of the Russian campaign, together with thousands of the most experienced aircrew. The ceaseless struggle for personal power among the Nazi leaders precluded the much more co-ordinated economic controls and policies adopted as a matter of course in Britain and America. 'The whole structure of the German administrative body was one of competing individuals and competing machines,' writes the economic historian Professor Milward,[4] 'which by 1942 represented a powerful collection of vested interests, each unwilling to relinquish its control of its own small part of the war economy.'

The prospect of imminent defeat had concentrated British minds wonderfully in 1940. There was no parallel confrontation with reality in Germany until at least 1943, but the Russian counter-offensive of November 1941 finally caused Hitler to concede that the days of the 'blitzkrieg economy' were ended. Fritz Todt's appointment as Minister of Munitions signalled the beginning of the reorganization and mobilization of German industry that was continued by Speer on Todt's death in an air crash in February 1942.

As Hitler's architect and a member of the inner circle of his intimates, for the next two years Speer worked with the overwhelming advantage of Hitler's personal support. He acted on the authority of the Führer Command directive 'Armament 1942', issued to Todt on 10 January 1942. To achieve the massive increase in production that he sought, Speer expanded Todt's system of industry-wide committees of businessmen, who were made responsible for meeting output targets by settling priorities, enforcing cooperation between companies, assigning raw materials. 'Directive Committees' were created to take responsibility for specific weapons, and 'Directive Pools', for the allocation of supplies.

Yet while Hitler had in principle accepted that arms production was now the overwhelming economic priority, it was another matter for Speer to make him accept the consequences of this decision. The new Minister fought an uphill struggle to induce Hitler to cut back on consumer production, and to import Germany's consumer needs from the Occupied Territories. Although in April 1942, 90 per cent of German industry was still working only a single shift, Speer was immediately concerned by the shortage of labour which was his overwhelming problem throughout the war. Conscript workers from the Occupied Territories were no substitute for native skilled workers drafted into the Wehrmacht. Speer and General Erhard Milch, State Secretary of the Air Ministry and the man responsible for aircraft production, were continuously at loggerheads with Sauckel, the Plenipotentiary for Labour, about the manpower shortage. In the first half of 1942 the aircraft industry was allocated 403,000 additional workers, but only 60,000 ever reached the assembly lines. Shortage of men – for the army, the factories, construction and reconstruction work – was the continuing nightmare of the directors of the German war effort until the end.

The British official historians of the strategic air offensive suggest that part of the German achievement must be attributed to 'the strong controls which could be employed in a totalitarian state'. Yet Speer himself and a succession of economic historians have marvelled at the inefficiency and lack of central control in the German war economy compared with that of Britain. In a speech to manufacturers on 6 October 1943, Speer commented acidly on the difficulties of preventing German industry from dissipating its energies on irrelevant production. He noted that in the preceding year, the Reich had produced 120,000 typewriters, 200,000 domestic radios, 150,000 electric blankets, 3,600 refrigerators, 300,000 electricity meters, 512,000 pairs of riding boots and 360,000 spur straps. 'It remains one of the oddities of this war that Hitler demanded far less from his people than Churchill and Roosevelt did from their respective nations,' Speer was later to write.[5] By the end of 1943, Britain had reduced her pre-war army of domestic servants by two-thirds. Yet in

Germany 1.4 million workers were still employed in household service, and Hitler was so anxious to maintain living standards that he decreed the import of a further half-million Ukrainian girls to reinforce this total. At the end of 1943 there were still six million Germans employed in consumer industries. Speer's efforts to cut back consumer output were repeatedly frustrated by Hitler's personal veto. Eva Braun intervened to block an order banning permanent waves and the manufacture of cosmetics.

Germany was inevitably doomed to lose a battle of production against the western Allies – they ultimately achieved a superiority of 9 to 2 in *matériel*. But almost until the end of the war, Speer's factories were producing more tanks and arms than there were men left in the Wehrmacht's combat divisions to use them. In the two and a half years following Speer's appointment, Germany increased her production of tanks sixfold; of ammunition, weapons and aircraft threefold. It is highly doubtful whether further increases of arms production would have significantly improved her strategic position. Manpower, always manpower, was Germany's central problem. 'Until the last six months of the war,' reported the United States Strategic Bombing Survey, 'the army was never critically short of weapons and shells.'

But where in all this was the Allied bombing of Germany? In 1943, Harris's great year of area attack, 200,000 tons of bombs fell on the Third Reich, five times the weight which had been dropped in 1942. In a minute to the Prime Minister dated 3 November 1943, Harris listed nineteen German cities which he claimed that been 'virtually destroyed', meaning that they had become 'a liability to the total German war effort vastly in excess of any assets remaining'. These were: Hamburg, Cologne, Essen, Dortmund, Düsseldorf, Hanover, Mannheim, Bochum, Mülheim, Koln Deutz, Barmen, Elberfeld, München Gladbach/Rheydt, Krefeld, Aachen, Rostock, Remscheid, Kassel and Emden. He also listed a further nineteen which were 'seriously damaged': Frankfurt, Stuttgart, Duisburg, Bremen, Hagen, Munich, Nuremberg, Stettin, Kiel, Karlsruhe, Mainz, Wilhelmshaven, Lübeck, Saarbrücken, Osnabrück, Münster, Rüsselsheim, Berlin and Oberhausen. In 1943, Bomber Command stated that 36 per cent of production had been lost in twenty-nine towns attacked.

In reality, the German armaments production index rose from 100 in January 1942 to 153 in July, 229 in July 1943, 322 in July 1944. The USSBS estimated after the war that in 1943, 9 per cent of German production had been lost as a result of bombing, and a further 17 per cent in 1944, mostly in the latter part of the year. Speer said: 'The total damage suffered by the armament programme as a result of air attack during the year 1943 was not considerable.' There was such enormous slack capacity in the economy to be diverted from consumer production that damage on this scale could readily be absorbed by the German war machine.

In 1942 it would have seemed incredible to most people in Britain had they known the relative comfort and normalcy of life in Germany. In 1943 the bombing of German cities swept away that air of normalcy for ever, and brought the German people face to face with the suffering they had inflicted upon so many others. Hitler's Reich had suffered a catastrophe:

Hamburg had put the fear of God into me [said Speer]. At the meeting of Central Planning on 29 July, I pointed out: 'If the air raids continue on the present scale, within three months we shall be relieved of a number of questions we are at present discussing. We shall simply be coasting downhill, smoothly and relatively swiftly . . .' Three days later I informed Hitler that armaments production was collapsing and threw in the final warning that a series of attacks of this sort, extended to six more major cities, would bring Germany's armaments production to a total halt.

'You'll straighten all that out again,' he merely said. In fact Hitler was right.[6]

Speer himself was astonished by the speed of Hamburg's recovery. The British official historians, weighing the various estimates made at the end of the war, suggest that 1.8 months' production was lost. Textile and food output suffered more than armaments. In 1943 thirty U-boats under construction were destroyed by bombing in all parts of Germany; the majority of these were lost in the damage to shipyards in the Battle of Hamburg. The Battle of the Ruhr, according to Webster and Frankland, the official historians, cost the region between one and one-and-a-half months' loss of output. Recalling the huge attacks on Essen, Krupps lost a total of three months' production from all air attacks up to and including the spring of 1944. The firm began to believe that they were intended to serve as a decoy for the bombers, since although their production of locomotives, tank bodies and artillery was important, it was nothing like as pivotal to the German war economy as the Allies obviously believed.

The Americans, meanwhile, fared no better. The detailed story of the 8th Air Force's attempts to 'sever Germany's jugular' by destroying the ball-bearing factories at Schweinfurt does not belong here. It is enough to say that their first attack on 17 August 1943 cost them a paralysing loss of 60 of the 376 aircraft dispatched. Production fell by a disturbing, yet not fatal 38 per cent. But the attack also awakened the Germans to the extreme vulnerability of their ball-bearing supplies, and by the time of 'Second Schweinfurt' on 14 October 1943, much had been done towards marshalling reserve stocks from all over Germany, and preparing to disperse production. Schweinfurt's output fell by 67 per cent after the 8th Air Force's extraordinarily gallant second attempt, but the Americans had lost another 60 Flying Fortresses out of 291 dispatched. They now suffered a major trauma about the future of their daylight operations, and, to Speer's overwhelming relief, Schweinfurt was not attacked again until 1944, by which stage its relative importance to German industry had been reduced. Harris had refused to allow his bombers to have anything to do with the Schweinfurt operations in 1943, which he dismissed as a further example of 'panacea-mongering'. The American failure greatly strengthened his hand in resisting further demands from the Ministry of Economic Warfare for precision attacks on allegedly exposed sectors of the German economy. Bomber Command only went to Schweinfurt in February 1944, when the pressure on Harris had become irresistible. By then it was too late.

The Americans had also spearheaded the assault on German aircraft production, notably by their attacks on airframe plants. Here, too, in the autumn of 1943, they had suffered overwhelming defeat. German aircraft production advanced by huge strides until the first serious check imposed by the 8th Air Force's 'Big Week' in February 1944. Even after this it reached new peaks. As Dr Frankland has said of the American assault on German aircraft production in 1943: 'The bombers were committed to a race between the destruction of the German air force in production by the bombers, and the destruction of the bombers by the German fighters in being. The result was a decisive victory for the German fighters in being.'[7]

After the war, Speer professed himself astonished by the inconsistency of the Allied air attack. 'The vast but pointless area bombing,' he said,[8] 'had achieved no important effect on the German war effort by early 1944. 'But at intervals the bombers had stumbled on a blind spot, a genuine Achilles' heel, only to turn aside and divert their attack elsewhere when they had done so. He marvelled at the American failure to repeat the two Schweinfurt attacks, at whatever cost. He was amazed that the British, having achieved remarkable success at Hamburg, neither returned to that city in sufficient force to prevent its recovery nor attempted to inflict the same treatment on any other city save Berlin, where the odds were impossible. He cited the example of the Dams Raid in May 1943. The Ministry of Economic Warfare in London correctly judged that the Mohne and the Sorpe dams were the key to the Ruhr water supplies. But after destroying the Mohne, 617 Squadron used their remaining mines to wreck the Eder dam, which was quite irrelevant. Bomber Command had merely judged it more easily breachable with Barnes Wallis's special mines than the Sorpe. It was the same reasoning process which had sent the bombers to Lübeck in 1942: a target was attacked because it was destructible, not because it was vital.

Throughout the war Speer's efforts were crippled by the lack of coherent economic thinking by the Nazi leadership. But he recognized that the Allies were as incapable as Hitler of assessing the fatal weakness of the German war machine. The RAF had discussed bombing electricity generating plants in the 1930s, yet no serious attempt was made against Germany's power supplies by Bomber Command. The British assumed that they were too sophisticated and too widely dispersed to succumb. Speer was astonished that the Allies only began their major attack on the synthetic oil plants in the spring of 1944, and even then Harris took no part. For a few weeks, it seemed that the German economy faced imminent collapse. But Speer exhorted his managers. On past experience, the Americans would persist for

271

a few weeks and then change policy: 'We have a powerful ally in this matter,' he said. 'That is to say, the enemy has an air force general staff as well.' His optimism was justified. It was another six months before the air attack on oil was pressed home.

Two further aspects of the British bomber offensive must be considered here. The first is the significant myth, fostered by the British official historians, that it contributed to the Luftwaffe's lack of bomber aircraft in 1944, and thus to its inability to intervene against the Allied armies on and after D-Day. It is perfectly true that Milch and Speer made great efforts to stop bomber production and concentrate exclusively on fighters from the summer of 1943. 'Gentlemen,' Milch told his staff after Hamburg, 'we are no longer on the offensive. For the last one and a half or two years we have been on the defensive. This fact is now recognized even at the highest levels of the Luftwaffe command.'[9] Galland, General of Fighters, fought determinedly for increases in the defences of Germany. Speer was in despair at the effort he considered wasted on bombers, each of which cost nine times the labour and resources of a fighter to build.

But they were all defeated by Hitler's overriding obstinacy. Until June 1944 he absolutely refused all proposals for the halting of bomber production, and by insisting that the jet Me262 meet the requirements of a bomber, delayed its appearance as a revolutionary fighter until too late. Hitler complained insistently about the Luftwaffe's inability to produce an adequate heavy bomber to carry out retaliatory raids upon England. All that Speer could do in the face of Hitler's obsession was to increase fighter production enormously, while maintaining that of bombers at a more or less static level. 'Milch's and my proposals that the manufacture of bombers be radically reduced in favour of increased fighter plane production was rejected until it was too late,' says Speer.[10]

Why was it, therefore, that whereas in September 1940 the Luftwaffe front line included 1,871 bombers and 1,162 fighters, by September 1944 the squadrons in Western Europe were reduced to 209 bombers against 2,473 fighters? There had been a long and disastrous series of design and development failures, beginning in the 1930s, when Goering, in his determination to create a tactical air force, ordered the destruction of the proto-types of the Do19 and Ju89 bombers. Germany entered the war with some superb aircraft, but since 1939 only the FW 190 fighter had appeared, to take the Luftwaffe into the next generation. Early in the war, immense development work had been wasted on the Ju288 and the FW191, which was intended to carry five tons of bombs and to replace the Ju88. Most futile of all was the Heinkel He177, an extraordinary aircraft with four engines gear-ed to two propellers which Milch christened 'the dead racehorse' in bitter judgement on the millions of hours wasted on flogging it. Several hundred were produced at enormous cost, but were a total operational failure.

The German aircraft industry was burdened with an impossible number of unproven and competing development projects – at the end of 1941 there were forty different types under active development or in production. The advanced version of the Ju88, the best Luftwaffe light bomber and night-fighter, required 50,000 design changes on the production line, and its problems were only resolved in 1943. Early in the war, in anticipation of the new generation of bombers, the production lines of the old He111 and Do17 had been running down. Yet, in the event, even in 1944 the Heinkel and the Ju88 were the only bombers that the Luft-waffe could get. They were still being produced in quantity, and destroyed in large numbers on the Russian front. There were still more than 1,400 serviceable bombers and dive-bombers on the Luftwaffe strength in June 1944, but few of them were adequate for their task. Speer was always a production rather than a development expert, and he sought to expand the output of what was available rather than risk slowing production to introduce new models. Germany's best scientists and engineers were work-ing on an impossibly extensive range of advanced weapons: the V-1 and V-2, the acoustic torpedo and half a dozen alternative jet aircraft. But if Germany had been able to build a satisfactory new bomber, Hitler would have insisted that the Luftwaffe be given it, whether they wanted it or not.

It is important to make one further point in this context: the essential tactical lesson of the war was that no bomber could operate effectively in the face of enemy air superiority. By early 1944 the Allies possessed the capability to create such an overwhelming air umbrella over the invasion that there was never the remotest possibility that the Luftwaffe could intervene effectively against the Allied armies. German airmen like to point out that while they put up nineteen aircraft in support of every German division attacking France in 1940 and twenty-six aircraft for every division invading Russia a year later, on D-Day the Allies launched 260 aircraft for every division landing.[11] Such was the pathetic plight of the Luftwaffe that it mounted only 319 sorties in northern France that day, and lost a thousand aircraft in Normandy alone in the month that followed. But the German air force had been brought to this pass by strategic and technical failures at home, followed by defeat in the air by the Allied air forces, not destruction in the factories. The fact that the Allies attained such absolute dominance of the skies, and yet faced a further eleven months of bitter fighting before victory, raises other questions about the limitations of air power which fall beyond the scope of this book.

The final issue about the effectiveness of the 1943–4 area-bombing campaign is that of its effect on the morale of the German people. When Bomber Command's great attacks on the cities began, the German leadership was deeply alarmed. 'Hitler had repeatedly exclaimed that if the bombings went on, not only would the cities be destroyed, but the morale of the people would crack irreparably,' wrote Speer.[12] 'Hitler was succumbing to the same error as the British strategists on the other side who were ordering mass bombings.'

After Hamburg, Milch said:

It's much blacker than Speer paints it. If we get just five or six more attacks like these on Hamburg, the German people will just lay down their tools, however great their willpower. I keep saying, the steps that are being taken now are being taken too late. There can be no more talk of night fighters in the East, or of putting an umbrella over our troops in Sicily or anything like that. The soldier on the battlefield will just have to dig a hole, crawl into it and wait until the attack is over. What the home front is suffering now cannot be suffered much longer.[13]

Since April 1942, Goebbels had been advocating reprisals, which the Luftwaffe was entirely incapable of carrying out:

I now consider it absolutely essential that we continue with our rigorous reprisal raids. I also agree that not much is to be accomplished with raids on munitions centres. Like the English, we must attack centres of culture, especially those which have only little anti-aircraft. Such centres should be attacked two or three times in succession and levelled to the ground; then the English probably will no longer find pleasure in trying to frighten us by their terror attacks.[14]

By March 1943, Goebbels was recording in his diary:

Reports from the Rhineland indicate that in some cities people are gradually getting rather weak in the knees. That is understandable. For months the working population has had to go into air raid shelters night after night, and when they come out again they see part of their city going up in flame and smoke. The enervating thing about it is that we are not in a position to reply in kind ... Our war in the east has lost us air supremacy in essential sections of Europe, and we are completely at the mercy of the English.[15]

Goebbels and his colleagues were intensely concerned to convey to the German people the notion that the British had unilaterally instituted terror bombing. British monitoring services noted that in one week of June 1943, 15 per cent of all German radio news output was given up to denunciations of the Allied air attack on German culture. In July a book was published under the auspices of the Propaganda Ministry, discussing the origins of strategic bombing, and entitled *England's Sole Guilt*. A plan was put forward for leafleting England with photographs of the grotesquely broken bodies of shot-down Bomber Command aircrew. A Party Chancellery directive[16] reminded newspaper editors that 'the concept of "terror raid" is intended to reflect the criminal behaviour of the enemy ... Therefore a German attack must never be called a "terror raid". Counter-measures of the German Air Force are to be designated as "retaliation measures".'

Yet, astonishingly, the Nazi leadership's fears were entirely unnecessary. The morale of the German people remained unbroken to the end, despite growing awareness that the war must be lost, and despite the increasing indifference of their Führer to their fate. Hitler refused to visit bombed cities, for all the exhortations of Goebbels and Speer. The Propaganda Ministry reacted nervously to every symptom that might suggest an impending moral collapse: reports from the Schweinfurt area of a decline in the general exchanging of the 'Heil Hitler!' salute; a growing resignation to subterranean life – 'Bunker fever' – as raids intensified; dismay about the news from the Russian front. But even in the ruined cities people queued to pay their taxes at temporary offices. After 'Big Week' in February 1944, Speer and Milch marvelled at the manner in which the aircraft workers laboured on temporary assembly-lines created in the open air in freezing winter weather, the heated factories having been reduced to rubble. Workers everywhere went back to their plant even after the firestorms. They repaired damage, restored production – even made their own shattered homes somehow habitable – with less assistance than the British authorities had provided for their own people during the Blitz. The 1940 German blitz on Coventry had destroyed 100 out of the city's 1,922 acres. In 1943, Krefeld lost 40 per cent of its housing in one night, yet continued to man its factories. Somewhere in the ruins of Hamburg, the vast majority of the million refugees who fled in the immediate wake of the firestorm returned and began to live again within weeks, even with 6,200 of the city's 8,382 acres apparently totally destroyed according to the reconnaissance photographs that were studied with such fascination at High Wycombe. What was achieved in Germany in the face of the bombing between 1942 and 1944 was not an economic miracle – Speer was extremely able, but he was not a genius. It was a triumph for the courage and determination of the German people in the face of the utmost suffering, paralleling that of the British in 1940. The assumption upon which the RAF had founded its area-bombing campaign – that Germans were liable to moral collapse in a way that the British had shown in 1940 they were not, was proved totally unfounded. In 1943, Dr Goebbels' department noted a marked stiffening of national morale in the face of raids, matched by the growth of a hitherto unknown popular hatred for the enemy.

In the burning and devastated cities we daily experienced the direct impact of the war [wrote Speer]. It spurred us to do our utmost. Neither did the bombings and the hardships that resulted from them weaken the morale of the populace. On the contrary, from my visits to armament plants and my contacts with the man in the street, I carried away the impression of growing toughness. It may well be that the estimated loss of 9 per cent of our production capacity was amply balanced out by increased effort.[17]

The British official historians looked back at 1943 and declared: 'For the first time in the war, Germany herself . . . began to pay the price of the fearful deeds which she had perpetrated and was yet to perpetrate, against others.[18]

Beyond any doubts, the area offensive punished Germany terribly. It destroyed centuries of construction and of culture, the homes and property of Germans who for the first time experienced the cost of Nazism. At the end of 1942 Goering had said: 'We will have reason to be glad if Germany can keep the boundaries of 1933 after the war.' By the end of 1943 production in every critical area of war industry – tanks, U-boats, guns, aircraft – was still expanding at a gigantic rate. But it had become apparent to the German people that they were beyond the hope of mercy. After three years of terrible sacrifice, this was the principal achievement of Bomber Command.

The defences

For the first year of the British bomber offensive that began in May 1940, the Luftwaffe who were responsible for every aspect of the defences of the Reich relied principally upon flak and searchlights. In 1939 the German air force possessed only one experimental night-fighter squadron equipped with Me109s – this was the first unit to engage Wing-Commander Kellett's Wellingtons on 18 December 1939. In June 1940, Goering himself admitted that the lack of night-fighters was 'the Luftwaffe's Achilles' heel'. That summer, the unsuitable 109s were withdrawn from night operations and progressively replaced by twin-engined Me110s. But their crews roamed the moonlit skies of Europe conducting visual searches for British bombers with almost the same sense of helplessness that afflicted many of the men in the Hampdens and Whitleys, of which they destroyed a bare handful.

But with the appointment of General Josef Kammhuber as General of Night Fighters in October 1940, Germany began to create the great defensive system against the bomber which came within an ace of victory in 1944. Through the winter of 1940–41, as his resources allowed, Kammhuber progressively extended a belt of searchlights and sound-locators across northern Germany and the Low Countries, between fifty and a hundred miles inland from the coast. Fighters patrolled sectors of this line, seeking to attack bombers which had been detected and illuminated. Kammhuber himself recognized that these were inadequate stop-gap measures until more sophisticated equipment came into service. By the time Hitler ordered the transfer of all searchlights from Kammhuber's belt to the direct defence of Germany in the spring of 1942, the new and much more deadly *Himmelbett* system, based on a chain of radar-guided fighter 'boxes', had been established the length of the European coast from north Germany to Belgium, and around the most important cities of Germany.

Dr R. V. Jones has described[19] how British Scientific Intelligence, through 1941 and 1942, progressively unravelled the mysteries of what they came to call 'The Kammhuber Line'. Each overlapping night-fighter 'box' was equipped with a *Freya* radar set, which provided early warning of Allied bombers and their course, although not of their height. But as the fighters scrambled and gained altitude to meet them, a bomber was picked up by a short-range *Würzburg* radar – the early model was effective up to something over twenty miles, which determined the radius of each 'box'. A second *Würzburg* meanwhile tracked the German fighter. On the ground, in the T-shaped control huts that now stood at intervals from Ostend to Denmark, the ground controllers plotted the position of fighter and bomber by green and red dots projected on to the *Seeburg* evaluation screen. At first, they sought to trap the bomber in the cone created by their supporting searchlight battery, for the fighter to attack. Later, in 1942, when *Lichtenstein* airborne radar had been fitted to the night-fighters, they sought to guide the fighter to the point within the two miles of the bomber at which the *Lichtenstein* could take over for the final approach.

The brilliant commando raid on Bruneval in March 1942 enabled the British to seize a *Würzburg* for examination, and the scientists were impressed by its quality and precision. German

278

standards of manufacture in electronics remained higher than those of the Allies throughout the war. But they lagged in design and application. British scientists and airmen preferred their own simpler techniques of tracking both fighter and bomber on the same radar screen. The German system also suffered the overwhelming limitation that each 'box' could direct only one interception at a time. It was in this knowledge that the British evolved their 'streaming' techniques, pushing the bomber force through a single 'box' at the utmost speed and density, to saturate the defences. The German control stations *Jaguar*, *Delphin*, *Lowe*, *Eisbar*, *Seidler* and the rest achieved a formidable total of successes, especially after the introduction in 1942 of the improved 'Giant *Würzburg*', with its range approaching fifty miles. But with the coming of the massive British attacks of 1942 and 1943, although the night-fighters were inflicting terrible losses on Bomber Command, it was evident that the Kammhuber Line was being hopelessly swamped by the scale of the offensive.

Kammhuber's greatest misfortune was that, on Hitler's orders, in October 1941 he was ordered to abandon his experimental 'intruder' operations against British bomber airfields. Hitler considered that only aircraft shot down over Germany were of value in convincing the German people that they were being defended. From late 1940 onwards, the general had been dispatching the largest force he could spare – never more than twenty Ju88 fighters, equipped with cannon and small bombs – to attack British bombers at their most vulnerable moments, as they took off and landed at their airfields. In 1940–41 they had been responsible for two-thirds of the Luftwaffe's night-fighter victories. Kammhuber was convinced that this promised to be the most effective means of causing casualties and chaos to the bomber offensive. Bomber Command shared his opinion. By 1943 the marshalling and dispatch of Harris's huge force had become an exercise of the utmost complexity, calling for precision timing at every airfield in eastern England. If Kammhuber's 'intruders' had been allowed to continue their operations, the consequences could have been overwhelming. But High Wycombe's nightmares went unfulfilled. With the exception of a single isolated incursion in October 1943, the Luftwaffe left the British airfields in peace. It was the greatest missed opportunity of the bomber war, and like so many other major tactical errors, it was a personal decision of the Führer.

It was only in the wake of the Battle of Hamburg that Germany's leaders began to perceive the scale of the threat to the Reich, and for that matter the enormous requirement for aircraft in total war. Ernst Udet, the former First World War flying ace who controlled aircraft production in the first years of the war made a series of disastrous errors and omissions before his suicide in November 1941. Milch, who took over his responsibilities, struggled to make good shortages and to gear the aircraft industry for all-out effort. He insisted that work be delayed on the Me262 jet in order to get the Me109F into urgent production. Yet in 1942 when he told Goering that he proposed to build a thousand fighters a month, the Reichsmarschall laughed heartily: 'Where would we use them all?'

But by late 1943 the Luftwaffe was losing more than a thousand aircraft a month, most of them on the Russian front. In June that year, the Luftwaffe's front-line strength on all fronts stood at some 7,000 aircraft. Until late 1944, when fuel shortages made the figures irrelevant, it hovered between 6,000 and 7,000. Yet for the night defence of Germany there were rarely more than 350 fighters, in six *Geschwaders* of four or five squadrons each. On a good night in 1943 or early 1944, the Luftwaffe could hope to mount between 200 and 250 sorties against a bomber attack. When the American Flying Fortresses began their massive daylight operations, the 8th Air Force from England and the 15th Air Force from Italy, the pressure on the Luftwaffe's home defence units became intolerable. Instead of the 400 or 500 dayfighters that were vital to meet the huge American formations on acceptable terms, there were never more than 300. To reinforce them, night-fighters and their highly trained crews were flung into the struggle, intensifying the pressure on aircraft serviceability, and losing a steady stream of experienced aircrew and their precious *Lichtenstein* sets. Again and again Milch, Speer, Kammhuber and Galland pleaded for increased resources for night defence, but until the summer of 1944 they were resolutely denied.

It was the Luftwaffe's misfortune to be under the command of Hermann Goering. For all his pleasure in the trappings of power, deep within himself this indolent sybarite had always regarded the war as a terrible error which had sown the seeds for Germany's destruction. Even as his own air fleets were launching their great attack on England in 1940, he crushed the bounding optimism of Jeschonnek, his Chief of Staff, about the prospects for an early British surrender:

'Do you think that Germany would give in if Berlin was in ruins?'

'Of course not,' said Jeschonnek.

'Then you think the British are different? That is where you are wrong...'

Goering's sense of doom became overwhelming when Hitler launched the invasion of Russia. For the remainder of the war he took refuge in drugs and delusions, exhibiting spasms of energy only when he felt his empire threatened by the expanding operations of Speer or Milch. The Luftwaffe was left without a dominant voice in the struggle around Hitler's throne. Goering was discredited and despised among his senior colleagues, but Hitler would not dismiss him because of 'The Fat Man's' public popularity, and Goering would not voluntarily abandon power. The Reichsmarschall quarantined himself from all unacceptable realities. When the news of the first 1,000 Raid was brought to him, he declined to believe it. He rejected reports of the American Mustang long-range fighter engaging the Luftwaffe over Germany, because he would not acknowledge that such an aircraft could be built. At a meeting at his Castle Veldenstein in the autumn of 1941, Goering brushed aside the proposals of Kammhuber, Molders and Galland for the defence of Germany: 'This whole phoney business won't be necessary any more once I get my squadrons back to the west.'[20] He continued to delude himself that the return of the vast Luftwaffe forces from the eastern front was imminent, just as he promised Hitler in 1942 that he could supply the beleaguered Sixth Army at Stalingrad from the the air. The night-fighters, meanwhile, were starved of numbers and aircrew, fuel and equipment.

'The defence of the Reich follows the latest bomb crater,' the pilots muttered cynically.[21] By 1943, pupils under training were finding themselves scrambled with their instructors to meet bomber attacks. When the former bomber pilot Major Hajo

Hermann formed his first 'Wild Boar' squadrons in July that year, he found himself obliged to recruit among failed bomber pilots and disgraced aircrew rejected by other line units. When *Lichtenstein* AI radar began to be fitted to night-fighters, the scientists had to overcome resistance from senior Luftwaffe officers who believed that its protruding aerials would have an unacceptable effect on speed and performance. From 1941 onwards the fuel allocation for aircrew training was quite inadequate, and the quality – though not the courage – of the Luftwaffe's pilots began the steady decline that continued until late 1944, when they were reaching line squadrons with only 150 hours' flying experience. It is generally accepted by former bomber pilots as well as by the Luftwaffe that the enormous scores claimed by a handful of pilots such as Lt-Col Helmut Lent – the veteran of Wilhelmshaven who scored 102 victories before he was killed in 1944 – were not far from the reality. A small minority of superb airmen such as himself, Major Heinz-Wolfgang Schnaufer (121 victories), Prince Lippe-Weissenfeld (51 victories) and Prince Sayn-Wittgenstein (83 victories) accounted for the overwhelming majority of bombers shot down by night-fighters, while hundreds of 'green' pilots landed night after night without a kill, even at the height of the 'Battles' in 1943–4.

After Goering, General Hans Jeschonnek, the Luftwaffe's Chief of Staff, bore much responsibility for the shortcomings of the defence of Germany, which he seemed to recognize by his suicide on hearing the news of the British raid on Peenemunde in August 1943. Jeschonnek was entirely in thrall to Hitler. He directed the Luftwaffe as he believed that the Führer wished, without thought for strategic or tactical reality. In the spring of 1942, in the face of fierce warnings about the long-term consequences for the Luftwaffe, Jeschonnek stripped training units and reserves of every man and aircraft to support the new offensive in Russia. 'The Luftwaffe must attack and not defend,' said Goering at the end of 1941, and Jeschonnek supported the fantasies of the Reichsmarschall and his Führer to the end of his life. Since the beginning of the war, the Luftwaffe had regarded flak and searchlights as the principal defence against strategic air attack, with fighters in a subsidiary role. Now, despite overwhelming evidence that the night-fighter was the decisive weapon in meeting the bomber offensive, there was still no major shift of priorities.

In July 1943, Kammhuber was replaced as GOC XII Air Corps after Hitler rejected his proposals for a massive new radar programme to meet the American air armadas which the general anticipated. Hitler dismissed his forecasts as fantasy, and in November Kammhuber was also removed from his post as General of Night Fighters and sent to Norway. Hajo Hermann, creator of the 'Wild Boars', replaced him.

But even in the face of enormous political and numerical difficulties, in late 1943 and early 1944 the German night-fighter force came close to the decisive defeat of Bomber Command, just as the Luftwaffe's day-fighters almost achieved the defeat of the 8th Air Force. It is impossible to overvalue the ingenuity and determination with which the German defences responded to the bomber offensive. Their knowledge of Bomber Command, chiefly derived from prisoner interrogation, was so comprehensive that they proposed to make a film depicting the planning and launching of a British attack, using actors to play the principals, for the training of Luftwaffe units. The script had been written and fell into the hands of the Allies in May 1945.

The 'Wild Boar' concept created by Hermann was short-lived, for the difficulties of operating single-engined fighters without blind-flying equipment at night proved overwhelming, and losses in landings and accidents became prohibitive. But the 'Wild Boars' had shown the way to the new approach for fighting the bombers, and the courage of the pilots who dived into their own searchlights and flak – which often ignored orders not to fire above a given height – to engage the bombers excited the respect of the British. The 'Wild Boars' were rapidly eclipsed by the 'Tame Boars', twin-engined fighters which were scrambled to orbit a visual beacon as soon as the approximate course of the bomber force was known. The British discovered that the Germans could often predict a raid by monitoring wireless operators' signals from all over eastern England during their morning air test, and 100 Group began to broadcast fake test signals on days when Bomber Command was not operating, to confuse the issue. But careful study of the weather predictions usually enabled the Germans to judge whether conditions were right for Harris to attack.

As the British approached Germany, the ground controllers directed the 'Tame Boars' into the stream by radio running-commentary. In the final stages of interception, the air turbulence created by hundreds of aircraft warned the fighters that they were close to the British. On a clear night, they then searched visually for the bombers. In moonless conditions they relied upon AI radar – by early 1944 they were being equipped with the *Lichtenstein* SN2, which was impervious to *Window* jamming. The blind spot of the British bombers below the fuselage had always been known to fighter pilots, but they had often been unable to exploit it until in the autumn of 1943 an ingenious fitter at a Luftwaffe airfield devised the prototype of the deadly *schrage musik* – 'jazz music' – a pair of fixed upward-firing cannon mounted behind the fighter's cockpit. The pilot had only to slide beneath the bomber and fire a short burst which was almost invariably lethal. A few lucky British survivors who came home to report that they had been flying peacefully over Germany until the world collapsed and they found themselves upside down in a wingless fuselage were treated as 'line-shooters'. It was not until the end of the war that British aircrew learned of the existence of *schrage musik*. It has been a matter of debate ever since whether the Canadian 6 Group, who alone fitted ventral turrets to many of their Lancasters to cover the blind spot, were justified in sacrificing speed and adding weight to do so.

But the most dramatic transformation of the bomber war in 1943 and 1944 was brought about by the decision of both sides to turn night into day. After years of rigorously blacked-out cities and oceans of darkness across Europe broken only by islands of light around a target, the most dazzling firework display in history now exploded every night over Germany. British Pathfinders dropped flares to light the target for their markers, while high above them Luftwaffe aircraft were laying their own lines of parachute flares to illuminate the bombers for fighter attack. On cloudy nights when the British were bombing blind, the searchlights arched upwards, seeking to turn the clouds into a layer of light against which the attackers were silhouetted for the fighters: 'The enemy bombers crawl across them like flies on a table cloth,' Milch told Speer with satisfaction.[22] From the five Divisional 'Battle Opera Houses', the Luftwaffe controllers maintained their running commentary to the fighters, based on information from ground observer stations that was processed and retransmitted inside one minute. The British adopted the most elaborate methods to stem their voices, with jammers mounted in the 'ABC' aircraft of Addison's newly formed electronic counter-measures force, 100 Group, or with interference by the huge British monitoring station at Kingsdown in Kent, where German-speaking men and women sought to deceive the fighters into breaking off or landing. When the Germans began to play selected music to direct the fighter pilots instead of voice transmissions, the British sought to match it. As the Germans strengthened their transmissions and altered their frequencies, the British followed them.

But for all the enormous effort that was mounted, Bomber Command never completely succeeded in breaking the controllers' communications with the fighters. When the Luftwaffe failed to intercept, it was almost invariably because the ground controllers had been deceived by the bombers' course changes, or by the 'spoof' force of Mosquitoes *Windowing* to resemble a Main Force attack. The Germans never got the measure of the Mosquitoes, even with the introduction in 1943 of a limited number of Ju88s boosted with nitrous oxide that were specifically intended for Mosquito interception. In the night-fighter squadrons, a pilot who shot down a Mosquito was allowed to count it as two 'victories'.

By the end of 1943 the radar war was also reaching a new pitch of intensity. The Germans had been impressed, almost awed, by their examination of captured British H2S sets and the cavity magnetrons that they contained. But having grasped the principle upon which the H2S aircraft dropped their blind markers, they embarked upon the herculean task of altering the H2S silhouette of the countryside around some key targets, for example by laying great strips of metal on rafts on the lakes around Berlin. They had also devised *Naxos*, a night-fighter radar which from early 1944 could home on H2S transmissions from British aircraft, and which at last caused Bomber Command to order that sets should only be switched on at short intervals over enemy territory. Just as British bombers had been fitted with *Monica*, which gave radar warning of aircraft approaching from the rear, so the Luftwaffe in turn fitted its fighters with *Flensburg*, which homed on *Monica*, and eventually led to its withdrawal. The Germans had also begun plotting the radar 'flames' from Allied IFF transmissions, about which Dr Jones and British Scientific Intelligence had been warning Bomber Command in vain for more than two years. Many crews were still convinced that IFF was capable of interfering with German radar, and kept their sets switched on from take-off to landing. Yet only in the spring of 1944 did the irrefutable evidence of Scientific Intelligence – supported by 'Ultra' intercepted German signals, of which the Luftwaffe's were throughout the war the most readily deciphered – compel Bomber Command to accept the reality of the threat and order crews to discontinue IFF emissions over enemy territory.

Yet whatever tactical antidotes Bomber Command could devise, by the winter of 1943 darkness had ceased to offer effective protection for the bomber, just as a few months earlier it had ceased to provide any safety for the cities of Germany. The night-fighter had achieved an alarming tactical dominance. It was the good fortune of the British that the leaders of Germany still had no grasp of the significance of the Luftwaffe's achievement. The bulk of the Reich's resources for the war against the bomber continued to be devoted to flak, searchlights and smoke generators. Something like a million people, albeit many of them women and schoolboys, were manning the defences each night. By September 1943, 8,876 of Germany's excellent 88-mm guns– which as Sir Arthur Harris often remarked would otherwise have been deployed against the advancing Russian tanks – were placed around the cities, supported by a further 24,500 light flak guns. Their chief value was in boosting civilian morale and forcing the bombers to fly high and bomb wide. In 1940 the Luftwaffe computed that its gunners expended 2,313 heavy and 2,458 light flak shells for every bomber destroyed, a ratio which increased later in the war.[28] One-third of the entire German optical industry was working to produce anti-aircraft defence equipment, half the electronics industry was building radar sets, most of them for the flak and the 7,000 searchlights supporting the guns. It was a formidable drain on German industry, and its value to the Allies must not be underestimated. Fifteen years after the war, Speer read the American official history of the USAAF's strategic bomber offensive, which expresses doubts about its achievement. He wrote in his secret diary in Spandau prison:

It seems to me that the book misses the decisive point. Like all other accounts of the bombing that I have so far seen, it places its emphasis on the destruction that air raids inflicted on German industrial potential and thus upon armaments. In reality the losses were not quite so serious ... The real importance of the air war consisted in the fact that it opened a second front long before the invasion of Europe. That front was the skies over Germany ... The unpredictability of the attacks made the front gigantic ... Defence against air attacks required the production of thousands of anti-aircraft guns, the stockpiling of tremendous quantities of ammunition all over the country, and holding in readiness hundreds of thousands of soldiers ... As far as I can judge from the accounts I have read, no one has yet seen that this was the greatest lost battle on the German side ...[24]

It is essential to quote this passage in any account of the bomber offensive, because the most enthusiastic defenders of the achievements of bombing, including Sir Arthur Harris himself, regard it among the principal testimony supporting their case. But in his memoirs *Inside the Third Reich*, published long after he wrote these words, Speer forcefully reasserted the view he had taken in his 1945–6 interrogations, that bombing had been ineffective in cracking Germany until the closing phase of the war. Speer was a manager, not a strategist. The balance of evidence suggests that in his Spandau writing, he overstated the importance of the German resources devoted to air defence, and underestimated the drain on the Allies of mounting the bomber offensive.

Germany's tragedy in the air war was that she lacked a coherent strategy, because of the lack of support and direction from the top. Her defences relied upon compromises and expedients. The resources that the Luftwaffe devoted to night-fighters were paltry by the standards of its own overall strength, far less when considered against the strength of the Allied air forces. Yet by the spring of 1944, in the face of every possible handicap, the German night-fighter force had inflicted a series of devastating blows on Bomber Command, culminating in the destruction of 108[25] aircraft on the Nuremberg raid of 30 March 1944.

However angered and dismayed were the leaders of Germany

by Allied bombing, they never considered it a sufficiently mortal threat to order a major withdrawal of aircraft from the east to reinforce the home front. Had they done so, had they lavished a fraction of the resources devoted to futile aircraft development or even ground defences upon the night-fighters of the Reich, had Jeschonnek or Goering forcefully supported Speer and Milch in their efforts to gain priority for home fighter defence, Bomber Command might by the winter of 1943 have suffered losses that would have brought its offensive against Germany to an abrupt conclusion.

10 Bomber Command headquarters, Buckinghamshire, 1943-44

Even in the bleakest nights of the bomber offensive it is remarkable how little dismay rippled the calm routine of Bomber Command headquarters at High Wycombe. Looking back over the war years later, staff officers remembered a thrill of excitement and triumph at the news of the 1,000 Raid on Cologne and the breaking of the Ruhr dams by 617 Squadron. In the wake of Hamburg in August 1943, there was a euphoric period 'when we really believed that we'd got it in the bag'.[1] But beyond these false dawns, there were few high surges or steep plunges of morale and enthusiasm. Week in and week out, eventually year in and year out, they walked or bicycled from their familiar billets in the morning to the quiet offices on No. 1 Site, poured forth the stream of orders and memoranda that clattered down the teletypes to Groups and Stations to launch seven thousand young men into the night sky over Germany and the following morning received back the paper harvest of signals and scrambled telephone messages, still-damp reconnaissance prints and provisional bomb-tonnage figures by which success or failure was measured. Their absolute remoteness from the battlefront has led some historians to compare High Wycombe with the French châteaux from which the generals of the First World War directed Passchendaele and the Somme, to liken Sir Arthur Harris to Sir Douglas Haig.[2]

Harris's eventual fall from grace was inevitable. He tossed too many hostages to fortune with his wildly exaggerated claims and promises, and attacked too many powerful interests with reckless rudeness. He was a warrior to the roots of his soul. He sought to engage and destroy the enemy by every means at his command, and it was this quality in him that undoubtedly appealed to Churchill, a like spirit. Harris had never been asked to determine the morality or desirability of a bomber offensive.

He had been appointed to attack Germany. If he fought fiercely for resources and support, this was not merely his privilege, but his duty. If he lost the confidence of the Prime Minister or the Air Staff, it was their business to sack him.

It is interesting that his aircrew, who never saw him, regarded him with rueful but enduring affection. His staff at High Wycombe respected and feared but, with a few exceptions, did not like him. He was too ruthless, too impatient of failure or disagreement, too devoid of endearing weakness. The stories of his abrasive encounters with authority were legion. Striding into the Air Ministry one morning, he passed one of the most senior civil servants with a bluff greeting of 'Morning, Abrahams, and what have you done to impede the war effort today?'[3] The Foreign Office sought Harris's help: 'Sam Hoare came bleating to me for a second aircraft to carry his diplomatic bags. But it just happened that one bag had burst open in the air on a previous run, and we found it full of lackeys' uniforms. I told Hoare that I did not consider these a fit cargo for my aircraft in the middle of the war.'[4] He made no secret of his loathing for the Royal Navy, and could contemptuously reel off details of the deluge of decorations awarded to sailors for some of their less successful operations. He said that there were three things one should never take on a yacht – a wheelbarrow, an umbrella and a naval officer. One day Churchill told Harris that Pound was deeply concerned about the continued survival of the battleship *Tirpitz*: 'Tell the First Sea Lord he need not worry,' said Harris blithely. 'I'll sink it when I have a spare moment.'

The mask never slipped from Harris, because there was no mask. Behind those piercing eyes, there was shrewdness but little tolerance. Those like Major Morton who recoiled from his philistinism were justified in the sense that he had no evident interest in culture. He had no small talk. He disliked physical activity – he often said that after his experiences in South-West Africa in the First World War, he made up his mind never to walk again unless he had to. At the same period, he formed a deep affection for mules and their ways, a joke against himself which he enjoyed. Few men have applied themselves to their duty even in war with the single-mindedness of Harris. Even Portal occasionally took a few days' fishing. In the course of more than three years at High Wycombe, Harris allowed himself only two weekends of holiday, with friends in Norfolk. Many of his staff officers were middle-aged men who found it possible to do their part to a not uncomfortable routine, but Harris lived with enormous strain. He often remarked that while most commanders in war were required to risk their forces in battle only at intervals of months, he was staking everything almost every night. He drowned his ulcers in Dr Collis Browne's mixture, and later in a potion supplied by the Americans. He chain-smoked Camels or Lucky Strikes through a battered holder. He gave vent to his inner tensions in moments of fierce anger that exasperated his equals and thoroughly frightened his subordinates.

But those who seek to present him as a latter-day 'Donkey', indifferent to casualties, do him an injustice. He was passionately concerned to give every man in his command the best possible chance of survival. A senior civil servant at the Ministry of Aircraft Production described vividly[5] an occasion on which Harris arrived to denounce the Stirling bomber and demand more Lancasters: 'It's murder, plain murder to send my young men out to die in an aircraft like that!' said Harris furiously. A good case can be made that he was slow to grasp the possibilities and limitations of radar. He was one of those men who refuse to accept any lesson until they have proved it for themselves. He was not a quick or indeed a first-class mind in the academic sense, but it is debatable whether first-class minds are wanted at the summit of operational commands in wartime.

The mainspring of all that Harris did was his determination to prove the unique qualities of strategic air power. Trenchard in the end came to regard Harris as his most perfect disciple, when other bright hopes such as Portal had been infected by unbelievers. Harris was a man of immense force and directness – though a good deal less frank than he sometimes appeared – whose overwhelming advantage was that he was quite indifferent to what the world thought of him. He reserved great warmth of heart for those who inspired his respect and affection, and was unswervingly loyal to his friends and those who served him well.

But he never took the precaution of cloaking what he was doing in the formal dress of circumspection and manners that the English traditionally cherish in peace and war. His Rhodesian background may explain something of this. He seemed to delight in assaulting social convention, in expressing the realities of the bomber offensive in the most brutally literal language. 'I wonder whether in Allied headquarters, as in ours, the talk was not of victory over the enemy, but of his "extinction" or "annihilation",' Speer mused in his cell at Spandau years later. 'How, for example, did Air Marshal Harris express himself?'[6]

Harris had performed a great service to England and to the Government in the first eighteen months of his command, when the bomber offensive was the Western Allies' greatest thrust against Germany. Now, strategic bombing had become a controversial matter. It is notable how much Churchill wrote about Bomber Command in the early chapters of his war memoirs, how little in the later. In his final volume, Harris himself is mentioned only once, *passim* and critically. It was Harris's reckless choice of language in writing and speaking of the bomber offensive during the war years that pinioned the levelling of Germany's cities to his back for good or ill for the rest of history, while men who chose their words more carefully – Churchill, Portal, even Cherwell – have somehow kept a distance from it.

From February 1942 until the end of the war Harris lived a few minutes' drive from High Wycombe, at the Commander-in-Chief's official residence, Springfield House. It was a remarkable *ménage*. He had married his second wife Therese only in 1938, and it had taken her some time to shrug off her natural initial shyness, a young woman suddenly thrust amidst the summits of the Royal Air Force. Now, at Springfield, she was bringing up their small daughter Jackie and entertaining ministers and celebrities of every nation in the war. De Gaulle came, and Ellen Wilkinson, the radical MP; there were Indians who needed special food, and Americans like Ira Eaker to be shown Harris's famous Blue Books – indeed his chief concern with every visitor was to indoctrinate them about the achievements and potential of Bomber Command. An RAF cook, Sergeant Simmonds, presided over the kitchen, although Harris himself was fond of taking over at the stove when there were no guests. There was a resident nucleus of Harris's staff. Harry Weldon, his Personal Staff Officer, was a philosophy don from Magdalen College, Oxford. It was Weldon who adapted Harris's language and sentiments into the forcefully expressed minutes and memoranda with which he bombarded the Air Ministry and the War Cabinet.

John Maze was posted to Harris at the completion of his tour of operations with 76 Squadron in the winter of 1943, one of a succession of ADCs throughout the war. Naturally nervous in his C-in-C's drawing-room after dinner, the gangling young man emptied his coffee over the pristine white carpet sent to Springfield from the *Queen Mary* when she was stripped to become a troopship. The Harrises liked to nickname the household and they knew their Damon Runyon, so Maze became 'Feets', just as Weldon was 'Harry the Horse'.

Harris's other permanent guest at Springfield was Air Vice-Marshal Sir Robert Saundby, first SASO and now Deputy C-in-C of Bomber Command. 'Sandy' Saundby was effectively Harris's Chief of Staff, an outstanding technician who was responsible for translating Harris's target decisions into operational reality, in liaison with the Group commanders. Saundby's family lived in Berkshire, too far from him to get home for more than occasional visits, so the Harrises invited him to live with them. Second only to his dedication to strategic bombing, he was a passionate naturalist. In his spare hours at High Wycombe, he stalked the hedgerows in pursuit of butterflies and plants. There was a legendary occasion on which he was arrested up a tree with his butterfly net, suspected by a local constable of attempting to catch sparrows for the London market. Saundby was also a superb fly-fisherman, drifting across West Wycombe lake in summer, rowed by any officer who would play boatman for him. Once he brought back a basket of trout for the Harrises, unconscious of their conviction that such horrors were a mass of pins and cotton-wool. It was Saundby's turn to shudder at dinner that night, when he found his beloved trout on the table as fishcakes.

The Deputy C-in-C's other passion was model railways. In a room above the mess at High Wycombe, he had an enormous layout on which he lavished all the attention that he could spare from nature and the bomber offensive. He was a genuine English eccentric, a placid, humorous, mild-mannered man who excelled at detail. He drove an old Rolls-Royce which he said he had bought as a lifetime investment, but never took shopping because it caused stores to overcharge him. He was almost old-maidishly careful about money, and the difficulty of catching him when it was time to buy a round of drinks was a standing joke in the mess at High Wycombe.

Saundby's crippling weakness was that he was totally in awe of Harris. A staff officer describes their relationship as that of headmaster and schoolboy.[7] It would never have occurred to Saundby to make a decision without consulting Harris, or to dispute policy with the C-in-C. Studying Bomber Command headquarters throughout the period of Harris's command, it is difficult to find evidence of any senior staff officer who took open issue with the C-in-C on a major policy matter. Harris was perfectly approachable on tactics and organization, but it would have been a brave man – and there were very few at High Wycombe – who touched the C-in-C on one of his exposed nerves. There appears to have been a chronic lack of open, critical debate. There were too many weak men and sycophants around the throne, and this situation must be attributed to Harris's choice and treatment of his subordinates. There was a fear of clear thinking if it led to unpalatable conclusions. If Harris had been able to call on more frankness from those close to him, some of Bomber Command's most serious misfortunes might have been avoided. Most important, perhaps, the Battle of Berlin might have been halted months before its eventual conclusion. 'Berlin had become a fixation with Bert, and we knew it,' said one of his staff officers thirty years later.[8] But it never occurred to himself or his colleagues to say as much to Harris at the beginning of 1944.

The routine at High Wycombe was a mirror-image of war on the stations: the day began as the crews went to bed, ended as they took off into the night. Each morning after breakfast Harris left Springfield in his black Bentley two-seater at 8.30, driven by the impeccable Maddocks, his chauffeur, with his distinctive patent-leather moustache. In his car Harris rushed everywhere, the way swept clear by the 'Cabinet Priority' badge on the bonnet. WAAFs and staff officers leapt for their lives as they saw the C-in-C's motor racing up the road of No. 1 Site. His office was situated at the corner of the solid redbrick two-storey building that housed Bomber Command's most senior officers, down the long ground-floor corridor. Lesser mortals were scattered over several acres of wartime huts. On Harris's arrival Peggy Wherry, his formidable WAAF secretary, brought him the most urgent signals and target folders. He retired to his morning ablutions to consider them, and there was often a hasty struggle to recall him when the Prime Minister came on the scrambler for details of the previous night's attack.

'I'm sick of these raids on Cologne,' growled Churchill testily one morning.

'So are the people of Cologne,' barked Harris.

If the C-in-C was not available, the call went through to some nervous staff officer in the Operations Room: 'How did the raid proceed last night?' inquired the most famous voice in England. 'Only 700 aircraft reached the target? Your C-in-C promised 800. And how many tons of bombs did you discharge?' The hesitant young man in the Ops Room might stumble on for several minutes before realizing that the Prime Minister, having learnt what he wanted, had long since noiselessly hung up.[9]

At 9 a.m. Harris left his office and was driven a few hundred yards across the base to the grass-covered mound that concealed the great underground bunker from which the bomber offensive was directed. The Operations Room, 'The Hole' as it was known, had been purpose-built for Bomber Command just before the outbreak of war. Here, at 'Morning Prayers' each day, Harris determined which city of Germany would suffer fire and high explosives that night. He took his seat at the desk in the midst of the big room, flanked by the great wall-maps of Europe and the target-priority list of dozens of cities and objectives, updated daily in accordance with the movement of the war, extensive enough to afford Harris enormous latitude. Around him stood Saundby, Magnus Spence the weather expert, the SASO, Deputy SASO, Group-Captain Operations, Group-Captain Intelligence, Navigation Officer, Captain de Mowbray of naval liaison, Colonel Carrington for the army, and a supporting cast of half a dozen wing-commanders and squadron-leaders from Operations and Intelligence.

After a brief report on the previous night's operations, it was invariably Spence who commanded the attention of the meeting. He might report that a front was moving up western Germany around midnight. Harris would say: 'In that case it's obvious that Hamburg, Bremen or Wilhelmshaven are our best bet for tonight' – he pronounced German names in obstinate English, so that Wiesbaden became 'Wysbaden' – 'Can we get there in time without too early a start?' If Spence approved, there was a hasty shuffling of target folders and photographs among the staff, and the possibilities were handed forward to the C-in-C. Occasionally Saundby reminded Harris of an urgent Air Ministry or Ministry of Economic Warfare request, but there was no controversy at 'Morning Prayers'. The decisions were unequivocally those of the C-in-C. The weather was both a dominant reality and an all-embracing alibi. Whatever target lists had recently been passed down by the Combined Strategic Targets Committee – on which the Americans, the Ministry of Economic Warfare and Bomber Command were all represented – Harris could and did plead the weather as an excuse for pursuing his own intentions, although often enough it genuinely restricted his options. He seldom lingered more than a few moments over the target folders at conference before closing the issue: 'Right. We'll send 800 heavies to Hamburg. Now what about some "gardening"? What do you want "gardened", de Mowbray?' Harris could never resist teasing the naval officer, not unkindly. The moment the key decision had been taken – targets and forces – Harris left the room and returned to his office.

It became Saundby's responsibility to organize the detailed planning of the operation. He had given every German city its codename as a fish: Berlin was WHITEBAIT, Munich CATFISH, Nuremberg GRAYLING. Now he reached for the DACE file on Hamburg. The key staff officers dispersed around the Operations Room to maps and telephones – most important to talk to Bennett, commanding the Pathfinders, and to Cochrane, commanding 5 Group. The two men detested each other, and invariably contested tactical suggestions offered by either. Bennett planned a route for his Mosquito 'Light Night Striking Force' to divert the defences. In telephone consultation with Saundby, he discussed the Main Force's course changes as they crossed Europe, aimed at concealing until the last possible moment the real objective of the attack. Addison's 100 Group were alerted to lay on their jammers and night-fighters. There might be weather problems in certain areas of England – perhaps

4 Group, in Yorkshire, were having difficulties clearing snow from their runways. On the wall, lights flickered like Christmas-tree illuminations on the great map that indicated the service-ability to Bomber Command's stations. Some squadrons might be ordered to carry extra fuel if there was doubt about a possible difficult landing on their return. Perhaps two hours after Harris had left The Hole, Saundby had noted precise routes, bombloads, take-off times and aiming-points in his meticulous handwriting, ready to be typed-up for Harris's final approval. Aiming-points were not infrequently changed late in the morning, in concession to *Pointblank*. It looked better on paper to send the Pathfinders to mark an airframe plant or a tank factory, however meaning-less such refinements became over the target. Then each Group Commander addressed his own conference, mirroring Harris's 'Morning Prayers', and the High Wycombe staff dispersed to their offices under the beech trees, to fix details department by department.

For the handful of senior officers directly concerned with the planning of operations, High Wycombe was a fascinating posting at the very heart of the war. For those of less exalted rank, it was a staid, formal, claustrophobic place, darkened by the over-hanging trees that dripped endlessly in the rain, corseted by the strictures of service bureaucracy. There were many elderly men like 'Daddy' Dawes, the Senior Personnel Staff Officer who con-trolled postings throughout Bomber Command, and relished every moment of his absolute power over so many men and women's service careers. The pace of work was hard, broken only by prolonged spells of bad weather that halted operations. There were none of the excitements and compensations of the operational stations. In their spare hours they walked across the fields to The Plough at Speen or hitchhiked into London. Every-body who could, lived off the base. Young wing-commanders posted to High Wycombe from 'ops' yearned to escape. Their opinions and advice were seldom heeded amidst so much 'brass'.

Perhaps the most preposterously unsuitable appointment at High Wycombe throughout the war was that of the Chaplain, Rev. John Collins, in future years the arch-radical opponent of Britain's nuclear bomb, and even in wartime a permanent thorn in the side of authority.

Bomber Command Headquarters [he wrote afterwards] was perhaps the most soul-destroying, the most depressing of the ... places in which I had to serve. For there, in contrast with the natural beauty of the surroundings, the evil ... policy of the carpet bombing of German cities was planned ... The majority of the personnel were simply clerks in uniform, for the most of whom any interest or glamour in being attached to Bomber Command headquarters had long since gone; and those not of this category were mainly officers who had been taken off operational duties or deadbeats.[10]

It was Collins who invited the socialist Minister of Aircraft Production, Sir Stafford Cripps, to give a talk at High Wycombe on the unlikely theme 'Is God My Co-Pilot?' which enraged the C-in-C and his staff, because Cripps suggested that officers

should send men on a bombing mission only if, with a clear conscience, they were convinced that such a mission was morally justified as well as justified on grounds of military strategy and tactics. At question time, he was accused by one or two officers of saying things that, if heeded, might threaten discipline and hinder the war effort ... The chairman found an excuse to call the meeting to an abrupt end.[11]

Harris fought back by sending Harry Weldon to give a lecture on 'The Ethics of Bombing', at which, according to Collins, attendance by all ranks was compulsory. When it ended, Collins stood up and said that he presumed he had misunderstood Weldon's title, which should have been 'The Bombing of Ethics'. It is difficult to understand how Harris and his chaplain stood each other's company in the same camp for the remainder of the war.

On the squadrons the bomber offensive was conducted without any great emotion except that of fear. But the staff at High Wycombe sought constantly to instil in the aircrew a suitable enthusiasm for their work. The Intelligence Department issued Briefing Notes for groups and squadrons. This is a sample from September 1943:

The history of MANNHEIM symbolizes on a small scale the evil history of Germany. The old town, decent and dignified, was designed in the seventeenth and eighteenth centuries as a setting for a riverside castle – the largest in Germany – for one of the innumerable but reasonably inoffensive little German states. Today it is one of the most important industrial centres of Hitler's Reich, its atmosphere darkened with the smoke of engineering plants and polluted by enormous chemical works. Vital war industries which together employ one-third of the total population (430,000) of MANNHEIM and its satellite town of LUDWIGSHAVEN. It is as though WINDSOR had sprouted a malignant growth of war factories, and one-and-a-half square miles of chemical works covered the playing-fields of ETON.[12]

The report goes on to assess the damage done by Bomber Command's latest attack, quoting a German broadcaster named Karl Rumpf:

The egregious RUMPF . . . rounded off his tale of woe with a tragedy enacted in the NATIONAL THEATRE in the centre of the town. It appears that this institution opened its new season on the night preceding the attack. The first night doubtless had an enthusiastic reception, but the following night all too literally brought the house down.[13]

Reports such as this made little impact on aircrew, but perhaps did something for the enlightenment and enthusiasm of the vast army of ground staff supporting the offensive. Just as it was the ground-based men and women who wrote the poems eulogizing the deeds of the aircrew, so it was they who also took the keenest interest in the Germany that they never saw.

Target Intelligence was one of the most vital departments at High Wycombe, and because Intelligence proved to have been the cardinal weakness of Bomber Command's offensive against Germany, it is necessary to explain at some length precisely how High Wycombe assessed the success or failure of their attacks. Harris's staff share responsibility for the huge misconceptions surrounding the strategic offensive with the Air Ministry and the Ministry of Economic Warfare, who failed at the outset to grasp the complexities of the German economy; the Secret Service, who never appear to have controlled agents inside Germany capable of providing useful economic Intelligence; and the Foreign Office, which throughout the war believed that the morale of the German people was crumbling. MEW and the Air Ministry never understood how widely critical industries were scattered: only 48 per cent of plant was located in the fifty-eight towns attacked in strength by Bomber Command, and by 1943 Speer and Milch were working energetically towards still greater dispersal, and locating vital assembly-lines underground. Although Hamburg was the third city of the Greater Reich, it accounted for only 3.6 per cent of Germany's production.

By far the most effective damage-assessment organization Britain possessed was RE8, the research department of the Ministry of Home Security, who reached their conclusions by projecting the British experience of lost production, absenteeism, de-housing and wrecked services in 1940 on to Germany's cities. They computed the number of German buildings lost or damaged beyond repair – 212,000 by the end of 1943 – with consistent accuracy. Their judgements on the probable injury to German production were also remarkably sound. The tragedy was that the airmen simply declined to believe them.

A typical Bomber Command Air Staff Intelligence report of February 1944, headed 'The Progress of the RAF bomber offensive against German Industry, 7 March 1943 to 31 December 1943' began with the following remarkable assertion: 'This paper is based on figures issued by RE8, but owing to difficulties in assessing certain factors, RE8 state that the calculated industrial loss is as much as 65 per cent underestimated.'[14]

In their six-monthly review of the achievements of the bomber offensive in mid-1943, the Ministry of Economic Warfare suggested that German production was 15 per cent down on the previous year, and in the Ruhr, 35 per cent down. By the end of 1943 they estimated that German output had fallen a further 10 per cent. As has been explained above,[15] they believed that this supposed loss represented a net absolute decline in war production, which was far from the truth. By mid-1944 they argued that Axis war production was being destroyed faster than it could be replaced.

These figures were, of course, largely based on information provided by the Royal Air Force. They did not perceive that aerial photographs overestimated damage. They regarded buildings with collapsed roofs as a total loss, while in fact the machinery beneath them could often be cleared of rubble and become operational again within days. They argued that vertical air reconnaissance must conceal vast damage. They never made adequate allowance for the fact that while the weight of area attacks was always directed against city centres, the heart of industry lay in the suburbs.

It is important to remember that all but the most senior officers at High Wycombe were as much amateurs, civilians in uniform, as the men who flew the aircraft. An officer of the key Target Intelligence department INT I recalled later: 'We made up the damage-assessment techniques as we went along, because there was no precedent for what we were doing.' The fatal error by the scientists and statisticians was their determination to establish an absolute mathematical relationship between acres of urban devastation (of which they were accurately informed) and loss of production to the German war economy. Bomber Command built its greater edifice of self-delusion about the plight of the German war machine on an astonishing foundation of graphs and projections. In 1943 they recorded that 'Efficiency' – as measured by 'acres of target devastated per ton of bombs claimed dropped – had risen from 0.038 at the end of 1942 to 0.126 by October 1943. 'Success', measured by 'acres destroyed per acre attacked', had risen from 0.032 in 1942 to 0.249 in 1943. Reports are strewn with such headings as 'Average monthly increase in number of industrial workers attacked.' From February 1944, they announced, 'The "Labour Target" now takes the place of the "Area Target", its dimensions being the number of industrial workers (which means exclusively factory workers) multiplied by the period of time which is being considered. . .' Another Air Staff Intelligence report from High Wycombe dated 19 February 1944 stated that in 1943

it will be seen that the enemy has *irretrievably lost** 1,000,000 man *years*.* This represents no less than 36 per cent of the industrial effort that would have been put out by these towns if they had remained un-molested . . . Expressing these losses in another way, 2,400,000,000 man-hours have been lost for an expenditure of 116,500 tons of bombs claimed dropped, and this amounts to an average return for every ton of bombs dropped of 20,500 lost man-hours, or rather more than one quarter of the time spent in building a Lancaster . . . This being so, a Lancaster has only to go to a German city once to wipe off its own capital cost, and the results of all subsequent sorties will be clear profit . . .[16]

Bomber Command Intelligence projected that by 1 April 1944, 33,760 acres – 40 per cent of 89,000 acres attacked – should have

*Emphasis in original text.

been destroyed, if average bomb tonnage remained static. But on the other hand, if the average monthly tonnage could be increased from 13,350 to 21,270, then 50 per cent of the 89,000 acres attacked could be destroyed…

The samples above are typical of the acres of paper filled by the Intelligence Staffs throughout the bomber offensive, and they are a powerful indication of Bomber Command's diminishing grasp on the reality of the German economy in 1943–4. Seldom in the history of warfare have attempts been made to measure victory or defeat by such remarkable mathematical yardsticks as those conceived in the huts and bunkers under the beech trees at High Wycombe.

But long before RE8's much more modest estimates had been reached and submitted, before even High Wycombe's own projections were compiled, Harris had been given an immediate provisional summary of results achieved, on the basis of reconnaissance photographs. Target Intelligence believed that the officer who presented this each day gave a consistently optimistic picture of what had been done. Often Harris seemed to make judgements from his own interpretation of the photographs on his desk. He frequently assessed a target destroyed which later proved to be merely damaged. Target Intelligence might suspect the truth, but they seem to have been unwilling forcefully to assert it. 'Has Eaker seen these?' Harris would say when some choice reconnaissance photographs of disroofed German urban areas appeared on his desk, and dispatch them for the American's delectation. In this, Harris and his staff were guilty of the same error as those earlier generals in Flanders who had been so awed by the magnificence of their own barrages that they found it inconceivable that the enemy could have survived them. Nor were the delusions confined to High Wycombe. On 2 February 1944, for instance, Air Vice-Marshal W. A. Coryton, Assistant Chief of Air Staff (Operations), wrote to Portal, commenting on a Ministry of Economic Warfare report:

The contribution Bomber Command has made to the reduction of German Air Force production as given in paragraph 9 of the attached report is remarkably low. I suggest that we should not treat these figures as firm, since the calculations on which they are based must invariably include assumptions based on guesswork. It is inconceivable that Bomber Command, in their attacks on the major industrial centres of Germany, have not caused acute bottlenecks in the production and supply of many items of equipment, e.g. machine tools, of which we are not aware.

Throughout the war Harris himself was wedded to his headquarters. He seldom left his office, with its barograph on the windowsill monitoring the fickleness of the weather, its charts and graphs on the wall concealed by shutters from insecure visitors. He lunched at home, then returned to his desk. His masters seldom troubled him in the flesh. Portal never came to High Wycombe. Instead, Harris drove once a week at his usual headlong pace to the Air Ministry for a conference, not infrequently involving the latest round of his feud with Bufton and the Directorate of Bomber Operations. 'Another paper from DB Ops?' Saundby would inquire schoolboyishly, lifting Bufton's file from the desk at arm's length. 'Tweezers. Pause for nausea.' Once a month the Group commanders assembled at High Wycombe, their meetings often punctuated by angry exchanges between Bennett and Cochrane. On very rare occasions Harris visited a bomber station. But the vast majority of his crews never saw him. It was not a matter of conviction that he toured stations so little: it was merely that when Bomber Command was laying on a raid almost every night, there was no one at High Wycombe to whom he cared to delegate the vital decisions if he went elsewhere.

The Royal Navy's most grievous grudge against Harris was his access to the Prime Minister. Chequers, Churchill's official country residence, was only a few miles from High Wycombe. Perhaps once in six weeks on a weekend evening, one of the Prime Minister's staff telephoned to invite Harris to dine. But Harris asserts most firmly[17] that it was unusual for him to have an opportunity to be closeted *tête-à-tête* with Churchill, and there is no reason to doubt him. He usually dined amidst a large party and general conversation. Later they adjourned to the house cinema to watch one of the Prime Minister's favourite films. Churchill called his C-in-C 'Bert', or 'Harris', or more ebulliently 'Bomber', according to his mood. Harris might have five or at most ten minutes' personal conversation with the Prime Minister. Churchill asked how the campaign was going, and what Harris planned for the future. Harris certainly used his opportunities to plead his own shortages of resources and the difficulties of meeting the claims of rival services. But Churchill never gave direct orders to Bomber Command. While Harris frequently expressed his own views on paper to Downing Street, Churchill almost invariable replied, with punctilious protocol, through Portal. Harris was sometimes irked by Churchill's impatience with his expositions: 'I wouldn't have called Winston a good listener.'[18]

The visits to Chequers gave vent to one of Harris's few private enthusiasms: driving horses. One day Churchill deplored the internal-combustion engine as the curse of the modern age. 'I entirely agree, Prime Minister,' said Harris, 'and what's more I think I'm the only man here who lives up to his principles.' He had driven himself over to lunch in a pony-trap.

But for all the courtesies between them, their respect for each other as dedicated warriors, there is no evidence of real personal warmth between Churchill and Harris, or that their meetings had any influence on the priority accorded to the bomber offensive. Harris, with his horror of 'panaceas' and his passion for the concentration of force, despaired of the Prime Minister's 'Parergonitis', as he called it, 'the search for soft underbellies' that had filled Churchill with enthusiasm for Gallipoli and North Africa. Harris would never forgive Churchill for his mute disavowal of the strategic offensive at the end of the war, when he declined to authorize a Bomber Command campaign medal.

Churchill, for his part, probably found Harris a convenient tool rather than a convivial companion. He always liked the sense of immediacy that he gained from meeting his C-in-Cs. In most cases they were too far afield to be readily available, but Harris was on hand. Contrary to much that has been written in the past, there is no reason to suppose that the course of the bomber offensive would have been any different if the two men had never met. Churchill invited Harris to dine because he was a keen supporter of bombing for reasons of his own. He did not become a supporter of bombing because Harris had his ear. There is no evidence that he was impressed by Harris's extravagant promises. By the spring of 1944 his enthusiasm for bombing was already waning. Harris continued to enjoy the memory of the Prime Minister's support and protection perhaps more in the minds of others than in reality. If Portal had chosen to put the matter to the test by sacking the C-in-C of Bomber Command at any time from the spring of 1944 onwards, he might have been surprised how passively Churchill acquiesced.

Harris's working day at High Wycombe ended at the same time as that of any businessman, around 6 p.m. Maddocks and the Bentley took him home to Springfield. Often there were guests to entertain, Americans or Russians to be invited to sit themselves at the stereopticon through which Harris gazed for so many hours on images of the ruined cities of Germany. Some evenings, the Harrises visited their close friends the Maurice Johns, a gynaecologist and his wife who lived next door to Springfield, with whom they could find some kind of release from the war. If they were at home and there were no guests, they dined with Saundby, Weldon and Maze, and in Harris's words, 'talked bombing until bedtime'.[19] Throughout the night the telephone by his bedside rang intermittently with reports of operations. Harris had the fortunate knack of being able to wake, listen, and instantly fall asleep again. It is one of the ironies of the bomber offensive that while the aircrew fought through the darkness over Germany, while the sleepless cities stood to their guns and searchlights and burst forth in their nightly torment of fire and blast, the Commander-in-Chief of Bomber Command lay dreamless in his bed among the Buckinghamshire woods.

11 Conflict and compromise, 1943–44

The Battle of Berlin

It is my firm belief [Sir Arthur Harris wrote to Portal on 12 August 1943] that we are on the verge of a final showdown in the bombing war, and that the next few months will be vital. Opportunities do not knock repeatedly and continuously. I am certain that given average weather and concentration on the main job, we can push Germany over by bombing this year . . .

It was the immoderation of Harris's expectations in the autumn of 1943 that provoked the scale of the subsequent disillusionment. If his promises had been less ambitious, his failure to fulfil them might have been forgotten. But until the last weeks before the invasion of Europe in June 1944, he continued to argue that Germany could be defeated by bombing alone. In the personal minute to Churchill of 3 November 1943 in which he listed the nineteen cities allegedly totally destroyed by Bomber Command, he went on to make the statement that would haunt his career to the end: 'We can wreck Berlin from end to end if the USAAF will come in on it. It will cost between 400 and 500 aircraft. It will cost Germany the war.'

This assertion, more than any other that he made throughout the war, surrendered Harris's reputation to his critics. It cast very serious doubts upon his judgement. Berlin was not to be wrecked 'from end to end' in the winter of 1943, and calm analysis of the tactical and industrial realities should have disposed of this fantasy at birth. It is anyway a mystery why Harris supposed that the destruction of Berlin would have caused the collapse of German resistance. By proclaiming his intention to launch the full weight of Bomber Command's resources against the enemy's capital, Harris also flaunted his defiance of the *Pointblank* directive. Attacking Berlin had only the most distant relevance to the defeat of the German air force in production, which was supposed to be the first duty of the Allied air offensive. It was absurd to imagine that the Americans were likely to join an attack that would entail renouncing *Pointblank*, which they had largely created. There is some evidence that the extent of the 8th Air Force's sense of defeat in the wake of Schweinfurt a fortnight earlier was still unknown to the British, and it was only to later historians that it became clear that the winter of 1943 was the critical low-water mark of the USAAF's fortunes in Europe. But Harris knew the scale of the Americans' losses. It is remarkable that he imagined that they were in the mood to embark on new deep-penetrations against the most heavily defended city in Europe.

It says much for the respect Harris had built up for his person-ality and achievements that the Prime Minister and the Air Staff did not at once lose confidence in a man capable of making such extravagant claims. On 5 November 1943, Air-Marshal F. F. Inglis, Assistant Chief of Air Staff (Intelligence), wrote to Portal commenting on Harris's letter to Churchill. It is interest-ing to see the C-in-C's ideas interpreted by an unflinching admirer:

We are convinced that Bomber Command's attacks are doing more towards shortening the war than any other offensive including the Russians' [began Inglis modestly]. The C-in-C's letter is the letter of a man with ONE AIM, the rightness of which is his obsession. It is neces-sary to take this obsession into account because, inevitably, it leads him to make statements which can be criticized even by those who are in sympathy with his plea for more help to finish the job. Its purpose is, apparently, twofold:

(1) To get the Prime Minister's support to speed up USAAF con-centration in the United Kingdom even at the expense of forgoing the strategic offensive from Italy.

(2) To get the Prime Minister to persuade General Eaker to bomb Berlin.

Our plan first to break the German air force defence and then to get on with the war does not appeal to a man who knows that it can be won by immediate offensive action long before our defensive plan has come near to completion. This is why the importance of industries in the Balkans and southern Germany does not appeal to him. Although he speaks of nine-tenths of German industry being nearer Norfolk than

Lombardy, we are sure he really means that nine-tenths of the German population is nearer Norfolk, and in the light of our new morale paper which is about to be published, it is the population which is the joint in the German armour. The C-in-C's spear is in it, but it needs a jolt to drive it home to the heart. Apparently, only the Americans can provide this additional thrust, and we believe he is right to ask for it.

Harris failed to persuade Portal or the Prime Minister to press the Americans to join Bomber Command's assault on Berlin. He has since said that he would never have embarked on the Battle had he known that the 8th Air Force would not take part, but it is impossible to believe that this was ever likely, or that the outcome would have been different had they done so. The winter weather would have made daylight blind-bombing as indecisive as night blind-bombing, and the heavy losses the Americans suffered when they finally attacked Berlin with powerful fighter escort in March 1944 suggest that their casualties would have been appalling if they had begun to do so four months earlier, before the Mustang long-range escort became available in quantity.

But it would be unjust to Harris to suggest that he could have begun his assault on 18 November 1943 without the support, indeed the active encouragement, of the Prime Minister and the Chief of Air Staff. Since August 1943, Portal had been asking when a major attack on Berlin could take place. If Harris flagrantly ignored *Pointblank* to pursue his own concept of air warfare, where was Portal, his superior, the man specifically charged by the Combined Chiefs of Staff with responsibility for *Pointblank* on their behalf? Throughout the autumn American concern about lack of progress with the destruction of the German aircraft industry had been mounting. May 1944, the provisional date for the invasion, was drawing inexorably closer. As their own losses and difficulties grew, the USAAF pressed harder for the full participation of Bomber Command in attacks on the aircraft factories. On 19 October 1943, Bufton, the Director of Bomber Operations, wrote to Portal:

Although General Eaker and the C-in-C Bomber Command had many reasons for not adhering more rigidly to the high priority German Air Force objectives in the Directive, I believe a greater concentration upon them to be possible if political pressure is brushed aside and the Commanders set their minds to the task.

A few days later Portal answered a letter from Arnold in Washington, who had been expressing his concern about the lack of concentration on *Pointblank*:

I would say at the outset that I agree with you that there have been diversions from priority objectives as laid down by the Chiefs of Staff. I had already become apprehensive about this dispersal of our effort. Last week I had a useful meeting with Eaker and Harris and stressed to them the urgency of concentrating the maximum effort on to the defeat of the German air force.

At first, it is difficult to reconcile this letter from Portal with Harris's opening of the Battle of Berlin less than a month later. The British airmen had repeatedly asserted their commitment to *Pointblank*, in the directives to Bomber Command of 10 June and 3 September 1943, signed by the Deputy Chief of Air Staff, Bottomley, who increasingly shared Bufton's misgivings about Harris. Portal was not so Machiavellian as wantonly to deceive Arnold about Bomber Command's intentions. How therefore did Harris defy him?

There are two answers. First, while history now sees the Battle of Berlin from November 1943 to March 1944 as a single entity – Harris's last undiluted effort to win the war by area bombing – at no time in these months did the Air Staff see the Battle in this light. A continuous struggle was being waged to induce Harris to conform to the objectives of *Pointblank*, although at no point was it suggested that Harris could not devote part of his available effort to attacks on the German capital. There was never a conscious surrender by the Air Ministry to Harris's point of view. He staved off his opponents on a week-by-week basis: with explanations of weather and tactical difficulties, fierce argument about policy, and undisguised prevarication. Meanwhile, each night he launched his aircraft against his chosen targets. He fought with such success that it was not until the end of February 1944 that Bomber Command at last staged five operations specifically directed against elements of the German aircraft industry. But throughout the winter the Air Staff had been waiting in almost daily expectation of Harris's acquiescence to his orders.

The second critical element in the struggle was the Prime Minister. Since Casablanca, he had displayed little interest in *Pointblank*. Bomber Command no longer occupied the prominent place in his mind that it had possessed in 1940 and 1941, but he was still greatly attracted by bringing fire and the sword upon Germany's cities, and he had been delighted by Harris's triumph at Hamburg. Throughout the war, Churchill had pressed for more and greater attacks on Berlin. On several occasions Harris had sensibly cooled his master's impatience. Now the airman promised to raze the Nazi capital. Churchill may not have shared his C-in-C's expectations about knocking Germany out of the war, but he was attracted by the vision of Berlin engulfed in a second firestorm. To a man who had not studied the difficulties closely, it seemed perfectly possible for Bomber Command, with its ever-increasing force of heavy aircraft and extraordinary new range of tactics and technology, to inflict a catastrophe on Berlin to match 'Operation Gomorrah'. By any measure, this would be a savage blow to the Nazi regime. Portal was increasingly dismayed by Harris's obduracy, but it was already apparent that the only way to defeat him was to sack him. Churchill would never have endorsed such an action in the winter of 1943. Portal knew this and Harris knew this. On 18 November, Bomber Command embarked on the Battle of Berlin.

Like the earlier battles of 1943, this was not to be merely an assault on a single city, but a convenient title for a sustained struggle embracing targets all over Germany. Between the first attack on Berlin on 18 November and the end of the series at Nuremberg on 30 March 1944, Bomber Command mounted 9,111 sorties against the German capital in sixteen major attacks, and 11,113 sorties against other cities, notably Mannheim, Stuttgart, Frankfurt, Nuremberg, Leipzig, Brunswick and Schweinfurt. Bomber Command lost 1,047 aircraft missing – 5.1 per cent of sorties dispatched – and a further 1,682 damaged or written off. After the second operation, it became apparent that it was suicidal to dispatch the wretched Stirlings against the devastating German defences, and they were removed from the attack on Berlin, as were most of the Halifaxes a few weeks later. The Stirlings were shortly afterwards withdrawn from all operations against Germany. The Battle of Berlin was fought overwhelmingly by the Lancasters, with support from the Mosquitoes, who flew 2,034 sorties for the loss of only ten aircraft, an astonishing tribute to the light bomber's invulnerability.

For the crews of the Lancasters, the Battle of Berlin was a nightmare. Northern Germany seldom enjoyed clear weather in mid-winter, and that year conditions were exceptionally bad. Night after night, Bomber Command took off through the rain, sometimes through the snow, into the upper atmosphere's freak winds and sudden icing conditions, loaded to the aircraft's limits with bombs and fuel for the 1,150-mile round trip. Very early in the Battle, Pathfinders began to report seeing crews dumping their 4,000-lb 'cookies' in the North Sea to gain height and speed.

By grossly underestimating the Germans' resilience [wrote a Pathfinder navigator] Command had given the impression that the war was almost over. Tactically, because of the longer nights, this was the only feasible time of the year for making regular deep penetrations. Psychologically and physically it was the worst. Long hours at sub-zero temperatures dulled the brain, reflexes were slowed and mistakes were made. Frostbite was common even among pilots and navigators; with the cabin that cold, conditions elsewhere in the aircraft had to be experienced to be believed . . .If there was one time in an operational tour when the crew felt they needed the best the aircraft could offer, it was on a sortie to Berlin. Crews could get neither height nor performance with the new all-up weight, and although performance was improved by getting rid of bombs either over the North Sea or Germany, psychologically the damage was already done. Pilots lost confidence in their aircraft, and crews who elsewhere would not have hesitated to go over the centre of the town became 'fringe merchants'.[1]

Command ordered the rewiring of bomb-release circuits so that the photoflash exploded automatically when a pilot released his 'cookie', to put an end to dumping. The heavily laden bombers were now meeting the German night-fighter force at the summit of its wartime effectiveness and strength. An enormous effort was mounted to thwart it. 100 Group's Intruder Mosquitoes sought out the night-fighters around their airfields, while *Serrate* Mosquitoes stalked the skies equipped with radar that homed on the German *Lichtenstein* transmissions. German-speaking men and women broadcast false orders to the fighters by the *Corona* technique, attacked their radio-telephone communications with *Cigar* jamming, interrupted the controllers with *Tinsel* transmissions. Halifaxes and Stirlings flew diversionary mining operations off the coast while OTUs and HCUs sent their aircraft to make *Bullseye* training flights over the North Sea to divert German early-warning systems. Airborne and ground-based *Mandrel* jammers sought to fog enemy radar frequencies, Bennett's Mosquito Light Night Striking Force flew spoof raids, dropping fake fighter-flares and route-markers, *Windowing* their way to a city upon which they dropped Target Indicators and 4,000-lb 'cookies' to drive the population to their shelters and simulate the opening of a Main Force attack. All these techniques contributed something sometimes to diverting the defences, but none of them were sufficiently successful consistently to protect bombers. Again and again the fighters broke into the stream and inflicted punishing casualties. Berlin, above all, was a very difficult target to conceal. For the last hundred miles of the route, it was clear that Bomber Command could be going nowhere else. The sky was lit by exploding aircraft as frozen gunners, numbed in their turrets, missed the shadow slipping below the fuselage that a few seconds later consigned them to oblivion.

But that winter, it was over the target itself that the bombers' difficulties became intolerable. Again and again, they fought their way to Berlin to find the city sheathed in impenetrable cloud. It was far beyond *Oboe* range. Unlike Hamburg, it represented no clearly defined H2S image. The difficulties of marking were enormous. The Germans had created huge, effective decoy fires. In the first attacks, the parachute sky-markers – cascading pyrotechnic candles – disappeared into the overcast within seconds. Later in the Battle, 8 Group evolved their 'Berlin Method', sustaining a barrage of both ground- and sky-markers throughout the twenty-five minutes or less of the attack. Crews were instructed to bomb on the ground-markers where they could see them, on the sky-markers where they could not. In the first six major attacks on Berlin that winter only 400 of 2,650 attacking aircraft reported sighting the ground-markers. The remainder bombed the sky-markers – or sometimes no markers at all – and came home without glimpsing the target. More serious even than the crews' inability to see what they were attacking by night was

Photographic Reconnaissance's inability to pierce the overcast by day to discover what they had or had not achieved. From November 1943 to March 1944, of thirty-seven PRU sorties to Berlin, only two were successful.

Yet throughout the battle, Bomber Command HQ continued to circulate to groups and stations the most melodramatic reports of the damage achieved in Berlin. On 29 December 1943, Air Staff Intelligence at High Wycombe distributed a progress report which asserted that a minimum of 320,000 Berliners had been de-housed.

and the word 'minimum' cannot be repeated too often in connection with any estimates based on the present photographic cover . . . Estimates of 500,000 to 800,000 are quite likely to be nearer the truth than the calculations made above . . . The following paragraphs describe the damage (in central Berlin only) as a London newspaper might have described it if the Luftwaffe had succeeded in inflicting corresponding damage in the central London area:

Government buildings in Whitehall have suffered severely. The Treasury is largely destroyed and the Foreign Office partially gutted. Scotland Yard is a soot-blackened ruin and so is the Ministry of Transport. The Cabinet Offices at No. 10 Downing Street are roofless, and fire has destroyed half of No. 11. Many other well-known landmarks in central London have disappeared. The British Museum Library and University buildings have been damaged. The Albert Hall and Drury Lane Theatre are smouldering wrecks. Big office blocks like Shell-Mex House and Bush House have been burnt out. The Ritz Hotel is no more and fire has damaged part of the Savoy. The Café Royal is gutted from roof to basement . . . Railway stations everywhere are besieged by crowds of evacuees, but many of them are so badly damaged that few trains, or none at all, are able to leave . . . It is difficult indeed to imagine devastation on such a scale in a modern capital.[2]

High Wycombe's Intelligence Section waxed lyrical for six pages about the situation in Berlin. When Bomber Command began its great assault, it had been justified on the grounds that the city contained some critical elements of the German war effort: one-tenth of all aero-engines and precision instruments, one-third of the electrical engineering output, a quarter of all tanks and half of all field artillery were built in Berlin. But the metropolitan area extended over 883 square miles. It was an impossible undertaking to cover it effectively with bombs in winter weather amidst the most formidable defences in Europe. Ministries and other public buildings were indeed razed to the ground. The Allkett tank plants were damaged. The Siemens electrical works were hit. The leaders of Germany including Speer and Milch were initially appalled by what Bomber Command was doing and threatened to do. But Berlin's industries continued to produce war material in scarcely diminished quantities, while the wreckage of a thousand British bombers littered the north German countryside. Harris had set out to achieve a second Hamburg. He came nowhere near this. Goebbels wrote on 28 November:

The British are greatly overestimating the damage done to Berlin. Naturally it is terrible, but there is no question of 25 per cent of the capital no longer existing. The English naturally want to furnish their public with a propaganda morsel. I have every reason to want them to believe this and therefore forbid any denial. The sooner London is convinced that there is nothing left of Berlin, the sooner they will stop their air offensive against the Reich capital.[8]

Since 1943 there has been acid controversy among airmen about the Pathfinders' alleged failure to mark their targets satisfactorily that winter. In reality, 8 Group did all that could be expected of themselves and their equipment. Their crews were often little better qualified or more experienced than those of Main Force, and were almost as prone to the problem of 'Creep-back', for all Bennett's harsh comments about Main Force letting down his men by 'baulking the jump' and bombing short. Looking back on the battle a year later, Bennett claimed that Bomber Command's crews had failed to destroy Berlin because they had failed to press home their attacks: 'There can be no doubt that a very large number of crews failed to carry out their attacks in their customary determined manner,' he wrote to Harris. He claimed that 50 per cent of Main Force crews never even troubled to use their bomb-sights.

It is certainly true that crews' determination suffered in the winter of 1943–4. Cochrane considered this the only moment of the bomber offensive at which morale was slipping dangerously: 'One of my squadrons had cracked and another was cracking until I took firm action.'[4] But flagging morale was not responsible for Bomber Command's failure to destroy Berlin. The truth was that the city was too sprawling to lend itself to a second 'Operation Gomorrah'; too deep in Germany to achieve the same sort of concentrated attack against heavy opposition; and too difficult to hit accurately by H2S. H2S was never an adequate tool for blind bombing, and throughout the war Bomber Command never achieved satisfactory results by bombing sky-markers, the 'Wanganui' technique, as Bennett had codenamed it. Even if the markers were satisfactorily placed on release, in a high wind they could be miles off-target within seconds. It is unreasonable to claim that the Pathfinders were responsible for Main Force's failure, just as it was absurd for the Pathfinders to blame the Main Force. The operation was simply beyond Bomber Command's capabilities.

Harris and his staff should have recognized this, but they did not. As late as 7 December 1943, when the difficulties of the task had become abundantly clear, Harris declared that by 1 April 1944 he could bring about the collapse of Germany if he was able to launch 15,000 Lancaster sorties against her vital cities. If it is necessary to acquit the C-in-C of Bomber Command of personal ambition, surely this extraordinary statement must do so. No man with the slightest instinct for professional self-preservation would have committed himself so recklessly to a specific date by which he would personally have won the war.

Harris almost got his 15,000 Lancaster sorties from the Battle of Berlin – 14,562, to be exact – but not without a bitter struggle that intensified through the winter months. Portal's concern and the pressure from the Americans was growing. There was no evidence of a collapse of the German defences, no slackening of losses, no holocaust engulfing Berlin. Yet still Harris resisted every proposal to shift the weight of his attack to those cities in which the aircraft industry was concentrated:

It is naturally impossible to state with arithmetical precision the acreage of German built-up area which must be destroyed to produce capitulation [he wrote to the Air Ministry on 28 December 1943]. However . . . it is surely impossible to believe that an increase by more than one half of existing devastation within four months could be sustained by Germany without total collapse.

In the Air Ministry directives of 14 and 28 January and 17

315

February 1944, Air Marshal Bottomley yet again forcefully urged the C-in-C of Bomber Command to address himself to the aircraft industry:

It is confirmed and emphasized that the closest co-ordination is essential to the successful prosecution of the Combined Bomber Offensive [Bottomley wrote on 14 January] and that without it, the reduction of the German fighter strength which is a prerequisite to the launching of *Overlord* as well as to the effective conduct of *Pointblank* may not be achieved in the time available. I am accordingly to request that you adhere to the spirit of the directive forwarded in the Air Ministry letter dated 10 June 1943, and that you attack, as far as practicable, those industrial centres associated with the German fighter-air-frame and ball-bearing industry.

Harris's refusal to attack the German ball-bearing factories at Schweinfurt had become the central *casus belli* of his escalating struggle with the Air Ministry. 'So far Bomber Command has done far more than was planned or could have been expected to give effect to *Pointblank*,' he wrote. 'I cannot continue this process and in addition carry out the part of the programme specifically allocated to the Americans.'

Bufton, the Director of Bomber Operations, was now foremost among those who believed that whatever tactical difficulties they were experiencing, the Americans' concept of strategic bombing by precision attack on key industrial targets was far more promising than Harris's area offensive. He was exasperated by Harris's repeatedly successful defiance of Air Ministry instructions:

The C-in-C states that there can be little doubt that the enemy would be caused to capitulate by the destruction of between 40 and 50 per cent of the principal German towns, and that the Lancaster force alone should be sufficient, but only just sufficient, to produce in Germany by 1 April 1944 a state of devastation in which surrender is inevitable [he wrote to Portal, early in January]. I am of the opinion that it would be sounder for Bomber Command to subordinate as far as may be necessary their efforts to achieve a quick victory in favour of helping the Americans to deploy their strength so that the Combined Bomber forces (and *Overlord*) may together achieve a certain victory.

One January morning at the Air Ministry, as Bufton waited to see the Chief of Air Staff, Portal's Personal Staff Officer, Bill

Dry, emerged from the office and murmured to Bufton: 'They're all gunning for Bert Harris.' The Americans, the Ministry of Economic Warfare and key departments of the Air Ministry were growing exasperated by the C-in-C of Bomber Command. The baldness of Harris's refusals to change policy added insult to insubordination. 'What do you think about the C-in-C then, Bufton?' Portal asked the Director of Bomber Operations that morning in King Charles Street. 'Do you think it might be good to have a change?' Bufton recalls that he told Portal that he was opposed to sacking Harris, which is remarkable. But the C-in-C of Bomber Command had achieved enormous prestige in the years of Hamburg and Cologne. To remove him now would be a great shock to public and service opinion. Nor was it yet apparent how far he was willing to go in defiance of orders. Harris was not sacked. Towards the end of February he grudgingly diverted his forces to carry out a series of moderately successful attacks in support of the American 'Big Week' onslaught on the German aircraft industry. But the overwhelming weight of Bomber Command's effort continued to be directed towards the area offensive.

If Portal and his colleagues had been confident of an alternative policy for Bomber Command, it is likely that Harris would have been sacked in January 1944. In the Air Ministry hostility to his behaviour was hardening. But how much visible success was an attack on the German aircraft industry under a new C-in-C likely to achieve, to compensate for the seismic shock of Harris's dismissal? What were the prospects of a definable, decisive success against key selected German industrial targets, as an alternative to Harris's assault on German cities? The Air Staff havered on these questions. They knew that they now doubted the efficacy of area bombing, but they did not know what they should substitute for it. It was their indecision that saved Harris, the one man unswervingly certain of his objectives and intentions. It required iron resolution to dismiss him, and Portal was not the man for confrontation if it could be avoided. Harris continued his battle.

It was only because Bomber Command was now receiving plentiful supplies of aircraft and crews that he could sustain his terrible losses into the New Year and the spring. Harris's average daily availability of aircraft, almost all 'heavies', rose from 948 in November 1943 to 1,043 in March 1944. It is important to remember that losses had to fall below 4 per cent for a crew to have a favourable chance of completing a tour of operations. In January 1944, Harris was losing 6.1 per cent of aircraft dispatched to Berlin, 7.2 per cent of those which went to Stettin, Brunswick and Magdeburg. On the operation against Leipzig in February he lost seventy-eight aircraft missing, 9.5 per cent of those dispatched. On 24 March he lost seventy-two aircraft – 9.1 per cent of those dispatched – against Berlin on a night of unpredicted fierce winds that blew much of the stream over the most heavily defended flak belts in Germany. It was not an unbroken slaughter: sometimes the diversions and 'spoofs' succeeded, the nightfighters failed to engage. On the night of 26 March, 705 aircraft went to Essen and only nine were lost. On the night of 1 March, 557 went to Stuttgart and only four were lost. But on the night of 30 March 1944, Bomber Command suffered its worst single disaster of the war, when ninety-six of the 795 aircraft dispatched to Nuremberg – 11.8 per cent – failed to return. Twelve more were fatally damaged.

The Nuremberg raid is one of Harris's most bitter memories, not for itself but for what posterity has made of it. The official historians, among others, have declared that it signalled the collapse of Harris's personal attempt to defeat Germany by razing her cities to ashes. Harris has remarked[5] that it is surprising that his forces did not suffer a score of Nurembergs. This was not a unique disaster, but a night on which an unhappy coincidence of clear skies to guide the fighters, and bad tactical planning that gave the German controllers an uncommonly easy task, led to losses that were statistically a little worse than those at Leipzig and Berlin in previous weeks. The Nuremberg casualties were in themselves acceptable in the context of Bomber Command's overall loss rate and the supply of replacement aircraft and crews.

But time had run out on Harris. He had commanded the centre of the stage for more than two years. Now other war machines were waiting impatiently in the wings: armies and fleets were gathering themselves for the invasion that dominated the minds of the leaders of the Grand Alliance. The generals and admirals had never cared for the 'bomber barons' and their all-consuming proposals. Now, at last, 'bombing operations were to be formally subordinated to the Supreme Allied Commander to support the invasion. From 14 April 1944, Harris and Eaker would take their orders from Eisenhower.

Bomber Command conducted further spasmodic operations against Germany through the late spring and summer of 1944, and amid these Harris could comfort himself with the delusion that if the invasion had not overtaken him, his attack on Germany could have continued. Indeed it is probably true that it would have done, for a few more weeks. But at the Air Ministry's morning conferences, the reports of Bomber Command's overnight casualties were greeted with growing dismay. In the year since he had begun his 'battles', Bomber Command had lost 4,160 aircraft missing and crashed in England. Harris's failure to bring Germany to her knees, and the cost of his failure, had become embarrassingly evident to every man but himself. And in a letter to the Air Ministry on 7 April 1944, he came as close as ever in his life to conceding that he was in deep trouble.

The strength of the German defences [he wrote] would in time reach a point at which night-bombing attacks by existing methods and types of heavy bomber would involve percentage casualty rates which could not in the long run be sustained . . . We have not yet reached that point, but tactical innovations which have so far postponed it are now practically exhausted . . .

This was the preamble to a demand for ten squadrons of night-fighters, to support his bombers. It was the final admission of defeat for the Trenchard doctrine. First Bomber Command, then the Luftwaffe, then the 8th Air Force had proved that daylight air bombardment was impossible unless air superiority had first been attained. Now Bomber Command had discovered that even night operations against Germany could no longer be continued on their existing basis unless the enemy's night-fighter force could be crippled or destroyed. The tactical possibilities of the single concentrated bomber stream protected by *Window* had been exhausted. Bomber Command was in a dilemma: to achieve decisive destruction it was necessary to attack a target repeatedly, yet to do so was tactical suicide. Only once, at Hamburg, had the début of *Window* provided the momentary tactical advantage to make possible a succession of saturation bombardments.

To the end of his life, Harris would continue to argue that had he been given the resources he sought and permitted to continue his assault on Germany into the summer of 1944, the war could have been ended months sooner. But many of his fellow airmen disagree with him. 'He was a gambler doubling up on each losing throw,' said Bufton, looking back on the Battle of Berlin.[6] 'In the operational sense, the Battle of Berlin was more than a failure. It was a defeat,' wrote Webster and Frankland.[7] 'Berlin won,' said Sir Ralph Cochrane,[8] AOC of 5 Group. 'It was just too tough a nut.'

The compulsory transfer of Bomber Command to tactical operations in support of the invasion, which Harris resisted so bitterly, saved him from confronting his own defeat. He had inflicted a series of catastrophes upon the enemy. But he had failed to achieve the decisive, war-winning thrust that had been at the heart of all his Trenchardian hopes.

The American breakthrough

On the day of the second disastrous American Schweinfurt operation, 16 October 1943, Arnold in Washington cabled to Eaker that the Luftwaffe appeared to be on the verge of collapse. Even in the wake of Schweinfurt, Eaker claimed ungrammatically that the Luftwaffe's victory had been 'the last final struggle of a monster in his death throes'. But in reality, the Americans had suffered an overwhelming and traumatic defeat. They had lost 148 aircraft in four operations. In the face of the Luftwaffe's massed assaults with cannon, rockets and bombs against their formations, the Fortresses and Liberators were taking intolerable punishment. Morale sagged in a manner unknown to Bomber Command at any period of the war. Attempts to revive aircrew spirit with periods of 'Rest and recuperation' at Miami Beach, Atlantic City and Santa Monica were scrapped when these were found to increase men's reluctance to return to operations. The practice of force-landing damaged aircraft in neutral territory became sufficiently common to cause serious controversy – by the summer of 1944 there were 94 8th Air Force crews interned in Sweden and 101 in Switzerland.

The Norden bombsight was useless in the persistent overcast of the European winter. While Harris fought the Battle of Berlin by night, the 8th Air Force, and the newly formed 15th Air Force operating under Spaatz's direction from Italy, were reduced to limited penetration blind-bombing missions by H2X, the American adaptation of H2S. In reality if not in theory, the Americans spent much of the winter of 1943–4 engaged in area-bombing operations. In the words of the American official historians: 'It seemed better to bomb low-priority targets frequently, even with less than precision accuracy, than not to bomb at all.'[9]

But with their limitless resources and unshakeable determination to succeed, the Americans persisted. The main handicap of their operations in the summer and autumn of 1943 had been that their fighter escort of Thunderbolts and Lightnings lacked the performance to meet the Luftwaffe on equal terms, and were compelled by lack of range to turn home at the German frontier. The Germans had thus been able to choose their own time and place to fall on the bombers. But in the wake of Schweinfurt, Arnold directed that the 8th and 15th Air Forces be given absolute priority for supplies of the remarkable new P-51B Mustang long-range fighter. The Mustang had originally been ordered from its American makers by the RAF in 1940. When it was delivered in 1942, they were disappointed by its lack of power. Rolls-Royce tried an experiment, replacing its Allison engine with one of their own Merlins. After various disappointments and modifications, they found themselves testing an aircraft that most airmen and designers had thought impossible, with the reach to fly deep into Germany equipped with disposable long-range drop-tanks, and with a speed of 455 mph at 30,000 feet that enabled the Mustang to match or out-perform every German fighter when it got there.

The Americans now began to take a keen interest in this extraordinary hybrid. The Packard company started building Merlin engines under licence, and a massive programme was undertaken to provide the USAAF with Mustangs. Progress towards a satisfactory drop-tank was hesitant, and it was not until the spring of 1944 that the Mustang element of 8th Air Force became formidable. But when it did so, the means at last existed to fight the Luftwaffe on highly favourable terms. As the tide of American aircraft production became a flood, with astonishing speed the huge Mustang escorts drove the German air force from its own skies. Whatever Speer was doing to increase German fighter-production in the factories, he could do nothing to halt the attrition of trained aircrew in the air battles. The Luftwaffe would continue to offer resistance to the end, and on occasion to inflict heavy loss on the Fortresses. But within four months of Schweinfurt, the Americans had overturned the balance of war in the air.

The escort fighter had been introduced to assist bomber operations. But through the spring of 1944, understanding grew among the American airmen that whatever they were or were not accomplishing against the German aircraft industry on the ground by bombing, by compelling the Luftwaffe to scramble to its defence they were winning a critical victory in the air. It was the ultimate vision of the *Circus* operations that the RAF had begun over northern France in 1941, intended to provoke the Luftwaffe to battle, but unsuccessful because the bombers' targets were not important enough to compel the Germans to rise to the bait. Now the Americans could force the defenders to meet the challenge. In 'Big Week', the immense effort by 8th and 15th Air Forces against the German aircraft factories that began on 20 February 1944, 3,800 Liberators and Fortresses dropped 10,000 tons of bombs for the loss of 226 heavy aircraft – 6 per cent of sorties dispatched – and twenty-eight escorting fighters. Bomber Command's five parallel night raids against aircraft-industry targets added a further 9,198 tons of bombs for the loss of 157 aircraft, 6.6 per cent of sorties dispatched. Between them, the Allies inflicted severe blows, but production continued to rise dramatically. In the last half of 1943 Germany produced an average of 851 single-engined fighters a month. In the first half of 1944, output rose to 1,581 fighters a month. The real impact of the Americans' daylight operations became visible in the Luftwaffe's air-loss figures: these rose from 1,311 aircraft destroyed from all causes in January 1944 to 2,121 in February, and 2,115 in March.

By March the Americans had consciously embarked on a policy of seeking targets which they knew that the Luftwaffe must defend. The skies over Germany were strewn day after day with the plunging wrecks of broken fighters and bombers, the black smears of flak, rocket trails, and amidst them all the glinting silver wings of the Fortress formations, cruising steadily onwards. Encounters continued for hours, with successive waves of Luftwaffe fighters landing to refuel and rearm, then engaging once more. On 6 March, 8th Air Force lost 69 of 660 bombers which attacked, and 11 fighters. The flak was intensifying and becoming more deadly – a quarter of all American bombers dispatched came home with shrapnel damage. But the enemy was tiring:

Viewed in retrospect [wrote the American official historians] the preceding sixteen months of bombing by American forces became a long period of preparation . . . The German air force could still offer serious resistance. Yet it was just such an air fight that the American commanders hoped to provoke, confident as they were in the ability of their airmen to impose a ruinous wastage upon the enemy . . . It is difficult to escape the conclusion that the air battles did more to defeat the Luftwaffe than did the destruction of the aircraft factories.[10]

But even as the USAAF was achieving the victory over the Luftwaffe that would enable Bomber Command eventually to dominate the night skies over Germany, the controversy over Allied bombing policy entered a new phase. *Overlord*, the plan for the Normandy landings, was now the chief preoccupation of the military and political leaders of the Grand Alliance. They were determined that the invasion would receive all the air support at their command to ensure its success. From the summer of 1943 until the spring of 1944, there was constant and acrimonious debate about how this could best be achieved.

The British were dismayed by the now inescapable American domination of the war, by the Americans' unconcealed determination to conduct the liberation of Europe with their commanders and by their strategy. They were no longer much concerned with smoothing British sensibilities. Their build-up in Britain and the Mediterranean was flooding bases, ports, airfields. Already the American bomber force outnumbered Bomber Command in aircraft, although not in bomb load. American policy was to concentrate forces within highly centralized command structures, inevitably controlled by their own generals. The

British sought by every means within their power to prevent their men from being engulfed in these monoliths. At the *Sextant* conference in Cairo in November 1943, the British were alarmed by the American announcement that they planned to put the 8th and 15th Air Forces under a single commander, and ultimately under the control of the American Supreme Commander of the invasion forces. Sir Douglas Evill, Vice-Chief of Air Staff, signalled London's reaction to Portal in Cairo in a Most Secret cipher telegram of 26 November.

After consultation with the Secretary of State, Permanent Under-Secretary and Deputy Chief of Air Staff, we are all of us agreed that everything possible should be done to resist any proposal that would end in the 8th and 15th Air Forces being placed under the command of the Supreme Allied Commander for North-West Europe. Such centralization would logically suggest inclusion of the RAF strategic night-bomber force, and there are insuperable operational and political objections to this.

There was considerable pathos in the efforts of the British to preserve their dwindling independence. One remarkable proposal to avoid placing Bomber Command under Eisenhower's control involved appointing an American Deputy Chief of Air Staff at the Air Ministry, to second Portal's direction of *Pointblank* on behalf of the Combined Chiefs of Staff. The British finally lost their fight to prevent the union of 8th and 15th Air Forces under the command of Spaatz, but they staved off a decision about Bomber Command's future place in the Allied command structure.

We were . . . able to secure some improvements in the organization originally proposed [Portal signalled to London on 7 December 1943]. This arrangement gives us essential general control and the new Commanding General will doubtless discover soon enough the difficulties of exercising detailed control of XVth Air Force from the United Kingdom. No commitments have been entered into about the date on which command passes to the Supreme Allied Commander.

But the principal officers and ministers of the Grand Alliance were not in the mood to concern themselves with the airmen's sensitivities when *Overlord* was at stake. Eisenhower insisted that, as Supreme Commander, he must have operational control of the strategic bomber forces. Among his colleagues even his Deputy,

Sir Arthur Tedder, himself an airman, was quite unwilling to trust the vital invasion air-support decisions to the discretion of Harris and Spaatz.

During the winter of 1943-4, acres of Air Ministry and Bomber Command paper were dedicated to demonstrating the scale of the British contribution to *Pointblank* against that of the Americans. Much has been made of Portal's fears that the programme for crippling the German air force before the invasion was falling behind schedule – three months was the stated lag.

[The achievements of the USAAF and Bomber Command] had to be considered always in close relationship to the strategic timetable [write Craven and Cate]. The important thing was to determine how near the operation was to achieving its assigned objectives within the time allotted; for although it was in a sense true that the success of *Pointblank* would determine the date of *Overlord*, there was a limit to how long the invasion could be postponed while awaiting the anticipated fatal weakening of the German air force.[11]

This seems grossly to exaggerate the concern of the Allied leadership about *Pointblank*, and about the threat that the Luftwaffe presented to *Overlord* by the winter of 1943. The Russian armies had already contributed immeasurably more than *Pointblank* could hope to achieve in bringing about the 'fatal weakening' of Germany in advance of the Western Allied invasion. As has been suggested earlier, the superiority of the Allied tactical air forces was already so overwhelming that it is impossible to believe that at this stage Washington or London considered postponing the invasion in the light of what *Pointblank* had or had not achieved. Naturally Eisenhowever, Marshall, Brooke and others were anxious to drive the German air force from the sky, and for that matter to inflict maximum damage on Germany. But they had long since lost any hope of finding the German ability to resist *Overlord* 'fatally weakened' by bombing. It was almost embarrassing to recall the plan codenamed *Rankin*, drawn up in the full flush of the airmen's enthusiasm months earlier, for a sudden occupation of Europe if German resistance collapsed under the weight of bombing or Russian offensives.

It was because the ground commanders doubted the airmen's judgement of what constituted the critical pressure-points of

German military and industrial strength that they insisted upon control of the strategic bombers being transferred to the Supreme Commander. There was a final pathetic wrangle provoked by the British, about the precise wording of Eisenhower's powers over Bomber Command: they refused to let him have 'command', but finally settled for giving him 'direction'. Then the issue was closed. From 14 April 1944 until further notice the Allied air forces would conduct strategic operations only with Eisenhower's specific consent. Their prime function would be the tactical support of the invasion. It was a total defeat for the wishes of the bomber commanders of Britain and America.

Air Chief Marshal Sir Trafford Leigh-Mallory had been appointed to nominal command of the Allied air forces at the invasion, and although he would never have the opportunity effectively to exercise it, in the winter of 1943 he had drawn up a plan for the bombing of key rail communications links in northern France and Belgium as a preliminary to D-Day. Professor Solly Zuckerman, co-author of the Hull and Birmingham Report which Cherwell had misquoted to such effect in 1942, had subsequently been posted to the Mediterranean. There he achieved considerable influence as a scientific adviser to Tedder, Eisenhower's air chief, particularly after he planned the bombing of the island of Pantellaria, which surrendered following the air attack. When Tedder was nominated Deputy Supreme Commander for D-Day in January 1944, Zuckerman came home to serve on his staff, and in particular to devise bombing plans. Zuckerman read the Leigh-Mallory plan, concluded that it was quite inadequate, and set out to devise a comprehensive strategy for the destruction of every key rail link in northern France. The fruits of his efforts became known as the Transport Plan, and unleashed a new bombing controversy that locked the leaders of the Allied war effort in fierce conflict until the last weeks before the invasion.

The Allied planners had concluded that the greatest threat to the invasion would come in the build-up period after the landings. Unless the Wehrmacht could be drastically impeded, they would be able to concentrate divisions around the Allied bridgehead more quickly than the Allies could reinforce it. Eisenhower and Tedder were rapidly persuaded that Zuckerman's plan represented the most promising means of wrecking the German army's communications with Normandy, and the most effective use of the strategic bomber force in the weeks before the invasion. Almost all the military leaders agreed, and Portal was willing to be convinced.

But deployed against the Transport Plan were the massed ranks of the other airmen; Lord Cherwell, who was still single-mindedly dedicated to the area offensive, which he cherished as his own brainchild; and the vital figure of the Prime Minister. Churchill was appalled by initial estimates from Cherwell and RE8 that bombing the railway centres could kill 40,000 French civilians.* This seemed to him – the Americans were less concerned – an utterly unacceptable manner in which to begin the liberation of Europe. Harris, who was resolutely opposed to the Transport Plan for a host of his own reasons, refused to give the Prime Minister any reassurance about possible civilian casualties: 'I was not about to start keeping a gamebook of dead Frenchmen.'[12] Throughout February the Prime Minister remained obdurate in his refusal to sanction the railway bombing, to the increasing alarm of Eisenhower.

But it was Harris and Spaatz who unleashed the most formidable revolt against the Transport Plan, or indeed against any tactical employment of the heavy-bomber force at all. Even at this late stage, neither officer had renounced his private conviction that *Overlord* was a vast, gratuitious, strategic misjudgement, when Germany was already tottering on the edge of collapse from bombing.

Overlord [Harris wrote to Portal on 13 January 1944] must now presumably be regarded as an inescapable commitment . . . It is clear that the best and indeed the only efficient support which Bomber Command can give to *Overlord* is the intensification of attacks on suitable industrial centres in Germany. If we attempt to substitute for this process attacks on gun emplacements, beach defences, communications or dumps in occupied territories, we shall commit the irremediable error of diverting our best weapon from the military function for which it has been equipped and trained to tasks which it cannot effectively carry out. Though this might give a specious appearance of 'supporting' the Army,

---

*In the event, approximately 12,000 French and Belgian civilians were killed in the pre-invasion bombing by Allied air forces.

in reality it would be the greatest disservice we could do to them. It would lead directly to disaster.

Harris professed to be unshakeably convinced that the only proper or possible use of his Command was for the area bombing of Germany, and the scientists of his Operational Research Section were driven to ever more tortuous statistical efforts to demonstrate that this was the case. While it may be argued that some of Harris's wartime misjudgements were only revealed with hindsight, in this matter his narrow-mindedness was astonishing. To any balanced observer of the Grand Alliance at the beginning of 1944, it was obvious that all other strategic priorities were dwarfed by the importance of *Overload.* Any success that the bombers might achieve over Germany that spring and summer by continuing the area offensive would be swept aside by the scale of disaster if the Allies failed to get ashore in Normandy and stay there.

But Harris was not alone in his obsession. Spaatz was convinced that victory over Germany was within his own grasp. He was exasperated by the prospect of giving the Luftwaffe a long respite while his aircraft attacked the French railway system. There was also another, even more critical factor. For two years of war, the USAAF had been groping for the throat of the German war machine, and now at last Spaatz believed that they had found it: the synthetic-oil system. In 1943, Germany's synthetic-oil plants produced 6.2 million tons of petroleum products from coal, in addition to the 2 million tons imported from Hungary and Rumania. The plants were dispersed among eighty locations, of which twenty-seven were notably important. Many of the targets were within range of 15th Air Force in Italy, if not of 8th Air Force in England, but hitherto the Allies had devoted barely 1 per cent of their entire wartime bombing effort to oil targets.

Now Spaatz's staff had drawn up a plan for the systematic destruction of Germany's oil resources by precision bombing. With the coming of the spring weather, with the enormous forces at his command, and with the Mustang to carve a path to the targets, Spaatz believed that he had the means to win the war. Professional rivalry with Harris also loomed large. He was haunted by fear that Bomber Command might somehow win the laurels while his Fortresses were reduced to running a bomb shuttle for Eisenhower. 'What worries me is that Harris is being allowed to get off scot-free,' he complained bitterly to Zuckerman.[13] 'He'll go on bombing Germany and will be given a chance of defeating her before the invasion, while I am put under Leigh-Mallory's command...'

By February, Tedder was in despair about the obstinacy with which each faction was fighting for its own triumph in the deployment of air resources. Like so much else to do with the strategic air offensive, the final decisions were a compromise. In March 1944, at the insistence of Portal – who was compelled to issue a direct order to Harris to gain his co-operation – the RAF carried out a series of experiments against the marshalling yards at Trappes, Aulnoye, Le Mans, Amiens/Lougeau, Courtrai and Laon. The attacks were a triumph for the aircrews of Bomber Command, who achieved a startling success while inflicting far lower civilian casualties than had been predicted. Harris stood confounded by the virtuosity of his own men. His most virulent opposition to the Transport Plan had been based on insistence that his crews were incapable of carrying it out. Instead they had proved capable of extraordinary precision. Zuckerman told Tedder that, far from Bomber Command assisting the invasion if it continued area attacks on Germany until D-Day, in his view they could only hope to reduce enemy production by a maximum of 7 per cent, which could not conceivably be decisive.

Churchill persisted with his opposition to the rail bombing until May, but he was overcome by pressure from Washington: Eisenhower had formally notified Roosevelt and Marshall that he considered the Transport Plan indispensable to the preparations for *Overlord*: 'There is no other way in which this tremendous air force can help us, during the preparatory period, to get ashore and stay there.' The Prime Minister at last bowed to the Americans' insistence. Bomber Command would undertake the principal burden of carrying out the Transport Plan. In March 1944, 70 per cent of British bombs were directed against Germany. In April this proportion fell to well under half; in May, to less than a quarter; in June to negligible proportions. The 'panacea merchants' had triumphed. Harris wrote artlessly in his memoirs:

'Naturally I did not quarrel with the decision to put the bomber force at the disposal of the invading army once the die had been cast; I knew that the armies could not succeed without them.'[14] The die had taken a long time to cast.

But while Harris fought his battle to continue area bombing, Spaatz was arguing in London and by direct appeal to Washington to be permitted to undertake his Oil Plan. On 19 April, Eisenhower authorized him to carry out two experimental attacks against oil plants, chiefly in the hope of bringing the Luftwaffe to battle. The weather was not suitable until 12 May, when Spaatz dispatched 935 bombers and a vast force of escorting fighters, losing forty-six bombers and ten of the escort. Further attacks followed on 28 and 29 May. Speer's nightmare had at last come to pass. Spaatz had touched the vital nerve of the German economy. In the months that followed, his aircraft were chiefly committed to attacking *Crossbow* targets to impede the German V-weapon attack on England, and providing tactical support for the Allied armies. In June only 11.6 per cent of his effort was launched against oil targets, in July 17 per cent, in August 16.4 per cent. But the results were dramatic. Petroleum available to Germany fell from 927,000 tons in March, to 715,000 tons in May, and 472,000 tons in June. The Luftwaffe's supplies of aviation spirit fell from 180,000 tons in April, to 50,000 tons in June, and 10,000 tons in August. All Speer's achievements in the aircraft factories went for nothing. By the late summer of 1944 the Luftwaffe lacked the fuel to fly anything like its available order of battle.

American airmen have since lamented the failure of the Allied command to understand the importance of Spaatz's achievement, to press home the Oil Plan and bring victory by the end of 1944. Bufton was among those at the Air Ministry who opposed the Transport Plan in favour of the Oil Plan. He described Zuckerman's scheme as 'a national disaster'.[15] He and many other airmen believed that the French rail links could have been destroyed with far less effort, had they been given the task and left to choose their own methods of executing it, by hitting bridges rather than marshalling yards. An American air force evaluation based on railway records concluded in 1945 that 'The pre D-Day attacks against French rail centres were not necessary, and the 70,000 tons involved could have been devoted to alternative targets.' The President of SNCF, the French rail network, said that he believed bridge-breaking would have been far more effective than hitting yards. The fact that the Germans indeed suffered enormous difficulties in reinforcing Normandy after D-Day must be attributed in substantial measure to the efforts of the Allied tactical air forces and the French Resistance, in addition to the strategic bombers.

But to make much of the fact that Spaatz's obsession with the Oil Plan was justified is a misuse of hindsight. By the spring of 1944 the credibility of the 'bomber barons' among the leaders of the Grand Alliance had sunk very low. Spaatz privately considered that Harris was 'all washed up' after the failure of the Battle of Berlin.[16] The British, in their turn, noted the yawning chasm between the Americans' past promises and achievements. The admiration of politicians and ground commanders for the airmen's powers of organization and leadership was now eclipsed by cynicism about their failures and their insatiable demands for resources. At one of the vital meetings to discuss the rival merits of the Oil and Transport Plans, Oliver Lawrence of the Ministry of Economic Warfare – who was much respected by both the British and the Americans – argued that on his estimate of German oil reserves, even if Spaatz's attacks were immediately effective against the production plants, it would be four to five months before the results benefited the battlefield. This projection was enough to damn Spaatz's hopes of undivided concentration of attack. The soldiers wanted results in days and weeks, not months.

The employment of the strategic bombers in the weeks preceding D-Day, and afterwards in support of the armies in Normandy, may today seem cautious and unimaginative. But it was vital insurance, and reflected a perfectly logical view of strategic priorities by the Combined Chiefs of Staff. *Overlord* had to succeed. Bomber Command and the USAAF were directed to do all in their power to see that it did so, and worked to that end with courage, dedication and professionalism. If their leaders were heard with insufficient respect in the councils of war, they had only their own past errors of judgement to blame. It is an indulgence of historians and armchair critics to pretend that, in the spring of 1944, there was a better way.

12 Pathfinders: 97 Squadron, Lincolnshire, 1944

'Usual flares and aircraft shot down on way in,' Flight-Lieutenant Charles Owen noted in his diary[1] after a Berlin operation on 26 November 1943:

Target was clear and we could see fires burning from an attack on the previous night. Hundreds of searchlights and very heavy flak, firing mainly into the cones. Flew over Hanover by mistake on return journey, and was coned for seven minutes, lost height from 20,000 to 13,000 feet during evasive action. Several holes in starboard wing and roof of cockpit, and the bomb-aimer wounded slightly in the leg. Also attacked by fighter when coned, but only damage was six inches knocked off one blade of the starboard outer prop.

The night of 16 December 1943 became known as 'Black Thursday' among Bomber Command crews, when on their return from Berlin they found their bases in England blanketed in impenetrable fog. Owen's note of his own and 97 Squadron's experience was typical:

Ten-tenths cloud over target. W/T and *Gee* packed up on way home, so homed across North Sea on D/F loop, which luckily was not jammed. Homed on to base on SBA beam, breaking cloud at 250 feet to find fog, rain and visibility about 300 yards and deteriorating. R/T then packed up, so after circling for ten minutes at 200 feet, landed without permission in appalling conditions. Six other aircraft landed at base, three landed away, three crews baled out when they ran out of fuel, four crashed when trying to land, and one was missing. Quite a night . . .

In order to understand the transformation that came over 97 Squadron and Bomber Command during 1944, the lightening of losses and the breakthrough to remarkable tactical success, it is necessary to remember the mood in which they emerged from winter, and from the Battle of Berlin. After losing one CO over Magdeburg, his successor did not live long enough to enter the squadron record book. Night after night, they took off into freak winds and fog, to face the flak and the night-fighters. A new pilot remembered arriving to join the unit at six o'clock one December evening, and moving into a hut with a crew dressing to operate that night. At 5 a.m. he was awakened by the clatter of boots as the Service Police arrived to collect his dead room-mates' possessions. There were many acquaintances and few close friends on Bomber Command stations that winter.

97 Squadron dispatched an average of twenty Lancasters a night, and almost invariably lost one, frequently two. On 28 January, of nineteen aircraft that took/off for Berlin one returned early, two were lost and one, piloted by a tough Australian named Van Raalte, came home having failed to find 'The Big City', bombed Kiel instead, and had his rear gunner decapitated by flak. In the first fortnight of February, they were briefed three times for Berlin, only to have the operations scrubbed by bad weather. When they finally went again on the 15th, they lost one out of seventeen. In March, they lost two out of fourteen against Frankfurt on the 22nd, two out of fourteen against Berlin on the 24th, and two out of fourteen against Nuremberg on the 30th.

97 was a Pathfinder squadron, one of Bennett's Lancaster units, based at Bourn in Cambridgeshire, in a straggling wasteland of mud and Nissen huts, where men slept in their greatcoats to fight the all-pervading damp and cold. But like the rest of Bennett's men, they took intense pride in their membership of 8 Group, a perverse pleasure in the ban on publicity about their 'ops', in Bennett's insistence that there should be no stars or professional heroes among his officers. 'There will be no living VCs in 8 Group,' the Australian had announced in 1942. His edict stood in 1944. But his men cherished the hovering eagle badge that they were forbidden to wear on operations, and the inscribed Pathfinder Certificate that survivors were awarded on completion of their double tour of forty-five operations. Bennett was a humourless, unrelenting man whom it was hard to like, but difficult not to respect as a professional airman. It was his achievement that he had created a genuine Pathfinder spirit among the men of his squadrons, pitchforked into 8 Group from every corner of Bomber Command under all manner of circumstances. They had their share of LMF cases, 'fringe merchants', poor pilots. But

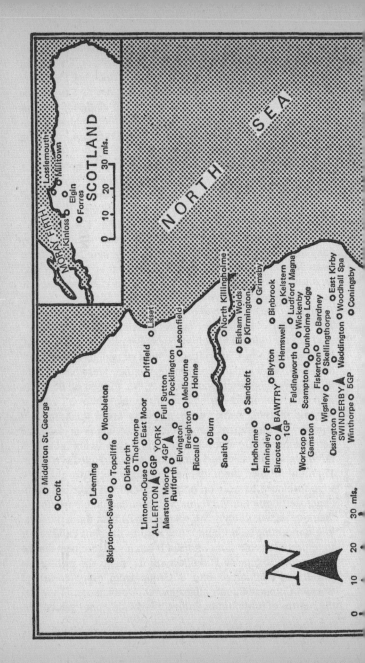

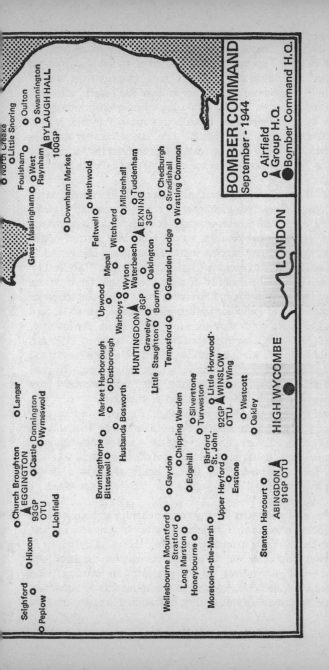

BOMBER COMMAND
September - 1944

o Airfield
▲ Group H.Q.
● Bomber Command H.Q.

o North Creake
o Little Snoring
Foulsham o   o Oulton
West   o Swannington
Raynham ▲ BYLAUGH HALL
        100GP

o Seighford
o Hixon   o Church Broughton
                 ▲ EGGINGTON
o Peplow   o Castle Donnington
                 o Wymeswold
                 o Lichfield

Great Massingham o

o Downham Market

Feltwell o o Methwold
Upwood   Witchford
Mepal o Mildenhall o
Warboys o Wyton o o Tuddenham
Market Harborough o Waterbeach o ▲ EXNING
o Desborough   Oakington o 3GP
Bruntingthorpe o ▲ HUNTINGDON
Bitteswell o   Graveley o 8GP o Chedburgh
                  Bourn o   o Stradishall
Husbands Bosworth Little Staughton o
                  Tempsford o Gransden Lodge o Wratting Common

Wellesbourne Mountford o o Gaydon
Stratford o   o Chipping Warden
Long Marston o o Edgehill   o Silverstone
Honeybourne o   o Turweston
                  Barford o o Little Horwood
Moreton-in-the-Marsh o St. John ▲ WINSLOW
                  Upper Heyford o 92GP o Wing
                  o Enstone   OTU
                               o Westcott
                               o Oakley

Stanton Harcourt o

ABINGDON ▲
91GP OTU

HIGH WYCOMBE ●

o Langar

LONDON

for the most part they were very conscientious young men. By 1944 Bomber Command's skills had come a long way from the Stone Age of 1940 and 1941. On most operations the bulk of Main Force bombed within three miles of the Target Indicators. The success or failure of a raid depended overwhelmingly on how these markers were placed, how successfully the Master Bomber corrected those that fell wide, how accurately the Supporters timed their back-up marking throughout the Main Force attack. Bennett's crews understood all this, and did their utmost to do their part.

But they were not a picked élite. 97's crews, like the rest of the Group, had reached Pathfinder Force by remarkably varied routes. Some were novices who had shown exceptional promise in training. Some were on their second, even third, tour of operations, men who had become supremely proficient bomber pilots and sought only to exercise their skills as long as 'The Reaper' allowed them. The majority of recruits had done ten or fifteen operations with a Main Force squadron, then volunteered or been drafted to Pathfinders when word came down to Groups that five or ten crews were required. Bob Lasham, for instance, was a pilot at 9 Squadron when he decided to go to PFF. His bomb-aimer and wireless operator were keen – the glamour and the temporary step in rank and pay appealed to them. His gunners acquiesced without enthusiasm. His navigator would have nothing to do with a 45-trip tour, and left the crew.

Pat Turner was a 44 Squadron flight engineer when his crew heard that they were being posted to Pathfinders. They did not mind going, but were conscious that they were not outstandingly talented fliers. It was not until later that they discovered that they had been 'volunteered' by station headquarters as a simple solution to their pilot's passion for the base commander's WAAF driver.

Charles Owen, after leaving public school, had been working at the Supermarine aircraft factory as a boy of seventeen in 1940, when he was badly injured in an air raid. He spent the winter in hospital, and came out at last old enough for the RAF. An exceptional pilot trainee, he was posted as an instructor, and served a year before transferring to operations with 97 Squadron, where he proved an outstanding operational captain. By 1944 he was a squadron-leader, celebrating his twenty-first birthday one January night over Stettin. He would end the war as a Master Bomber with a string of decorations.

Tony Aveline left France through Dunkirk with the British army in 1940, and after an eternity at training camps in Scotland, volunteered for the RAF in 1941. He was washed out of pilot training in Florida, but qualified as a navigator in Canada. On his first operation as a passenger with an experienced crew, they were coned over Berlin and attacked by a fighter. They lost two engines and caught fire in one wing. The hydraulics failed and their wireless went dead. Blaspheming continuously in their fear, they staggered across Holland and the North Sea to crash in a field in Lincolnshire. They crawled out of the wreck and Aveline asked: 'Is it always like this?' But when his pilot volunteered for PFF, Aveline went with him, and flew the rest of his tour with 97 Squadron in a mood of cynical fatalism: 'I never thought about the value of it all. I just hoped it would end.'

Pathfinder recruits went from their Main Force stations for a two-week course in marking techniques at Warboys before they were posted to a squadron. They concentrated on the use of H2S, and much of the new responsibility fell on the bomb-aimer. Bennett addressed every new intake personally. Most Bomber Command aircrew were indifferent to which Group they nominally belonged. Bennett's men shared with Cochrane's 5 Group an intense sense of identification, loyalty, and rivalry. At the beginning of April 1944, when 97 were abruptly informed that they were being transferred to 5 Group under Cochrane's command, their anger and resentment were unbounded.

Sir Arthur Harris had always mistrusted the concept of a single élite Pathfinder Group in Bomber Command. As his force expanded and its range of operations widened, he was increasingly impressed by Cochrane's insistence that given the chance, 5 Group could attempt targets and techniques that 8 Group could not. To Bennett's undisguised scorn, Cochrane advocated low-level marking. The Australian argued that it was impossible to map-read flying below a hundred feet, and above a hundred feet the marker aircraft would be annihilated by light flak. But Cochrane persisted. It was his 617 Squadron which had carried out the greatest precision-bombing feat of the war, breaking the

Ruhr dams from a height of sixty feet. Despite their subsequent failure against the Dortmund–Ems canal, during the winter of 1943, 617 had carried out further experiments in bombing accuracy; on 16 December, nine of their Lancasters using the Stabilized Automatic Bomb Sight achieved an astounding error of only ninety-four yards against a V-weapon launching site at Abbeville. On 8 February 1944, Leonard Cheshire marked the Gnome and Rhône engines factory at Limoges from a height of 200 feet, supported by Micky Martin, and the rest of 617 then demolished the works with extraordinary accuracy. They failed against the Antheor Viaduct in February, but both Cheshire and Cochrane were convinced that there was enormous scope for precision bombing guided by low-level marking, especially if Mosquitoes were available to do it. At the beginning of April, in one of his more imaginative decisions, Harris decided to give Cochrane the chance to prove his point. He ordered Bennett to transfer 627, one of his cherished Mosquito squadrons, together with 83 and 97 Lancaster squadrons, to 5 Group. They would remain administratively responsible to 8 Group and would retain their PFF badges and ranks. But they would operate under Cochrane's command.

Bennett fought until the last moment to retain his squadrons, in his most bitter clash of the war with Harris. He rang Saundby at High Wycombe to demand furiously where 8 Group were to get more Mosquitoes when Cochrane's had all been shot down. Some of his staff urged him to resign, but he pointed out grimly that he had no intention of vacating his chair in order to let Cochrane move into it. In the end he swallowed his pride, but the enmity between 5 and 8 Groups was redoubled. 'I'm afraid I was rather tactless with Bennett,' admitted Cochrane afterwards.[2] But both were dedicated men, convinced of their own points of view.

97 Squadron's Movement Orders were issued and cancelled three times before they finally flew their Lancasters to Coningsby in Lincolnshire, a pre-war permanent station at the heart of a web of 5 Group airfields. There was friction at the outset: the Tannoy summoned all aircrew to the cinema, where the base commander gave them a terse talk about shedding their 8 Group habits and learning that they were in 5 Group now. A plaintive voice called

from the back: 'We're fighting the Germans, you know, sir, not 8 Group.' The base commander announced that they would begin training immediately. Jimmy Carter, 97's CO, stood up and said: 'I'm sorry, sir, but my chaps were operating last night, and they're not going out to train now.'

It was weeks before the first tensions relaxed. On 17 April two pilots, one of them Charles Owen, went to the Juvisy marshalling yards with 617 Squadron, to study the 5 Group technique: 'It seemed to work well enough against no opposition,' Owen wrote presciently in his diary, 'but I decided it might not be so much fun against a heavily defended German target.' The essence of the 5 Group method was that no aircraft attacked until the Master Bomber was satisfied with the placing of the markers, and gave the order by radio-telephone. The hazards were that it was only practicable in clear visibility, and that it entailed delay for the bomber force in the target area. But these difficulties would become unpleasantly apparent as summer went on.

8 Group's prestige undoubtedly declined in the shadow of 5 Group's achievements in the last year of the war, so much so that a medical officer at one of Bennett's stations considered that morale suffered.[8] He reported a conversation in the mess one day, when a group of officers were discussing whom Princess Elizabeth might marry. A voice in the corner muttered gloomily. 'It's bound to be somebody from 5 Group. . .' But Cochrane was fortunate in his timing. Had he embarked on his low-level marking operations during the Battle of Berlin, or against heavily defended German targets, he would almost certainly have met disaster. On 24 April 1944, Cheshire and three other 617 Squadron pilots carried out their extraordinary roof-level marking of Munich in Mosquitoes for which Cheshire received the Victoria Cross. But Harris has remarked that 'any operation which deserves the VC is in the nature of things unfit to be repeated at regular intervals'.[4] The Munich exercise was proof of the extraordinary determination of Cochrane and his pilots, but not of the possibilities of regular low-level marking against heavy defences.

5 Group's luck was that their breakthrough came at exactly the right moment to meet the unique problem of the French invasion targets, where accuracy was vital not only to destroy the objective but to save civilian lives, and where ground defences

were generally negligible. In the first month of their independent operations, 5 Group almost halved the normal 680-yard error for effective aimed bombs dropped on *Oboe* ground marking. In May, when Cochrane introduced 5 Group's famous 'offset' technique, the average error fell to 285 yards. Cochrane was the most imaginative of Harris's Group commanders, perhaps the man who should have occupied Harris's chair at High Wycombe in the last phase of the war. He created 'offset' marking to contend with the problem of markers obliterated by smoke and flame in the midst of an attack. The principle was to mark a clearly visible point some distance short, beyond or wide of the target. Crews were anyway required to feed an allowance for wind into their bombsight computers. By adjusting this allowance to compensate for the markers' distance from the aiming-point according to radio-telephone instructions from the Master Bomber, the bomb-aimer hit the target without obscuring the brilliance of the marker.

Although 5 Group continued frequently to bomb with the rest of Main Force, and although 8 Group continued to mark targets with considerable success, Cochrane had made his point. In the last year of the war, his 'Independent Air Force' became a rueful focus of controversy among those of Bomber Command who were restricted to a more pedestrian role. Cochrane had introduced 'the 5 Group corkscrew', his own variation of the defensive manoeuvre against night-fighters (and compelled all his station and squadron commanders to go into the air and experience it), and 'the 5 Group quick landing scheme' to cut the delay in bringing down squadrons on their return from operations. He waged remorseless war against all that he considered undisciplined in the air and on the ground, checking navigators' logs, seeking to purge smoking on operations and intercom chatter in which crews referred to each other by their first names rather than the proper 'Captain', 'Navigator', and so on. He insisted that aircraft captains should be commissioned, to have the authority over their crews that he thought essential. This able martinet fumed when, after the introduction of 'Secretary aircraft' carrying wire recorders to monitor radio-telephone conversation over the target, he heard the informality and unprofessionalism (as he considered it) that sometimes broke out in the stress of an operation.

But Cochrane's outstanding virtue was his receptiveness to ideas and innovations, from whatever source they came. He could behave arrogantly, but he had no professional conceit. 5 Group's unique broadcast link-up between headquarters and the squadrons made a real contribution to briefings, with flight and squadron COs encouraged to offer suggestions and tactical changes. It is hard to believe that it was coincidence that Cheshire, Gibson, Willie Tait[5] and Micky Martin were all 5 Group officers who came to the fore under Cochrane's command. He has a good claim to be considered not merely the outstanding Group AOC, but the outstanding British bomber commander of the war.

In April, 97 Squadron lost only two crews in ninety-eight sorties. After Bomber Command's early experiences against the French targets, the success in hitting the marshalling yards and the weakness of the Luftwaffe response, the spring brought lengthening odds on each man's survival. Berlin and the winter were behind them. But their spirits plunged when word came that High Wycombe planned to recognize the ease of attacking French targets by making each sortie count only one-third of an 'op' towards a man's tour. Crews with only three or four trips left were appalled by the prospect that these might stretch to nine, twelve.

Then, on 3 May, they went to Mailly-Le-Camp.

Bright moonlight night [wrote Charles Owen] and Jerry pilots had a field day. Went in at 8,000 feet, but circled outside target at 4,000 feet waiting for order to bomb. Saw several fighters but was not attacked until on the bombing run at 5,000 feet. Luckily he was a rotten shot and we were able to carry on and drop our markers. We were attacked again coming out of the target, and he shot away our mid-upper turret and made a few holes elsewhere. The mid-upper gunner, miraculously, was only slightly wounded, but had to leave what was left of his turret. The fighter came in again, but the rear gunner drove him off and claimed him as damaged. I came home at 0 feet.

Of 362 aircraft that attacked, forty-two, or 11.3 per cent, were destroyed, overwhelmingly by night-fighters. One of them came from 97 Squadron. On 10 May, 5 Group sent eighty-nine Lancasters to Lille. There was a prolonged delay in the midst of the attack, when the Target Indicators were blown out and the target had to be remarked. Twelve aircraft, 13.5 per cent, were destroyed. 97 lost two out of eight dispatched. There was no more talk of French targets counting a third of an 'op'. These were two exceptionally bad nights, but they were a tough reminder of what the Luftwaffe could still do, given the chance. Lingering around a target for accurate visual marking could be fatal.

It was the beginning of a summer of intense effort by Bomber Command, vastly different in kind and scale from everything that had gone before. In June 1944, they carried out 15,963 sorties against the 5,816 of June 1943. Huge numbers of aircraft no longer attacked a single target in a concentrated stream. The objectives required great accuracy from limited forces of aircraft. To obscure the Allies' intentions in Normandy, it was necessary to attack marshalling yards, airfields, radar and wireless installations with equal intensity, from Belgium to the Cherbourg peninsula. There were still failures caused by weather and bad luck: on 19 May the Master Bomber cancelled the attack on Amiens as they circled the target, for lack of visibility. Three nights later, 97 Squadron went to Brunswick, a confused and unsatisfactory attack on which Cliff Chatten was badly damaged by a night-fighter while coned over the target, and somehow brought his aircraft home without instruments or cockpit canopy, circling the Wash until it was light enough for a crash landing. He was awarded the DSO and ceased to be a teetotaller.

On 31 May they went to a gun battery at Maisy near Cherbourg, but once again were sent home when they found the target shrouded in cloud. On 3 June they hit a wireless station at Ferme D'Urville. On the evening of 5 June they were briefed to attack a gun battery on the French coast at St Pierre du Mont. They were told nothing of the special significance of the occasion, but their orders were unusual: no aircraft was to fly below 6,500 feet; no bombs were to be jettisoned in the Channel; no IFF was to be used. In the early hours of 6 June, they flew south across the Channel, and broke cloud to see the great invasion armada below them. 'The army had pulled its finger out at last, and D-Day was on,' wrote Owen. 'We bombed at 0500 hrs just as it was getting light, and had a grandstand view of the Americans running in on the beach.' 3,467 heavy and 1,645 medium and light bombers flew in support of the landings that day. Bomber Command's Operation *Flashlamp* put a hundred aircraft on to each of ten major German coastal batteries. Some of the attacks were hampered by poor visibility and the guns went into action, but in most cases the German crews were paralysed by the bombing for long enough to enable Allied forces to overrun them.

As 97 Squadron turned for home, they saw the huge formations of American aircraft following them into attack. There was a holiday excitement about the fantastic spectacle below them, and perhaps this contributed to a moment of tragedy when the German fighters made one of their few effective interventions of the day. Jimmy Carter, 97's CO, went down hit by a Ju88, taking with him the squadron gunnery and signals leaders. Another aircraft from 97 followed. Yet even the losses could not suppress their satisfaction at taking part in one of the great days of the war. They turned on the mess radio as they landed at Coningsby, and hung fascinated around it all day.

On 13 June the Germans launched the first of the 30,000 V-weapons with which they bombarded Britain before the end of the war. For the rest of the summer, Bomber Command and the USAAF added the 'ski-sites' and V-weapon storage depots to the target list of barracks, airfields and marshalling yards that they were already attacking daily. American experiments had indicated that low-level fighter-bomber strikes were the most effective weapon against the 'ski-sites', but in their desperate anxiety to save the British people from another Blitz, the Government insisted that the 'heavies' be thrown into the counter-attack as well. Senior airmen reminded the War Cabinet that even at maximum intensity, the V-weapons – 'those damn silly rockets', as Harris called them – could do less damage than a single Bomber Command attack on a German city. But this was no consolation to the Prime Minister. Like many aircrew, he saw the V-weapons as somehow unique cowardly weapons, launched by men who did not risk their own lives in the killing of others. In his anger, he seriously considered reprisal gas attacks against Germany, and several Bomber Command squadrons were specially trained to carry them out. But Eisenhower and Tedder were foremost among those who dissuaded Churchill. The V-weapons continued to cause much pain and fear, although very limited material damage to Britain. Bomber Command continued to be compelled to divert aircraft to the ineffectual counter-offensive against them.

On 24 June, amidst one of 97's strikes against a 'ski-site' at Prouville, they met the German fighters in force. Tony Aveline suddenly felt the stink of his bomb-aimer's vomit surge up from the nose, as their pilot hurled the Lancaster into a corkscrew under attack. The squadron lost one aircraft. In the three summer months of June, July and August, barely one-sixth of Bomber Command's effort was directed against German targets, compared with more than a third of the USAAF's tonnage. Spaatz had been more successful than Harris in convincing Eisenhower that his operations against Germany would yield early dividends to the Allied armies. Harris, on the other hand, was playing his usual forceful hand in fighting off unwelcome proposals. To the C-in-C of Bomber Command, the German oil plants were merely the latest in the long line of 'panacea targets' with which so many knaves and fools sought to divert him from the task of destroying Germany. His fierce opposition to the pre-*Overlord* deployment of Bomber Command forgotten, he also expected greater public recognition of the achievements of the Transport Plan. He wrote to Portal on 1 July.

I think you should be aware of the full depth of feeling that is being aroused by the lack of adequate or even reasonable credit to the RAF in particular and the air forces as a whole, for their efforts in the invasion. I have no personal ambition that has not years ago been satisfied in full, but I for one cannot forbear a most emphatic protest against the grave injustice which is being done to my crews. There are over 10,500 aircrew in my operational squadrons. In three months we have lost over half that number. They have a right that their story should be adequately told, and it is a military necessity that it should be. Yours Ever,
    Bert

The Air Ministry now asked what resources Harris would need to destroy ten selected oil targets in the Ruhr. On 13 June, he replied that his staff estimated that 32,000 tons of bombs would be required – scarcely less than Bomber Command had dropped on all operations in the entire month of May.

Yet as a sop to the 'panacea merchants', of whom there seemed to be disagreeably many on the matter of oil, Harris agreed verbally with Tedder that Bomber Command would divert its spare effort to oil targets through the summer. On the night of 21 June, 97 Squadron was part of the force that went to the oil plants at Gelsenkirchen, their only operation against Germany between June and late August. There was a marked lack of enthusiasm among the crews for their return to the Ruhr. They bombed amidst heavy flak and thick overcast, and on the way home met the night-fighters as the moon rose. 'Not at all a nice trip, and a lot of chaps missing,' wrote Charles Owen. One of 97's aircraft failed to return, and two more were badly damaged. That month, Bomber Command launched four major attacks on German oil plants, 832 sorties in all, and paid heavily – extraordinarily so compared with casualties against the French targets. Ninety-three aircraft were missing.

Then the word came down that daylight sorties, abandoned by Bomber Command in mid-1943, were to be resumed. Training was to begin immediately. Formation-flying is a difficult art, which it had taken the Americans years to perfect. The British in 1944 had neither the stable, heavily armed and armoured aircraft, nor the highly trained crews to compete with the USAAF over Germany. But as the Allies approached absolute daylight air superiority over France, there was obviously a strong case for Bomber Command to take advantage of the situation, especially after Lille and Mailly-Le-Camp.

On the morning of 23 June, 97 Squadron's aircrew were in a boisterous mood as they waited for the trucks to take them to the dispersals for a formation training flight. They suddenly fell on a tiny Fiat car owned by a pilot named Perkins, and by force of fifty pairs of arms hauled it to the top of a big air-raid shelter. It was still perched there, and they were still laughing when they took off. High over Lincolnshire they took up their unaccustomed positions in formation. Then Van Raalte momentarily allowed his Lancaster to drift into the slipstream of Bill Gee's aircraft in front. The huge bomber was tossed fiercely aside, plunging into that of Perkins beside it. The two aircraft fell steeply out of the sky, breaking up as they went. The rest of the squadron landed and walked to the air-raid shelter to lift down the little Fiat, much sobered young men. The remains of only eleven bodies were found, but they filled twelve coffins for the funerals. The twelfth turned up in a field weeks later. The thirteenth man, a wireless operator, miraculously survived. Six weeks later another crew took him into the air for a training flight. He landed shaking, was later diagnosed as a tuberculosis case, and never flew again. In the first weeks after D-Day, the casualties of Bomber Command were higher than those of the British Second Army in Normandy. The scent of victory had gone out of the air again.

On 25 June the new CO arrived. Wing-Commander Anthony Heward had been commanding 50 Squadron when he was summoned to see Cochrane: 'I want you to take over at 97 and train them to concentrate on the task of target illumination,' said the AOC. He made no secret of his opinion that the squadron did not conform to the standards of discipline and efficiency that he was looking for. The taste of 8 Group was still too strong at Coningsby for Cochrane's liking. By the same token, 97 Squadron at once sensed that Heward had been sent to shape them to the 5 Group mould, and resented him accordingly. They also resisted the feeling that here was a career RAF officer, sent to impose meaningless service routines upon experienced operational aircrew. A sharp, clever, rather chilly man, who flew brilliantly when he chose to go into the air, his initial impact on Coningsby was dramatic. He sacked the squadron adjutant within hours of his arrival, and summoned the flight commanders for an icy lecture on untidiness, indiscipline and inefficiency: 'Nobody was bothering about the length of their hair. They dressed like Desert Rats, in their own idea of uniform.' Some of his officers were angry and resentful, and indeed Heward won little of their affection. He had more success in moulding novices to his ways than converting the 'Old Lags' from 8 Group. But he quickly became aware that 97 Squadron's aircrew were markedly superior to the general run of Bomber Command in ability and qualifications.

For no apparent reason, there were a surprising number of officers of private means and comfortable background among

346

them: Charles Owen; Heward himself; Arthur Ingham, the tall, balding son of a northern wool-merchant's family who was older than most and said little about his experiences, but was a superb operational captain. Lionel Wheble and Gordon Cooper, the H2S leader, were both members of Lloyd's, the London under-writers. Jock Simpson had been an accountant with the Bank of Scotland. Most exotic of all was Pete de Wesselow, a surgeon's son of Hungarian origins who had transferred to the RAF from the Brigade of Guards. The precise, immaculate de Wesselow spoke several languages fluently, collected antique glass, and could call on a rower's physique for throwing his Lancaster around the sky. He could also claim the almost unique distinction of having twice walked home through Occupied France and Spain after being shot down on operations.

These men of unusually elegant background for Bomber Command were leavened by the host of Australians, New Zealanders, Canadians, Norwegians, South Africans and Eng-lishmen who made every squadron such a melting-pot of youth and experience: Noel Parker, an Australian who had already been shot down over France and walked home to return to operations; 'Killer' Booth, the primeval little rear gunner who had somehow survived over a hundred operations with ruthless relish, and had an axe dripping blood painted on the wall of his billet; Pat Broome, the bombing leader, who decorated the mess with his cartoons, and who never seemed to be without his dog Virginia and the WAAF of the moment; Steve and Dave – Bow-man and Crugeon – two inseparable Australians who were finally killed on the same night in different aircraft; Bill Clayfield, the debonair signals leader who raced his Singer to the Gliderdrome dancehall in Boston so many nights of Stand-Down; Watson, with the spaniel that he always took on operations, and which finally fell from the night sky over Germany beside him; Perkins's two wild Canadian gunners, who were sent to Sheffield in punish-ment for smashing the sergeants' mess one night and thus missed the crash that killed their pilot. These and 150 or so other aircrew made up 97 Squadron in 1944.

Coningsby was one of the crack stations of 5 Group, the hub of '54 Base'. Bomber Command had sub-divided its Groups into base commands, each centred on a station with several 'satellite' airfields. 97 shared Coningsby with 83 Squadron. The two units worked in close partnership, indeed were usually briefed together by the little base commander, Air Commodore Bobbie Sharpe. There was also a tiny, élite force at Coningsby known as 54 Base Flight, which comprised 5 Group's Master Bombers. A hut on the station housed the Jordan Trainer, a sophisticated device for training Master Bombers. Pupils sat in their 'cockpit' in a gallery, while below them a fifteen-foot darkened model of a German city revolved to create its image as seen from a circling aircraft, with steam producing cloud, lights and small pyrotechnics imitating Target Indicators and smoke. To be a Master Bomber was intensely dangerous, circling the target throughout an attack, often descending to very low level to correct markers that had fallen wide. Visually marked attacks depended heavily on the Master Bomber, and when he was shot down or suffered technical failure, the whole raid often ended in fiasco.

97 Squadron still carried out marking and bombing attacks according to well-established 8 Group techniques. But their most notable contribution to 5 Group's operations was as an Illuminating Force, lighting up the target for the Mosquitoes who followed them. Routines varied in detail from operation to operation, but a typical 5 Group raid in the late summer of 1944 sent selected aircraft of 83 and 97 Squadrons to open the attack by laying lines of parachute flares over the target blind by H2S, at seven-second intervals, with a margin of error seldom much above 200 yards. Meanwhile the Primary Blind Marker dropped his Target Indicators, also by H2S, to give the Mosquitoes an approximate line on the target. 627's Mosquitoes then came in low with their Target Indicators or Red Spot Fires – more precise but less brilliant markers. The first pilot to see the marking-point called 'Tally-Ho!' on the radio-telephone, and dived in to mark. It was then the Master Bomber's business to assess its accuracy and call for correction and support as required, before letting loose the Main Force. Supporting illuminators were available to reinforce the flares as necessary, but often went home without being required to act. In both 5 and 8 Groups, there was a distinct hierarchy of importance and efficiency among marking crews, who were promoted to 'Flare Force I', or demoted to become 'Supporters' according to their operational performance.

There was now an extraordinary profusion of marking and aiming techniques: visual; by *Oboe*; by H2S; by a new device called G-H, of the *Oboe* family but with greater range and capable of use by a hundred aircraft simultaneously. Often a combination of more than one of these would be employed. Sometimes the Pathfinders would decide only on the run-up to the target whether to mark visually or by radar. They were equipped with multi-stage Target Indicators which changed colour through the attack to defeat German decoys. At 97 Squadron, the bomb-aimer's vital function had become that of 'Set Operator', manning the H2S from a seat beside the navigator as the aircraft ran up to the target. Flight engineers had been retrained as 'Visual bomb-aimers', and it was they who customarily handled the Mk XIV bomb-sight on a visual attack. Each squadron aircraft carried its own individual combination of Target Indicators, flares, 'Wanganui' sky-markers, high-explosive bombs and incendiaries, according to its place in the attack.

At a crack Pathfinder unit there was intense professional dedication to improving technique. Gordon Cooper, the H2S leader at 97, had devised a range of new methods of handling the set. The squadron engineering officer discovered that by applying a high polish to the bulging H2S dome below the fuselage, it was possible to add 5 mph to a Lancaster's speed. Each radar set was individually tuned. Highly-skilled *Gee* operators found that they could use their equipment almost to the Ruhr despite the German jamming, getting the vital blip at extreme range by calling on their pilot to waggle his wings.

But it is important not to allow admiration for the sophistication of Pathfinder techniques at this stage of the war to obscure one central fact: Bomber Command never overcame the problem of the weather. Until the very end, there were failed attacks and unsatisfactory marking when the cloud-base was low. The weather remained almost as central an element in the bomber offensive in April 1945 as it had been in September 1939. Despite the FIDO burners that were established at key airfields to clear runways of fog, crashes on take-off and landing remained a major cause of lost aircraft. With the approach of winter, the sortie rate declined severely even in the last year of the war.

One of Cochrane's most intensely held convictions was that

training must never stop, even when crews were operating constantly. Heward kept 97 Squadron in the air by day and night all that summer. They dropped bombs at Wainfleet, practised H2S technique on blind 'cross-countries', tested their gunners in the air against drogues and targets. Some of the crews resented the pressure when they felt entitled to relax between operations. Most were sufficiently dedicated to improving their art to accept it with reasonably good grace, although somebody wrote an acid note in the operational record book at the end of June: 'The Group "Exercise" which was laid on for tonight was once more cancelled at a late hour. One gets the impression that these "Exercises" are laid on and cancelled at such late hours to prevent the aircrews ever having an evening out of camp to themselves.'

Operations reached a peak of intensity in August, when they sortied by day or night on eighteen occasions. Some men found the daylight trips a pleasant change, forging across France in a great loose gaggle, gazing down at the unfamiliar sunlit scenery. Most, however, were deeply wedded to the night. They hated the sense of nakedness in daylight, the horror of watching aircraft fall from the sky in slow motion, of being able to identify each man's funeral pyre, to see the collisions, the bursting flak and attacking fighters, seldom though it was that they now encountered the Luftwaffe.

On 18 August, they were ordered to the U-boat pens at Bordeaux. They took off that morning in uncommonly easy mind. They had had little trouble with French targets for weeks, and this trip had been laid on at short notice, almost as an afterthought by High Wycombe. Then as the group of Lancasters curved in towards the town and the vast, unbroken concrete mass that housed the U-boats, a terrifying blanket of flak opened before them. Instinctively, pilots edged outwards to skirt it, their course widening away from the pens. Arthur Ingham, in 97's lead aircraft, drove unswerving onwards, calling furiously down the radio-telephone: 'Come in, come in. Support me. Support me.' The flak began to kick and rock the aircraft. Ingham locked his arms on the yoke and said grimly to his crew: 'We are going through.' There was intense nervous chatter between aircraft on the R/T, somebody calling in bewilderment: 'There are some Germans down there pushing out what looks like a wheelbarrow.'

The 'wheelbarrow' erupted as its crew brought their quad AA guns into action. Beside Ingham sat Pat Turner, a flight engineer who had volunteered for Bordeaux because he was a few trips behind the rest of his usual crew, and 'this one sounded dead cushy'. The flak bracketed them in earnest as they came in to bomb, tearing through wings and fuselage, wrecking the electrics and flaps, holing five tanks, wounding the navigator and mid-upper gunner. They came home through the bright sunshine with the wind rushing through 160 holes in the aircraft, two engines gone, Pat Turner bent over the bleeding squadron navigation leader with a morphia syringe. They crashed at Fighter Command's airfield at Tangmere, where their survivors were grudgingly found sleeping space on the mess floor.

Bill Clayfield, 97's signals leader, came home in an aircraft with a badly wounded bomb-aimer. The ambulance met them as they landed, and rushed him away. Only when the others reached the mess did they realize that they were a man short. They raced back to the Lancaster, to find their mid-upper gunner slumped unconscious over his guns. He had been hit in the backside by shrapnel, but when he recovered later he said that knowing of their difficulties in the cockpit with the bomb-aimer, he had not wanted to add to them by reporting his own injuries.

It was, inevitably, a dangerous business using heavy bombers with a mean aiming accuracy of three miles to support ground operations. But that summer the Allied armies called repeatedly for assistance from Bomber Command and 8th Air Force to blast open the German lines in advance of an attack. Until the end of the war, many airmen and some thoughtful soldiers argued that it was counter-productive to send in Bomber Command, for the devastation could cause serious problems for advancing armour, and bombing was not accurate enough to pinpoint German positions. And even with good marking, there were fatal errors. In an incident on 14 August during the battle for Falaise, Bomber Command hit Canadian troops, causing several hundred casualties. It was largely a failure of liaison, because the men on the ground had fired Colours of the Day unknown to the airmen, but closely resembling Target Indicators. There had also been some careless bombing, however, and on most ground-support sorties thereafter, there was a 'long stop' controller to ensure that no aircraft bombed beyond a certain point near the Allied lines. Tactical support bombing became a central part of the summer's operations, as the army called repeatedly for preparation by heavy bombers, if only to boost the morale of the Allied assault troops.

On 16 August, 97 Squadron carried out their first operation against a German target since June. Bomber Command dispatched 461 aircraft on a deep penetration to Stettin. While the Main Force attacked the city, 97 and 83 Squadrons went to mine the nearby Swinemunde Canal. It was an exceptionally difficult low-level operation, and before they left Coningsby they had long consultations with Guy Gibson, drawing on his dam-busting experience. Gibson recommended that the three marking aircraft make one low-level run down the canal before turning to drop their flame-float markers. At tea in the mess, there were some gloomy jokes about Heward's refusal to allow crews to take part in swimming exercises at the local baths, on the grounds that the chlorine might have damaged their night vision. Ed Porter, approaching the end of his second tour, was Master Bombing with a scratch crew. He would mark the middle of the canal, Parker the south end, Reid the north. Then somebody remembered that Reid could not swim. To their intense dismay, for it was to be the last trip of their tour, Harry Locke's crew were detailed instead.

Locke's aircraft lost its *Gee* on the outward run, but approached the canal dead on time at 300 feet, to find the five flak ships moored beside the channel already hosing up fire. On their second run, their flame floats had just fallen away when they were hit by ground fire, and plunged towards the water. 'Pull out,' yelled the wireless operator, Tony Boultbee, as he glanced from his window to see the water rushing up at them. They called Porter on the R/T as they climbed away: 'Permission to break off?' Porter assented. They turned for home. Crossing Denmark at 6,000 feet, they reached the English coast with leaking hydraulic fluid swamping the H2S, and all radar aids out of action. Locke belly-landed at Coningsby with the crew huddled behind the main spar, haunted by the usual terror of fire on impact. Somehow they all walked away. Locke was awarded an immediate DSO.

But the furious flak caught Porter's aircraft as he hung over the canal, coned by a dense knot of searchlights. With an unshakeable calm that every crew listening remembered for the rest of their lives, he said on the R/T: 'I'm afraid we have had it. I shall have to leave you now. Baling out. Good luck everybody.' But they were too low for parachutes. Going home that night, one of 97's crews looked down on the bright lights of neutral Sweden, and for several minutes they talked seriously among themselves about the possibility of baling out into internment. Later, they felt ashamed and never mentioned their conversation to each other again. But that night fear had sunk deep into their reserves of courage.

In August 1944, 97 Squadron carried out 193 sorties for the loss of only three aircraft missing. Faces that came to the squadron were now lingering long enough to become familiar. There were often more crews than aircraft for them to fly, and with an establishment of twenty, on some 'maximum effort' nights they sent out twenty-four Lancasters, some of their novices carrying bombs with Main Force. But the declining graph of losses, the rise in the fortunes of Bomber Command, were more readily apparent to the statisticians at High Wycombe than to the aircrew on the stations. The unending exhaustion; the dirtiness; the stink of aviation spirit and the lonely ride through the darkness to the dispersals; the monotony of the air broken only by moments of intense concentration or fear, felt the same in the summer of 1944 as in 1943 or 1942. It is only to historians that it is so readily apparent that the nature of the battle changed profoundly in this last year of the war.

With such a strong contingent of Colonials on 97 Squadron, Coningsby's senior officers fought a losing battle to enforce discipline on the ground. These men were not career airmen. Whatever dedication they brought to operational flying, they had no patience with rigid restriction away from their aircraft. Elsewhere in Bomber Command, disgruntled Canadians had been known to ring up their High Commission in London when confronted, for example, with official efforts to prevent NCOs from addressing officers by their christian names. 'No bullshit!' said the Canadians defiantly, and when all aircrew at Coningsby were confined to camp in punishment for the sawing-down of the base flagpole by a crew completing their tour, general impatience came close to explosion. Gordon Cooper slept with a pistol under his pillow to protect himself from the two New Zealanders with whom he shared a room, who were utterly careless whom they assaulted after a few drinks. In the early hours of one August morning after an operation, all 97's crews were hauled out of bed to take part in a post-mortem about the failure of the attack. They listened to Bobbie Sharpe's incisive questioning for a few minutes, then Harry Locke, one of the Australians, called in disgust: 'This is a heap of horseshit.' They were allowed to go back to their beds.

Heward, the CO, was known as 'Smiler' in deference to the chilly mask that he presented to the world. It was said that in his days at 50 Squadron, a pilot interrupted one of the base WAAFs who said how much she would like to do something special for the war effort: 'Marry the CO, then, because he's giving us absolute hell.' Heward's crew reported for duty one morning in severe pain after a heavy social night at a local American base. His face cracked into a frostly smile: 'Fighter affiliation for us this morning, I think.' For the next hour he hurled the Lancaster through the Lincolnshire sky until the cockpit floor was awash with rebellious breakfasts. But unknown to the squadron, Heward was conducting one exercise that was quite out of step with the character they had drawn of him: laying siege to Clare Wainwright, a general's daughter who was Code and Ciphers Officer at Coningsby, and by common consent the most beautiful WAAF on the base. There was little opportunity for going out together in the town, but instead they went for long walks across the flat Lincolnshire fields. They were married late in 1944.

Coningsby had all the facilities of a pre-war station, but was grossly overcrowded with aircrew. Officers were sleeping in double-banked bunks, eating at long tables in a self-service mess, sharing a batman between six. Discomfort that would have been tolerable for men working regular hours in undemanding jobs became insufferable to aircrew permanently weary, coming and going at all hours of day and night. They discovered that the mess funds had accumulated enormously in five years of war, and threw them all into two massive parties. It was always possible to laugh and find the war funny when you were among exuberant colleagues. But once they left the throng, most men's faces relapsed into that mask of mingled earnestness, tiredness and strain that is apparent in so many photographs of wartime briefings. On Stand Down evenings, they lounged on the grass outside the Leagate Arms in the village, conducting inter-crew drinking contests in which victory was measured by the length of each team's line of beer bottles stretching down the lawn, or dashed into Boston and Lincoln, or drank around the mess piano.

Coming out of briefing,
Get into the kites,

they sang, to the tune of 'Lili Marlene',

Down the f—ing runway,
And off into the night,
We've left the flarepath far behind,
It's f—ing dark but never mind,
We're pressing on regardless
For the Wingco's DFC . . .

Often that summer, targets and bombloads were changed at short notice, and operations were laid on and cancelled at a few hours' warning. They played cricket in the sunshine outside the flight offices, or joined the high poker school in which Tony Aveline was a monotonously steady winner. Fewer men were dying, but the tension and discomfort of night operations were unchanged. Fred Hendry, one of the navigators, suffered chronically from air sickness, but was haunted by fear that he might be considered 'Lacking Moral Fibre'. Trip after trip, he flew with his topographical map folded into a sick-bag, throwing up his heart despite all the pills that he took before take-off, at last completing his forty-five amidst the admiration of 'the Navigators' Union'. One night Bob Lasham's flight engineer fell unconscious in the aircraft when he accidentally unplugged his oxygen. When he was reconnected and brought round, he tried to attack the wireless operator with a fireaxe. He thought that they had crashed, and that the man bending over him was a German soldier.

Billy Russell was a Scots rear-gunner, who had come to the RAF from the mines. One night on the way to the target, his electrically heated suit failed. On his return, he had to spend two days in hospital with frostbite. Russell flew with Noel Parker, an intensely professional Australian of much experience. On the trip to Mailly-Le-Camp, with the sky lit by tracer and exploding aircraft, Russell suddenly saw a shape in the darkness behind him, and swung his guns. He hesitated for a moment until he could see clearly, then sagged with relief, for it was another Lancaster. Back on the ground, he told Parker about the near-disaster, and was astounded by the Australian's explosion: 'You stupid bastard – you thought it was an Me110 and you hesitated. You should have fired the second you saw it!'

'But I was wrong,' said Russell in confusion.

'Next time you may not live to know that,' said Parker curtly. 'Fire every time.'

Some crews took chances and got away with it. One night, a 97 Lancaster landed back at Coningsby ahead of the Mosquitoes. At the ensuing inquiry, it emerged that its crew had ignored the stream's dog-leg route home, and flown a direct course in order to get to a mess party. Some men fell asleep in their aircraft on the way back. Others smoked, used torches carelessly to read the instruments, switched on IFF or even landing lights over enemy territory without noticing. A few came back, but many of these men lie in the cemeteries of France and Germany. Billy Russell was appalled one night, coming home from a trip to Germany with a novice captain, to hear the man say: 'OK, we're over our own lines now. You can come out of the turrets and have a smoke.' Survivors of Bomber Command needed luck, but also sanity, discipline and utter concentration.

One of the saddest episodes at Coningsby that autumn concerned the station commander, the huge, popular teddy-bear figure of Group-Captain Evans Evans. Evans Evans felt a deep respect for aircrew. At Bourn, there had been a superstitious tradition that no one ever came to watch the aircraft take off, but at Coningsby 97 were surprised and at first alarmed to see Evans Evans saluting by the runway at the head of a crowd of waving WAAFs and ground staff. He was there without fail, every trip. Then one day in August, Evans made up his mind that it was his duty to fly an operation himself. He was a man of such enormous dimensions that he had difficulty getting into a Lancaster cockpit, far less controlling the aircraft. Bob Lasham's crew went to the squadron CO and flatly refused to fly with the station commander after a hair-raising cross-country flight in his hands. Instead, Evans took a scratch crew, flew to Caen and somehow came back to tell the tale. He was awarded a DFC. But instead of delighting him, this played on his mind. He felt that his 'gong' had been easily earned by comparison with those of the aircrew. He decided that he must fly another operation. He took off for Germany one night with all 97's specialist 'Leaders' in his crew, including Jock Wishart, the navigation leader, who was on his eighty-fourth trip. They somehow drifted into a 'Diver' area, where the Allied gunners had orders that any flying object must be treated as hostile. The aircraft was blown to pieces by American flak. Only the Australian rear gunner baled out in time to survive and tell the tale. Coningsby was torn between regret for Evans Evans, and sympathy for those who had been obliged to die with him.

But war on a bomber station was always a cruel business, in which the laws of natural selection were pushed to the limit. Throughout the offensive, a large proportion of casualties were novice crews on their first six trips. Yet because they were new to their squadrons, they found their inexperience compounded by the fact that they had to fly the aircraft nobody else wanted, the oldest and most vice-ridden. Beyond even this, by 1944 the best crews were concentrated overwhelmingly in the crack units – 8 Group, 5 Group, the Mosquito squadrons. 'Main Force' had become a term of condescension. New and mediocre crews in other Groups lacked a sufficient leavening of knowledge and experience in their flights and squadrons. It was a situation that Harris had anticipated with the formation of the Pathfinders in 1942, but which there was now no momentum in Bomber Command to reverse.

The experienced had little pity to spare for the newcomers in the mess. Statistically, seven or fourteen or twenty-one of us have to die tonight, so please God, let it be the nervous young face in the corner whom I do not know, rather than Harry, or Bill or Jack laughing at the bar, who are my friends. Thus their jokes: 'Killer' Booth walking over to the new crew having their pre-op meal in the mess at Coningsby, looking them up and down and declaring with cold certainty: 'You're for the chop tonight.' Or the familiar chestnut of putting a chopper cut out of perspex into a navigator's mapcase, for the man to find as his pilot ran up engines at dispersal. It was part of their defences against their own fear, of the schoolboy immaturity that was always close to the surface among so many young men of eighteen, nineteen and twenty, who still thought it the greatest sport in the world to pull somebody's trousers off after dinner. It was this same feather-light tread of youth that enabled so many thousands of their generation to fly for Bomber Command through six years of war, amidst the terrible reality that, statistically, most of them were dead men.

The early autumn of 1944 was the last false dawn of the war for the Allies, before the crushing disappointments of Arnhem and the German counter-offensive in the Ardennes, followed at last, belatedly, by victory. After months of delay, the armies had broken out of Normandy, sweeping across France and Belgium. It seemed perfectly possible to end the war in Europe by Christmas.

For Bomber Command, the path into Germany that had been fraught with such loss and disappointment only five months before suddenly reopened. It was a remarkable twist of war that *Overlord*, which the airmen had sought to supplant as the key to victory, now made possible the reopening of the strategic air offensive with devastating results, at vastly reduced cost:

The Combined Bomber offensive as planned in the spring of 1943 was ... primarily a campaign to defeat the Luftwaffe as a prerequisite to *Overlord* [wrote Crave and Cate]. Ironically enough, it was not until the Allies had gained a firm foothold on the continent ... that the bombing of Germany's vital industries, originally considered the purpose of a strategic bombing offensive, was systematically begun.[6]

The German early-warning radar and observer stations, together with their vital forward airfields in France, were gone. The attrition of the summer against the American strategic and the Allied tactical air forces had destroyed much of the Luftwaffe's remaining corps of trained aircrew, and wrecked its aircraft at the rate of 500 a week. The German air force continued to inflict loss on Bomber Command until the very end of the war, but Harris's casualties fell to 1 per cent of aircraft dispatched. In January 1944 he had lost 314 aircraft for 6,278 dispatched. In September, losses fell to 96 missing for 6,428 night sorties, in October to 75 in 10,193 night sorties. Casualties on daylight operations were negligible.

With the benefit of hindsight, it is remarkable how much Allied nerves relaxed after the Normandy bridgehead had been secured. D-Day had been the climax of so many hopes and fears. By 11 July, Portal found time to preside over a meeting at the Air Ministry to discuss, of all things, means by which the Royal Air Force might gain more publicity in the Press. The Chief of Air Staff opened the discussion himself:

In the second stage of the war, RAF operations might be to a large extent overshadowed by army and naval operations and by the Americans, and so would receive comparatively little national publicity. There was accordingly a genuine danger that the part which it had played in the earlier part of the war would be forgotten by Ministers and by the public.

The Director of Public Relations said that the Admiralty were obstructing publicity for Coastal Command. The Chief of Air Staff said that he would take this matter to the highest levels if necessary . . .

In August the Air Ministry issued a long memorandum to all Commands concerning preparations for the end of the war. They were anxious that there should be no destructive or extravagant celebrations, and pointed out that it was advisable to ensure that when the time came, personnel had no unauthorized access to firearms, explosives or pyrotechnics. There was expectancy in the air at the highest levels of command: the Russians had seized great areas of Poland and Rumania including the vital oilfields, and seemed to be driving all before them. On every side there was a feeling that one more push could suffice to topple the Nazi edifice.

This impatience contributed significantly to the Allies' failure in the last nine months of war to devise and prosecute a consistent strategic-bomber strategy, with the enormous resources now at their command. Had they but known it, Spaatz's oil offensive was succeeding beyond the Americans' wildest expectations. By the end of September, German fuel supplies had fallen to less than a quarter of their January total, and a fatal crisis was threatening the German armed forces. But once again, as throughout the bomber offensive, a failure of Intelligence led to tragic misjudgements. For four years the airmen had exaggerated the achievements of bombing because they possessed no satisfactory means of assessing them. Now, Spaatz's dramatic prognostications of impending victory fell on sceptical ears, because he had no conclusive means of proving what he had done. Generals might gain ground, admirals might sink ships, but the airmen were forced back on the measurement of success or failure by aerial mosaic and mathematical projection. The Allied leadership did not dispute Spaatz's progress, nor the potential of his attacks. But they were by now far too well-versed in the apparent realities of the bomber offensive to accept that the oil attack offered a chance of early and absolute victory. Spaatz continued his campaign – with the support of Portal, of which more will be heard later. But at no point did it seem likely that the undivided weight of the Allied strategic-bomber force would be committed to the assault on the German oil industry.

By late summer many of the Allied leaders behaved as if the German military collapse was so close that it no longer mattered greatly what the bombers attacked, as long as they provided tactical support for the advancing armies on demand. In July, the British Chiefs of Staff produced the minute to the Prime Minister which sowed the seeds of Operation *Thunderclap*, ultimately executed in a modified form against Dresden:

The time might well come in the not too distant future when an all-out attack by every means at our disposal on German civilian morale might be decisive [they wrote] . . . The method by which such an attack would be carried out should be examined and all possible preparations made.

The importance of this minute was not that it resulted in any immediate drastic action, but that it confirmed that the candle of support in high places for area bombing, which had all but expired in March 1944, was once again flickering by July. The fact that it was signed by all the Chiefs of Staff is a reminder that the concept of inflicting mass death and destruction on Germany's cities was not a unilateral air-force enthusiasm. The Directorate of Bomber Operations did some calculations about the possibilities of *Thunderclap*:

If we assume that the daytime population of the area attacked is 300,000, we may expect 220,000 casulties. 50 per cent of these or 110,000 may expect to be killed. It is suggested that such an attack resulting in so many deaths, the great proportion of which will be key personnel, cannot help but have a shattering effect on political and civilian morale all over Germany . . .

Tedder showed great interest in the possibilities of pursuing the attack on morale. Portal seemed for a time to favour it. There was intense discussion of a possible four days and nights round-the-clock air assault on Berlin, to precipitate the collapse of the Nazi regime.

The critical point is that none of the Allied leaders resolutely opposed a renewal of area bombing in some form or other, and this was more than enough of a mandate for Sir Arthur Harris. The C-in-C of Bomber Command had never lost faith in the principles by which he had set out to level Germany two and a half years before. He had bowed to overwhelming pressure to commit his forces to support *Overlord*, and this they had done wholeheartedly and with great effect. As the German air defences crumbled and losses fell, Harris found himself with more than a thousand first-line aircraft daily available, a surplus of crews so great that by autumn trainees found themselves employed shifting coal, and a range of devices and techniques formidable beyond the dreams of two years before.

Harris was still obliged to seek the authorization of SHAEF headquarters for every operation by his Command, but Tedder himself agreed by August that the army had become far too careless in their demands for strategic-bomber support even in the most unsuitable circumstances, and must be 'weaned from the drug'. In August, Harris gained SHAEF's approval for twelve area attacks on German cities, when his forces were not required elsewhere. The biggest raids were those of 16 August, when 809 'heavies' staged a two-pronged attack on Kiel and Stettin.

By early September, the French marshalling-yard campaign had ended, the 'ski-sites' had been largely overrun by the armies, and the Chiefs of Staff were addressing themselves to the future of the strategic air offensive. On 14 September a new bombing directive was issued, of which more will be heard later. But by the end of that month, Arnhem had ended, and the entire mood of the Allies was changing.

In the period of strategic hiatus for the airmen in late August and early September, however, they were for a few weeks astonishingly free to pursue their personal inclinations. Spaatz addressed himself to oil. On 11, 12 and 13 September, for example, he launched three great attacks on synthetic plants by 1136, 888 and 748 aircraft respectively, in which the Luftwaffe once more lost heavily in air battles, their defeat unredeemed by the half-hearted intervention of a few jet fighters. Bomber Command returned, inevitably, to Germany's cities. On 29 August they gave terrible proof of their new effectiveness in an attack on Königsberg. A mere 175 Lancasters 'de-housed' 134,000 people in a single night. They lost four aircraft.

Harris was going back to the ground that he had so reluctantly abandoned in April. He was able to do so, quite simply, because there was no one among the Allied directors of the war sufficiently determined to stop him.

13 'A quiet trip all round': Darmstadt, 11–12 September 1944

'A quiet trip all round, with everything going according to plan.'
83 Squadron debriefing report, 12 September 1944

On the night of 11 September 1944, three days before the Combined Chiefs of Staff issued their directive restoring Bomber Command to Portal's control and establishing new priorities for the strategic offensive, 5 Group bombed the German town of Darmstadt. 218 Lancasters and 14 Mosquitoes delivered an exceptionally effective attack in which somewhere between eight and twelve thousand people – about a tenth of the town's population – were killed. In the words of the *United States Strategic Bombing Survey* in 1945:

This was an area raid of the classic saturation type, which had so effectively razed Cologne and Hamburg . . . The mechanics of the raid, between the 'Target Sighted' and the 'Bombs Away', were almost perfunctory, and as a consequence Darmstadt was virtually destroyed.

From the British point of view, this was not an important operation – it rates only a footnote in the four volumes of the official history. But I propose to describe it in some detail, partly to show the destruction of which Bomber Command was capable by late 1944, but chiefly to give some impression of what it was like to suffer one of the most devastating forms of assault in the history of war. I have tried to convey the courage and dedication of the aircrew who flew over Germany. In any story of Bomber Command it is also appropriate to show something of the spirit of the enemy below.

Darmstadt was a prosperous provincial town set in rolling farmland studded with woods, some fifteen miles south of Frankfurt. It was primarily a residential and small-business centre, where shopkeepers and craftsmen plied their trades from stores and workshops beside their homes. The heart and pride of Darmstadt was the old town, a maze of narrow, cobbled streets radiating outwards from the seventeenth-century *landgraf*'s castle, whose grey walls and tall bell-tower over-looked the central market square. Among the gabled baroque and renaissance houses stood two theatres, a celebrated museum and a cluster of lesser palaces and great houses built in the days when Hesse was among the most notable independent German principalities. It was 'typical' in the sort of way that made pre-war English tourists nod and exclaim on the charm of the German bourgeoisie. It was a survivor of the greatest age of German culture and architecture.

The old town gave way at its edges to modern houses and widening streets, squares and small parks and a scattering of factories. The south suburb was the smart residential area. Most of the industrial workers lived on the north side, close to the town's two largest factories, E. Merck and Rohm & Haas, family businesses which between them employed almost half the total workforce of Darmstadt making chemicals and pharmaceuticals. A number of V-2 rocket technicians were being trained at the Technical University. Almost one in ten of the town's workers were employed in government offices; the remainder worked in shops, the printing business, or the small factories making photographic paper, leather goods and wood products. Most of the factories were working only a single eight-hour shift a day. According to the post-war USSBS survey, 'Darmstadt produced less than two-tenths of 1 per cent of Reich total production, and only an infinitesimal amount of total war production. Consequently, it had a low priority on labour and materials. Nor was the city important as a transportation centre, because it had no port and was bypassed by the principal rail arteries.' In all, 18.5 per cent of the workforce was employed on production that directly assisted the German war effort.

Situated as it was in western Germany, Darmstadt had always been readily accessible to Bomber Command, and indeed as early as October 1940 Portal had placed it on his list of German cities suggested for proscription. In November 1943, Sir Arthur Harris had included it in his great list of towns that he claimed had been damaged by Bomber Command, in his letter to the

Prime Minister. But in reality very few bombs had ever hit Darmstadt, whether aimed or not. Over the years, a few crews had jettisoned their loads there. There had been two 'nuisance' raids against the town in the spring of 1944. On one occasion, fifteen USAAF Flying Fortresses had attempted a precision attack on the Merck works, without significant effect. On the night of 25 August 1944, 202 aircraft had been dispatched from 5 Group to bomb Darmstadt, but by a series of extraordinary flukes the Master Bomber was compelled to go home with technical failure, both his deputies were shot down en route to the target, and the Illuminating Force dropped their flares well wide. The Main Force arrived to find the VHF wavelength silent, the flare lines already dying. Most aircraft diverted to join the other Bomber Command attack of the night, on Rüsselsheim. Only five crews bombed Darmstadt itself, and a further twenty-five dropped their loads within three miles.

The Darmstadters were not even aware how close they had come to extinction that night. They assumed that the bombs which fell upon them were either jettisoned, or intended as a further nuisance raid, to drive them into the shelters. Before the night of 11 September they had suffered only 181 people killed in air raids. They were vividly aware that this was a trifle by the standards of every great city in Germany, and, to tell the truth, they had become complacent, almost careless about the peril of air attack.

The Allied armies were now scarcely a hundred miles west. To the very end of the war, few Germans sensed the depths of their Führer's alienation from them, his indifference to their suffering, his deranged determination to drag them with him to Wagnerian cataclysm. But there was little faith left in secret weapons or miraculous deliverance in Darmstadt. Its people had become fatalists, living out their lives in the hope of some ending of the war at tolerable cost in pain and pride.

But they cherished one terrible delusion. After four years of the Allied air offensive, Darmstadters believed that their town had been deliberately excluded from the Allied target lists. Their great treasure trove of paintings and works of art had not been evacuated from the city. Night after night they had watched the terrible fireworks displays over Mannheim, Frankfurt, Ludwig-

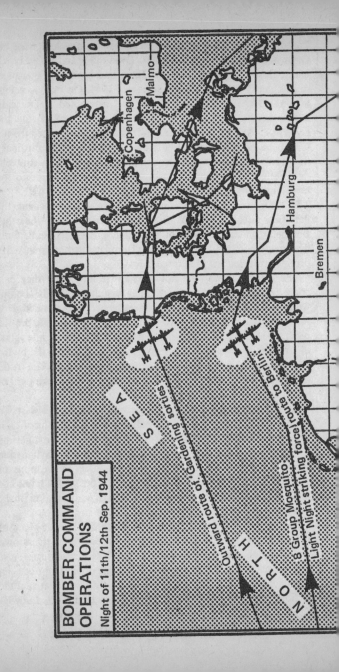

BOMBER COMMAND
OPERATIONS

Night of 11th/12th Sep. 1944

NORTH SEA

Copenhagen
Malmo
Hamburg
Bremen

Outward route of Gardening sorties
8 Group Mosquito route to Berlin
Light Night striking force

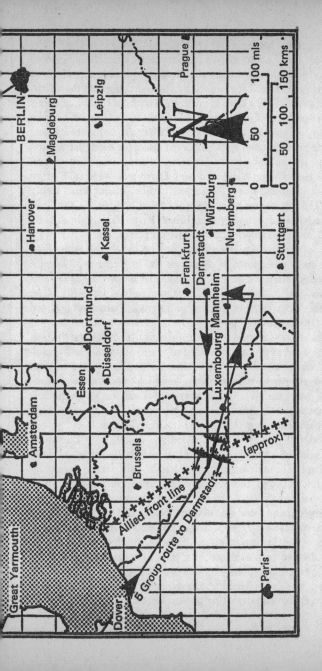

Great Yarmouth

Amsterdam

BERLIN

Hanover

Magdeburg

Leipzig

Dover

Essen
Dortmund
Düsseldorf

Kassel

Brussels

Frankfurt

Würzburg
Darmstadt
Mannheim

Nuremberg

Luxembourg

Stuttgart

Prague

++++++
Allied front line

+++++ (approx)

6 Group route to Darmstadt

Paris

N

0   50   100   150 kms
0   50   100 mls

shaven. They had seen the great glow in the sky as other cities burned; the 'Christmas trees', as they called them, floating down from the Pathfinder aircraft cascading light; the burning bombers plunging to earth. They had felt the earth shaking with the torrent of explosives falling around them. Yet Darmstadt stood, and they often discussed why. Some people said that with the Allied armies already closing on the borders of Germany, the enemy had selected certain cities to be preserved intact for headquarters and billets, and as a sop to the advocates of preserving German culture. Heidelberg, Wiesbaden and Darmstadt were said to be foremost among these. There was another quaint local theory that Darmstadt was marked for salvation because the Prince of Hesse, who was related to the British Royal Family, lived close to the town and still owned extensive property there.

In fact Darmstadt had always been on the British target lists. Like every other town of significant size in Germany, it was included in MEW's *Guide to the Economic Importance of German Towns and Cities*, subtitled with macabre jocularity 'The Bomber's Baedeker'. According to the guide, Darmstadt included one Grade I target, the Merck factory: 'It is believed that this works is now concentrating on products of direct war interest at the expense of its production of pharmaceuticals and chemicals,' declared the May 1944 edition. The Eisenwerk Eberstadt Adolf Riesterer, manufacturing grinding machines and stone saws, was listed as a Grade 3 target. So was the Motorenfabrik Darmstadt AG, 'who are now reported to be making diesel engines'. Rohm and Haas rated as a Grade 2 target.

Today it is impossible to determine exactly why Darmstadt was selected for attack on 25 August and finally destroyed on 11 September in preference to the scores of other area targets of far greater industrial and military significance. On a given night, a city was chosen from the vast target list generally after verbal discussion, and those who decided the fate of Darmstadt are now dead, or have long forgotten one unmemorable night among six years of war.[1] It is possible, as many historians have sought with Dresden, to seek evidence of a prolonged and rational debate leading to a consciously momentous decision. In reality, in the heat of war and in the midst of a campaign that was waged nightly over period of years, target choices were made with what might now seem remarkable carelessness. A succession of Air Ministry, Ministry of Economic Warfare and Bomber Command HQ committees had placed a city on the target list, perhaps years before. On a given night a compound of weather, forces available and the state of the German defences determined which was chosen for attack. In September 1944, 5 Group were seeking previously undamaged area targets of manageable size upon which to test the accuracy and effectiveness of various marking and bombing techniques at tolerable cost – in other words at limited penetration inside Germany. Darmstadt met all their criteria perfectly.

On the night of 11 September, 5 Group experimented with a new aiming technique designed to cause maximum devastation. Because Darmstadt had never before been seriously scarred by bombing, it was easy to reach a verdict on the new method and its achievements. When *The Times* reported the raid the following morning, it was able to state, according to the Air Ministry public-relations brief: 'This is a centre of the enemy's chemical industry.'

Late on the morning of 11 September, the teletypes from 5 Group headquarters at Swinderby began to clatter out the long winding sheet of orders for its bases and squadrons. This was to be an operation exclusively by Cochrane's men, and thus most of the detailed planning had been done by his own staff rather than High Wycombe.

AC864 SECRET Action Sheet 11 September
Target: LUCE
8 Group to WHITEBAIT
MONICA not to be used at any time
Aim: to destroy an enemy industrial centre
2359 H Hour
Aircraft to attack between 12,500 and 16,000 feet
Main Force 1 x 4,000 lb plus maximum 4 lb incendiary clusters . . .

5 Group's attack on LUCE – one of Saundby's countless fish codenames – was to be the main Bomber Command operation of the night. Bennett was dispatching forty-seven Mosquitoes of his Light Night Striking Force to Berlin. Seventy aircraft from 100 Group would be in the air, putting up the usual *Mandrel*

radar-jamming screen, interrupting the night-fighter controllers, sending twenty-six Intruder Mosquitoes to attack the Luftwaffe airfields, and a further eighteen *Serrate* Mosquitoes to stalk the night-fighters in the sky. 3 Group would also be dispatching mining sorties to area GERANIUM, in the Baltic.

At 4 p.m., 5 Group's squadron and flight commanders gathered in the operations rooms of their bases across Lincolnshire. The familiar crisp, patrician voice began to echo down the broadcast link from Swinderby: 'Good afternoon. This is the AOC. The target for tonight is Darmstadt...' After Cochrane's introduction his weather man gave the provisional forecast for western Germany: clear skies and strong westerly winds. Then the little groups of men in the ops rooms listened intently as they heard the tactical plan for the night. Darmstadt was a 900-mile round-trip from Lincolnshire as the crow flies, but their dog-leg deception course would take them 1,083 track miles there and back. They would be carrying the usual fire-raising mix of 'cookies' to blast open the walls and windows, and incendiaries to ignite the households and factories thus exposed. Darmstadt would receive in all 399 tons of high explosive and 580 tons of incendiaries.

Marking would be offset, the marking-point being an old army parade-ground, the *Kavallerie Exerzierplatz*, a mile west of the city centre. It had been chosen because its white, chalky soil showed up vividly by day or night on the reconnaissance photographs that they all had before them. But the most remarkable part of the plan was now to come: when the ten squadrons of 5 Group's Main Force ran in to bomb, rather than approaching as usual along a single common axis, tonight they would bomb along no less than seven different aiming-lines at varying heights, spreading out from the marking-point in what Darmstadters were later to call *Der Todesfächer* – 'The Death Fan'. Every aircraft would vary its delay in bombing after passing the marking-point by between three and twelve seconds. Instead of a single mass of devastation, tonight 5 Group sought to spread its attack evenly and fatally the entire length and breadth of Darmstadt. Finally, to ensure that the key industrial targets were destroyed, after the Main Force attack seven of 627 Squadron's Mosquitoes – the less proficient marking crews – would go in low with all-incendiary loads to deliver precision strikes on the key factories.

83 and 97 Squadrons, the Illuminating Force, took off from Coningsby a few minutes before 9 p.m., 2100 hrs. Crossing the Channel, they flew down the Franco-Belgian border, high above Luxembourg, within earshot of tens of thousands of Allied and German soldiers confronting each other in the forward positions miles below. The bombers were on track for Karlsruhe, perhaps, or Mannheim or Stuttgart. German radio began its nightly running-commentary for millions of civilian listeners, huddled behind the blackout in their bedrooms or sitting-rooms, fully dressed with their suitcases and valuables beside them. Programmes were interrupted at regular intervals for the terse bulletins:

2216: Enemy bomber formations over and approaching Denmark in an easterly direction [this was the 'Gardening' force].

The reported fast-bomber formation is still approaching Schleswig-Holstein and Denmark – [these were Bennett's Mosquitoes].

The sirens wailed in Copenhagen as people left the cinemas and bars for the shelters. The first Bomber Command casualty of the night, one of the 'gardening' Halifaxes, was hit by a night-fighter and crashed into a farmhouse near Vordinborg. Its mines blew up, killing the farmer, his wife and three children, most of their livestock and seven young Englishmen.

2309: The reported bomber formation is now approaching Pomerania. The reported fast bomber formation is over Mark Brandenburg. A new formation of fast bombers is approaching west Germany.

Here at last were 5 Group's marking Mosquitoes, overtaking the Lancasters and tracking fast down the Franco-Belgian frontier.

2332: The reported formation continues to approach Pomerania. The bomber formation reported over and approaching western Germany is now over west and south-west Germany. The reported bomber formation over Mark Brandenburg is flying off north-westerly.

Eight minutes earlier, the air-raid sirens had sounded in Darmstadt, for the fourth time that day – the Americans had passed overhead during the afternoon. Wearily but without great fear, families gathered their children, their possessions, their helmets and a little food, and trooped down to the cellars, remembering to switch off the gas and unlock the emergency exits to their houses as they went. Many had been listening to the night's radio broadcast of Strauss's *Der Rosenkavalier*. They chatted to the neighbours as they slipped down from their apartments. There were the usual air-raid warning jokes.

North-west of Karlsruhe, 5 Group suddenly swung up through a steep 75-degree turn to port. Now they were tracking north, straight for Darmstadt. The city had laughed for the last time for many days.

Darmstadt had always been low on the priority list for civil defence, flak and searchlights. 'Looking back,' said Jacob Glanzer, one of the survivors of this night, 'our precautions were ridiculously dilettante.' The great cities of Germany possessed an elaborate and efficient hierarchy for the control of air-raid reporting and rescue, reaching down from each city's Police President to individual house wardens. Darmstadt possessed the structure, but not the effectiveness. Few of its children had been evacuated to rural areas. No deep public shelters had been dug. While in the embattled industrial centres the Nazi Party under the personal direction of Dr Goebbels had taken over many of the rescue and relief functions – a shrewdly calculated propaganda move – in Darmstadt these had been left to the municipality. Communal shelters existed in the basements of offices and public buildings and in the cellars of the local brewery, but the overwhelming majority of Darmstadters relied exclusively on their own cellars for protection. Reinforced slit-trenches had been dug in and around the railway station, and 'safety holes' had been knocked through the brickwork of adjoining cellars in many rows of houses. But these things had been done without the terrible sense of urgency and expectancy that moved Berliners and Hamburgers. Many of the flak batteries around Darmstadt had been removed to cover seriously embattled cities. The local fire-brigade was just 150 men strong, and on the night of 11 September their thirteen engines were arrayed as usual in the courtyard of the castle, ready to move on the orders of Max Jost, the fire chief, in his underground bunker. It was not unlike preparing a tugboat to save the *Titanic*.

At 2346 hrs, a local hairdresser named Emil Thier rang the bunker from his observer post on Hochzietsturm, to report

'Christmas trees in the west'. 17,000 feet above, 97 and 83 Squadron's Flare Force droned over the city, laying in their wake five lines of parachute-borne light. The green proximity Target Indicators of the Primary Blind Markers, aimed by H2S, burst on the city at the same moment. Those who were still above the ground in Darmstadt heard the flares burning. Some described a rustling sound, others a persistent hiss. The town seemed frozen in the still, icy glare. Then the light flak began to clatter angrily into the sky, the heavier 88s burst into their barrage. Somebody in the control bunker said flatly: 'Now it's us.'[2]

5 Group were not very impressed by Darmstadt's flak and searchlights. One pilot in his report described the light AA as 'meagre'. 83 Squadron assessed the heavy 88-mm fire as 'light to moderate'. The three 'Windfinder' aircraft, circling at 22,000 feet a few miles from the city with their special equipment, maintained reports to the Master Bomber on VHF, chattering a good deal too much according to the marking aircraft crews, straining to catch R/T instructions across the busy ether. The windspeed was forty-three knots, and Main Force were instructed to feed their bombsight computers accordingly. Flare Force I had scarcely begun illuminating when there was a crackled 'Tally-ho!' from one of 627's circling Mosquitoes, and the pilot swung in to mark the *Kavallerie Exerzierplatz*. Wing-Commander Woodroffe, the Master Bomber, orbited at a thousand feet. The red Target Indicators were perfectly positioned. Crews could see one German dummy green TI in the distance, perhaps ten miles westwards, and some decoy incendiaries burning furiously in a nearby wood. But none of these threatened to disturb the attack on a clear night with only the slightest haze.

Woodroffe ordered the rest of his marking pilots to back up the red TIs with greens, halted Flare Force II in the midst of their run at 2352 hrs, and a few moments later sent all the marking aircraft home. At 2356 hrs, he called in Main Force to bomb on their aiming lines as ordered, attacking by the red TIs if they could see them, by the greens if they could not. Two hours later, the Mosquitoes were back on the ground at Woodhall Spa. The Lancasters had no difficulties in bombing, but ran into nightfighter trouble as they turned away from Darmstadt. 5 Group lost twelve aircraft that night, including two crews from 97 Squadron. But those who came home described the operation without notable excitement or dismay. 'Should prove a very successful raid,' said Flying Officer Birdling of 83 Squadron at debriefing. 'Marking was done quickly and without a hitch. Opposition was slight.' 627 Squadron's report was brief and contented: 'Objective: Town centre, Darmstadt. All TIs were within 400 yards of the Marking Point. Main Force bombing was well-concentrated.' Squadron-Leader Twigge of 83 Squadron aaid: 'A quiet trip all round.'

The raid on Darmstadt lasted fifty-one minutes, from the fall of the first Target Indicator to the release of the last Mosquito incendiary load. In the cellars and shelters of the city, almost a hundred thousand people lay numbed by the continuous concussions, the dust swirling in through the ventilators, the roar of falling masonry all around them. The lighting system collapsed almost immediately, and as foundations trembled cellar-doors buckled, brickwork began to fall. The civil defence organization disintegrated as streets were blocked and bombs cut the vital cable links to the control centre on Hugelstrasse and the emergency control on lower Rheinstrasse. The firemen were without orders. The fire-watching centre behind the city church was itself ablaze. Gas, water and power mains were severed. In the first minutes of the attack, Darmstadt lost its identity as a coherent body of citizens, capable of mutual assistance. It became a splintered, blazing, smoking battlefield upon which a hundred thousand men, women and children each struggled to save themselves as best they might. This, of course, was precisely the purpose of saturation air attack on cities. But it was very rarely, even in this last year of the war, that the intention was as comprehensively fulfilled as on the night of 11 September in Darmstadt.

In the cellars, thousands of isolated clusters of humanity lay unmoving, limbs limp, stomachs shrunken by terror. The heat grew, and burning embers began to drift through the ventilators. Most people lay in silence, huddled with their private nightmare. But where Jacob Schutz sheltered a child cried endlessly through the attack as the walls shook: 'Jesus, my Jesus, Mercy, Mercy . . .' Schutz imagined the bombers above, strewing their loads upon Darmstadt like men sowing a field. A Dutchman who had been upstairs suddenly rushed into their cellar with his hair awry shouting, 'Everything, everything is burning!'

There was a dreadful crash, the walls shook, we heard masonry cracking and collapsing, and the crackle of flames [wrote Martha Gros]. Plaster began to fall and we all thought the ceiling would collapse . . . About thirty seconds later there was a second terrible explosion, the cellar-door flew open, and I saw, bathed in a brilliant light, the staircase to the cellar collapsing and a river of fire pouring down. I shouted: 'Let's get out!' but the Hauptmann gripped me: 'Stay here, they are still overhead.' At that moment, the house opposite was hit. The armoured plate in front of our cellar flew up in the air, and a tongue of fire about fifteen feet long shot through at us. Cupboards and other furniture burst and fell on to us. The terrible pressure hurled us against the wall. Now somebody shouted: 'Get out and hold hands!' With all his strength he pulled me out from under the wreckage, I dropped my cash box and pulled the others with me. We climbed through the hole leading to the back . . . More bombs were already falling into the garden. We crouched low, each of us beating out the small flames flickering on the clothes of the one in front. Phosphorus clung to the trees and dripped down on us . . . The heat was terrible. Burning people raced past like live torches, and I listened to their unforgettable final screams . . .

Gerhard Hartmann sat on a chair in a shelter crowded with his family's most precious furniture, a huge cupboard behind him 'rolling like a ship at every blast'. Carolin Schaefer clung to her two sons in the cellar of her home in Weiterstedtstrasse, the children burying their heads deeper in her breast at each explosion. Her husband was with the army on the western front. On most nights, they spent air-raid alarms in her father-in-law's strongly built cellar a few streets away, but tonight they had been unable to get there in time, so they were packed into the basement of their apartment building. They shared their refuge with an elderly couple and a girl with a baby, who cried continuously about the lack of bedclothes for her child. At last Frau Schaefer passed her sons to the woman, and ran upstairs to fetch some covers. She opened the door from the cellar to be met by a cascade of flame. She seized a sand bucket and threw it in a futile gesture into the blaze. Then there was another roar of explosives as a 4,000-lb bomb exploded nearby. She fled once more to the cellar empty-handed.

In the shelter where Karl Deppert lay near the main post office, the lights survived through the first stage of the attack. Then there was a single heavy explosion, and blackness descended. There was a choked cry from the next cellar: 'Break through – we're trapped.' The men scrambled to the jumble of brickwork and struggled in the glimmering torchlight to clear a hole. After a few minutes' fevered labour, dust-covered bodies began to crawl through the wreckage. A sudden strong draught of air brought behind them a rush of smoke and sparks. Somebody yelled: 'Get out! The town's in flames!' Deppert picked up his small son in his arms, seized his wife's hands and gave her the bag holding the most vital family papers and some bread, then stumbled up the steps into the night.

All around them, flames were roaring through houses, shops, offices. Timbers sagged, window-frames and doors gaped empty, furniture blazed furiously. The 40 per cent slaked-lime fire-proofing of roof timbers which had saved acres of Kassel in the great raid a year before could do nothing for Darmstadt. A paper factory crumbled and collapsed before the Depperts' eyes. They stood hesitating for a moment, uncertain which way to go for safety. They thought of the castle, then saw that upper Rhein-strasse, which led to it, was already an inferno. They began to run the other way, up Mathildenhohe. Their hair smouldered as embers fell upon their heads, and they brushed them away. A girl ran to them begging: 'Take me with you – I've just come from the pastry shop, and all the sugar is melting and no one dares to get out.' They linked arms to avoid falling among the debris, and fled through the spirals of fire and the corpses that already filled the streets.

Young Hanna Schnaebel crawled from the cellar beneath her family's little shop on Elizabethstrasse when the heat became un-bearable, into that of the house adjoining, and then on down the cellars of the street. She ran up the stairs of the last one, into the midst of a shop whose counters were already on fire. An un-known man forced open the door for them to escape, then she stood alone on the streets shouting for the rest of her family and their little shopgirl, Annie. She began to run, a wet blanket over her head. She saw people crowding for shelter into a little work-man's hut in the midst of the grass of the Palaisgarten. She ran to join them, and together they cowered panting and silent with their terror until someone shouted: 'The hut's on fire!' They staggered out, to find flames entirely encircling them, leaping towards the sky:

Suddenly I saw my mother. It was a miracle. We embraced, then we got to the wall of the Palaisgarten and crept beneath it. My blanket had been swept away. I lay half across her to shield her. Suddenly the bushes around us began to burn. We crawled to a big tree. I began to shake, to feel sick. Then I was sick, and I felt better. There was a momentary blast of icy air before the heat descended again. There was a gale of ashes as houses collapsed. No one spoke. All we could hear were the terrible screams for help from the cellars of the streets around us. But no one could move . . .

The first fatal misfortune for the people of Darmstadt after the departure of 5 Group that night was that an ammunition train in a siding near the central station began to burn. At intervals for the next hour, its cars exploded, convincing the terrified city that the bombardment was continuing either from aircraft above, or from delayed-action bombs, whose value Bomber Command had learnt from the Luftwaffe in the 1940 blitz on Britain. Thousands of Darmstadters lay motionless, apathetic in their cellars when their only hope of survival lay in flight. The last of 627's Mosquitoes had dumped its incendiaries more than half an hour before the fires of the *Todesfacher*, fuelled by the superlative tinder of the old town and the stiff breeze, combined to create a firestorm.

This was the terrible hurricane of flame and wind that had destroyed Hamburg, and which was to raze Dresden. As the fires leapt a mile into the sky, they sucked in cold air to bellow the blaze, sweeping from street to street in an irresistible rush of heat. Darmstadt was overwhelmed by a great roaring sound that induced deadly paralysis among the thousands in the shelters. They peered briefly out at the city, light as day amidst the flames, and lacked the will to step forth. So there, in their underground refuges, they died – whether of suffocation or by incineration it mattered little. The only people who lived that night were those who summoned the courage to fly.

Even among those who tried to escape, hundreds were sucked

into the fires by the force of the wind, a snowstorm of ashes whirling around their heads. By 2 a.m., a Force 10 gale was driving through Darmstadt, while at the heart of the fires temperatures reached an incredible 1,500, perhaps 2,000 degrees centigrade. No one knew with certainty which way to run for safety. After Hamburg, the big city streets had been everywhere adorned with arrows pointing the way to flight in a firestorm, but there were no such refinements in Darmstadt. Those who sought to carry their great bundles of possessions or pull their handcarts behind them were doomed. Many fell as they ran, and could not rise again. Their corpses sank into the asphalt as it melted, and were mummified long before morning. Jacob Schutz, the man in whose cellar a child had appealed for divine intervention, dipped his coat in the water tank in the shelter, then ran up the stairs and down the street, clutching it to his head. After a few minutes, he sank down to rest by a garden fence. Looking up past the flames, for a curiously tranquil moment he marvelled, like so many bomber crews, at the sight of the stars and the thin moon, crystal clear and wonderfully cool above Darmstadt's fires. Then he regained his composure, and ran back to the cellar.

I urged the others to move. Four women had already gone, led by another man. No one else would go. I went back to lie under a big advertising hoarding in the street. For perhaps fifteen minutes I stayed among the children there, trying to help to make them feel safe, wrapping them in blankets. Then I went to look for a better place for us. I was forced back again and again by the smoke and the flames. Then I found a wall in Heinrichstrasse where perhaps a hundred people were sheltering. When I returned to the hoarding, it was in flames. With one child in my arms and leading another by the hand, I took twenty people to the wall. I saw a few faces I knew: a husband and son who had lost his wife and daughter. A cow had wandered in from somewhere, and stood calmly among the people . . .

Schutz found his way to a nearby fountain, and threw himself into its blissful coolness. Then he filled his helmet with water, and carried it carefully back to the beleaguered survivors in Heinrichstrasse. They dipped their scarves and handkerchiefs into the water, and pressed them to their lips to deaden the terrible heat beating at their faces. Again and again Schutz made the journey to the fountain. At last, when all the group had been tended, in a moment of pity he went back once more for water for the cow. He met a friend who had recently given him two packets of precious tobacco. Now it lay in the abandoned embers of his house. They laughed absurdly about the tragic loss. Then they lay down to wait for the dawn. 'It was not death that was terrible that night,' said Schutz, 'but the fear of death – the whimpering, the shrieks, the screams. . .'

All over Darmstadt, men, women and children were being asphyxiated where they sheltered, slowly slipping away into unconsciousness. One cellar lay beneath a house that received a direct hit from a 'cookie'. Every inhabitant was killed instantly by blast except a single survivor, a chemist. He was found later with a razor in his hands. He had slit his own throat. Fifty people took refuge in one fountain, lying amidst the surrounding smoke and flame in a few inches of water beneath a great statue of Bismarck. In the morning, twelve survived. In a communal shelter beneath an apartment block in Rheinstrasse, a central-heating boiler burst, drowning sixty people whose bodies were discovered in the morning, perfectly cooked. Two pregnant women collapsed as they fled through the streets and gave premature birth. Their bodies and those of their infants were found incinerated where they lay. Corpses were everywhere, the horror increased by the remains of long-dead Darmstadters blasted from their graves by a 4,000-lb bomb that had exploded in a cemetery. Schutz saw the body of a young woman 'lying like a statue, her cold heels in their shoes stuck up in the air, her arms raised, parts of her face still visible, her mouth and teeth gaping open so that you did know whether she had been laughing or crying. . .'

There were the usual multi-coloured corpses, stained every shade of the rainbow by pyrotechnics. 'One fat air-raid warden lay, his little lantern beside him, his hands peacefully folded on his enormous chest. He looked like a sleeper replete after a banquet in some wonderful country.' Since the earliest raids on Germany's cities, there had been strict laws forbidding the storing of solid fuel in cellars, which had contributed to so many terrible fires in the wake of bombing. But in this as so much else, Darmstadt had been complacent. Many cellars were packed with wood, coal and coke. Now these fuelled their owners' funeral pyres.

The castle, with its priceless library, was blazing furiously. In

MAI

Railway Station

Kavallerie
Exerzierplatz

5 Group
line of approach
from ½ ml.
marking point

ESCHOLLBRUCKERSTRASSE

WOODLAND

HEIDELBERGER STRASSE

HEINRICHSTRASSE

Central
Market Square

Bomb loads fell outside this area

AGRICULTURAL

RESIDENTIAL

AREA

MARKERS

ROLSDORFER STRASSE

N

0   ¼   ½   ¾   ml
0   ½   1km

WOODLAND

Flugplatz
(Aerodrome)

Bomb loads fell outside this area

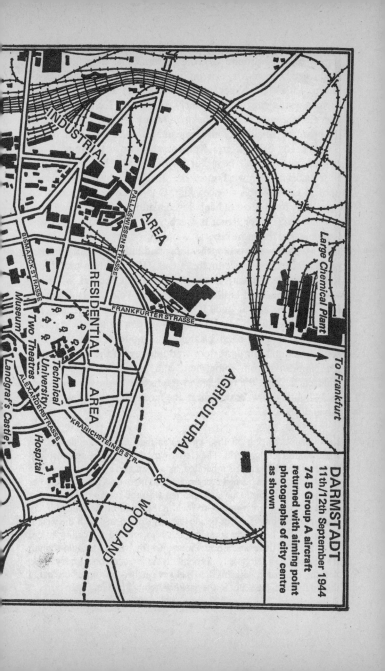

INDUSTRIAL AREA

Large Chemical Plant

To Frankfurt

PALLASWIESENSTRASSE

RESIDENTIAL AREA

FRANKFURTER STRASSE

BISMARCKSTRASSE

Museum

Two Theatres

Technical University

ALEXANDERSTRASSE

Hospital

Landgraf's Castle

KRANICHSTEINER STR.

AGRICULTURAL

WOODLAND

DARMSTADT
11th/12th September 1944
74 5 Group A aircraft
returned with aiming point
photographs of city centre
as shown

Mathildenplatz, seven stallions which had broken out of their stables careered around the ring of flame encircling the square, maddened with terror, striving in vain to break out. Seven of Darmstadt's eight Evangelical churches had already gone, and firemen were struggling hopelessly to save the Technical University, the museum and the theatres. Georg Dumas had to watch the priceless panelling of his home in Mathildenhöhe burn before his eyes. His beloved grand piano sank into the flaming floorboards 'with a final beautiful chord like the last trump'. His little dachshund crawled under the stove and whined hysterically until at last the fires silenced him. One of his neighbours cried ceaselessly for the loss of her beloved paintings, including a Tintoretto and a Salvator Rosa. It was beyond her to grasp what was happening to the entire city.

In Maria Tevini's cellar, the doors had burst from their frames after a near-miss early in the attack. Her eighteen-month-old son was hidden beneath a cushion in a laundry basket, while her 4½-year-old huddled beside her. She heard voices outside yelling to them to escape at once if they hoped to live. Clutching the children, she stumbled out into the garden to see their rabbit hutch and chicken-coop blazing, and molten debris from the roof of the museum next door smouldering on the grass. A fireman appeared from somewhere, and helped her to carry the children through the rubble and the flames to the Herrengarten park, fighting to walk upright in the face of the gale of wind and ash and heat.

I saw people tearing off their clothes as they caught fire, amidst the terrible music of the storm. The Herrengarten looked like an enormous medieval military camp, inhabited by the most ragged army in the world. Incendiaries burned everywhere, and no one was certain whether they were dangerous. Our eyes smarted with the smoke. I was given a handkerchief – a great prize – to soak in the water of the fountain. My son hung motionless, silent beside me. My arms ached with the weight of the baby. Then I met some women who soothed the children, and promised that there was a house intact nearby where we could shelter. It sounded like a fairytale . . . I found my father, sunk on a grassy bank, sleeping exhausted with his steel helmet perched on top of his hat. I should have laughed. But in the past few hours, I had forgotten how . . .

Ludwig, Prince of Hesse, was at his castle outside Darmstadt when he heard the assault on the city begin. He went outside and stood in the darkness, watching the sky lightening into a great red and yellow glow over the town. Too old for this war, he still possessed his army uniform from the last. Now, he went indoors and put it on, together with his helmet and jackboots. There was no petrol for the cars, so he helped his old coachman Helmuth to harness the horses to a cart. They loaded two bicycles in the back. Then with great fear in their hearts, they climbed aboard and Helmuth whipped the team towards the fires.

Darmstadt Castle was still burning as they approached, beside its grey walls a huge charred Wellingtonia, decapitated by blast. 'My only satisfaction was that the New Palace which I had sold to the Gestapo was utterly destroyed. It had always been a terrible thought to me that in cellars where my brother and I had played so happily as children, people were now tortured and imprisoned. . .' They moved among numbed survivors checking piles of corpses. One woman said, 'Is that father?' but her son shook his head: 'He was wearing different trousers.' The Prince helped an enormous old lady to clamber over a wall from the ruins of her house:

I told her to imagine that we were both a few years younger, and that I was a charming cavalier into whose arms it would be a pleasure to fall. The old lady instinctively wanted to go to the old cemetery, where she joined hundreds of people sitting amidst the graves on rescued sofas and mattresses, gazing hypnotized into the fires . . .

A Russian prison-camp at the edge of the town had been totally destroyed. 200 Italian internees sought to escape from the Concordia Hall in Waldstrasse through a narrow archway into the street. It collapsed upon them as they battered at the doors. The town treasury was gutted. A soldier on leave from the Russian front stood crying by the burning castle: 'I have never seen this,' he said. 'This is hell.' Else-Marie Ullrich was a sixteen-year-old lawyer's daughter who had been sheltering with her parents in the basement of the Dresdner Bank, above which they had an apartment. They were a cheerful, easygoing family who seldom bothered to go down to the shelters when there was an alarm, and joked about it when they did. After attempting to escape and finding flames and debris all around them, they made a conscious decision that it was better to suffocate than to burn. One woman who tried to flee was never seen again. The others sat in silence as the air thickened and grew stifling. Else-Marie's sister suddenly blurted out: 'Oh! I've found my lucky penny! It's all right, we're all going to be all right!' But water was pouring into the cellar from the wrecked boiler-room next door. They lay on the floor, gasping for the dwindling breaths of air. One by one they lost consciousness. They were very close to death when at the instigation of a bank employee, in the early hours of daylight, a gang of soldiers dug through the wreckage to free them. 'Many people struggled to help and gave unstintingly that night,' said Fraulein Ullrich. 'Others, who had much, offered nothing. We have forgotten neither kind.'

One of Darmstadt's principal tragedies that night was that no outside help could reach the city through the ruins and the flames until the firestorm was far beyond checking. There was an elaborate nationwide organization to support local town fire-brigades in crises such as this. There were fifty-three Luftwaffe fire-fighting battalions, and the men of the Mobile Reserve Service – part of the Fire Protection Police – were stationed at strategic points all over Germany to race down the *autobahns* to a city under attack. There were also relief columns which went to the assistance of devastated cities with personnel and equipment capable of providing 30,000 meals a day. All these organizations worked with efficiency and dedication until the last weeks of the war, but on the night of 11 September they could do nothing. By 3 a.m. the following morning, a great mass of vehicles and men from neighbouring towns and villages and from as far afield as Mannheim, Mainz and Frankfurt stood helpless on the *autobahn* that the Führer had opened himself almost exactly ten years before, gazing towards the tormented city. In Darmstadt itself, the fire service did its pathetic best. But they were without orders and short of petrol for their pumps. Scores of fire hydrants were blocked by rubble. Scores more were linked only to fractured mains.

In the Marienhospital in the midst of the city, doctors and nurses worked amidst the blast-broken window frames to do

384

what they could for thousands of terribly injured Darmstadters. The hospital's patients had been evacuated to the cellars when the attack began, and there in the candlelight they remained. Two babies were delivered in the basement even as 5 Group delivered their attack. Now, queues of adults and children sought treatment for eyes tormented by the smoke and fumes. The doctors worked by emergency lighting from batteries – mains power and water were gone. For scores of horribly burned casualties, there was nothing to be done but ease their dying. Nurses soaked their sheets in salad oil to calm the pain. Most had ended their sufferings by morning.

The firestorm died around 4 a.m. A yellow-grey light began to break over the city. Houses and public buildings still burned, but without the ferocity of the night. Prince Ludwig met a friend near the Inselstrasse who described how his old tutor, Professor Eugen Koser, had run headlong through the blazing darkness, cursing the rulers of Germany. People began to pick their way between the smoking buildings, through the melted asphalt of the streets to their houses, searching for life or property. The first terrible discoveries were made: cellars crammed with suffocated bodies – worse still, with amorphous heaps of melted and charred humanity. There were whole families whose remains could be removed in a laundry basket. Some bodies had shrunk to a quarter of life-size. Dr Fritz Kramer had been in France with the Kaiser's army thirty years before, 'yet this was worse than anything I had ever seen in Champagne'. There were blue corpses and purple corpses, black heaps of flesh and protruding bones. Kramer saw a man carrying a sack containing the heads of his entire family; the body of a girl lay on a pavement with one naked leg broken off beside her, 'looking like some obscene joint of cold meat'. Loose hands and legs, the head of a man buried in rubble to the chin with his eyes open and empty, lay in Ludwigstrasse. Bodies were already piled in the Palaisgarten. The bleak humour of disaster began to assert itself. 'Well, at least we have nothing to worry about now,' said Ernst Luckow's wife Wilma, 'because we have nothing left at all...'

Rudolf Vock ran into the Mayor of Wamboldt, one of the outlying suburbs of Darmstadt. 'Vock,' said the Mayor, 'you've got to get a hundred spades and go at once to the Waldfriedhof cemetery. There are a hundred Russian prisoners who've got to be started digging graves.' As he went, Vock passed a column of lorries in Rheinstrasse already piled with corpses. Two French prisoners who had been ordered to help the sisters at the Marien-hospital to remove their dead had been too nauseated by the stench to do the job, and now the nurses pushed a cartload of corpses to the Waldfriedhof themselves. At the cemetery, a silent crowd of men and women watched as the Russians unloaded the corpses, and began dumping them in hastily dug pits, each covered with a layer of quicklime. A squad of armed SS troopers guarded the prisoners. Police detectives were stripping bodies of valuables and placing them in envelopes, labelled if there was any clue to identity. Hour after hour, the lorryloads trundled in. They laboured on, without food or rest. A gang of Gestapo prisoners were brought to reinforce the Russians, and that after-noon 5,000 men of the Wehrmacht moved into the city to support relief operations.

In four years of bombing, Germany had evolved a detailed procedure for dealing with the unspeakable realities of mass death. In the wake of the great raid on Kassel in 1943, the local Police President had circulated a long list of suggestions that he believed other cities might find helpful: protective overalls, rubber gloves, goggles and disinfectants were essential for hand-ling corpses; supplies of alcohol, candles, tobacco and torch batteries should be stockpiled for use in the first days after the raids; as many witnesses as possible should be brought to central collecting points to assist with identification of bodies. Identifica-tion teams should be equipped with shears and bolt-cutters for removing jewellery. It was useful to print in advance supplies of corpse-registers, corpse-cards and pro formas for individual personal descriptions, and to prepare supplies of envelopes for valuables. Bodies were best labelled in pencil, for ink ran in the rain. Dismembered corpses should be recovered whenever possi-ble, to avoid double-counting of loose limbs if they became separ-ated. The Darmstadt authorities, therefore, had a useful body of case-history to draw upon. They needed it all in the days that followed.

At lunchtime on 12 September, Wilhemine Wollschrager hurried into the city from her suburban home to look for her grandparents, equipped with bread and a thermos of tea. She made her way down the narrow avenue through the rubble on Rheinstrasse, a moistened pad over her mouth amidst the lingering smoke. She was awed by the tramlines hung crazily over the road, the stream of empty-eyed refugees fleeing down the street against her, seeking the East Station. On the corners, little knots of blackened firemen and rescue workers sat exhausted, while others still laboured amidst the debris. At last she reached her grandparents' house.

Thank God! The cellar windows were open. In my excitement I ran forward calling, 'Grandmother! Grandfather!' Then I looked through the windows and saw small flames licking at the floor. Somebody pulled me back, shouting that the building could collapse at any minute. I rushed through the yard to the neighbour's house next door. I saw him lying dead in the yard, his bicycle and briefcase against a tree beside him. I never saw my grandparents again.

'There was a deathly silence in the town, ghostly and chilling,' wrote Martha Gros, the doctor's wife who had fled from her blazing cellar at the height of the attack.

It was even more unreal than the previous night. Not a bird, not a green tree, no people, nothing but corpses . . . We climbed over the wreckage into the garden and proceeded to the burnt-out cellar. The ashes were almost two feet deep. I found the place where I had dropped our cash box, picked it up and opened it. The 1,000 Reichsmark note which I had saved for emergencies was a heap of ashes. The little boxes of jewellery had been burned. The best piece, a large emerald, had cracked. Around our safe lay large lumps of melted silver, and in the wine-racks there were melted bottles hanging in bizarre long ribbons. For this to have happened the temperature must have been something like 1,700 degrees.

'One was afraid of losing one's reason,' said Jacob Schutz:

People from the rescue service were collapsing into nervous hysteria. It was a privilege to have a coffin, or even the means to make one oneself. Most of the bodies were put on a lorry or wheeled in little handcarts to the mass graves in the cemetery.

The hospitals were crammed. All preparations counted for nothing. You could travel without a ticket on the train, bicycle on the pavements. There were no windows in the trains, no schools, no doctors, no post, no telephone. One felt completely cut off from the world. To meet a friend who survived was a wonderful experience. There was no water, no light, no fire. A candle was of priceless value. Little children and old people collected wood from the ruins for cooking. Every family dug its own latrine in the garden. There was no more absolute ownership of anything. Many people moaned about their losses, yet others seemed almost relieved by their freedom from possessions. This had suddenly become a city of proletarians . . .

Half-dressed people struggled to the stations in the great surge of anxiety to flee. Loudspeaker cars toured the city broadcasting evacuation instructions. The relatives of pregnant women who had given birth under the strain of the night sought desperately for a doctor or a midwife. Carolin Schaefer had covered the eyes of her children as they fled through the corpse-strewn streets 'because I felt that if the boys were to see this, they could never grow up to lead happy lives'. But by dawn she was compelled to abandon her efforts to save them from the sight of horror, because it was everywhere. A friend passed her in the streets pushing a bicycle, the melted rubber on its rims all that was left of the tyres. On the luggage rack was a soap box. Silently she embraced me. Then she began to cry, pointing to the box. "In there is my husband,' she said. Frau Schaefer's father and sister heard on the radio about the fate of Darmstadt, and travelled the breadth of Germany from their home in Chemnitz to look for her. Her husband was granted five days' leave from the front, and reached home in a Wehrmacht staff car: 'When he arrived, he said that nothing he had seen on the battlefield had ever pained him so much.' She found her father-in-law in the crowded ward of a city hospital, blind and terribly injured, 'a wreck of a man looking expressionlessly through his bandages'. He had been found wandering, dazed and unseeing, through the streets.

Chalk scribbles on buildings were the only indication of the fate of thousands of Darmstadters. 'Where is Doctor Kutz?' Jacob Schutz saw scrawled on the broken wall of a house. Another hand had written briefly beneath: 'DEAD'. Men, women, children wandered the streets, searching for lost relatives and friends, struggling to save a few charred possessions from the ruins of their houses. Others were more fortunate. Passers-by were enraged to see a working-party of prisoners from the jail, under guard and in prison-striped uniform, labouring to rescue hundreds of cases of wine from the cellar of the local *Kreisleiter*'s house.

The troops who cleared the city of its corpses were openly plied with alcohol to enable them to complete their ghastly task. The living stumbled through the streets pushing handcarts laden with luggage, or piled their remaining sticks of furniture until some vehicle could break through to collect them. People of every age and background pillaged ruthlessly what they needed to survive. When Martha Gros miraculously found a coffin for one of her relations, she was compelled to chain it to the railings outside the house until they could carry out the burial.

Soup kitchens had been established at strategic points, and businessmen and lawyers, shopkeepers and industrialists learnt to commute in a new pattern, from canteen to cellar, cellar to canteen. Many left the city altogether, some walking miles past the crowds of awed spectators who had come from scores of surrounding villages to gaze on Darmstadt. 'And so we went like gypsies out of our dear, burning town,' wrote Hanna Schnaebel. Thousands of people clogged the railway station, where, by the afternoon of the 12th, packed refugee trains were running out of the city. Vast numbers of postcards were distributed, supposedly to let distant relatives know the fate of their families, but although they were filled in and collected for postage, none seemed to reach its destination.

At lunchtime on 13 September, to the stupefied disbelief of the survivors amidst the ruins, there was an air-raid warning. A great cry went up: 'They're coming again!' Carolin Schaefer saw the shattered faces around her in the street gaze appalled into the sky. Voices shouted in horror: 'Why have they come back?' 'What do they want?' 'There's nothing for them here.' High in the clear sky, they saw the glinting wings of a formation of the 8th Air Force's Flying Fortresses. The black puffs of flak began to burst around them. Moments later, the earth shook once more with explosions as people huddled with their hands to their ears, cowering amidst the rubble of the city, for only a few surviving deep shelters cut into rock were still of value to the people of Darmstadt.

The Americans had come for the marshalling yards, but when

they bombed they were also able to destroy a pocket of housing on the north side of the city that had somehow survived the attack thirty-six hours before. Fritz Kramer noted the ironic case of a man who had returned to Darmstadt on compassionate leave from the front to see his mother after the night raid. He was killed when the American bombs hit the railway station.

Psychologists who studied the effects of bombing on morale after the war concluded that it was a terrible experience to be bombed, but that once one had been bombed once, successive treatments had less and less rewarding impact on morale. So it seemed in Darmstadt. A passivity, an apathy gripped the city, as if its people were no longer capable of feeling. Overnight they had become hardened, even brutalized. Jacob Schutz met a man who had lost a son, but simply said: 'I thank God I have two more of them.' Another man was bemoaning the loss of his wife and child to an officer, who interrupted him with a shrug: 'In that cellar over there you'll find a family of ten who all caught it together.' When it rained, the hastily piled earth slipped away from some of the mass graves, exposing the bodies once more. Fungus grew upon them. But it was days before anyone could be troubled to bury them again.

Bomber Command's report of the attack on Darmstadt was no more dramatic than that on scores of other targets, past and future: 'Photographic Reconnaissance Unit cover shows industrial part not covered, but remaining part shows large areas of complete devastation. Damage Assessment shows Rohm & Haas severely damaged; E. Merck – slight damage; diesel engine works has had nine buildings gutted.' On the night of 11–12 September Bomber Command lost sixteen aircraft, including the twelve from the Darmstadt force. A *Serrate* Mosquito claimed to have shot down an Me110 north of Darmstadt. An Intruder Mosquito claimed a Ju88 damaged. A surprisingly large number of Bomber Command aircraft – forty-three in all – claimed to have seen German fighters at some point before, during or after the attack on Darmstadt. 218 of the 236 aircraft dispatched claimed to have bombed the target.

It was not until the end of the war that a scientific attempt could be made to assess the achievement of 5 Group's attack on Darmstadt, by the USSBS. Even this cannot be examined without emphasizing the degree of guesswork and statistical projection that went into the Survey's work, coupled with an enthusiasm to prove that USAAF 'precision' had been more effective than British 'area' bombing. But the USSBS 'Detailed Study of the effects of the Bomber Command raid on Darmstadt' is the only collated evidence that exists, and thus it should be quoted:

The area raid of 11/12 September came when industrial employment had already started on a general decline [stated the report]. The raid accelerated this decline. Its principal disruptive impact on the city's labour was felt in small commercial enterprises, who lost some 50 per cent of their workers. The most disruptive factor in the labour situation was not the air raids, but the withdrawal of German men into the army . . . Industrial labour remained adequate, although a shortage of skilled labour was generally acknowledged . . .

Disruption of essential services such as gas, water, electricity and local transportation was not sufficient to interfere with production. The effects on industrial production of the 11/12 September raid were sufficient to have caused an overall production loss to the city of one month. The loss in the chemical industry was 1.4 months, and 1.1 months for the iron and metal production and fabrication industries. However, in a period of general economic decline this loss seems to be overstated in that it does not give proper weight to the downward trend which would have continued even without the raid. Therefore, by means of another computation . . . it was estimated that the overall loss can more fairly be stated as 0.4 months, i.e. 0.5 months for the chemical industry and 0.4 months for iron, metal production and fabrication.

Without accepting the detailed statistical conclusions of the report, it is possible to state that the raid of 11–12 September devastated the city of Darmstadt without seriously damaging the war production which theoretically prompted the bomber attack. Darmstadt's output fell from 8.3 million Reichsmarks in August 1944 to 3.7 in September, but then rose to 5.2 in October. In November it was still 4.5 million, despite the general national industrial decline, and in December 4.3. Thereafter, it collapsed completely in the wake of a further massive raid. But in the words of the USSBS: 'The production loss for the area raid of 11–12 September 1944 was remarkably small for a city experiencing a 49 per cent housing destruction.' During 5 Group's attack, the left-hand axis of attack had achieved insufficient weight and concentration. While the old town had been fatally hit, the industrial north-west had escaped remarkably lightly, even after the low-level Mosquito attacks. It was a characteristic shortcoming of Bomber Command area raids: city centres burned readily, but the overwhelming weight of industry was in the suburbs, which were far harder to hit and destroy.

Yet there could be no doubt of the effective impact of the 5 Group attack on Darmstadt as a society. Where the abortive 25 August attack had destroyed only 327 buildings, that of 11 September totally destroyed 4,064 out of 8,401 dwellings. A further 462 had been rendered uninhabitable. 570 of the town's 888 shops had ceased to exist. The old town had simply been erased from the face of the earth. The prison and the post office were the only notable buildings to survive. From Lord Cherwell's point of view, the operation had been a major success: 70,000 people had been 'de-housed'. 49,200 fled the city as refugees. In 1939 Darmstadt and its outlying villages mustered a population of 115,211 people. By December 1943 conscription had reduced the total to 98,440. By 1 March 1945, there were only 51,750 people on the city's official ration strength. The remainder had joined the vast army of refugees, 'displaced persons' and corpses. What was done to Darmstadt – virtually unnoticed by the Allied leadership, far less the public of Britain and America – vastly exceeded the devastation in Cologne created by the trumpeted 1,000 Raid of 1942.

It will never be certain exactly how many people died on the night of 11 September, because so many bodies were never identified and so many records were destroyed. Contemporary Nazi statistics showed that of every 100 deaths, 15 were caused by blast, 15 by incineration, 70 by suffocation. 181 women and children died for every 100 men. One in five of the dead was a child under the age of sixteen.

The best estimate is that 12,300 Darmstadters were killed in air raids up to the end of the war, the overwhelming majority of them on the night of 11 September. In the immediate wake of the attack, the authorities counted 6,049 confirmed dead, 4,502 missing and 3,749 wounded. When the figure of those confirmed dead had reached 8,433, the count broke down as follows:

936 military
1,766 civilian males

2,742 civilian females
2,129 children
  368 prisoners of war
  492 foreign labourers

It would be absurd to imagine Darmstadt as a town somehow possessed of a unique innocence, its people free of the taint of Nazism, its factories producing cuckoo clocks or cigarette boxes. Darmstadt was a provincial centre no more and no less devoted to supporting Hitler's war effort than scores of others. It was unusual only in that it was so little prepared to save and defend itself, and that its contribution to the war was slight in proportion to the Allied resources deployed to destroy it. What happened to Darmstadt was merely a supremely efficient demonstration of the kind of destruction meted out to so many towns for so long by the armed forces of Germany. The horrific tales of Darmstadters' experiences in September 1944 were only a later reflection of those of millions of Poles, Frenchmen, Dutchmen, Englishmen and Russians since 1939. For Bomber Command, it had now become possible to administer such blows almost nightly to the cities of Germany. They would do so until the last month of the war.

The American 8th Air Force visited Darmstadt once more, on 19 September, just a week after Bomber Command. They delivered a precision attack on the Merck works, with considerable effect on production and further devastation of the pockets of buildings still standing around them. It might have seemed impossible that by then there was anything left to destroy in the city, but on 12 December the B-17s came once more – 446 of them, delivering 1,421 tons of explosives to the industrial area on the north-west of the town. The Allied armies then inherited the ruins.

A friend of Jacob Schutz, a very old man, wrote to him after the destruction of Darmstadt:

At the turn of the century, I came through Germany's towns, and each one had its own soul and its own face. Shortly before the war I came through the same towns, and it seemed that their souls were gone, as if they were dead within themselves.

Now, as I walk through the ruins of these same towns, I am overcome by the terrible awareness that they have fulfilled the promise that was made before the war. Instead of living corpses, they have become truly dead ones.

14 Saturation, 1944–45

You would think the fury of aerial bombardment
Would rouse God to relent; the infinite spaces
Are still silent. He looks on shock-pried faces
History, even, does not know what is meant

Richard Eberhart

In the last phase of the war, between October 1944 and May 1945, the Allied strategic bomber forces played a dominant part in bringing the German economy to the point of collapse. Against only ineffectual resistance from the Luftwaffe, they attacked Germany by day and night on an unprecedented scale. Bomber Command alone dropped more bombs in the last quarter of 1944 than in the whole of 1943. The air forces' destruction of Germany's oil resources was chiefly responsible for the breakdown of the Ardennes offensive at the end of 1944, and must have hastened the end of the war at least by several weeks. The bomber attack on German rail and water communications was choking industry to death by the last weeks of 1944. However, it is more difficult to argue that the Transport Plan had a decisive effect, since although munitions production was doomed to extinction, the German armies continued to possess tolerable supplies of arms and ammunition almost until their capitulation.

The airmen's misfortune was that their triumphs came too late, in the context of the advance of the Allied armies across Germany, to be accepted as a decisive contribution to victory. By September 1944, with a degree of assistance from Bomber Command, the USAAF had brought German oil production almost to the point of extinction. Aviation spirit production, for instance, had fallen from 156,000 tons in May to 54,000 in June, 34,700 in July, 17,000 in August and 10,000 in September, measured against Luftwaffe consumption of 165,000 tons in April. Pilot training had all but ceased; the Luftwaffe could not operate the aircraft Speer was still producing with such huge exertions. Total supplies of all fuel products had fallen to less than a third of their January levels. The German armies were largely driven back on horse-drawn transport; diesel trucks towed petrol vehicles; whole tank formations were immobilized; tactical battlefield mobility was being seriously affected, and stockpiles were rapidly becoming exhausted.

But with the onset of winter weather that often made precision bombing impossible, and the herculean efforts of Speer's repair squads at the oil plants, the Allied bombing offensive lost momentum. Aviation spirit production rose to 21,000 tons in October, 39,500 tons in November, and 24,500 tons in December. Germany was able to husband the slender reserves with which it became possible to mount the Ardennes offensive. Thereafter, the bombing pressure became finally unbearable, and by the end of January 1945 the Allied victory over Germany's oil resources was all but complete. But the airmen had missed their moment. They were never to receive undisputed credit for an achievement that came so late. There has been a continuing controversy about responsibility for the failure to press home their assault in the summer and autumn of 1944, when a marginal increase in bombing effort might have tipped the balance to make the oil campaign decisive and to end the Second World War in Europe months earlier.

In previous chapters, it has been suggested that in the spring of 1941 the airmen's credibility was too low for Spaatz's enthusiasm for the Oil Plan to be wholeheartedly accepted by the Allied High Command. By autumn, however, there was widespread understanding of the success and potential of the attack on fuel. How was it, then, that against the USAAF's overall wartime effort of 131,000 tons of bombs dropped on oil targets, Bomber Command with its greater lifting capacity contributed only 94,000 tons, most of this in the last stages of the campaign?

The answer lies in the decisive breakdown of the RAF's internal command structure which took place in the winter of 1944, when the Chief of Air Staff, Sir Charles Portal, finally showed himself unable to exercise authority over Sir Arthur Harris. At the Quebec *Octagon* conference in September 1944, Portal proposed to the Combined Chiefs of Staff that the strategic air forces should be removed from control of SHAEF now that the Allied armies were fully established in Europe. The Americans demured – they thought that Eisenhower and Tedder had directed the bombing effort admirably since June. They also believed, according to their official historians, that behind the smokescreen of British arguments about effective command, 'perhaps the crucial issue was one not mentioned in the official British proposals: a desire of the Air Ministry to re-establish its control of Harris's Bomber Command'.[1] That September, the Chiefs of Staff still envisaged the European war coasting to a reasonably smooth conclusion by Christmas. The British Air Staff were acutely conscious that Bomber Command had thus far failed to make the 'decisive' contribution to victory that they sought. They sensed time running out on them. Portal had become completely committed to the attack on German oil. He clearly believed that by re-establishing his control of Bomber Command, it might yet be possible for the RAF to play a leading part in the conclusive attack of the war on German oil supplies. Air Ministry papers of 1944 refer repeatedly to the danger that unless Bomber Command addressed itself urgently to the oil attack, the 8th Air Force would complete the task single-handed. The British would be left to rest on the withered laurels of their area campaign against the cities.

Portal finally got his way in Quebec, perhaps not least because the Americans had already transferred their chief attentions to the Pacific. The British, with their Bomber Command, were to have a last opportunity to make an independent contribution to the defeat of Germany. On 14 September, Arnold and Portal issued a new joint directive on behalf of the Chiefs of Staff to Sir Norman Bottomley, Deputy Chief of Air Staff, and General Spaatz, the USAAF's commander in Europe. Control of the strategic-bomber forces was henceforth to revert from SHAEF to Bottomley and Spaatz as representatives of Portal and Arnold. The priority of *Pointblank* 'to bring about the progressive destruction and dislocation of the German military, industrial, and economic systems' was reasserted, save only that the Luftwaffe had ceased to be an important consideration. Support of the armies remained a major responsibility, and 'important industrial areas' were to be attacked 'when weather or tactical conditions are unsuitable for operations against specific primary objectives'.

It was a clumsy command arrangement, which placed Portal at one remove from his notoriously wayward C-in-C. But the directive issued by Bottomley on Spaatz to Bomber Command and 8th Air Force on 25 September, translating the Chiefs of Staff's instructions into formal orders, ranks among the most emphatic and specific of the war. There were no more wordy equivocations: oil became sole First Priority target, with transport links, tank and vehicle production as Second Priority. Perfunctory mention was also made of area targets, in the same terms as in the directive of 14 September.

The new orders were a disappointment to Sir Arthur Tedder, Deputy Supreme Commander at SHAEF. He had fought a fierce battle to concentrate the air attack on Germany's rail and water transport links. Tedder had been persuaded by the evidence presented to him by Professor Zuckerman and others that what the pre-*Overlord* bombing had achieved in breaking French transport links could now be repeated against those of Germany, producing speedy and dramatic paralysis reaching forward to the battlefield. But to be effective, Tedder's Transport Plan called for the concentration of bomber effort. This was not to happen. During the winter of 1944 the 8th Air Force poured bombs on to marshalling yards and communication centres by H2X when the weather was too bad for oil targets, but in reality this amounted to nothing more than American participation in the area-bombing campaign on the cities. Germany's rail and water links were indeed hit with devastating effect by all the strategic air forces, including a series of notable precision attacks by Bomber Command, three of which breached the Dortmund–Ems canal. But it was only in March 1945 that the effects of transport bombing became terminal for German industry. Most of the senior airmen and the members of the Combined Strategic Targets Committee had become wholehearted advocates of the oil offensive. It was their view that prevailed in Quebec, and to their purposes that the 8th Air Force addressed its dedicated efforts in the winter of 1944.

Awareness seems only to have grown slowly on Sir Charles Portal, back in London, that Bomber Command was contributing less than its utmost energies to fulfilling the September directive. As Arnhem was fought and lost and the Allied ground offensive slithered into the tragic winter stalemate, Harris's aircraft were hitting again and again at Germany's cities. In the last three months of 1944, the C-in-C waged his last and greatest Battle of the Ruhr, with complete and terrible success within his chosen compass. 14,254 sorties were dispatched to the great industrial centres at which he had hammered for so long – Duisburg, Essen, Cologne, Düsseldorf and their lesser brethren. 60,830 tons of bombs were dropped – 85 per cent high-explosive now, for almost anything that would burn in these towns had long since gone to Harris's bonfires. Only 136 aircraft were lost. The transmitting stations for *Oboe* advanced into Europe with the armies, vastly extending the range of accurately-guided marking. With the decline in the defences, accuracy and concentration rose among the great bomber force of more than a thousand 'heavies' which could now set forth nightly. With the fall in casualties, aircrew experience and competence rose.

Yet in October, 6 per cent of Harris's effort was directed against oil targets, less than in June. Between July and September 1944, 11 per cent of Bomber Command's sorties were dispatched to oil plants, 20 per cent to cities. Between October and December, 14 per cent went to oil, 58 per cent to the cities. It was impossible to believe that Harris was applying himself to the September directive. He had merely returned to the great area-bombing campaign precisely where he had left it in April, despite the almost unanimous conviction of the Air Staff that the policy had long been overtaken by events. Harris now embarked on a correspondence with Portal in defence of his convictions and operations, in the course of which the Chief of Air Staff first requested, then demanded, and at last pleaded with Harris to obey the orders that he had been given.

Harris fired his opening salvo in this last great bombing controversy of the war on 1 November 1944. In a letter to Portal, he violently protested the range of demands on his forces, the 'number of cooks now engaged in stirring the broth'. The Admiralty and the ball-bearing experts were tunnelling at his resources again, 'and even the nearly defunct SOE* has raised its bloody head and produced what I hope is now its final death rattle'.

In the past eighteen months, Bomber Command has virtually destroyed forty-five out of the leading sixty German cities. In spite of invasion diversions we have so far managed to keep up and even to exceed our average of two and a half cities devastated a month . . . There are not many industrial centres of population now left intact. Are we going to abandon this vast task, which the Germans themselves have long admitted to be their worst headache, just as it nears completion?

To complete his great design, said Harris, all that was required was the destruction of Magdeburg, Halle, Leipzig, Dresden, Chemnitz, Nuremberg, Munich, Coblenz, Karlsruhe and the surviving areas of Berlin and Hanover. Portal replied on 5 November: 'At the risk of your dubbing me "another panacea merchant", I believe the air offensive against oil gives us by far the best hope of complete victory in the next few months. . .' The next day, Harris dispatched a long answer in which he expressed his agreement about the importance of the oil plan, and offered tactical justification for the launching of great raids on Cologne and Bochum, which had been questioned by Portal. But, on the 12th, Portal returned to the fray:

You refer to a plan for the destruction of the sixty leading German cities, and to your efforts to keep up with, and even to exceed, your average of two and a half such cities devastated each month; I know that you have long felt such a plan to be the most effective way of bringing about the collapse of Germany. Knowing this, I have, I must confess, at times wondered whether the magnetism of the remaining German cities has not in the past tended as much to deflect our bombers from their primary objectives as the tactical and weather difficulties which you described so fully in your letter of 1 November. I would like you to reassure me that this is not so. If I knew you to be as whole-hearted in the attack on oil as in the past you have been in the matter of attacking cities, I would have little to worry about . . .

In November the weight of bombs delivered against oil targets increased to 24.6 per cent of all Bomber Command effort, and even outstripped the 8th Air Force's tonnage at the end of the month. But by 12 December, Harris was once more writing to

---

*SOE: Special Operations Executive, for whom Harris reluctantly provided aircraft from his Special Duties squadrons to parachute arms and agents into occupied Europe.

Portal to declare his renewed scepticism about the value of the oil offensive. 'The MEW experts have never failed to overstate their case on "panaceas". . . The oil plan has already displayed similar symptoms.' Portal replied on 22 December that he was 'profoundly disappointed that you still appear to feel that the oil plan is just another "panacea". . . Naturally, while you hold this view you will be unable to put your heart into the attack on oil.' Harris replied on 28 December.:

It has always been my custom to leave no stone unturned to get my views across, but when the decision is made I carry it out to the utmost and to the best of my ability. I am sorry that you should doubt this, and surprised indeed if you can point to any precedent in support of your statement. I can certainly quote precedent in the opposite sense.

This was truculence of a very high order, even by the standards of Sir Arthur Harris. Yet instead of seeking now to exert his authority, Portal chose to try to continue a rational debate with his C-in-C about the merits of razing cities: 'While area bombing, if it could have been continued long enough and in sufficient weight, might in the end have forced the enemy to capitulate,' he wrote on 8 January 1945, 'his counter-measures would have prevented us from maintaining such a policy to the decisive point.'

But for the favourable air situation created by the Americans, said Portal, 'it is possible that the night blitzing of German cities would by now have been too costly to sustain upon a heavy scale'. Here was a remarkable admission from the British Chief of Air Staff – that it was only the success of American air policy which had spared that of Britain from visible and humiliating defeat. Not surprisingly, Harris totally rejected Portal's criticism of the area campaign. He now asserted flatly that he had no faith in selective bombing, 'and none whatever in this present oil policy'.

Then he threw down the glove.

I will not willingly lay myself open again to the charge that the lack of success of a policy which I have declared at the outset . . . not to contain the seeds of success is, after the event, due to my not having tried. That situation is simply one of heads I lose, tails you win, and it is an intolerable situation . . . I therefore ask you to consider whether it is best for the prosecution of the war and the success of our arms, which alone matters, that I should remain in this situation . . .

In their judgement on the C-in-C of Bomber Command, the British official historians wrote:

Sir Arthur Harris made a habit of seeing only one side of a question and then of exaggerating it. He had a tendency to confuse advice with interference, criticism with sabotage and evidence with propaganda. He resisted innovations and was seldom open to persuasion. He was sceptical of the Air Staff in general, and of many officers who served upon it he was openly contemptuous. Seeing all issues in terms of black and white, he was impatient of any other possibility, and having taken upon himself tremendous responsibilities, he expected similar powers to be conferred.[2]

Harris saw his own role in the ultimate Trenchardian sense, as the independent director of a campaign that he was entitled to wage in his own way for as long as he possessed the confidence of his superiors. He had now made it brutally apparent that if Bomber Command was to advance from an area force to a precision one, he himself must be sacked. The moment of truth had come for Portal.

Yet in these last months of the war, how could the British public be reconciled to the dismissal of 'Bomber 'Harris, whom Press, newsreel and radio publicity had built into one of the most celebrated British leaders of the war? It has been often and emphatically argued above that the great difficulty throughout the bomber offensive was to find sensibly defined and generally acceptable criteria by which success or failure might be measured. Even after the war, it was to prove difficult to do so. For what specific defeat was Harris now to be sacked? It was unthinkable to reveal the nature, far less the course, of the dissension between the Chief of Air Staff and his C-in-C.

In all this it is important to stress what was at stake. No one familiar with the tactical and weather problems could have expected Bomber Command's aircraft to maintain an unbroken offensive against Germany's oil plants – the Americans failed to do so, despite their total commitment to the policy. Throughout the winter, the Allied armies were pressing their own urgent and almost compulsory demands on the strategic bomber force. There were targets to be attacked at the behest of the Admiralty, alarmed by a late surge in U-boat activity, and at the urging of the politicians with their own preoccupations. Tedder himself had pressed for a concentrated attack on the Ruhr in October, the *Hurricane* plan. But having made allowances for all these elements, there were still many mornings when Harris sat at his desk confronted with the long list of targets of every kind, together with a weather forecast that – as usual throughout the war – made the C-in-C's decision a matter of the most open judgement. And again and again, Harris came down in favour of attacking a city rather than oil plants. He sincerely believed that the use of massed bomber forces against oil installations was a waste of available effort.

The difference between the actual and potential effort Bomber Command concentrated on oil targets may have been only a matter of ten or twenty thousand sorties. But it is essential to reiterate what dramatic consequences might have stemmed from a real determination by Harris to put everything into oil, and even fractionally to increase Bomber Command's contribution: 'By the narrowest of margins, the strategic air offensive failed to smash Germany's economy by this one method of attack,' wrote the economist Professor Milward.[3] 'The most successful operation of the entire Allied strategical air warfare was against Germany's fuel supply,' wrote Galland of the Luftwaffe. 'Looking back, it is difficult to understand why the Allies started this undertaking so late. . .'[4] 'Thus the Allies threw away success when it was already in their hands,' wrote Speer, of the slackening of the oil offensive as far back as the summer of 1944. 'Had they continued the attacks of March and April with the same energy, we would quickly have been at our last gasp.'[5]

Speer testifies that when Bomber Command did attack oil plants, the larger British bombs caused greater damage than those of the 8th Air Force. But beyond Harris's underlying contempt for the oil plan, High Wycombe also suffered grievously in the winter of 1944 from the perennial difficulty of damage assessment. Again and again oil plants were judged destroyed when Speer's extraordinarily effective and courageous repair squads proved able to restore some level of production. 18.9 per cent of the RAF's bombs dropped on oil plants failed to explode. The winter weather hampered effective photographic reconnaissance, just as during the Battle of Berlin a year before. When pictures did become available, Harris personally studied them, and often drew unwarrantably sanguine conclusions.

Nor was his lack of perspective confined to oil. A senior officer who attended the regular air meetings at SHAEF in 1944–5 has described Harris's remorseless jibes at the Allied armies on the ground. One morning he detailed his plans for a bombing strike against Walcheren island, ordered by SHAEF to pave the way for a massive ground attack. 'When the bombing is over,' he concluded, with a scornful glance at the battery of generals deployed around the table, 'I shall send my batman to occupy Walcheren.' Yet for all his braggadocio, when the bombing was over, the taking of Walcheren cost the Allies some of the hardest fighting of the war.

In the last quarter of 1944, 14 per cent of Harris's effort fell on oil targets against 53 per cent on cities, 15 per cent on transport targets, 13 per cent on army-support operations, 5 per cent on naval targets such as U-boat and E-boat pens. Between January and May 1945, 26 per cent of Harris's effort was directed towards oil, 37 per cent against cities. The cost of his stubbornness to the Allied war effort at this last stage was almost certainly grievous. The Oil Plan will be remembered by history as one of the Allies' great missed opportunities. Harris himself said thirty years later:[6]

The only serious row I ever had with Portal was about the Oil Plan. I was against putting everything into oil. It was using a sledgehammer to crack a nut. I remember Portal ringing me up, the only time in the war that he lost his temper with me. I simply told him that if he didn't want me, I was quite prepared to go.

Long after the war, Portal sought to argue that his dispute with Harris had been grossly inflated.

Harris's offer of his resignation (by no means the only one I had from him) was not, I knew, intended seriously, but was made in a moment of exasperation [he wrote in 1959[7]]. His good qualities as a commander far outweighed his defects, and it would have been monstrously unjust to him and his command to have tried to have him replaced on the ground that while assuring me of his intention to carry out his orders, he persisted in trying to convince me that different orders would have produced better results.

It is impossible to accept this view. Portal in his own wartime correspondence made it abundantly clear that he was not satisfied that Harris was wholeheartedly seeking to carry out his orders. The issue at stake was one of profound significance for the conduct of the war. The evidence is clear that Harris never conformed single-mindedly to his instructions, and the margin by which he failed to do so may have been decisive.

But the simple fact was that at the end of 1944, Harris enjoyed far wider fame and greater public prestige than Portal, and knew it. He believed, rightly or wrongly, that he could count on the support of the Prime Minister. He was certain of his own rightness. He inspired considerable open and tacit admiration for pursuing a defiantly British policy at a moment when American dominance of the Alliance was everywhere being made painfully apparent: 'By 1945 he was one of the very few senior British officers who seemed able to ignore, let alone to deny the American predominance in the conduct of grand strategy.'[8] In those last months of the European war, it seemed to Portal that the uproar that would have surrounded Harris's removal was not justified by the strategic benefits that would result. He flinched from sacking his C-in-C, and having shown his own weakness, had no further sanctions against him. His letter of formal surrender to Harris on 20 January 1945, which effectively acknowledged his subordinate's right to continue bombing cities as he saw fit, bears a note of almost pathetic resignation:

I willingly accept your assurance that you will continue to do your utmost to ensure the successful execution of the policy laid down. I am very sorry that you do not believe in it, but it is no use my craving for what is evidently unattainable. We must wait until after the end of the war before we can know for certain who was right, and I sincerely hope that until then you will continue in command of the force which has done so much towards defeating the enemy, and has brought such credit and renown to yourself and to the Royal Air Force.

Portal's retreat, which greatly disminishes his stature as a director of war, was the negation of all that he had sought to achieve at

Quebec by the transfer of authority from SHAEF. He had proved too weak to impose his will on the command structure he himself had created. It is hard to believe that had Bomber Command continued under SHAEF's orders, Tedder would have tolerated the same degree of defiance from Harris. Whether or not Tedder would have insisted that Bomber Command dedicate itself single-mindedly to the Transport Plan, it is at least likely that a single policy would have been consistently pursued.

Harris's behaviour towards the Air Staff in this last phase almost certainly influenced the fact that he received no peerage and was offered no further employment at the coming of peace, much more than any notion of making him a scapegoat for Dresden. If he had shown the flexibility in the autumn of 1944 to acknowledge that the usefulness of area bombing was ended, that his force was now capable of better and more important things, history might have judged him more kindly. But he did not. With the single-mindedness that even one of his principal advocates at the Air Ministry had termed obsession,[9] he continued remorselessly with his personal programme for the levelling of Germany's cities until the very end. In the first four months of 1945, 181,000 tons of bombs were delivered to Germany, a fifth of the tonnage dropped throughout the entire war.

In this final phase, from the winter of 1944 to May 1945, Bomber Command reached the zenith of its strength: a daily available average of 1,609 aircraft, drawn from a force that included 1,087 Lancasters, 353 Halifaxes and 203 Mosquitoes. Sir John Grigg, the Army Minister, said in the House of Commons in the Army Estimates debate of 1944: 'We have reached the extraordinary situation in which the labour devoted to the production of heavy bombers alone is believed to be equal to that allotted to the production of the whole equipment of the army.' Every heavy bomber was equipped with H2S, *Gee* and other sophisticated electronic equipment. Belatedly, some Lancasters were being fitted with 0.5 calibre rear-turret guns, and a handful even with gun-laying radar. The advanced successor to the Lancaster, the Lincoln, was being prepared for operations in the Far East with the RAF's 'Tiger Force' when the European war ended. There was a vast surplus of aircrew, many of whom were never called upon to fly operations. Cochrane and Carr were transferred from command of their Groups early in 1945, merely in order that two other promising officers might gain experience of battle command before the end. Amidst the deep national weariness that afflicted Britain by 1945, Bomber Command at last tasted operational victory.

Until the final days, the Luftwaffe offered resistance, and Bomber Command's overall loss rate of 1 per cent masked individual nights of operations when casualties of 5 per cent, even 10 per cent were inflicted by the dwindling band of German night-fighters. But stripped of their early-warning systems and swamped by the mass of Allied jamming and radar devices, the defences were in ruins. After losing 31,000 aircrew between January 1941 and June 1944, the Luftwaffe had lost 13,000 between June and October 1944 alone. In 1944, the USAAF had destroyed 3,706 enemy aircraft merely in daylight operations over Germany.[10] No air force could stand losses on this scale. As Bomber Command's operations became more and more a nightly exercise of technique and professionalism, amidst the monotony of the long trips to and from Germany, for the first time a significant number of crews felt sufficiently lightened of their own fear to pity those who lay beneath. The standards of marking, of bombing, of devastation had risen enormously since the previous winter of the Battle of Berlin. Huge forces of aircraft set forth, and the cities beneath were levelled in due measure. In the first four months of 1945, there were thirty-six major Bomber Command operations against German urban areas, twenty-four by night and twelve by day: 528 and 1,107 aircraft went on two nights to Dortmund, 717 and 720 to Chemnitz, 276 to Kassel, 805 to Dresden, 654 to Munich, 521 and 293 to Nuremberg, 597 to Wiesbaden, 349 to Worms, 458 to Mainz, 478 to Mannheim, and 238 to Bonn.

Night after night the huge palls of smoke and fire rose from the cities. 'The situation grows daily more intolerable and we have no means of defending ourselves against this catastrophe,' wrote Goebbels on 2 March.[11] 'Reports sound almost monotonous but they tell of so much sorrow and misery that one hardly dares think about them in detail.'[12] Had Hitler not maintained his spellbinding influence over the German people to the very end, it is impossible to believe that they would have continued the war through these months, if the opportunity had existed for them to surrender. It is almost beyond belief that the German army continued to resist so effectively even amidst the rubble of the nation. The Wehrmacht's dogged retreat, and the continued output from the factories until the last weeks, rendered the concept of morale bombing finally absurd.

Beyond the great area attacks, Bomber Command delivered 17,621 tons of bombs – more than half the total dropped by all the Allied strategic and tactical air forces – in the campaign against Germany's communications. Thousands more sorties were carried out in support of the Allied armies, although some argued that these were self-defeating, because of the mountains of rubble that they created in the face of advancing armour. On 12 November 1944 the *Tirpitz* was finally capsized in Tromsö Fjord by Lancasters of 617 and 9 Squadron – the victims of Wilhelmshaven on 18 December 1939. The *Admiral Scheer* was capsized in Kiel harbour during an attack on 9 April 1945. A vast ten-ton 'Grand Slam' bomb, created by Barnes Wallis and delivered by 617 Squadron, finally severed the Bielefeld Viaduct linking Hamm and Hanover on 14 March 1945, and 617 Squadron dropped forty more of these monstrous weapons on hitherto impregnable installations before the end of the war. Altogether in 1945, Bomber Command launched 67,487 sorties for the loss of 608 aircraft. It is a measure of the scale of the strategic air offensive in its final months that such casualties could be regarded as a small price.

There will never be a definitive judgement on the contribution of the strategic bombers to the final collapse of Germany, because there are so many impenetrable uncertainties. Speer and his army of managers and workers struggled through the winter of 1944 against the tides of disaster breaching their industrial sandcastle on every side, and by the beginning of 1945 it was clear to him that it was being overwhelmed. 'From July 1944 to May 1945 the German economy was tried with so many stresses applied from different directions that it is impossible to say which was the heaviest stress and which caused the final break,' writes Professor Milward.[18]

The advancing Allied armies had cut off Germany from the raw materials on which her industries were dependent. There would be no more chrome from Turkey. The Swedes were belatedly cutting the flow of high-grade steel to the Reich. The Rumanian oil-fields were in the hands of the Russians. Germany had been desperately short of manpower throughout the war, but in October 1944 Hitler made clear his own priorities by decreeing the creation of the *Volkssturm* and calling up every German male between sixteen and sixty for some degree of part-time military training. Hitler and most of his colleagues perceived clearly that unless they could achieve a decisive success on the battlefield within months, the achievements of industry would have become irrelevant. Thus they ignored the desperate protests of Speer about the effects of the call-up on production. After the autumn of 1944, Speer was probably the only leading man in Germany still concerned for the long-term future of the armaments industry, or indeed of any industry at all.

Beyond the final success of the oil offensive, the Allied bombing of German communications and especially of the Ruhr's rail and canal network was strangling coal output and thus steel production by the end of November 1944. It is impossible to separate the achievements of precision air attacks on rail yards, bridges and canals from those of the Allied area attacks on the Ruhr cities. The end result, in any event, was catastrophic. 80 per cent of Germany's coal came from the Ruhr, and to maintain supplies to industry it was necessary for 22,000 wagonloads a day to leave the pits. By the end of November, this flow had been cut to 5,000 a day. In the last quarter of 1944, it was essential for Germany to produce more than 9 million tons of steel. Largely in consequence of the coal famine, less than 4 million tons were produced, barely enough to sustain ammunition production, far less to create new armaments. Allied bombing of the Ruhr links relaxed sufficiently that winter to allow coal flow to increase to 8,100 wagons a day by February, but after another deluge of explosives early in March the Ruhr was totally isolated from the rest of Germany by the middle of the month, a few days before the arrival of the Allied armies.

From September 1944, Speer's economic edifice had passed its peak and was doomed to decline as labour, raw materials and plant in fallen territories were taken from him. By 30 January 1945, with remarkable courage, he conceded openly to Hitler

408

that the game was played out: 'It is a matter of estimating with certainty the final collapse of the German economy in four to eight weeks. . . After this collapse the war can no longer be pursued militarily.' Thereafter Speer devoted most of his labours to frustrating Hitler's orders to destroy German industry in the face of the advancing armies.

The strategic-bomber offensive contributed overwhelmingly to the destruction of Germany's ability to continue the war after the spring of 1945. It is simply a matter for speculation whether the German army would have been capable of prolonging its resistance thereafter, had it been provided with more weapons with which to do so. It seems extraordinarily doubtful. Even in the midst of disaster, tank production was maintained almost to the end, although the tactical air forces made it difficult to move finished armour from the works to the battlefield. Jet aircraft continued to be produced underground despite the best efforts of the Allied bombers to stop them, and shortage of fuel and pilots contributed more than bombing to preventing their effective use in the air.

By the end of January 1945, Germany's gas, power, water and rail systems were in chaos. Fuel of every kind was in desperately short supply on the battlefield and across the nation. Railway signalling and telephone systems and industrial communications had almost totally broken down. Yet the strategic-bomber offensive continued for ten more weeks. It became overwhelmingly an area attack in the final stages, because beyond maintaining the ruin of the oil plants there were pitifully few selective targets to justify the employment of the huge air forces available. In one of the most telling phrases of his dispute with Portal the previous autumn, Harris had declared: 'In Bomber Command we have always worked on the assumption that bombing anything in Germany is better than bombing nothing.' Whatever their post-war assertions of principle, in these months the American airmen joined wholeheartedly with the British in devastating the last remaining undestroyed cities of Germany, because to leave their great forces idle on the ground would have been an intolerable alternative.

The Americans erected a smokescreen of strategic bluster to conceal their part in the area-bombing campaign, which was much less attractive than Harris's open commitment. Even before the Americans unleashed the ultimate area attacks at Hiroshima and Nagasaki, the distinction between the respective national bombing policies had grown to seem very threadbare indeed. But in January 1945 the 8th Air Force's commander, Ira Eaker, could still declare fervently that 'We should never allow the history of this war to convict us of throwing the strategic bomber at the man in the street.'[14]

General Carl 'Tooey' Spaatz, until March 1945 the senior American airman in Europe, consistently opposed proposals that were openly terroristic, such as *Thunderclap* in the summer of 1944, but proved perfectly willing to commit his aircraft to bombing cities if some credible window-dressing could be erected around their purpose, such as 'blind-bombing of transportation centres'. By early 1945 the 8th Air Force had achieved an average circular probable error of two miles on operations guided by H2S. All its blind-bombing missions through the winter of 1944, therefore, amounted in reality if not in name to area bombing. Yet still the American official historians wrote:

It is not surprising that proposals for all-out attacks on Berlin, the Ruhr or other critical areas of Germany always seemed to come from the British, who had undergone the German raids of 1940–41, and were now enduring the punishment of V1s and V2s. All proposals frankly aimed at breaking the morale of the German people met the consistent opposition of General Spaatz, who repeatedly raised the moral issue involved, and American air force headquarters in Washington strongly supported him on the ground that such operations were contrary to air force policy and national ideals.[15]

Throughout the war the American airmen were driven by determination to win their place as an independent third service alongside the army and navy. Spaatz had gained a great degree of freedom to prosecute the war in his own way by the end of 1944, and great forces with which to set about doing so. He was determined to concede nothing to the RAF in the bombing competition that continued until the end of the war, and as Harris heaped explosives on to Germany's cities, in the last stages Spaatz's bombers matched the British ruin for ruin.

It was the most futile and the most distasteful phase of the bomber offensive, and it was also that in which the airmen disastrously damaged their place in history. They did not then know the exact date upon which Germany would concede defeat, but it was apparent for months beforehand that the end was so close that the razing of cities could do nothing to hasten it. The vast American fire-raising attacks on Japan, in which Lemay's Super Fortresses killed 84,000 people in a day before the atomic bomb was heard of, have escaped the widespread censure of posterity, perhaps because the Japanese then seemed so far from capitulation. But the attacks on Dresden by Bomber Command and the American 8th Air Force between 13 and 15 February 1945, which destroyed the city and killed a minimum of 30,000 and perhaps as many as 100,000 people, aroused a revulsion even in the dying days of the war which has not been diminished by the passing of a generation.

It is ironic that while Harris and Spaatz must accept much responsibility for continuing the area offensive after it had ceased to have any strategic meaning, the Allied attack on Dresden cannot be laid at their door. Dresden had indeed been on Harris's target lists for months, but the final impetus to launch the raid on the great East German city came from the Prime Minister and the Chief of Air Staff. Since the end of 1943, with the exception of his role in the pre-*Overlord* debate, Churchill had displayed diminishing interest in bombing, as so many other great issues of war and diplomacy unfolded around him. He continued occasionally to invite Harris to dine,[16] but as has been suggested above, the C-in-C's real influence upon and protection from the Prime Minister may not have been nearly as great as both Portal and Harris supposed, by the winter of 1944.

Yet now, as Churchill prepared to leave for Yalta for the last great Allied conference of the European war, he turned almost impulsively to consider what evidence he could offer the Russians of Western support for their great offensives in the East. He talked to Sinclair on the night of 25 January 1945. The next day the Air Minister informed the Air Staff that the Prime Minister wanted to know Bomber Command's proposals for 'blasting the Germans in their retreat from Breslau'. The old *Thunderclap* plan for delivering a series of overwhelming raids to bring about the collapse of German morale was taken out and dusted down. Yet Portal was not keen to divert the Allies' massed air resources from the tasks he considered pre-eminent: hitting jet-aircraft factories, and maintaining the ruin of Germany's oil plants. He said that he thought the Allies might merely commit 'available effort' to 'one big attack on Berlin, and attacks on Dresden, Leipzig, Chemnitz, or any other cities where a severe blitz will not only cause confusion in the evacuation from the east, but will also hamper the movement of troops from the west'. Sinclair submitted a long memorandum to the Prime Minister outlining these possibilities. He received a crisp reply:

I did not ask you last night about plans for harrying the German retreat from Breslau. On the contrary, I asked whether Berlin, and no doubt other large cities in East Germany, should not now be considered especially attractive targets. I am glad that this is 'under examination'. Pray report to me tomorrow what is going to be done.

Sir Norman Bottomley immediately dispatched an official letter to Harris, pointing out the implications of the Russian advance, and reporting that Portal favoured one big attack on Berlin, with related operations against Dresden, Leipzig and Chemnitz, 'subject to the overriding claims of oil and other approved targets within the current directive'. At Yalta on 4 February the Russians submitted a memorandum in which they formally requested strategic air attacks against Germany's eastern communications, especially such centres as Berlin and Leipzig. On 6 February, Portal signalled Bottomley that the Air Ministry proposals for the eastern air attacks had been approved by the Chiefs of Staff. Thus on the night of 13 February Bomber Command launched its great fire-raising attack on Dresden, to be followed up by those of the 8th Air Force. Little but the railway yards escaped destruction. Chemnitz was fired the next night. Berlin, already heavily attacked by the 8th Air Force earlier in the month, was hit with devastating effect on the night of 24 February by Bomber Command.

It is important to stress that to those who planned and directed it, the raid on Dresden was no different from scores of other operations mounted during the years of war. Bomber Command's attacks had reached an extraordinary pitch of technical efficiency, but it was impossible to anticipate the firestorm which developed, multiplying the usual devastation and deaths a hundredfold. To the staff at High Wycombe, Dresden was simply another German town. Here are Bomber Command's hitherto unpublished briefing notes, issued to Groups and squadrons on the eve of the Dresden raid:

Dresden, the seventh largest city in Germany and not much smaller than Manchester, is also far the largest unbombed built-up area the enemy has got. In the midst of winter with refugees pouring westwards and troops to be rested, roofs are at a premium, not only to give shelter to workers, refugees and troops alike, but to house the administrative services displaced from other areas. At one time well known for its china, Dresden has developed into an industrial city of first-class importance, and like any large city with its multiplicity of telephone and rail facilities, is of major value for controlling the defence of that part of the front now threatened by Marshal Koniev's breakthrough.

The intentions of the attack are to hit the enemy where he will feel it most, behind an already partially collapsed front, to prevent the use of the city in the way of further advance, and incidentally to show the Russians when they arrive what Bomber Command can do.[17]

Much of this, of course, was fantasy. Dresden was not a city of major industrial significance. And unlike so many of Bomber Command's targets of the past five years which had been mere names to the British public, symbols of Nazi power such as Nuremberg or of enemy industrial might such as Essen, Dresden was a city which an important section of educated Englishmen had heard and read of, and perhaps seen. Since the eighteenth century, the old town had stood for all that was finest, most beautiful and cultured in Germany, a haven where Trollopian heroines sought exile, visited by generations of young English noblemen on the Grand Tour. For the first time since the bomber offensive began, on the news of the destruction of Dresden a major wave of anger and dismay swept through Whitehall and the Air Ministry, echoed in Parliament, and finally reached the gates of High Wycombe. Urgent questions were asked by important people about the reasons for destroying the city.

Concern was heightened by the release of an Associated Press dispatch from SHAEF on 17 February, in which a correspondent reported that 'Allied air chiefs' had at last embarked on 'deliberate terror bombing of German population centres as a ruthless expedient to hasten doom'. The attacks on Dresden, Chemnitz and Berlin had been launched 'for the avowed purpose of heaping more confusion on Nazi road and rail traffic, and to sap German morale'. This dispatch – which of course was perfectly accurate, although its news was three years old – was hastily suppressed by the censor in Britain. But it had already been widely distributed in America, causing a major public controversy whose echoes soon reached London. Popular concern might have been even greater had it been known that at the end of February the entire resources of British and American tactical and strategic air power had been committed briefly to the execution of the consciously terroristic American operation *Clarion*, attacking local transport centres the length of Germany in a kind of inverted *Thunderclap*, designed to create moral collapse by bringing the war into even the smallest centres of population. *Clarion* tailed off without achieving any measurable success. Concentrated attacks on the cities, the airmen believed, were a far more effective method of sowing despondency than widely dispersed local raids.

But February 1945 marked the moment when farsighted airmen and politicians began to perceive that history might judge the achievements of strategic air power with far less enthusiasm than their own Target Intelligence departments. General Marshall asserted publicly that Dresden had been bombed at the specific request of the Russians. In the midst of the controversy, General Arnold cabled Spaatz, seeking to be informed of the distinction between 'moral bombing' and radar attacks on transportation targets in urban areas. Spaatz replied that 'he had not departed from the historic American policy in Europe, even in the case of Berlin, and Arnold expressed himself as entirely satisfied with the explanation'.[18] This, of course, was cant. But its incessant repetition would do much to spare Spaatz and Eaker from the criticism heaped upon Harris in the post-war era.

Churchill also sensed the new climate. On 28 March 1945 he composed a memorandum for the Chiefs of Staff Committee and the Chief of Air Staff:

It seems to me that the moment has come when the question of bombing of German cities simply for the sake of increasing the terror, though under other pretexts, should be reviewed. Otherwise we shall come into control of an utterly ruined land. We shall not, for instance, be able to get housing materials out of Germany for our own needs because some temporary provision would have to be made for the Germans themselves. The destruction of Dresden remains a serious query against the conduct of Allied bombing. I am of the opinion that military objectives must henceforward be more strictly studied in our own interests rather than that of the enemy.

The Foreign Secretary has spoken to me on this subject, and I feel the need for more precise concentration upon military objectives, such as oil and communications behind the immediate battle-zone, rather than on mere acts of terror and wanton destruction, however impressive.

It is impossible to regard this memorandum as anything other than a calculated attempt by the Prime Minister to distance himself from the bombing of Dresden and the rising controversy surrounding area bombing. The airmen were not unreasonably angered and dismayed. At Portal's instigation, Churchill was persuaded to withdraw his paper and substitute a new one, dated 1 April 1945:

It seems to me that the moment has come when the question of the so-called 'area bombing' of German cities should be reviewed from the point of view of our own interests. If we come into control of an entirely ruined land, there will be a great shortage of accommodation for ourselves and our Allies; and we shall be unable to get housing materials out of Germany for our own needs . . . We must see to it that our attacks do not do more harm to ourselves in the long run than they do to the enemy's immediate war effort. Pray let me have your views . . .

In the years that followed, many of the airmen who wrote their memoirs – Tedder and Slessor prominent among them – prevaricated about both area bombing and their own part in it. Harris alone never sought prudent cover, nor made excuse or apology for what his forces had done. 'I would not regard the whole of the remaining cities of Germany as worth the bones of one British grenadier,' he wrote to Bottomley on 29 March 1945, at the height of his anger about Churchill's draft memorandum. 'The feeling over Dresden could easily be explained by any psychiatrist. It is connected with German bands and Dresden shepherdesses.'* Alone he stood on the parapet of his trench, facing the slings and arrows of posterity with the same unflinching

*This fascinating memorandum, Harris' fullest and frankest personal revelation, is printed in full as Appendix G p. 450

defiance with which he had received those of his critics and enemies throughout the bomber offensive.

The Chiefs of Staff formally decreed the ending of area bombing on 16 April 1945. Yet it was intolerable to the airmen that Bomber Command should sit out the last weeks of the war in idleness. Harris's aircraft bombed Berchtesgaden and a few remaining oil plants and the coastal guns on the north German island of Wangerooge. One of Bomber Command's last operations of the war was carried out on 16 April, against the German island fortress of Heligoland, where naval radar had first detected Wing-Commander Kellett's Wellingtons before their terrible defeat five and a half years earlier.

More than 900 aircraft were dispatched, a force great enough to level three cities. There were three aiming-points: the main island, the airfield and the naval base. 'Marking, from the initial *Oboe* TIs to the last backer-up, was of a high standard, and the Master Bombers kept a tight rein on an enthusiastic Main Force,' recorded the History of 8 Group.[19] 'The next day, thirty-three Lancasters of 5 Group, six carrying Grand Slams and the remainder Tallboys, sent to flatten anything left standing, reported that the centre of the island was still ablaze.'

The means, which had for so long been lacking to fulfil the airmen's great ambitions, had at last overtaken the ends.

15 The balance sheet

We want – that is, the people who served in Bomber Command of the
Royal Air Force and their next of kin – a categorical assurance that the
work we did was militarily and strategically justified.
Wing-Commander Ernest Millington
MP, House of Commons, 12 March 1946

At the end of the war, Bomber Command received the courtesies
of victory. There was a letter from Buckingham Palace for High
Wycombe, on receiving the final version of Harris's beloved
Blue Books:

The King has asked me to thank you for the two volumes of Bomb
Damage Diagrams which were brought here this morning . . . These
reports have been a constant source of interest to His Majesty since
they started, and provided an admirable record of the great part played
by Bomber Command in winning the war. The King hopes that you
will express to those who have compiled the records His Majesty's
appreciation of the neatness and accuracy of the work . . .[1]

But beneath a thin layer of perfunctory goodwill, it was soon
apparent not only at High Wycombe but throughout Bomber
Command, that in the safety of peace the bombers' part in the
war was one that many politicians and civilians would prefer to
forget. The laurels and the romantic adulation were reserved for
Fighter Command, the defenders. The men of the Army of
Occupation were first awed, then increasingly dismayed, by the
total devastation of Germany. As more pictures and descriptions
of the effects of area bombing began to appear in Britain,
especially concerning what had taken place in Dresden, public
distaste grew. Among the vanquished, those who had launched
air attacks on civilians were prominent in the dock at Nuremberg.
'Was not your purpose in this attack to secure a strategic advan-

tage by terrorization of the people of Rotterdam?'² asked Sir
David Maxwell Fyfe damningly, as he examined Kesselring
about his part in the 1940 offensive. 'I decided on Coventry
because there the most targets could be hit within the smallest
area,' declared Goering,³ on trial for his life, with his direction
of the Blitz on Britain among the principal prosecution issues.
The Reichsmarschall was sentenced to hang. Kesselring went with
Milch and Speer to begin a long imprisonment.

Sir Arthur Harris was offered no further employment in the
Royal Air Force, and departed for South Africa at the end of
1945. To Churchill's undying discredit, he declined to exert his
influence to secure Harris a peerage, which many lesser men were
being rewarded. Only in 1953 did Harris received a baronetcy,
the sort of honour usually granted to time-serving Members of
Parliament. Whatever posterity may make of Harris, he had
served Churchill well, and given all that he could offer to the
service of the Royal Air Force. It was an oddly ungenerous
gesture by the Prime Minister and tends to support Major
Morton's contention about Churchill's lack of personal affection
for the C-in-C of Bomber Command. Of the offensive as a whole,
Churchill had only this to say in the final volume of his war
memoirs:

In judging the contribution to victory of strategic air power it should be
remembered that this was the first war in which it was fully used. We
had to learn from hard-won experience . . . But although the results of
the early years fell short of our aims, we forced on the enemy an elaborate, ever-growing but finally insufficient air-defence system which
absorbed a large proportion of their total war effort. Before the end,
we and the United States had developed striking forces so powerful that
they played a major part in the economic collapse of Germany.⁴

By the last months of the struggle, Churchill the politician was
already reasserting himself over Churchill the director of war.
When the Americans began to pour thousands of economists and
scientists into captured territory to compile their massive
Strategic Bombing Survey, the RAF hoped to do likewise. But
Churchill angrily rejected their proposals, on the grounds that
they would waste skilled manpower. It is not possible to accept
his argument at face value. It is easier to imagine that he wished

to put the strategic air offensive behind him, with as little resort as possible to further statistical fantasies and noisy claims by the airmen. The British Bombing Survey Unit was grudgingly granted token resources. American and British airmen competed for German documents and access to the top captured Nazis, notably Speer, in their anxiety to prove the triumph of 'precision' or 'area' bombing. Professor Solly Zuckerman, who wrote the 'Overall Report' of the BBSU, had always been an advocate of attacking communications links rather than cities. When his work was completed, it was received without enthusiasm at the Air Ministry, although Zuckerman's old chief Sir Arthur Tedder was now Chief of Air Staff.

The main fault of commission in the combined bomber offensive [wrote the scientist] would undoubtedly appear as the launching of the offensive against German aircraft assembly plants, and the continuation of 'area attacks' on German towns beyond the point where they were necessitated by the operational limitations of inaccuracy in navigation and bombing. Even the more accurate and devastating raids on the Ruhr that took place towards the end of the war were an extravagant means of achieving a fall in steel production compared to the direct attack on communications . . .[5]

Originally a biologist by training, Zuckerman had been staggered to discover, on arriving in Germany at the end of the war, that most zoos which had not suffered direct damage were still feeding a full complement of animals. In Britain such useless mouths had been ruthlessly destroyed early in the war. It was a striking example of the gulf between the desperate plight of Germany as Allied Intelligence had perceived it and the reality as it now emerged. Zuckerman's 'Overall Report' was suppressed by the Air Ministry, as was Sir Arthur Harris's final dispatch on the work of Bomber Command 1942–5. Meanwhile, across the Atlantic a similar uncertainty and controversy about the bomber offensive had broken out among Americans:

Even General Arnold had doubts about how effective the air war had been. The British and American strategic air forces had blasted factories and cities from one end of the Reich to the other. Unquestionably the destruction had not had the effect on the enemy's war effort that Arnold had expected or hoped for, the effect 'we all assumed would result'.[6]

The Royal Air Force entered the Second World War committed to demonstrating that the air-dropped bomb was a weapon of unique potential. Political, social and professional pressure on the infant service had driven the airmen to a passionate level of belief, and it is precisely for these reasons that some historians have argued that the RAF should never have become an independent service in 1918. The airmen, desperately jealous of their freedom, became obsessed with their need for an independent function, and only a strategic-bomber offensive seemed able to provide it.

The technical failings of Bomber Command in the first years of the war were no worse than those of the army and the Royal Navy. The bombers made an important, perhaps critical contribution in 1941 and 1942 to keeping alive the morale of the British people, and to deterring the Americans from a premature second front. The casualties suffered by the airmen would have been far exceeded by the Allied armies if they had been compelled to face the Wehrmacht head-on in 1942 or 1943.

The Allies' possession of a heavy-bomber force was an important military asset, seen to most advantage in support of *Overlord*. But Churchill made a major error of judgement in the winter of 1941–2 by committing British industry to the enormous heavy-bomber programme that came to fruition at the end of 1944. The Prime Minister could have achieved his strategic purpose with a far less extravagant outlay of resources. Instead, although they were denied their '4,000 Plan', the airmen were allowed to embark on their own ambitious war aims. Tizard said after the war: 'No one thinks now that it would have been possible to defeat Germany by bombing alone. The actual effort expended on bombing Germany, in manpower and resources, was greater than the value in manpower and resources of the damage caused.'

Whether or not this is precisely true, the British investment in Bomber Command was immense. Webster and Frankland suggest that the bomber offensive employed only 7 per cent of the nation's manpower, but this figure can hardly be accepted literally, since it discounts the exceptional quality and skills of those concerned. It is difficult to compute the exact proportion of the nation's war effort that was involved, but A.J. P. Taylor, one of the critics of the bomber offensive, argues around one-third. Bomber Command took the cream of Britain's wartime high technology, and the true cost of a Lancaster fitted with H2S, *Gee*, the Mark XIV bombsight and other supporting equipment must have been staggering. The fact that Britain was compelled to buy from America all its transport aircraft (and enter post-war civil aviation at a serious disadvantage), most of its landing craft, a large proportion of its tanks and vast quantities of ammunition stemmed directly or indirectly from the weight of British industrial effort committed to the bomber offensive. The simple fact was that only America possessed the industrial resources to embark on strategic air warfare on the necessary scale to have decisive results within an acceptable period.

Lord Trenchard is entitled to the undying gratitude of the Royal Air Force for keeping the service in being between the wars, but all the key strategic principles upon which he built air-force doctrine were found wanting. It was a terrible experience to be bombed, but German morale never came near to collapse until the very end. In any event, as Liddell Hart perceived, morale bombing was incompatible with the Allied doctrine of enforcing unconditional German surrender.

The 'de-housing' paper, a document which leaves an ineradicable sense of distaste surrounding the name of Lord Cherwell, was itself curiously mealy-mouthed. If moral considerations were to be discarded, the most rational policy for Bomber Command would have been to regard its campaign as a straightforward attempt to kill the largest possible number of Germans, rather than dally with such compromises as making them homeless. Supplies of arms were never critically lacking in Germany, but there was a chronic shortage of hands to bear them.

By the spring of 1944, it was clear that Harris's area-bombing campaign had failed to bring Germany even within distant sight of defeat. That winter, when Harris made clear his continuing commitment to the area offensive despite the major reservations of the Chief of Air Staff, he should have been sacked. The obliteration of Germany's cities in the spring of 1945, when all possible strategic justification had vanished, is a lasting blot on the Allied conduct of the war and on the judgement of senior Allied airmen.

'We had a surfeit of air staffs,' Lord Zuckerman has written,[7] 'presided over by chiefs who were not called "the air barons" for nothing. They ruled their commands like feudal lords, rarely changing their conventional views or their personal allegiances. What mattered was the ability to destroy. . .' By his indecision and weakness in handling Harris and the bombing offensive in the last eight months of the war, Sir Charles Portal disqualified himself from consideration as a great, or even as an effective, commander of air forces, whatever his merits as a joint-service committee-man.

The bomber offensive compelled the Germans to divert resources to the defence of their own cities. If Hitler had been a reasonable man, the pressure upon him to do this on a much larger scale might have had important strategic consequences. Reason demanded that major forces of day- and night-fighters be deployed against the bomber offensive as Speer, Milch and Galland demanded. But Hitler was not a reasonable man, and did not comply with their wishes until the means to do so were gone.

Economic historians agree that German industry proved astonishingly resilent in the face of bombing:

There can be no doubt that active interference of this nature in the work of the German economy hastened the decline in production [wrote Professor Milward[8]]. But the overall importance of bombing, as well as the importance of particular aspects of the offensive, has been exaggerated, often for the purpose of demonstrating the success of different kinds of bombing policy.

The two great achievements of the Allied strategic air offensive must be conceded to the Americans: the defeat of the Luftwaffe by the Mustang escort-fighter, and the inception of the deadly oil offensive. 'The British inflicted grievous and bloody injuries upon us,' said Milch after the war, 'but the Americans stabbed us to the heart.' Even the American breakthrough came late in the overall context of the war. The most common fault among air historians since 1945 is that they have examined the strategic-bomber offensive in isolation. The course of the war must be considered in its entirety. It is gratifying to airmen, but historically irrelevant, that the destruction of the German economy would have been decisive granted another few weeks of hostilities. Many of their greatest feats of precision bombing such as the sinking of the *Tirpitz* – which would have been a vital strategic achievement in 1941, 1942, even 1943 – had become no more than marvellous circus-tricks by the time they were achieved in 1944 and 1945. The pace of the war had overtaken them.

By late 1944, Bomber Command and the USAAF possessed the means to undertake what Harris had attempted in 1942 and 1943: the wholesale destruction of Germany's cities. But it was too late. When they had the strategic purpose – in 1942 and 1943 – they lacked the means. By the winter of 1944, when they had gained the means, the purpose was gone, for the Allied armies were evidently on the verge of complete victory on the ground, and it was only a combination of their own shortcomings and the Wehrmacht's genius that delayed the end so long. In the last months of the war Bomber Command contributed to the punishment of Germany more than to the defeat of the enemy. No one disputed Germany's guilt. Arguably it is because of what the German people suffered from bombing in the Second World War that they are so unlikely to embark on such a national adventure again. But it is difficult to accept in cold blood that the Allied air forces were appropriately employed as a punitive force. Contrary to the view of the British official historians, most civilized men would agree that there *is* a significant moral distinction between the incidental and deliberate destruction of civilian life in war, and it is hard to look back across a generation on such a night's work as the destruction of Darmstadt with any pride.

Bomber Command was very well served by its aircrew, and with a few exceptions very badly served by its senior officers, in the Second World War. The gulf between the realities in the sky and the rural routine of headquarters was too great for most of the staff to bridge. Cochrane and Bennett were the only men among Bomber Command's leaders to do so. High Wycombe was fatally isolated both from the front and from sharp critical debate on policy. Even after all their bitter experience in the early years of war, senior officers were unwilling to face unacceptable realities. Dr Noble Frankland has written that 'the whole belief that the bomber was revolutionary in the sense that it was not subject to the classical doctrines of war was misguided',[9] and this should have been apparent to the airmen by 1942. The air-dropped bomb had shown itself no more potent than any other conventional explosive object. For all the technology embodied in the bomber aircraft, its load once released was an astonishingly crude and imprecise weapon.

The airmen's great error, in which they have persisted to this day, was their refusal to admit that they had overstated their case. Had they chosen to stand on Bomber Command's un-disputed achievements and marvellous courage, their short-comings and excesses might have been forgotten. Instead, many prominent British airmen have fought doggedly since the war to prove that the bomber offensive was the decisive factor in Allied victory. Their imprecision about what they sought to achieve has persisted through the intervening generation. The four-volume official history prints forty-nine sets of statistics covering every aspect of German production, hundreds of pages of data on British aircraft and losses, and yet not a single appendix giving details or estimates of German civilian casualties or even numbers 'de-housed' by the bomber offensive. The Federal Statistical Office in Wiesbaden computed after the war that 593,000 German civilians died and 3.37 million dwellings were destroyed, including 600,000 in Berlin alone, from 1939 to 1945.

The strategic offensive partly fulfilled some important purposes for the Allied war effort. Bomber Command entirely satisfied Churchill's hopes as I have interpreted them at the beginning of 1942, by fighting a long holding action to buy time to launch *Overlord* on overwhelmingly favourable terms. If the air marshals had pitched their demands for resources, their own hopes and their subsequent claims more modestly, history might have judged them more kindly. As it was, the cost of the bomber offensive in life, treasure and moral superiority over the enemy tragically outstripped the results that it achieved.

Beyond those who died flying for Bomber Command, many more outstanding young men somehow used themselves up in the Second World War, leaving pathetically little energy and imagina-tion to support them through the balance of their lives. Surviving aircrew often feel deeply betrayed by criticism of the strategic offensive. It is disgraceful that they were never awarded their own Campaign Medal after surviving the extraordinary battle they fought for so long against such odds, and in which so many of them died. One night after I had visited a much-decorated pilot in the north of England in the course of writing this book, he drove me to the station. Suddenly turning to me in the car, he asked: 'Has anybody else mentioned having nightmares about it?' He said that in the past ten years he had been troubled by increasingly vivid and terrible dreams about his experiences over Germany.

A teacher by profession, he had thought nothing of the war for years afterwards. Then a younger generation of his colleagues began to ask with repetitive, inquisitive distaste: 'How could you have done it? How could you have flown over Germany night after night to bomb women and children?' He began to brood more and more deeply about his past. He changed his job and started to teach mentally handicapped children, which he sees as a kind of restitution. Yet still, more than thirty years after, his memories of the war haunt him.

It is wrong that it should be so. He was a brave man who had an outstanding record in the RAF. The aircrew of Bomber Command went out to do what they were told had to be done for Britain and Allied victory, and subsequent judgements on the bomber offensive can do nothing to mar the honour of such an epitaph.

Appendix A

Bomber Command sorties dispatched and aircraft missing and written off, 1939–45

		Sorties		Missing		Crashed	
		NIGHT	DAY	NIGHT	DAY	NIGHT	DAY
1939	September	83	40	2	12	3	0
	October	32	0	2	0	2	0
	November	15	4	0	0	1	0
	December	40	119	0	17	0	2
1940	January	38	6	0	0	0	0
	February	54	4	1	0	2	0
	March	239	53	5	1	6	0
	April	489	167	18	15	8	0
	May	1,617	802	21	49	3	3
	June	2,484	812	26	31	7	1
	July	1,722	616	40	32	3	4
	August	2,188	417	52	18	11	0
	September	3,141	98	65	1	21	0
	October	2,242	172	27	1	32	0
	November	1,894	113	50	2	34	0
	December	1,385	56	37	2	23	0
1941	January	1,030	96	12	3	12	1
	February	1,617	124	16	2	32	2
	March	1,728	162	35	4	36	0
	April	2,249	676	56	23	12	7
	May	2,416	273	39	20	14	3
	June	3,228	531	76	22	15	3
	July	3,243	582	91	66	28	3
	August	3,344	468	121	35	45	5
	September	2,621	263	76	14	62	1
	October	2,501	138	68	17	40	1
	November	1,713	43	83	0	21	0
	December	1,411	151	28	7	16	0
1942	January	2,216	24	56	0	32	0
	February	1,162	252	18	15	14	1
	March	2,224	131	78	2	21	0
	April	3,752	246	130	13	29	2
	May	2,702	105	114	1	21	0
	June	4,801	196	199	2	39	1
	July	3,914	313	171	19	22	0
	August	2,454	186	142	10	16	5

		Sorties		Missing		Crashed	
		NIGHT	DAY	NIGHT	DAY	NIGHT	DAY
	September	3,489	127	169	6	39	0
	October	2,198	406	89	14	27	0
	November	2,067	127	53	11	23	0
	December	1,758	200	72	16	22	2
1943	January	2,556	406	86	15	18	3
	February	5,030	426	101	6	22	3
	March	5,174	284	161	7	25	1
	April	5,571	316	253	12	24	1
	May	5,130	360	234	19	27	4
	June	5,816	0	275	0	15	0
	July	6,170	0	188		31	
	August	7,807	0	275		33	
	September	5,513	0	191		34	
	October	4,638	0	159		21	
	November	5,208	0	162		48	
	December	4,123	0	170		47	
1944	January	6,278	0	314		38	
	February	4,263	45	199	0	24	0
	March	9,031	18	283	0	39	0
	April	9,873	10	214	0	25	0
	May	11,353	16	274	0	29	0
	June	13,592	2,371	293	12	30	0
	July	11,500	6,298	229	12	29	4
	August	10,013	10,271	186	35	22	1
	September	6,428	9,643	96	41	15	0
	October	10,193	6,713	75	52	26	0
	November	9,589	5,055	98	41	34	0
	December	11,239	3,656	88	31	43	0
1945	January	9,603	1,304	121	12	57	0
	February	13,715	3,685	164	9	60	0
	March	11,585	9,606	168	47	76	10
	April	8,822	5,001	51	22	29	6
	May	349	1,068	3	2	0	1

These statistics are admittedly incomplete because they do not include minelaying or Special Duties sorties and casualties, and because some squadron and Group record books were carelessly kept, but they are the best figures that the Royal Air Force is ever likely to compile. The totals for crashed aircraft before February 1942 are unreliable, and it is not clear which were damaged and which were totally written off.

Appendix B
Specifications and performance of the principal aircraft of Bomber Command and Luftwaffe night-fighters, 1939–45

It is impossible to detail the immense number of different Marks of each aircraft. I have therefore chosen those which relate to the events most closely described in the text. Performance figures are only the most approximate guide, since individual aircraft varied immensely in efficiency and handling. Some Lancasters, for instance, were modified to carry a bombload of ten tons, with front and mid-upper turrets removed.

British aircraft

Vickers WELLINGTON IC. Type: twin-engined medium bomber, crew: 6; length: 60.8 feet; height: 18.75 feet; wing-span: 86 feet; maximum loaded weight 30,000 lb; ceiling: 15,000 feet; cruising speed: 165 mph; maximum speed: 235 mph; bombload: 4,500 lb (with fuel for 1,200 miles)/1,000 lb (with fuel for 2,550 miles); armament: twin .303s in front and rear turrets, single free .303s on beam mountings;* engines: Pegasus XVIII.

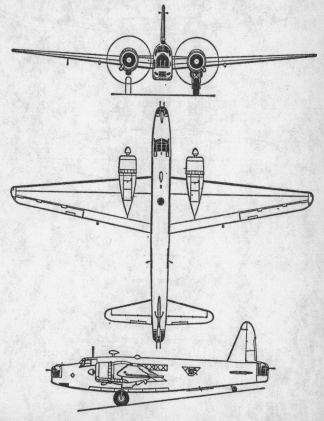

*3 Group Wellington Is of 18 December 1939 lacked beam guns and carried only a single gun in forward turret.

Bristol BLENHEIM IV. Type: twin-engined light bomber; crew: 3; length: 40 feet; height: 9.2 feet; wing-span: 56 feet; maximum loaded weight: 15,800 lb; ceiling: 22,000 feet; cruising speed: 180 mph; maximum speed: 266 mph; bombload: 1,000 lb (with fuel for 1,460 miles); armament: twin .303s in forward under nacelle*; single .303 in rear turret, single .303 rearward fixed firing from engine nacelle; engines: Mercury XV.

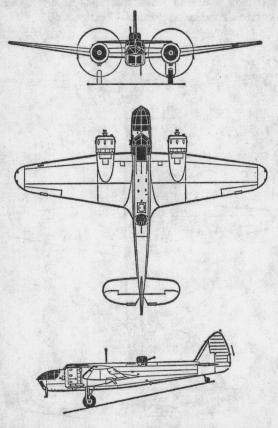

*Not shown.

Armstrong Whitworth WHITLEY V. Type: twin-engined medium bomber; crew 5; length: 69.3 feet; height: 12.75 feet; wing-span: 84 feet; maximum loaded weight: 33,500 lb; ceiling: 17,600 feet; cruising speed: 165 mph; maximum speed: 202 mph; bombload: 8,000 lb (with fuel for 630 miles)/3,500 lb (with fuel for 1,930 miles); armament: single free .303 in forward turret, four .303s in rear turret; engines: Merlin X.

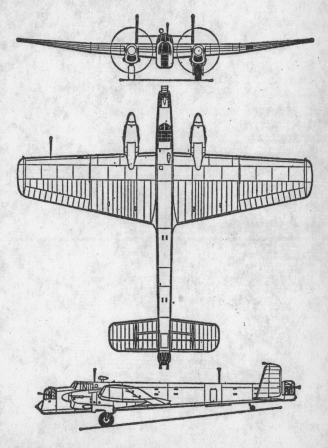

Handley Page HAMPDEN. Type: twin-engined medium bomber; crew: 4; length: 53.3 feet; height: 14.9 feet; wing-span: 69.3 feet; maximum loaded weight: 22,500 lb; ceiling: 20,000 feet; cruising speed: 155 mph; maximum speed: 243 mph; bombload: 4,000 lb (with fuel for 1,200 miles)/2,000 lb (with fuel for 1,885 miles); armament: single fixed and single free .303 in nose, single or twin free .303s in rear and mid-under positions; engines: Pegasus XVIII.

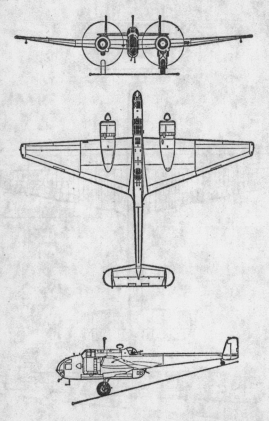

Avro MANCHESTER. Type: twin-engined heavy-medium bomber; crew: 7; length: 68.8 feet; height: 19.5 feet; wing-span: 90.1 feet; maximum weight: 50,000 lb; ceiling: 19,200 feet; cruising speed: 185 mph; maximum speed: 258 mph; bombload: 10,350 lb (with fuel for 1,200 miles)/8,100 lb (with fuel for 1,630 miles); armament: twin .303s in front and mid-upper turrets, quad.303s in rear turret; engines: Vulture II.

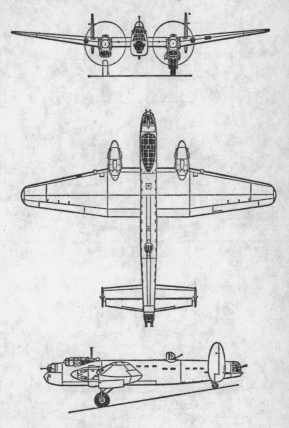

Short STIRLING III. Type: four-engined heavy bomber; crew: 7; length: 87 feet; height: 22.75 feet; wing-span: 99 feet; maximum loaded weight: 70,000 lb; ceiling: 17,000 feet; cruising speed: 200 mph; maximum speed: 270 mph; bombload: 14,000 lb (with fuel for 590 miles)/2,010 lb (with fuel for 3,575 miles); armament: twin .303s in front and mid-upper turrets, quad .303s in rear turret; engines: Hercules VI.

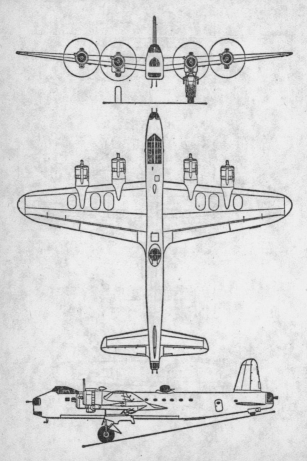

Handley Page HALIFAX III. Type: four-engined heavy bomber; crew: 7; length: 70.1 feet; height: 20.75 feet; wing-span: 104 feet; maximum loaded weight: 65,000 lb; ceiling: 20,000 feet; cruising speed: 225 mph; maximum speed: 277 mph; bombload: 13,000 lb (with fuel for 980 miles)/6,250 lb (with fuel for 2,005 miles); armament: single or twin .303s in front turret, quad .303s in mid-upper turret, quad .303s in rear turret; engines: Hercules XVI.

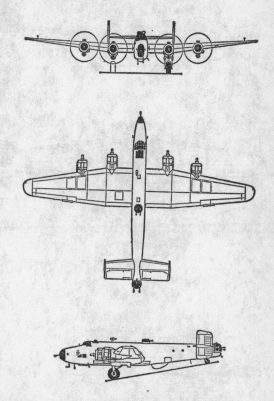

*76 Squadron in 1943 were equipped with the earlier Halifax II or V.

Avro LANCASTER I and III. Type: four-engined heavy bomber; crew: 7 (sometimes 8 in PFF aircraft and 6 Group aircraft with ventral turrets); length: 68.9 feet; height: 19.5 feet; wing-span: 102 feet; maximum loaded weight: 68,000 lb; cruising speed: 216 mph; maximum speed: 266 mph; ceiling 20,000 feet; bombload: 14,000 lb (with fuel for 1,660 miles); armament: twin .303s in front and mid-upper turrets, quad .303s in rear turret; engines: Merlin 22, 28, or 38.*

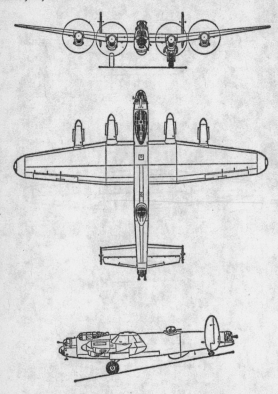

*Note H2S dome under fuselage below mid-upper turret.

De Havilland MOSQUITO Mk IV. Type: twin-engined light bomber; crew: 2; length: 40.5 feet; height: 12.5 feet; wing-span: 54.17 feet; maximum loaded weight: 21,462 lb; ceiling: 33,000 feet; cruising speed: 265 mph; maximum speed: 362 mph; bomb-load: 2,000 lb (with fuel for 1,620 miles) – some aircraft were modified to carry a 4,000-lb bomb; armament:none; engines: Merlin 21 or 23.

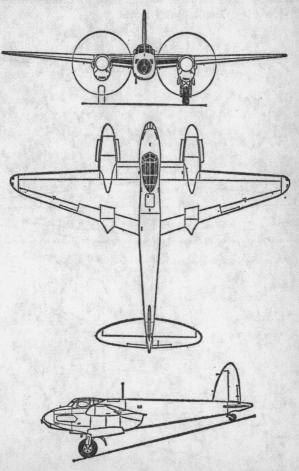

German aircraft

Messerschmitt Bf110G. Type: twin-engined night-fighter; crew: 3; length: 42.8 feet; height: 13.7 feet; wing-span: 53.4 feet; maximum weight: 21,800 lb; ceiling: 26,250 feet; cruising speed: 250 mph; maximum speed: 342 mph; range: 1,305 miles; armament: two 30-mm cannon and two 20-mm cannon in nose: twin 7.9 mm machine-guns in rear; some aircraft fitted with *schrage musik* in 1944; engines: Daimler-Benz DB 605B.*

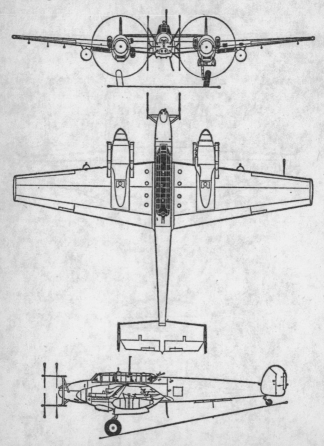

*Note *Lichtenstein* aerials at nose.

Messerschmitt Bf109G. Type: single-engined day-fighter used as 'Wild Boar', July 1943 – March 1944; crew: 1; length: 29 feet; height: 8.2 feet; wing-span: 32.5 feet; maximum weight: 7,491 lb; ceiling: 37,890 feet; cruising speed: 260 mph; maximum speed: 386 mph; range: 620 miles; armament: one 30-mm cannon or one 20-mm cannon plus two 13-mm machine-guns; engines: Daimler-Benz DB 605A.

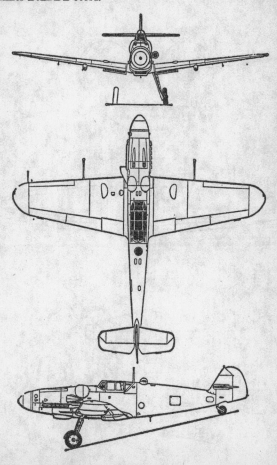

Junkers Ju88C. Type: twin-engined night-fighter; crew: 2 or 3; length: 49.4 feet; height: 16.6 feet; wing-span: 65.8 feet; maximum weight: 27,225 lb; ceiling: 32,480 feet; cruising speed; 263 mph; maximum speed: 307 mph; range: 1,230 miles; armament: three 20-mm cannon and three 7.9-mm machine-guns in nose, one 13-mm machine-gun in rear of cockpit; some aircraft in 1944 fitted with *schrage musik*;* engines: 2 Junkers Jumo 211J.

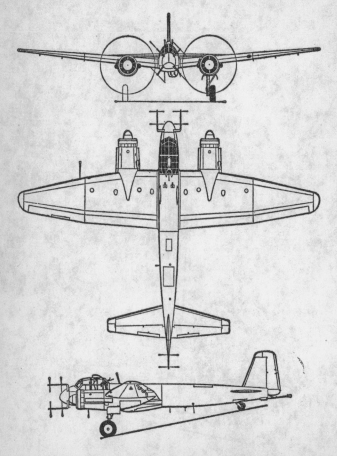

*Illustrated here. Note also *Lichtenstein* aerials at nose.

US aircraft in service with Bomber Command

Boeing B-17 FORTRESS III.* Type: four-engined heavy bomber; crew: 7; length: 73 feet; height: 15.6 feet; wing-span: 104 feet; maximum weight: 64,000 lb; ceiling: 31,500 feet; cruising speed: 230 mph; maximum speed: 280 mph; bomb-load: 12,800 lb (with fuel for 1,140 miles); armament: nine .50 in turrets and free-mounted; engines: 4 Cyclone GR1820-97.

*Deployed by 100 Group, 1944–45.

Appendix C

The Target Indicator Board at Bomber Command HQ High Wycombe, at the beginning of February 1945

Order of Priority

ARMY SUPPORT	
Bielefeld Viaduct	1
Altenbeken/Neuenbeken Viaduct	
Krefeld/Uerdingen	
Hohenbudberg	
Köln/Gremberg	
Breisach Bridge	

OIL		2
Bohlen (S. of Leipzig)		A
Ruhland (N. of Dresden)	1	E
Lutzkendorf (Halle)		B
Magdeburg		B
Poelitz (Stettin)		D
Brux (Czecho-slovakia)	1	E
Leuna (Merseburg)		C
Zeitz	1	E
Rositz		C
Harburg-Rhenania	1	E
Misburg		D
Wanne Eickel	1	E
Sterkrade Holten	2	E
Hansa (B)		B
Carolingluck (B)		B
Bruckhausen (B)	1	E
Prosper (B)		B
Nordstern (B)		B
Kaiserstuhl (B)		B
Ministerstein (B)		A
Gneisenau (B)		A
Consolidation (B)		A
1 Scholven (B)		B
Alma Pluto (B)		A
Meidrich (B)		B
Osterfeld (B)		A
Rauxel Tar (B)		C
Salzgitter (B)	1	E
Fortsetzung (B)	1	E
R. Muser (B)	1	E

Note: In addition to the above, the A.M. Directif lists a number of oil plants at a lower priority than the Benzol plants, but as they are of such slight current importance, they are not included with list shown above.

TRANSPORTATION	3
Lohne	
Wesel Railway Bridge	
Wesel Road Bridge	
Hohenzollern Bridge	
Dusseldorf/Neuss Bridge	
Rheinhausen Bridge	
Hochhalen Bridge	
Stuttgart/Kornwestheim	
Rothensee	
Paderborn	
Hamm	1
Rheine	2

Osnabruck North	1	Friedberg	
Munster		Dillenburg	
Schwerte		Mannheim	2
Arnsberg		Ludwigshaven	
Köln/Gremberg		Frankfurt A/M East	
Siegen		Aschaffenburg	
Niederlahnstein		Mainz HBF	
Wetzlar		Bebra	
Marburg		Darmstadt	
Bonn		Wiesbaden	
Troisdorf		Gemunden	
Betzdorf		Alzey	
Limburg		Niedernhausen	

Order of Priority (2)

RUHR	4	HEAVILY DAMAGED BUT WITH LARGE INTACT AREAS	
TOWNS CONTAINING SCATTERED UNDAMAGED SECTIONS		Nurnberg	
Essen		Leipzig	
Dortmund		TOWNS CONTAINING SMALL OR SCATTERED UNDAMAGED AREAS	
Duisburg		Stuttgart	
Oberhausen		Kassel	
Gelsenkirchen		Karlsruhe	
Neuss		Harburg	
Hagen		Ludwigshaven	
Witten		Munster	
AREA TARGETS	5	Bielefeld	
UNDAMAGED OR ONLY SLIGHTLY DAMAGED TOWNS		Osnabruck	
Chemnitz		TOWNS AWAIT P.R. COVER	
Halle		Hanover	1
Dessau		Hanau	1
Dresden		Magdeburg	1
Erfurt		Munich	1

Order of Priority (9)

CROSSBOW TARGETS 6
DIVER AIRFIELDS
Schleswig/Land
Leck
Wittmundhafen
Zwischenahn
Eggebek
Husum/Narrenthal

'JET' FACTORIES WITHIN
OBOE RANGE 7

Niedersachswerfen (U)
Muldenstein
Dessau
Bettenhausen
Leipzig/Gautzsch
Leipzig/Taucha
Baumenheim
Leonberg (U)
Schwabisch-Hall
Neuburg

Obertraubling
Schwabmunchen
Leipheim
Lechfeld
Lonnewitz
Wittenberge

Zuffenhausen

NAVAL TARGETS 8
FIRST PRIORITY

Hamburg-Blohm & Voss 1
Hamburg/Finkenwarder 1
Bremen Deschimag
Bremen Shelters
SECOND PRIORITY
Kiel/Germania
Kiel/Deutsche Werke
Kiel/Howaldts Werke
Vegesack/Vulkan Werke
Farge

SPECIAL TARGETS 9
Ijmuiden Pens
Maassluis/Poorterhaven
Bergen Pens
Trondheim Pens

Author's note: Letters against oil targets denote plant type and state of damage; numbers denote special priority targets.

Appendix D

British and German production of selected armaments, 1940-44

	1940 Germany	1940 UK	1941 Germany	1941 UK	1942 Germany	1942 UK	1943 Germany	1943 UK	1944 Germany	1944 UK
Military aircraft										
Total (numbers)	10,200	15,000	11,000	20,100	14,200	23,600	25,200	26,200	39,600	26,500
Total structural weight										
(million lb)	59	59	64	87	92	133	138	185	174	208
Bombs (filled weight in 1,000 tons)		48	245	143	262	241	273	309	231	370
Armoured vehicles										
Tanks	1,600	1,400	3,800	4,800	6,300	8,600	12,100	7,500	19,000	4,600
Others	500	6,000	1,300	10,500	3,100	19,300	7,800	24,200	9,900	22,600
Wheeled vehicles (thousands)										
Heavy type		112	62	110	81	109	109	104	89	91
Light cars and vans		21		17	29	16	36	17	26	13
Motor cycles		68		71		75	38	79	33	75
Heavy guns (75 mm and over)										
Field, medium and heavy	4,400	1,000	4,700	3,800	5,100	4,000	11,700	3,000	24,900	2,800
Tank	470	–	650	–	2,200	2	9,500	4,600	20,400	7,500
Anti-tank	–	–	–	–	2,100	500	9,900	3,300	13,800	1,900
Anti-aircraft	1,400	900	2,400	1,500	4,200	2,100	6,900	1,300	8,200	200
Total	6,300	1,900	7,800	5,300	13,600	6,600	38,000	12,200	62,300	12,400
Light guns (under 75 mm, excluding 20 mm)										
Tank	–	240	100	6,000	3,000	22,000	900	10,400	700	1,700
Anti-tank	430	1,500	2,100	2,700	4,500	9,100	2,600	9,800	–	1,100
Anti-aircraft		1,100	1,200	2,700	2,100	5,300	4,600	5,600	7,700	800
Total		2,800	3,400	11,400	9,600	36,400	8,100	25,800	8,400	3,600

Appendix E

Schedule of German cities subjected to area attack by Bomber Command, 1942-45

Town	Date of first Main Force attack	Date of last Main Force attack	Total number of Main Force attacks	Tonnages (Short) claimed dropped (including Mosquito attacks) Jan. 1942–May 1945	Acreage 40 per cent or more built-up (Target) area	Acreage destroyed in built-up (Target) area	Destroyed percentage of built-up (Target) area
Aachen	5/6.10.42	13/14. 7.43	2	3,930	1,030	605	59
Augsburg	25/26. 2.44	–	1	2,076	1,535	445	29
Berlin	16/17. 1.43	24/25. 3.44	24	49,400	19,423	6,427	33
Bochum	29/30. 3.43	4/5.11.44	6	10,207	640	532	83
Bonn	18.10.44	4/5. 2.45	5	2,317	708	240	34
Bremen	3/4. 6.42	22. 4.45	12	9,709	1,744	1,042	60
Bremerhaven	18/19. 9.44	–	1	968	375	297	79
Brunswick	14/15. 1.44	14/15.10.44	5	6,803	1,400	655	47
Chemnitz	14/15. 2.45	5/6. 3.45	2	4,574	1,452	590	41
Coblenz	6/7.11.44	–	1	896	523	303	58
Cologne	13/14. 3.42	2. 3.45	22	28,699	3,250	1,994	61
Darmstadt	25/26. 8.44	11/12. 9.44	2	1,726	745	516	69
Dessau	7/8. 3.45	8/9. 4.45	2	2,017	542	331	61
Dortmund	14/15. 4.42	12. 3.45	9	18,295	1,720	923	54
Dresden	13/14. 2.45	–	1	2,978	2,844	1,681	59
Duisburg	13/14. 7.42	21/22. 2.45	18	29,010	2,955	1,424	48
Dusseldorf	31/1. 8.42	2/3.11.44	10	18,099	3,115	2,003	64
Emden	6/7. 6.42	6. 9.44	5	2,834	485	270	56

Essen	8/9. 3.42	11. 3.45	28	39,907	2,630	1,319	50
Frankfurt A/Main	24/25. 8.42	28/29.12.44	11	23,139	2,200	1,145	52
Freiburg	27/28.11.44	–	1	1,900	694	257	37
Friedrichshafen	27/28. 4.44		1	1,234	148	99	67
Gelsenkirchen	25/26. 6.43	22/23. 1.45	4	7,386	757	360	48
Giessen	2/3.12.44	6/7.12.44	2	549	398	130	33
Hagen	1/2.10.43	15/16. 3.45	4	4,515	486	325	67
Hamburg	15/16. 1.42	13/14. 4.45	17.	16,089	8,315	6,200	75
Hamm	5.12.44		1	514	355	140	39
Hanau	6/7. 1.45	18/19. 3.45	2	3,059	275	190	69
Hanover	22/23. 9.43	25. 3.45	16	15,299	2,519	1,517	60
Harburg	11/12.11.44	–	1	–	286	153	53
Heilbronn	4/5.12.44	–	1	1,254	430	351	82
Hildesheim	22. 3.45	–	1	1,168	378	263	70
Kaiserslautern	27/28. 9.44		1	909	369	134	36
Karlsruhe	2/3. 9.42	2/3.2 .45	6	8,178	1,237	398	32
Kassel	27/28. 8.42	8/9. 3.45	6	6,175	905	620	69
Kiel	27/28. 2.42	23/24. 4.45	10	10,875	1,466	725	50
Konigsberg	26/27. 8.44	29/30. 8.44	2	1,053	824	435	53
Krefeld	2/3.10.42	21/22. 6.43	2	2,779	1,529	714	47
Leipzig	20/21.10.43	10/20. 2.44	3	5,714	3,183	625	20
Lubeck	28/29. 3.42	–	1	441	633	190	30
Magdeburg	21/22. 1.44	13/14. 2.45	4	4,166	1,884	774	44
Mainz	11/12. 8.42	27. 2.45	4	3,295	971	593	61
Mannheim-Ludwigshaven	14/15. 2.42	1. 3.45	13	14,319	1,911	1,213	64
Mulheim	22/23. 6.43	–	1	1,848	303	193	64

Appendix E – continued

Munchen-Gladbach and Rheydt	30/31. 8.43	1. 2.45	4	4,115	1,176	633	54
Munich	19/20. 9.42	7/8. 1.45	9	8,755	3,634	1,547	42
Munster	28/29. 1.42	25. 3.45	6	3,769	997	650	65
Neuss	23/24. 9.44	28/29.11.44	4	5,744	225	17	8
Nuremberg	28/29. 8.42	16/17. 3.45	11	13,807	2,255	1,146	51
Oberhausen	14/15. 6.43	4.12.45	3	3,065	502	100	20
Osnabruck	9/10. 8.42	25. 3.45	5	4,437	658	441	67
Pforzheim	23/24. 2.45	–	1	1,825	369	304	83
Plauen	10/11. 4.45	–	1	1,344	712	365	51
Potsdam	14/15. 4.45	–	1	–	559	75	13
Remscheid	30/31. 7.43	–	1	871	339	281	83
Rostock	23/24. 4.42	26/27. 4.42	4	990	634	200	32
Saarbrucken	29/30. 7.42	5/6.10.44	4	2,986	866	418	48
Schweinfurt	24/25. 2.44	26/27. 4.44	2	3,321	293	126	43
Solingen	4.11.44	5.11.44	2	2,048	343	169	49
Stettin	20/21. 4.43	29/30. 8.44	4	5,261	1,386	736	53
Stuttgart	4/5. 5.42	12/13. 2.45	18	21,246	2,514	1,152	46
Trier	21.12.44	23.12.44	2	1,436	492	48	10
Ulm	17/18.12.44	–	1	1,449	562	155	28
Wiesbaden	2/3. 2.45	–	1	2,483	605	90	15
Wilhelmshaven	10/11. 1.42	15/16.10.44	9	7,354	972	130	13
Witten	18/19. 3.45	–	1	1,081	207	129	62
Worms	21/22. 2.45	–	1	1,116	328	127	39
Wuppertal-Barmen	29/30. 5.43	13. 3.45	2	3,448	1,139	655	58
Wuppertal/Elberfeld	24/25. 6.43	–	1	1,979	929	870	94
Wurzburg	16/17. 3.45	–	1	1,127	477	422	89

475,363
7,074
Total 482,437

All area attacks prior to January, 1942

Source: British Bombing Survey Unit report. Figures do not seek to include tonnage dropped and damage achieved by USAAF attacks.

Comparative average quarterly Allied and German aircraft production, 1939–45

Date	Single-engined fighters			Twin-engined aircraft*			Four-engined aircraft		
	German	British	United States	German	British	United States	German	British	United States
1939 1st quarter	128 (avg)	70	—	219 (avg)	134	—	0.5 (avg)	—	Not known
2nd quarter		82	—		141	—		—	5
3rd quarter		74	—		153	—		—	—
4th quarter		114	—		174	—		—	6
1940 1st quarter	156 (avg)	155	—	382 (avg)	151	24	3 (avg)	—	9
2nd quarter		340	12		288	24		1	8
3rb quarter		563	91		365	28		3	17
4th quarter		420	156		339	20		11	18
1941 1st quarter	160	452	146	366	375	51	5	25	64
2nd quarter	326	491	152	353	428	106	5	34	125
3rd quarter	242	550	174	454	438	169	6	50	182
4th quarter	221	559	320	373	407	224	3	57	237
1942 1st quarter	396	625	395	434	465	326	12	89	329
2nd quarter	349	692	473	504	511	376	20	142	457
3rd quarter	420	681	517	521	503	526	24	191	700
4th quarter	449	659	484	555	517	575	27	232	914
1943 1st quarter	642	697	525	698	488	625	31	321	1,134
2nd quarter	865	687	741	683	472	808	45	387	1,435
3rd quarter	932	672	993	743	443	707	34	383	1,516
4th quarter	763	661	1,205	663	452	1,010	54	428	1,383
1944 1st quarter	1,236	663	1,320	567	525	1,010	64	483	1,113
2nd quarter	1,927	666	1,320	779	489	1,138	72	481	1,066
3rd quarter	2,779	563	1,290	795	476	1,185	36	460	
4th quarter	2,645	534	1,394	554	434	1,067	Nil	412	
1945 1st quarter	2,078	483	1,221	492	421	908	Nil	350	
			1,283			837			

Source: *BBSU Effects of Bombing the German Aircraft Industry.*

* German twin-engine aircraft were mostly bombers pre-1943 and mostly fighters thereafter.

Appendix G
Letter to Sir Norman Bottomley from Sir Arthur Harris

AIR 20/3218
Headquarters, Bomber Command
High Wycombe, Bucks
29th March 1945

ATH/DO/4B
PERSONAL & TOP SECRET

Dear Norman

It is difficult to answer indictments of which the terms are not fully revealed and for this reason I cannot deal as thoroughly as I should like with the points raised in your CAS.608/DSAS of March 28th. I take it, however, that it is unnecessary for me to make any comment on the passages which you quote and which, without the context, are abusive in effect, though doubtless not in intention.

To suggest that we have bombed German cities 'simply for the sake of increasing the terror though under other pretexts' and to speak of our offensive as including 'mere acts of terror and wanton destruction' is an insult both to the bombing policy of the Air Ministry and to the manner in which that policy has been executed by Bomber Command. This sort of thing if it deserves an answer will certainly receive none from me, after three years of implementing official policy.

As regards the specific points raised in your letter, namely the adverse economic effects on ourselves by increasing yet further the material havoc in Germany and the destruction of Dresden* in particular the answer is surely very simple. It is already demonstrated in the liberated countries that what really makes any sort of recovery almost impossible is less the destruction of buildings than the complete dislocation of transportation. If, therefore, this objection is to be taken seriously I suggest that the transportation plan rather than the strategic bombing of cities is what needs to

*The feeling, such as there is, over Dresden could be easily explained by any psychiatrist. It is connected with German bands and Dresden shepherdesses. Actually Dresden was a mass of munition works, an intact government centre, and a key transportation point to the East. It is now none of those things.

be considered, as I understand it has been, and for precisely that reason. You will remember that Dresden was recommended by the Targets Committee as a transportation target as well as on other grounds.

I do not, however, stress this point since I assume that what is really at issue is (a) whether our strategic bombing policy up to date has been justified (b) whether the time has now come to discontinue this policy. I will therefore confine myself to these questions.

As regards (a) I have on previous occasions discussed this matter very fully in official correspondence with the Air Ministry and to avoid repetition I refer you to the following correspondence:

 (i) Bomber Command letter BC/S.23801/Press/C.-in-C. of October 25th 1943.
 (ii) Air Ministry letter CS.21079/43 of December 15th 1943.
 (iii) Bomber Command letter BC/S.23801/Press/C.-in-C. of December 23rd 1943.
 (iv) Air Ministry letter CS.21079 of March 2nd 1944.
 (v) Bomber Command letter BC/S.31152/Air/C.-in-C. of March 7th 1944.

I have always held and still maintain that my Directive, which you quote, 'the progressive destruction and dislocation of the German military, industrial and economic systems' could be carried out only by the elimination of German industrial cities and not merely by attacks on individual factories however important these might be in themselves. This view was also officially confirmed by the Air Ministry. The overwhelming evidence which is now available to support it makes it quite superfluous for me to argue at length that the destruction of those cities has fatally weakened the German war effort and is now enabling Allied soldiers to advance into the heart of Germany with negligible casualties. Hence the only question which I have to answer is this: would 'confining ourselves to more precise concentration upon military objectives such as oil and communications behind the immediate battle zone' tend to shorten the war more than persistence in attacks on cities? The answer appears to me to be obvious; but, even if it is not, I must point out as I have frequently done before that we have by no means always a free choice in this matter. Weather conditions frequently constrain me to decide between attacking cities and not attacking at all. When this happens it is surely evident that it is expedient to attack the cities. I can only find, pinpoint and hit small targets with a small part of my force at a time, and I have not enough fighter escort to do more than two such small attacks daily.

I have thus disposed of point (a). We have never gone in for terror bombing and the attacks which we have made in accordance with my Directive have in fact produced the strategic consequences for which they were designed and from which the Armies now profit.

Point (b) is rather difficult to follow. It can hardly mean that attacks on cities no longer produce dislocation in the German war effort. Quite the contrary is the case. The nearer Germany is to collapse the less capable she is of reorganizing to meet disasters of this kind and we ought logically to make a special effort to eliminate the few cities which still remain more or less serviceable.

I therefore assume that the view under consideration is something like this: 'no doubt in the past we were justified in attacking German cities. But to do so was always repugnant and now that the Germans are beaten anyway we can properly abstain from proceeding with these attacks'. This is a doctrine to which I could never subscribe. Attacks on cities like any other act of war are intolerable unless they are strategically justified. But they are strategically justified in so far as they tend to shorten the war and so preserve the lives of Allied soldiers. To my mind we have absolutely no right to give them up unless it is certain that they will not have this effect. I do not personally regard the whole of the remaining cities of Germany as worth the bones of one British Grenadier.

It therefore seems to me that there is one and only one valid argument on which a case for giving up strategic bombing could be based, namely that it has already completed its task and that nothing now remains for the Armies to do except to occupy Germany against unorganized resistance. If this is what is meant I shall no doubt be informed of it. It does not however appear to be the view of the Supreme Commander. Until it is, I submit that the strategic bombing of German cities must go on.

Some final points. As you know Transportation targets are now largely off. Oil has had, and is getting, all we can practically give it in consideration of weather and escort factors. We answer every army support call and, as Monty tells us, in a 'decisive manner'. We have asked for more but there aren't any. H.E. is seriously limited in supply. Incendiaries are not. All these factors must therefore also be considered, and the inevitable answer is that either we continue as in the past or we very largely stand down altogether. The last alternative would certainly be welcome. I take little delight in the work and none whatever in risking my crews avoidably.

Japan remains. Are we going to bomb their cities flat – as in Germany – and give the Armies a walk over – as in France and Germany – or going to bomb only their outlying factories* and subsequently invade at the cost of 3 to 6 million casualties? We should be careful of precedents.

Yours Ever,
  Bert

Air Marshal Sir Norman Bottomley, KCB, CIE, DSO, AFC,
Air Ministry, Whitehall, SW1

*Largely underground by the time we get going.

Bibliography and a note on sources

The principal sources of original material for this book have been the AIR files in the Public Record Office, notably those of the Chief of Air Staff, the C-in-C Bomber Command, the Directorate of Bomber Operations and the Secretary of State for Air, although sadly most of the latter's papers have been lost or destroyed. I have also relied heavily on group and squadron Operational Record Books, *Bomber Command Quarterly Review*, and that stand-by of the wartime Target Intelligence department, *The Bomber's Baedeker*. At the end of the war, High Wycombe's Intelligence Section devoted great labour to compiling a remarkable two-volume file entitled 'A Review of the Work of Int I', which I can only describe as a handbook for the use of any future planner who might be called upon to organize a strategic bomber offensive. It gives a fascinating flavour of High Wycombe's staff work, and I am deeply indebted to the officer who loaned me his almost unique copy. *The United States Strategic Bombing Survey* is vast, uneven, often unreliable but indispensable. So is the British official history, *The Strategic Air Offensive against Germany*, especially the final volume of appendices, selected documents and statistics. A good study of the strategy of the campaign is Anthony Verrier's *The Bomber Offensive*, to which I am indebted for many important lines of thought. *Hansard's* reports of the parliamentary debates on the Royal Air Force both during and immediately after the war make fascinating reading. No novelist writing of the air war of 1939–45 has matched the genius of V. M. Yeates's *Winged Victory* or Cecil Lewis's *Sagittarius Rising* on the First World War, but I have included below several works of fiction which either paint a vivid picture of operational bomber flying, or cast interesting light on contemporary wartime attitudes to Bomber Command.

I have omitted many relevant volumes on the general conduct of
the Second World War, which are invaluable background reading,
but deal only peripherally with Bomber Command. Asterisked
titles are notable for their exceptional photographs of operational aircraft.

Air Ministry, *Bomber Command* (HMSO 1941)
Bates, H. E., *The Stories of Flying Officer X* (Cape 1952)
Bekker, Caius, *The Luftwaffe War Diaries* (Macdonald 1964)
Bell, George, *The Church and Humanity* (Longmans 1946)
Bennett, D. C. T., *Pathfinder* (Muller 1958)
Birkenhead, The Earl of, *The Prof in Two Worlds* (Collins 1961)
Blackett, P. M. S., *Studies of War* (Oliver & Boyd 1962)
Bond, Brian, *Liddell Hart: A Study of His Military Thought*
(Cassell 1977)
Boyle, Andrew, *Trenchard* (Collins 1962)
Bowyer, Chaz, *The Mosquito at War** (Ian Allan 1976)
—, *Hampden Special** (Ian Allan 1975)
Bowyer, Michael, *A History of 2 Group, RAF* (Faber 1974)
—, *Mosquito* (Faber 1967)
Braddon, Russell, *Cheshire VC* (Evans 1954)
Cheshire, Leonard, *Bomber Pilot* (Hutchinson 1943)
Churchill, Winston, *The Second World War* (Cassell 1948–54)
Clark, Ronald, *The Rise of the Boffins* (Phoenix 1962)
—, *Tizard* (Methuen 1965)
Collier, Basil, *A History of Air Power* (Weidenfeld 1974)
Deighton, Len, *Bomber* (Cape 1970)
—, *Fighter* (Cape 1977)
Divine, David, *The Broken Wing* (Hutchinson 1966)
Frankland, Dr Noble, *The Bombing Offensive against Germany*
(Faber 1965)
Galland, Adolf, *The First and the Last* (Methuen 1955)
Garbett and Goulding, *The Lancaster at War** (Ian Allan 1971)
Gibson, Guy, *Enemy Coast Ahead* (Michael Joseph 1946)
Goebbels, Josef, *The Goebbels Diaries* (Hamish Hamilton 1948)
—, *The Goebbels Diaries: The Last Days* (Secker & Warburg
1978)
Groves, Brigadier P. R. C., *Our Future in the Air* (Harrap
1935)

Hansell, Major-General H. S., *The Air Plan that Defeated Hitler* (Atlanta 1972)

Harris, Marshal of the RAF Sir Arthur, *Bomber Offensive* (Collins 1947)

Hornsey, Denis, *The Pilot Walked Home* (Collins Blue Circle 1946)

Hyde, Montgomery, *British Air Policy between the Wars* (Heinemann 1976)

Irving, David, *The Destruction of Dresden* (Kimber 1963)

—, *Nicht Und Deutschlands Stadte Starben* (Schweitzer, Zurich 1963)

—, *The Mare's Nest* (Kimber 1964)

—, *The Rise and Fall of the Luftwaffe* (Weidenfeld 1973)

—, *Hitler's War* (Hodder & Stoughton 1977)

Jones, Geoffrey, *Raider: The Halifax and its Fliers* (Kimber 1978)

Jones, H. A., *The War in the Air* (Oxford 1937)

Jones, Nevill, *Origins of Strategic Bombing* (Kimber 1973)

Jones, R. V., *Most Secret War* (Hamish Hamilton 1978)

Lawrence, W. J., *No. 5 Bomber Group RAF* (Faber 1951)

Lee, General Raymond, *The London Observer* (Hutchinson 1972)

Lewin, Ronald, *Ultra at War* (Hutchinson 1978)

Liddell Hart, B. H., *Paris, or The Future of War* (Kegan Paul 1925)

—, *When Britain Goes to War* (Kegan Paul 1935)

—, (*and see* Bond, Brian)

Lumsden, Alex, *Wellington Special** (Ian Allan 1974)

Middlebrook, Martin, *The Nuremberg Raid* (Allen Lane 1973)

Milward, Alan, *The Germany Economy at War* (London University 1965)

—, *War, Economy and Society* (Allen Lane 1975)

Mosley, Leonard, *The Reichsmarschall* (Weidenfeld 1973)

Muirhead, J. T., *Air Attack on Cities* (Allen & Unwin 1938)

Musgrove, Gordon, *Pathfinder Force* (Macdonald & Janes 1976)

Price, Alfred, *Instruments of Darkness* (Kimber 1967)

Revie, Alasdair, *The Lost Command* (David Bruce & Watson 1971)

Richards, Denis, *Portal of Hungerford* (Heinemann 1978)

Richardson, Frank, *Fighting Spirit* (Leo Cooper 1978)

Roskill, Captain S. W., *Churchill and the Admirals* (Collins 1977)

Rumpf, Hans, *The Bombing of Germany* (Muller 1963)

Saint-Exupery, Antoine de, *Airman's Odyssey* (Reynal & Hitchcock, New York 1942)

Saundby, Air Marshal Sir Robert, *Air Bombardment* (Chatto & Windus 1961)

Saward, Group-Captain Dudley, *The Bomber's Eye* (Cassell 1959)

Schmidt, Klaus, *Die Brandnacht* (Reba Verlag, Darmstadt 1964)

Seversky, Major Alexander, *Victory through Air Power* (Hutchinson 1942)

Slessor, Marshal of the RAF Sir John, *The Central Blue* (Cassell 1956)

—, *Air Power and Armies* (London 1936)

Snow, Lord, *Science and Government* (Oxford 1961)

Spaight, J. M., *Air Power and Cities* (Longmans 1930)

—, *Air Power and the Next War* (Bles 1938)

—, *The Sky's the Limit* (Hodder & Stoughton 1940)

—, *Bombing Vindicated* (Hodder & Stoughton 1944)

Speer, Albert, *Inside the Third Reich* (Weidenfeld 1970)

—, *Spandau: The Secret Diaries* (Collins 1976)

Tedder, Lord, *Air Power in War* (Hodder & Stoughton 1948)

—, *With Prejudice* Cassell 1965)

Thomson, R. W., *Churchill and Morton* (Hodder & Stoughton 1976)

Verrier, Anthony, *The Bomber Offensive* (Batsford 1968)

Watson, John, *Johnny Kinsman* (Cassell 1956)

Winfield, Roland, *The Sky Belongs to Them* (Kimber 1976)

Zuckerman, Lord, *From Apes to Warlords* (Hamish Hamilton 1978)

Officia lhistories

The Royal Air Force 1939–43, Richards, Denis (HMSO 1953)

The War At Sea, vols I & II, Roskill, Captain S. W. (HMSO 1954 and 1956)

The Strategic Air Offensive against Germany, vols i-iv, Sir Charles Webster and Noble Frankland (HMSO 1961)

The Design and Development of Weapons, Postan, Hay and Scott (HMSO 1958)
RAF Medical Services, Rexford Welch (HMSO) 1955
The United States Army Air Forces in World War II, Craven and Cale (Univ. Chicago Press 1948-58)

It may be useful to add to the above list the following books which were published after the manuscript was completed, but which it was possible to consult while *Bomber Command* was still at proof stage. All contain important relevant material on the bomber offensive, although none caused me to wish to make significant changes to what I have written:

Dean, Sir Maurice, *The RAF and Two World Wars* (Cassell 1979)
Faber, Harold (ed.), *Luftwaffe* (Sidgwick & Jackson 1979)
Hinsley, F. H., *British Intelligence in the Second World War*, vol. i (HMSO 1979)
McLaine, Ian, *Ministry of Morale* (Allen & Unwin 1979)

Notes and references

All letters and documents quoted in the text are from the AIR files in the Public Record Office unless otherwise stated.

Foreword
1 Harris, *Bomber Offensive* (Collins 1947), p. 176.
2 *Quarterly Review*, vol. 300, p. 428.

Prologue
1 3 Group report on the events of 18 December 1939.
2 Quoted Bekker, *The Luftwaffe War Diaries* (Macdonald 1964), p. 74.
3 Grant to author, July 1978.
4 ibid.

Chapter 1
1 Webster and Frankland, *The Strategic Air Offensive against Germany* (HMSO 1961), vol. 1, p. 10.
2 Fuller, *Tanks in the Great War* (London 1920), p. 314.
3 Liddell Hart, *Paris* (Kegan Paul 1925), p. 47.
4 Shaw, *Adventures of the Black Girl in Search of God* (Constable 1932).
5 Spaight, *Air Power and Cities* (Longmans 1930).
6 Robert Rhodes James, *The British Revolution* (Hamish Hamilton 1977), vol. II, pp. 258–9.
7 Sir Barnes Wallis to author, 8 November 1976.
8 Slessor, *Air Power and Armies* (London 1936), p. 65.
9 Quoted in full in the Appendices to H. A. Jones's *The War War in the Air* (Oxford 1937), along with Sir John Haig's equally interesting remarks.
10 R. V. Jones, *Most Secret War* (Hamish Hamilton 1978), p. 45.

Chapter 3
1 Denis Hornsey, unpublished MS 'Here Today, Bomb Tomorrow'.
2 Air Vice-Marshal S. O. Bufton to the author, 12 November 1976.
3 Webster and Frankland, op. cit., vol. I, p. 154.

459

4 Denis Richards, *Portal of Hungerford* (Heinemann 1978) p. 166.

5 Hornsey MS, op. cit.

6 Letter to the author, March 1978.

Chapter 4

1 Churchill to John Lawrence, cited interview with the author, 7 July 1978.

2 Taylor, *The Second World War* (Hamish Hamilton 1975), p. 129. Some airmen claim that a much smaller proportion, as low as 6 per cent of the war effort, was devoted to the bomber offensive, but this is quite unconvincing.

3 Raymond Lee, *The London Observer* (Hutchinson 1972), pp. 372–3.

4 Quoted Roskill, *Churchill and the Admirals* (Collins 1977), p. 139.

5 ibid., p. 206.

6 Quoted A. J. P. Taylor, *Beaverbrook* (Hamish Hamilton 1972).

7 Kennedy, *The Business of War* (Hutchinson 1957).

8 Roskill, op. cit., p. 137.

9 Craven and Cate, *The Army Air Forces in World War II* (University of Chicago Press 1949), vol. II, p. 735.

10 Webster and Frankland, op. cit., vol. I, p. 180.

Chapter 5

1 Webster and Frankland, op. cit., vol. I, pp. 15–16.

2 ibid., p. 336.

3 Sir Barnes Wallis conversation with the author, November 1976.

4 I must differ with the view expressed by Ronald Clark in his excellent biography of Tizard: even if Tizard was not questioning the principles on which the bombing offensive was based, he was convinced that it could not yield results in proportion to the effort being expended upon it. His disagreement with Cherwell does indeed seem 'fundamental'.

5 See Zuckerman's autobiography, *From Apes to Warlords* (Hamish Hamilton 1978), pp. 139–46.

6 Harris, op. cit., p. 147.

7 Harris conversation with the author, 25 April 1978.

8 Harris, op. cit., pp. 15 and 52.

9 Quoted Thompson, *Churchill and Morton* (Hodder & Stoughton 1976), p. 44.

10 ibid., pp. 48 and 86.

11 Anthony Verrier, *The Bomber Offensive* (Batsford 1968), p. 4.

Chapter 6

1 The Empire Training Scheme handled 200,000 aircrew in the course of the war.

2 Owen conversation with the author, November 1976.

3 Feelings of Esmond Romilly as quoted by Philip Toynbee, *Friends Apart* (McGibbon & Kee 1954), p. 68.

4 Harris to David Irving, 1961.

5 Webster and Frankland, op. cit., vol. I, p. 392.

6 S/Ldr Ronald Barton, *Hampdens from Swinderby* (published privately).

7 Webster and Frankland, op. cit., vol. I, pp. 394–5.

8 Dudley Saward, *The Bomber's Eye* (Cassell 1959), p. 126.

9 Lee, op. cit., pp. 378–9.

10 ibid., pp. 379–80.

11 Hornsey MS, op. cit.

12 Yeates, *Winged Victory* (Cape 1973).

13 Information to the author from a German-speaking aircrew POW who saw story and photograph in German Press. I have interviewed a WAAF who was once taken as a passenger on an operation.

Chapter 7

1 See Anthony Trythall, '*Boney*' *Fuller* (Cassell 1977), p. 226.

2 See Brian Bond, *Liddell Hart: A Study of his Military Thought* (Cassell 1977), pp. 146–8.

3 Harris, op. cit., p. 58.

4 Seversky, *Victory through Air Power* (Hutchinson 1942).

5 As far as I am aware, this remarkable paper from the 4 Group files in the PRO has never before been published. It is a major reflection on Harris's tactical judgement, and it is for-tunate that he was dissuaded from pursuing his faith in day-light operations at this stage.

6 Or so the Air Ministry believed: Harris himself says that he never actually set eyes on *Pointblank* until it reached his desk in its final form in June 1943 (conversation with the author, 25 April 1978).

7 Webster and Frankland, op. cit., vol. II, p. 5.

8 Churchill, *The Second World War* (Cassell 1950), vol. II, p. 314.

9 Robert Rhodes James, *The British Revolution* (Hamish Hamilton 1976).

10 Webster and Frankland, op. cit., vol. II, p. 7.

11 Harris, op. cit., p. 143.

12 Harris, op. cit., p. 49.

13 Harris conversation with the author, 14 October 1976.

14 Bennett conversation with the author, July 1978.

15 Harris, op. cit., p. 144.

Chapter 8

1 Craven and Cate, op. cit., vol. II, p. ix.

2 Hank Iveson conversation with the author, 17 June 1978.

3 Hornsey MS, op. cit.

4 Webster and Frankland, op. cit., vol. II, p. 142.

5 Professor Derek Jackson, one of the scientists most closely involved in wartime radar development, has stated (letter to the *Sunday Telegraph*, 12 March 1978) that insufficient supplies of *Window* existed to enable its introduction before July 1943. But Air Vice-Marshal Addison, then commanding 80 Wing, possessed supplies stockpiled in his HQ at Radlett golf club, Herts, in mid-1942 (conversation with the author 11 November 1976).

6 Sir Barnes Wallis conversation with the author, 8 November 1976.

7 Kirkham to the author, 20 March 1978.

8 Conversation with the author, February 1977.

9 Conversation with the author, February 1978.

10 Cochrane conversation with the author, November 1976.

11 Cheshire, *Bomber Pilot* (Hutchinson 1943), p. 9.

12 Kirkham to the author, 12 November 1978.

13 Hornsey did publish one book, on his escape from France

after being shot down: *The Pilot Walked Home* (Collins Blue Circle 1946).

Chapter 9

1 *Goebbels Diaries* (Secker & Warburg 1978), p. 86 (9 March 1945).
2 See David Irving, *Rise and Fall of the Luftwaffe* (Weidenfeld 1973), p. 82.
3 See Appendix F for comparative figures.
4 Milward, *The German Economy at War* (London University 1965), p. 10. Milward is invaluable for any study of German industry at this period.
5 Speer, *Inside the Third Reich* (Weidenfeld 1970), p. 214.
6 ibid., p. 284.
7 Frankland, *The Bombing Offensive against Germany* (Faber 1965), p. 76.
8 See Speer Interrogations 24.
9 Irving, op. cit., p. 230.
10 Speer, op. cit., p. 209.
11 Irving, op. cit.
12 Speer Interrogations, op. cit.
13 Irving, op. cit., p. 230.
14 *Goebbels Diaries*, pp. 138–9.
15 ibid., p. 208.
16 Dated 7 July 1942.
17 Speer memoirs, op. cit., p. 278.
18 Webster and Frankland, op. cit., vol. II, p. 95.
19 R. V. Jones, *Most Secret War* (Hamish Hamilton 1978).
20 Galland, *The First and the Last* (Methuen 1955), p. 188.
21 ibid., p. 198.
22 Irving, op. cit., p. 153.
23 ibid., p. 153.
24 Speer, *Spandau: The Secret Diaries* (Collins 1976).
25 Total includes aircraft missing and crashed in England.

Chapter 10

1 Former High Wycombe staff officer in conversation with the author, June 1978.

2 For instance, see Taylor, op. cit., p. 130.
3 Harris himself denies this story, but it was offered to the author by one of his personal staff who claimed to have been present.
4 Harris conversation with the author, 14 October 1976.
5 To the author, November 1978.
6 Speer, *Spandau Diaries*, op. cit., p. 29.
7 To the author, May 1978.
8 ibid.
9 Lord Elworthy conversation with the author, March 1977.
10 Collins, *Faith under Fire*, p. 69.
11 ibid., p. 89.
12 From the original text in possession of the author.
13 ibid.
14 From the internally circulated 1945 'Review of the Work of Int I', loaned to the author by a former High Wycombe staff officer.
15 See Chapter 9.
16 'Review of the Work of Int I', op. cit.
17 Harris conversation with the author, 25 April 1978.
18 ibid.
19 ibid.

Chapter 11

1 Musgrove, *Pathfinder Force* (Macdonald & Janes 1976), pp. 85 and 87.
2 From 'Review of the Work of Int I', op. cit.
3 *Goebbels Diaries*, op. cit., p. 438.
4 Cochrane conversation with the author, November 1976.
5 To the author, April 1978.
6 To the author, July 1978.
7 Webster and Frankland, op. cit., vol. II, p. 193.
8 To the author, November 1976.
9 Craven and Cate, op. cit., vol. III, p. 11.
10 ibid., vol. III, pp. 51, 63 and 730.
11 ibid., vol. III p. 715.
12 Harris conversation with the author, October 1976.
13 Zuckerman, op. cit., p. 276.

14 Harris, op. cit., p. 192.
15 Bufton conversation with the author, July 1978.
16 See Zuckerman, op. cit., p. 352.

Chapter 12

1 Loaned to the Author by Group-Captain C. B. Owen.
2 Cochrane conversation with the author, November 1976.
3 8 Group post-war Station MO's report in PRO.
4 Harris, *Bomber Offensive*.
5 Tait, CO of 83 Squadron and subsequently of 617 Squadron, was among the most distinguished and decorated Bomber Command pilots of the war.
6 Craven and Cate, op. cit., vol. III, p. 666.

Chapter 13

1 In his book *The Destruction of Dresden*. David Irving suggests that Darmstadt was bombed at the prompting of a Jewish former resident of the town, who in 1944 lived in the same Surbiton apartment block as an officer of the RAF's target selection staff. There is no reason to doubt that the refugee spoke to the staff officer, but it seems open to question whether their conversation directly provoked the attack of 11 September. The RAF had been well aware of Darmstadt's chemical plants since 1940. I am more inclined to believe that the raid was inspired by tactical considerations such as those discussed in the text.
2 Klaus Schmidt *Die Brandnacht*, Darmstadt 1965. For this and all other quotations from the stories of the people of Darmstadt in this chapter, I am indebted to the above collection of first-hand accounts, especially valuable because so many of those who contributed have since died.

Chapter 14

1 Craven and Cate, op. cit., vol. III, p. 320.
2 Webster and Frankland, op. cit., vol. III, p.82.
3 Milward, op. cit., p. 170.
4 Galland, op. cit., p. 279.
5 Speer, *Inside the Third Reich*, p. 286.

6 Harris conversation with the author, 14 October 1976.

7 Portal to the Air Ministry, 30 September 1959, commenting on draft of Webster and Frankland. Quoted Richards, *Portal*, op. cit., p. 330.

8 Verrier, op. cit., p. 283.

9 See Chapter 11 above, Inglis to Portal.

10 Milward, op. cit., p. 188.

11 *Goebbels Diaries*, ed. Trevor-Roper (Secker & Warburg), p. 24.

12 *Goebbels*, op. cit., p. 96.

13 Milward, op. cit., p. 188.

14 Eaker to Spaatz, 1 January 1945, quoted Craven and Cate, op. cit., vol. III, p. 733.

15 Craven and Cate, op. cit., vol. III, p. 638.

16 For instance, Harris to Churchill, 30 August 1944: 'I would much have liked to give you my views personally in response to your invitation to dine, but I have the sort of cold which I would not bring within ten miles of you and yours . . .'

17 Quoted in 'A Review of the Work of Int I,' op. cit.

18 Craven and Cate, op. cit., p. 727.

19 Musgrove, op. cit., p. 181.

Chapter 15

1 Transcribed from the original in possession of S/Ldr Ronald Barton.

2 Churchill, op. cit., vol. VI, p. 434.

3 Nuremberg hearings, 13 March 1946.

4 ibid., 15 March 1946.

5 Quoted as Appendix 5 of Zuckerman, op. cit.

6 Craven and Cate, op. cit., vol. III, p. 716.

7 Zuckerman, op. cit., p. 353.

8 Milward, op. cit., p. 163.

9 Frankland, *The Strategic Air Offensive against Germany*, p. 106.

Glossary
Royal Air Force commissioned ranks with their army equivalents

Marshal of the RAF	Field-Marshal
Air Chief Marshal	General
Air Marshal	Lt-General
Air Vice-Marshal	Major-General
Air Commodore	Brigadier
Group Captain	Colonel
Wing-Commander	Lt-Colonel
Squadron-Leader	Major
Flight-Lieutenant	Captain
Flying Officer	Lieutenant
Pilot Officer	Second Lieutenant

A British bomber squadron in the Second World War was commanded by a wing-commander with squadron-leaders as flight commanders. Fighter squadrons were commanded by squadron-leaders.

Abbreviations, codenames and technical terms

AOC	Air Officer Commanding
ABC	AirBorne Cigar – aircraft-mounted transmitter which jammed German fighter frequencies
AI	Airborne Interception radar equipment fitted to fighters
ASV	Air to Surface Vessel radar
Boozer	Radar warning device against fighters, fitted to bombers
CAS	Chief of Air Staff
Circus (operations)	Fighter-escorted daylight bomber sorties by the RAF against short-range French targets, chiefly in 1941, intended to provoke the Luftwaffe to battle
Clarion	American plan to disrupt German communications and morale by wide-ranging bomber attacks in February 1945
Corona	Counterfeit orders to German fighters broadcast by the British 100 Group

467

Crossbow	Countermeasures against German V-weapons
DR	Dead Reckoning navigation
Duppel	German word for *Window*
ETA	Estimated Time of Arrival
Fishpond	British early-warning radar against fighters, fitted to some bombers in 1944
Flak	*Fliegerabwehrkanonen* – German anti-aircraft gun
Flensburg	German radar device fitted to night-fighters, homing on British bombers' *Monica* transmissions
Freya	German early-warning radar
Gee	Radio navigational aid introduced in 1942
G-H	Blind bombing device based on ground-station transmissions to aircraft introduced in 1944
Glycol	Aircraft engine coolant
Grand Slam	22,000-lb penetrating bomb
HCU	Heavy Conversion Unit
Himmelbett	German controlled night-fighting system
H2S	British radar navigation and blind-bombing aid fitted to some bombers from 1943 onwards*
H2X	American name for H2S
Husky	Allied invasion of Sicily in 1943
IFF	Identification Friend or Foe, transmitting a blip to British radar screens.
Knickebein	German radio-beam navigational system introduced in 1940

*The German habit of giving their radar appropriate-sounding codenames to suit the nature of the device was of vital assistance to British scientific Intelligence in interpreting the enemy systems. The British thus learned to be more careful about their own equipment. H2S was originally christened 'TF' until Dr R. V. Jones pointed out that this plainly stood for 'Town Finding'. The name was changed to H2S, popularly believed to stand for 'Home Sweet Home', but in reality for Hydrogen Sulphide. It earned its evil-smelling acronym when at an early meeting to discuss its progress Lord Cherwell showed scepticism and declared gloomily, 'It stinks!' The name stuck.

Lichtenstein	German night-fighter radar introduced in 1941
Mandrel	British 100 Group swamping of German early-warning radar from 1944 onwards
Monica	British radar early-warning device against fighters fitted to bombers from 1943
Naxos	German night-fighter radar homing on British H2S transmissions
Newhaven	Pathfinder codename for target marking blind by H2S, supported by visual backers-up
Oboe	British blind-bombing device fitted to Pathfinder aircraft, controlled by transmissions from ground stations
OKW	*Oberkommando der Wehrmacht* – High Command of the German armed forces
OTU	Operational Training Unit
Overlord	The Allied invasion of France, 6 June 1944
Paramatta	Pathfinder codename for target marking by blind-dropped ground-markers (with prefix '*Musical*', *Oboe*-guided)
Pointblank	The June 1943 directive from the Combined Chiefs of Staff for the Combined Bomber Offensive
PRU	Photographic Reconnaissance Unit
Razzles	Air-dropped incendiary device for igniting crops and forests, employed by Bomber Command August–September 1940
R/T	Radio/Telephone, i.e. voice communication
SASO	Senior Air Staff Officer
SBA	Standard Blind Approach
Schrage musik	Upward-firing cannon fitted to some German night-fighters from late 1943 onwards
Sealion	German codename for the invasion of Britain in 1940
SHAEF	Supreme Headquarters Allied Expeditionary Force 1944–5
Tallboy	12,000-lb penetrating bomb developed by Barnes Wallis

Tame Boar	German tactic for guiding night-fighters from orbit around a visual beacon into bomber stream by running-commentary from ground controller
Thunderclap	1944 Allied plan to deliver overwhelming *coup de grâce* to Berlin and/or other leading German cities by sustained bomber attack
Tinsel	Technique by which British bomber wireless-operators fed jamming noise on to German night-fighter frequencies
Torch	Allied invasion of French North Africa in 1942
VCAS	Vice-Chief of Air Staff
Wanganui	Pathfinder codename for target marking by blind-dropped sky-markers (with prefix '*Musical*', *Oboe*-guided)
Wild Boar	Freelance German single-engined fighter guided into bomber stream by ground controller's running-commentary, July 1943–spring 1944
Window	Tinfoil strips dropped by Allied bombers to fog German radar
W-Mines	Small air-dropped mines for use against locks and river traffic, employed briefly by Bomber Command in 1940
W/T	Wireless transmission, i.e. morse signal rather than voice
Würzburg	German tactical radar for gun-laying, searchlight and night-fighter direction
X-Gerat, Y-Gerat	German beam-guided blind-bombing systems

Acknowledgements

I have received generous help in writing of this book from a great range of people directly and indirectly concerned with the Royal Air Force. Among them I must mention Group-Captain E. B. Haslam, until 1978 head of the Air Historical Branch of the Ministry of Defence, and his colleague Mr Humphrey Wynn; S/Ldr 'Jacko' Jackson and the RAF's Battle of Britain Flight, who flew me in one of the few remaining airworthy Lancaster bombers, and enabled me to get the feel of the aircraft from every turret and crew position; Freddy Lambert of the Public Record Office, who was tireless in answering my endless demands; Dr John Tanner and his staff at the RAF Museum, who enabled me to explore the Wellington and the Mosquito.

The *Daily Telegraph*, the Pathfinder Association journal *The Marker*, the Air Gunners' Association journal *Turret*, the Australian Pathfinders' *Marker*, the RAF Association's *Air Mail*, the Goldfish Club newsletter and the RAF POW Association newsletter *Kriegie* published the appeals which enabled me to contact more than three hundred survivors of Bomber Command, over a hundred from the squadrons which I had chosen for special study.

Mrs Joan Hornsey and her daughter Mrs Carol Wain allowed me to read and to quote extensively from the late Denis Hornsey's remarkable unpublished manuscript on his service in Bomber Command, '*Here Today, Bomb Tomorrow*'.

This book would never have been written without the inspiration of my publisher James Wade in New York, and the support of my editor at Michael Joseph in London, Alan Samson. David Irving is one of the most controversial of contemporary historians, but he is also one of the most generous, and allowed me to borrow for many months his extensive files on the bomber war. Andrea Whittaker helped me with the German translations.

I am indebted to the following for permission to quote from published works and private letters: Lord Salisbury for the letter of the 4th Marquess of Salisbury reproduced on page 204; the Rt Hon. Sir Geoffrey Shakespeare for his letter to Sir Archibald Sinclair on page 147; the Controller of Her Majesty's Stationery Office, for extracts from Webster and Frankland's

The Strategic Air Offensive against Germany; the Keeper of the AIR files; the University of Chicago Press for extracts from Craven and Cate's *The Army Air Forces in World War II*; Messrs Hutchinson for the extracts from General Raymond E. Lee's *The London Observer*; Oxford University Press, for permission to quote from 'Aristocrats' from *The Complete Poems of Keith Douglas*, edited by Desmond Graham; A. D. Peters & Co. Ltd, for permission to quote from *Men at Arms* by Evelyn Waugh; Faber & Faber Ltd, for permission to quote from 'Lincolnshire Bomber Station' by Henry Treece; Denis Richards and William Heinemann Ltd, for the extract from *Portal of Hungerford*; and Chatto & Windus Ltd and Richard Eberhart, for permission to quote from 'The Fury of Aerial Bombardment'.

I would also like to thank: the Air Ministry; Michael Bowyer; Chaz Bowyer; George Carter; Keith Creswell; G/Capt. L. C. Deane; G/Capt. J. R. Goodman; the Imperial War Museum and especially their photographic library; H. M. Irwin, RN retd; Tom Jones; A. Killingley; the London Library and its indefatigable librarians; Doug McKinnon; K. J. Reinhold, editor of the *Darmstadter Echo*; Alun Richards; Captain Stephen Roskill, RN retd; T. A. Stern; W. G. Uprichard; and John Winton.

And now for the principal witnesses of the story of Bomber Command who have assisted me in the past two years; I have omitted ranks below that of Wing-Commander, and a plethora of decorations which would otherwise overwhelm these pages.

The Air Ministry, Bomber Command and Group headquarters
Air Vice-Marshal E. B. Addison; Ronald Barton; Air Vice-Marshal S. O. Bufton; Air Vice-Marshal D. C. T. Bennett; the late Air Chief Marshal Sir Ralph Cochrane; Canon John Collins; Marshal of the RAF Lord Elworthy; Wing-Commander F. A. B. Fawsett; Marshal of the RAF Sir Arthur Harris; Air Commodore W. I. C. Inness; John Lawrence; Fred Lloyd; Miss Barbara Morton; the late Sir Barnes Wallis; Miss Peggy Wherry; Lord Zuckerman.

3 *Group, December 1939*

D. Beddow (99 Squadron); E. T. Butcher (37 Sq.); I. P. Grant (9 Sq.); J. R. Greaves (37 sq.); Frank Hargreaves (51 Sq. weather reconnaissance); H. J. Hemsleyhall (37 Sq.); L. E. Jarman (9 Sq.); Harry Jones (37 Sq.); Wing-Commander J. Lovell (9 Sq.); Air Marshal Sir Hugh Pughe Lloyd (9 Sq.); J. T. Reynolds (9 Sq.); Herbert Ruse (37 Sq.); L. Russell (pupil at North Coates); Eric Scott (115 Sq.).

82 *Squadron, 1940–41*

Wing-Commander L. V. E. Atkinson; J. W. D. Attenborough; the late Air Chief Marshal The Earl of Bandon; Eric Chandler; Kenneth Collins; L. C. Davey; J. Harrison-Broadley; T. C. P. Hodges; F. W. S. Keighley; W. J. Q. Magrath; D. W. McFarlane; Wing-Commander John McMichael; F. H. Miller; N. W. Orr; R. J. Rumsey; Air Vice-Marshal Ian Spencer; Air Commodore Philip Sutcliffe; George Whitehead; Mrs E. M. Wilkins.

10 *Squadron, 1940–41*

F. Ashworth; Bob Dodd; Peter Donaldson; Group-Captain Pat Hanafin; Norman Gregory; Wing-Commander H. J. Heal; J. M. Poole; Group-Captain A. V. Sawyer; Air Vice-Marshal W. E. Staton; A. E. Smith; P. G. Whitby.

50 *Squadron, 1942*

C. W. Gray; Mrs M. A. Hamilton; Stewart Harris; H. S. Hobday; Gus Macdonald; Air Marshal Sir Harold Martin; J. H. Mitchell; L. O'Brien; Ken Owen; G. A. Philips; Reg Raynes; S. D. Stubbs; John Taylor.

76 *Squadron, 1943*

Sidney Ashford; V. G. Bamber; Fred Beadle; Group-Captain Leonard Cheshire; P. C. Chipping; Pamela Finch; Eric Freeman; Group-Captain D. Iveson; C. A. Kirkham; Etienne Maze; R. G. McCadden; B. McNulty; Ferris Newton; C. Rathmell; Cliff Ramsden; S. W. Palmer; E. A. Strange; A. L. Tame; Air Marshal Sir John Whitley.

97 Squadron, 1944

Tony Aveline; Mrs Dorothy Bird; A. Boultbee; F. Broughton; Ron Buck; Wing-Commander W. E. Clayfield; Gordon Cooper; J. A. M. Davies; F. W. A. Hendry; Air Chief Marshal Sir Anthony and Lady Heward; R. L. C. Lasham; T. H. Makepeace; J. W. Nedwich; Group-Captain C. B. Owen; Arthur Tindall; P. R. Turner; Jack Watt.

Index

Freeman, Sir Wilfred 210, 226
Freya radar 278
Fuller, J. F. C. 47, 207–8
FW190 273

Gadsby 80
Galland 272, 280, 281, 402, 422
Gallantry, Flight-Sergeant 233
Garbett, Dr 209
Gaulle, Charles de 58, 292
Gawler, Stan 188
Gee, Bill 345
Gee 149, 157, 162, 173, 174,
  182, 223, 228, 229, 349
Gelsenkirchen 97, 117, 235, 344
Gembloux 68, 70
Germany: economy 264–6;
  industrial production 264–71;
  lack of manpower 268; fighter
  production 270, 272; bomber
  production 272–4; defences
  277–88; production losses
  301; oil supplies 328, 330,
  331, 360, 395; *see also*
  Luftwaffe
G-H 349
Gibson, Guy 168, 249, 256, 341,
  352
Gillchrist 105
Giortz, 'Wilfred' 236
Glanzer, Jacob 372
Gneisenau 16, 120, 127, 128,
  130, 148, 171
Goebbels, Josef 176, 246, 264,
  274–5, 314, 372, 404
Goering, Hermann: German
  economy 265–6; destroys
  Do19 and Ju89 prototypes
  272–3; sense of doom 277,
  280–81; lack of night
  fighters 277, 287; aircraft
  production 282; raids on
  Coventry 418
Goldsmith, Norman 194
Gollob, Gordon 30
Gomorrah, Operation 242, 310
Goodwin, Group-Captain 18

Gould 105
Grafton, Duke of 20
Grand Slam bombs 407
Grant, Peter 19, 23, 30, 32, 35,
  36, 38
Greaves, Jack 23, 26, 31, 32
Greenwood 84
Grizel, Peggy 188
Gros, Martha 375, 387, 389
Guderian, Heinz 58
Guernsey 102
gun turrets, power operated 16
gunners 189, 193
Guthrie, Squadron-Leader 22, 26,
  30, 37

H2S radar 211, 228, 285, 315,
  337, 348, 349
H2X 321
Hagen 268
Halifaxes 58, 149, 184, 232;
  come into service 138;
  production 166; faulty rudder
  design 258; specifications 435
Halle 399
Halton 23
Hamburg 77, 112, 122, 230,
  236, 268, 269, 276, 299–300
Hamburg, Battle of 243,
  245–6, 274, 280, 289, 310
Hamm 97, 407
Hampdens, as stop-gap
  bomber 58; need for
  replacement 97;
  specifications 432
Hanafin, Pat 101, 103–4, 106
Handley Page 258
Hands Off Britain Air
  Defence League 49
Hanover 101, 157, 249, 268, 332,
  399, 407
Harris, Arthur 94, 224, 286;
  daytime bombing 38;
  discipline of Trenchard 46,
  56; target marking 50; area
  bombing 56, 155, 159, 163,
  222, 361, 397–405, 409, 415,

481

Harris, Arthur *continued*
421; takes over Bomber
Command 157; background
157-8; character 158-9, 162,
290; 4,000-bomber plan
160; relations with Churchill
160-61, 289, 304, 418;
effectiveness of bombing 161;
popularity 161; precision
bombing 162; proscription
172; public relations 172,
177, 201, 210; attack on
Lübeck 173; '1,000 plan'
177, 180; establishes
reputation 181; bides his time
against industrial targets
186; and the Navy's demands
211; impressed by US
bombing 216; supports
USAAF against other
services 217; Eaker Plan
219; and American
dominance in the air 220;
Casablanca Conference 221;
Pointblank directive 221-2,
308, 309, 316; disdain for Air
Ministry 224; and the setting
up of Pathfinder Force 224-8,
337, 357; begins strategic
offensive 230; assault on
the Ruhr 231, 232;
introduction of *Window* 243;
Battle of Hamburg 245;
cities destroyed 268; attacks
on Schweinfurt 270; fall
from grace 289, 306, 315-18,
331; relationship with
colleagues 289-90, 294;
contempt for Navy 290;
Battle of Berlin 294, 306-10,
313-15, 331; planning raids
295-7; assessment of results
302; Eisenhower takes over
command 319; Nuremburg
raid, 318; Transport Plan
327-30, 344; and operation
Overlord 327-8, 344, 360;

moves squadrons from
Bennett to Cochrane 338;
renewal of area bombing 361;
raid on Darmstadt 364-5;
Portal's problem with 395-6,
398-405; Battle of the Ruhr
398 oil-targets 398-405; offers
resignation 400-401, 403;
jibes at Allied armies 403;
Dresden raids 410-14, 415;
leaves RAF 418; final
dispatch 419
Harris, Jackie 293
Harris, Squadron Leader 30,
31, 36
Harris, Stewart 195, 197, 199
Harris, Therese 291-93
Hartmann, Gerhard 375
Haw-Haw, Lord 83, 84
Hay, Bob 169
Hayward 105
He111 273
He177 273
Heathcote 29
Heidelberg 368
Heligoland 17, 416
Heligoland Bight 92
Hendry, Fred 355
Hermann, Hajo 281-2, 283
Heward, Anthony 346, 350,
352, 354
High Wycombe 289-305
Hill, A. V. 132
Hill, Jock 257
Himmelbett system 278
Hitler, Adolf: obession with
tactical aircraft 58; domestic
political support 264-6;
economic policies 264-6;
bomber production 272, and
Allied bombing of cities 274;
refuses to visit bombed cities
275; 'intruder' operations
279; tactical errors 280; and
Goering 281; dismisses
Kammhuber 283; influence
over Germans 406; creates

Guy Gibson
Enemy Coast Ahead £1.25

'A book more truly racy, or fuller of vitality, gaiety, high spirits and native good sense, is not likely to be written of the RAF . . .
Here is the very accent and idiom of Bomber Command, and an emotional picture as complete as we are likely to get of the way its aircrews contrived to do their duty'
TIMES LITERARY SUPPLEMENT

'Everyone should read this unforgettable book' PUNCH

Paul Brickhill
The Dam Busters £1

The epic story of the RAF's most famous squadron . . . Again and again they hit targets that demanded extreme courage and pinpoint accuracy! Hitler's last secret weapon, the V3 . . . the battleship *Tirpitz* . . . and the giant Moehne and Eder dams — in the most audacious raid of the War.

Over one million copies sold in Pan.

'In all the history of arms there is no finer epic'
DAILY EXPRESS

Karl August Muggenthaler
German Raiders of World War II £1.95

Who were those mysterious and silent ocean marauders, prowling the South Atlantic and Indian Ocean? Numbering less than a dozen, these brilliantly disguised German freighters sank almost one million tons of Allied shipping in the battle for ocean supremacy which they were destined to lose. This vivid and fascinating account, fully illustrated, is based on interviews with the Raiders' officers and men and their Allied adversaries — the first complete history of a little-known but crucially important theatre of the last war.

'Full and fascinating' DAILY MAIL

Lord Kilbracken
Bring Back My Stringbag £1.50
a Swordfish pilot at war

Vigorous, honest, at times hilarious, this account by Lord Kilbracken of his five years in the Fleet Air Arm during the last war provides a remarkable picture of the Swordfish aircraft (jokingly known as 'Stringbags'), seemingly 'left in the war by mistake', and the oddball characters who flew them. The author experienced every hazard that could confront a shipborne pilot — torpedo and bomb attacks, mines, flak-filled skies and ditching in mid Atlantic, coming through with his courage and offbeat humour undaunted.

Michael Pearson
Tears of Glory £1.25
the betrayal of Vercours

The Vercours Massif, 1944: two days after the Normandy landings this vast natural fortress was the scene of the most tragic action in the bloodstained annals of the French Resistance. The Tricolor fluttered briefly over the Frenchmen who had flocked to the Maquis in the face of twenty thousand German troops. The promised Allied air support on which their success depended never arrived — Vercours was betrayed, and the outcome was inevitable.

'An enthralling though tragic narrative . . . crystal-clear description of tactics, fighting and terrain' DAILY TELEGRAPH

H. R. Trevor-Roper
The Last Days of Hitler 75p

'An incomparable book, by far the best written on any aspect of the second German war: a book sound in its scholarship, brilliant in its presentation, a delight for historians and laymen alike.'
A. J. P. TAYLOR

'Absolutely enthralling . . . It is all there, the fantastic comings and goings, Hitler's last-minute marriage to Eva Braun and the supposed suicide and ritual burning of the corpse'
DAILY WORKER

B. H. Liddell Hart
History of the First World War £2.25

'Immensely readable and informative . . . belongs in the possession
of anyone interested in what the greatest British military thinker
of the century has to say' THE SOLDIER

'It was always his special talent to be able to express military
situations in telling and limpid phrases which would stick in the
reader's mind' DAILY TELEGRAPH

'Remarkable for its clarity and objectivity, and for analysis
undistorted by professional prejudice or by bitterness over the
unrecallable past. It remains outstanding: for those familiar with
its subject, illuminating and thought-provoking; for those new to
it and wishing to know what happened in the First World War,
the best place to begin' WESTERN MAIL

History of the Second World War £2.95

Liddell Hart brought his brilliant and original mind to this
magnificent narrative of the war – a task which occupied him for
over twenty years. Trenchant, searching, thought-provoking,
it is military history written with realism and learning, and
illuminated with flashes of insight.

'The book has the mark of the author's genius – a lucidity and
insight such as no other military writer can match . . . it will long
be read with profit and enjoyment by all interested in the
military art' ARMY QUARTERLY

Bestselling Fiction and Non-Fiction

☐ **Fletcher's Book of Rhyming Slang** — Ronnie Barker — 80p
☐ **Pregnancy** — Gordon Bourne — £2.50p
☐ **A Sense of Freedom** — Jimmy Boyle — £1.25p
☐ **The Thirty-nine Steps** — John Buchan — 80p
☐ **Out of Practice** — Rob Buckman — 95p
☐ **The Flowers of the Forest** — Elizabeth Byrd — £1.50p
☐ **The 35mm Photographer's Handbook** — Julian Calder and John Garrett — £6.95p
☐ **Women Have Hearts** — Barbara Cartland — 70p
☐ **The Sittaford Mystery** — Agatha Christie — 85p
☐ **Lovers and Gamblers** — Jackie Collins — £1.50p
☐ **Sphinx** — Robin Cook — £1.25p
☐ **The Life** — Jeanne Cordelier — £1.50p
☐ **Soft Furnishings** — Designers' Guild — £5.95p
☐ **Rebecca** — Daphne du Maurier — £1.25p
☐ **Peter Finch** — Trader Faulkner — £1.50p
☐ **The Complete Calorie Counter** — Eileen Fowler — 50p
☐ **The Diary of Anne Frank** — Anne Frank — 85p
☐ **Flashman** — George MacDonald Fraser — £1.25p
☐ **Wild Times** — Brian Garfield — £1.95p
☐ **Linda Goodman's Sun Signs** — Linda Goodman — £1.95p
☐ **The 37th Pan Book of Crosswords** — Mike Grimshaw — 70p
☐ **The Moneychangers** — Arthur Hailey — £1.50p
☐ **The Maltese Falcon** — Dashiell Hammett — 95p
☐ **Vets Might Fly** — James Herriot — 95p
☐ **Simon the Coldheart** — Georgette Heyer — 95p
☐ **The Eagle Has Landed** — Jack Higgins — £1.25p
☐ **The Seventh Enemy** — Ronald Higgins — £1.25p
☐ **To Kill a Mockingbird** — Harper Lee — £1.25p
☐ **Midnight Plus One** — Gavin Lyall — £1.25p
☐ **Chemical Victims** — Richard Mackarness — 95p
☐ **Lady, Lady, I Did It!** — Ed McBain — 90p
☐ **Symptoms** — edited by Sigmund Stephen Miller — £2.50p
☐ **Gone with the Wind** — Margaret Mitchell — £2.95p
☐ **Robert Morley's Book of Bricks** — Robert Morley — £1.25p

☐	**Modesty Blaise**	Peter O'Donnell	95p
☐	**Falconhurst Fancy**	Kyle Onstott	£1.50p
☐	**The Pan Book of Card**		
	Games	Hubert Phillips	£1.25p
☐	**The New Small Garden**	C. E. Lucas Phillips	£2.50p
☐	**Fools Die**	Mario Puzo	£1.50p
☐	**Everything Your Doctor**		
	Would Tell You If He		
	Had the Time	Claire Rayner	£4.95p
☐	**Polonaise**	Piers Paul Read	95p
☐	**The 65th Tape**	Frank Ross	£1.25p
☐	**Nightwork**	Irwin Shaw	£1.25p
☐	**Bloodline**	Sidney Sheldon	95p
☐	**A Town Like Alice**	Nevil Shute	£1.25p
☐	**Lifeboat VC**	Ian Skidmore	£1.00p
☐	**Just Off the Motorway**	John Slater	£1.95p
☐	**Wild Justice**	Wilbur Smith	£1.50p
☐	**The Spoiled Earth**	Jessica Stirling	£1.75p
☐	**That Old Gang of Mine**	Leslie Thomas	£1.25p
☐	**Caldo Largo**	Earl Thompson	£1.50p
☐	**Future Shock**	Alvin Toffler	£1.95p
☐	**The Visual Dictionary of**		
	Sex	Eric J. Trimmer	£5.95p
☐	**The Flier's Handbook**		£4.95p

All these books are available at your local bookshop or newsagent, or can be ordered direct from the publisher. Indicate the number of copies required and fill in the form below

Name _____
(block letters please)

Address _____

_____

Send to Pan Books (CS Department), Cavaye Place, London SW10 9PG
Please enclose remittance to the value of the cover price plus:

25p for the first book plus 10p per copy for each additional book ordered to a maximum charge of £1.05 to cover postage and packing Applicable only in the UK

While every effort is made to keep prices low, it is sometimes necessary to increase prices at short notice. Pan Books reserve the right to show on covers and charge new retail prices which may differ from those advertised in the text or elsewhere